The Authoritarian Specter

The Authoritarian Specter

BOB ALTEMEYER

HARVARD UNIVERSITY PRESS
Cambridge, Massachusetts
London, England
1996

To M. Brewster Smith

Permission has been granted by Oxford University
Press to quote from C. D. Batson and W. L. Ventis,
*The Religious Experience: A Social Psychological
Perspective* (1982).

Library of Congress Cataloging-in-Publication Data

Altemeyer, Bob, 1940–
The authoritarian specter / Bob Altemeyer,
      p.   cm.
Includes bibliographical references and index.
ISBN 0-674-05305-2 (alk. paper)
1. Authoritarianism.   2. Fascism.   3. Right-
wing extremists.   4. Right and left (Political
science)
JC481.A48   1993
320.5'3—dc20   96-21389

Acknowledgments

This book ratchets up the number of publications on my *curriculum vita* to nearly double digits. And I have been an academic for only 30 years. A colleague, noting this furious pace, once urged me to slow down. I thought he was worried about my "Type A" personality. But he explained that he did not think I really had that much to say.

Fortunately, many people near and dear encouraged me to persevere. When my wife, Jean, learned I had written a third book, she joyfully exclaimed, "Why?" Seeing I was determined, she suggested a title: *Yet Another Book about Authoritarianism: Still More Studies, Trudging along Like the Seven Dwarfs to the References and Index.* When I pointed out the first part of this title would abbreviate to "YABAA" and that people might then confuse me with Fred Flintstone, she realized the likely misidentification. "Fred would also buy his clothes from Mr. Short and Dumpy," she conceded.

However, one of my former acquisition editors responded to my new manuscript as follows: "You already have two books . . . don't cause trees to be cut for the sake of 'stubborn vision.' "

I then showed the manuscript to a dear friend who so liked my last book, he read it aloud to his wife each night when they went to bed. He encouraged me to seek a publisher; he also told me his wife has left him.

More comforting, Jean and I have become friends with a couple who once asked about my research, so I now tell them *all* my findings. In turn, they keep inviting me to go on wilderness canoe trips with them, even though they know I cannot swim. I think they want to show their appreciation.

I was mightily buoyed when I saw that, even though I began publishing my discoveries only fifteen years ago, they have already been reported in a textbook: David Martin's introductory *Psychology: Principles and Applications*. I was so thrilled, I went right next door to Dave's office and thanked him. I even paid him the money I borrowed in 1983. I hope that someday Dave will write a text for personality or social psychology courses, so my work might get mentioned to students in these fields too.

A number of people have written me asking how to get a copy of my first book, the one published fifteen years ago. It is supposedly out of print. But the publisher still has seventeen copies left that it will gladly sell. And I have the other three.

I think one reason my work has gone unappreciated is that most people already knew everything I have discovered. I had a good demonstration of this one night when a fellow professor, from the humanities, stated that authoritarianism was obviously caused by one's upbringing. I told him that some researchers had evidence now that it is caused by our genes. He quickly responded. "Of course, one intuitively knows this."

Some people's intuitions led them to ask whether my research is secretly funded by the Left-Wing Eastern-Establishment Communist-Front Atheistic-Subversive Un-American Foundation. However, I have not had a research grant since 1971. I mainly cover expenses by having my university set aside part of my pay check as a "grant in lieu of salary." But one year, when I requested that $6,400 be devoted to this, the university would allocate only $6,000. Their attitude seemed to be, "Nobody should spend $6,400 on your research, not even you."

This brings up the sticky subject of my lack of promotion. I rose rather quickly to the rank of associate professor by—coincidentally—1971, but have gone no farther in the twenty-five years since. Most of my former Ph.D. students now outrank me. (Well, all of them do, if you count the one who's a prison warden.) They do not rub it in. But my university keeps sending me announcements of Retirement Planning workshops.

I have done research with my first Ph.D. student, Bruce Hunsberger, for many years now and Bruce could easily be coauthor of Chapter 6 in this book. So if you do not like that chapter, blame him. (To give credit where credit is due, it was Bruce who came up with "Mr. Short and Dumpy." Somehow, he has become quite sassy since receiving his Ph.D.)

As for the rest of the book, as usual any mistakes are someone else's fault.

Lewis Goldberg complained that I did not mention him in the Acknowledgments of my last book. He says he is my "biggest fan." I told him flattery would get him nowhere.

Since I have promised everyone, including the trees, that this will be my last book on authoritarianism, I should say a few appreciative words about the advantages I have had in life. I was born white and male in the richest country in the world. It was also a free country, especially for people like me, because others had given their lives to make it so. I attended a great university where a great teacher, Chris Argyris, changed my life. I married an almost "perfect match." Within a few years of receiving my Ph.D., I was granted tenure and have spent the rest of my life teaching and studying whatever interested me. I never lived through a Depression. I always knew where my next dollar was coming from, and it always came. I was never called to war, and neither was any of our children. I owe a lot. I have used up far more than my fair share of the earth's resources, and an even larger chunk of my local Introductory Psychology subject pool (undoubtedly the biggest asset I have had as a scholar besides the scientific method).

Among my blessings has been a long friendship with M. Brewster Smith, who has served as my mentor all the way to my fifty-sixth birthday. (When you're my mentor, the job takes the rest of your life.) Without his support, you would be reading something else now. He has encouraged many other researchers as well, and become one of the great persons in contemporary psychology.

If you are ever in Brewster's office, you will find hanging on its walls most of the honors and awards that psychologists give. Mine is quite minor in comparison, but the best I can do. I gratefully dedicate this book to him.

I am grateful to Linda Howe at Harvard University Press for supporting this book during the acquisition phase. Clover Archer did a fine job drawing the illustrations, especially the one on p. 292 that nearly did her in. Elizabeth Hurwit had the thankless job of editing the manuscript of an author who thinks that every word he writes, even when misspelled, is perfect. By the end I had a deep appreciation of her gifts and friendship. As production editor, Kate Brick competently turned that manuscript into the volume before you now.

Contents

Introduction:
Twenty Stories

In the fall of 1993, when I began writing this book, the following stories appeared in the news.

Bosnian Serbs continued their genocidal policy of "ethnic cleansing" by raping, torturing, and murdering Muslims.

In the United States, President Clinton began building political support for a national health plan that would reduce the vast inequality in medical care Americans receive.

The Chinese government, hoping to host the Olympics in 2000, released its most famous dissident from jail. Wei Jingsheng had been imprisoned for nearly fourteen years for "publishing counterrevolutionary propaganda." Meanwhile, the American government struggled to decide whether to renew China's most-favored-nation trade status in light of Beijing's "abysmal human rights record."

In Florida, a murder trial was set for an anti-abortion activist who shot a doctor in the back outside his abortion clinic. Supporters of the murderer said he had done a good thing.

In Washington, a federal appeals court struck down the old Pentagon policy barring gays from military service, saying, "the government cannot discriminate against a certain class in order to give effect to the prejudice of others." The ruling, should it stand, would cast doubt upon the legality of the Pentagon's new "Don't ask, don't tell" policy as well.

In Brazil, some thirty military policemen stormed into a Rio de Janeiro shantytown and killed twenty-one people in a shooting rampage. A month earlier, the police had murdered eight children believed to be thieves, with considerable public approval.

Newsweek featured Pat Robertson's efforts to build a new generation of "religious conservatives" to win control of the Republican Party. Oliver North, favored to win the Virginia GOP nomination for the Senate, sent out a fund-raising letter stating that an "arrogant army of ultrafeminists dominates U.S. politics."

In many countries around the world, governments wrestled with massive debts by cutting back on social programs.

A German court sentenced a neo-Nazi to life imprisonment for the fire-bombing that killed three Turkish immigrants. German "skinheads" also beat a white American athlete who came to the aid of a black teammate being taunted. It was discovered that most neo-Nazi German-language propaganda originates in North America. Meanwhile, American skinheads continued to grow in number and violence.

Pope John Paul issued a 179-page encyclical, "Splendor of Truth," in which (among other things) he reaffirmed the church's traditional teachings on the sinfulness of birth control, premarital sex, married priests, and female priests.

It was learned that most of the Salvadoran military officers implicated in the 1989 murder of six priests had been trained at the U.S. Army's School of the Americas at Fort Benning, Georgia. Officers connected to death squads in many other Latin American countries were also found to have been trained at the same school.

The U.S. Census Bureau reported that in 1992 the rich got richer, and the poor got more numerous.

In Russia, 150 "right-wing" lawmakers armed and barricaded themselves in the Parliament building and urged supporters to storm television stations and government offices. Troops loyal to President Yeltsin eventually repelled the rioters and attacked the Russian White House, routing the insurgents. Two months later, "fascist" leader Vladimir Zhirinovsky proved the big winner in parliamentary elections.*

At another White House, Israeli and Palestinian leaders signed an agreement intended to end nearly fifty years of enmity and warfare. Jewish hard-liners vowed violent opposition. So did Islamic fundamentalists, who were also putting terrorist pressure on Muslim governments from North Africa to the Persian Gulf to establish fundamentalist Islamic states.

In Canada, federal elections reduced the Conservative Party's seats in the

---

*Terms such as "right-wing," "fascist," "conservative," "fundamentalist," (as well as "left-wing," "liberal," and so on) convey general meanings that elude scientific precision. I hope eventually to sharpen their usage in this book. In the meanwhile, I could fence them in with quotation marks each time, to show my honest hesitation at their employ. But that would turn your reading into a kind of steeplechase. So I shall usually omit the qualifying quotation marks and we shall canter along over smoother ground, pretending we know what we are talking about.

House of Commons from a dominating 153 to 2. A Quebec separatist party formed the Official Opposition to the Liberal government. In western Canada, former Conservative supporters flocked to the banner of the Reform Party, which promised to eliminate the deficit, oppose Francophone policies, and reduce immigration.

In South Africa, Nelson Mandela and F. W. de Klerk agreed on a plan for holding democratic elections involving blacks and whites. Afrikaner extremists and Zulu nationalists vowed to oppose the elections with force.

In Northern Ireland, the members of the Irish Republican Army and the Ulster Defense League continued to kill each other, and others who happened to be around.

In Somalia, Canadian peacekeeping troops beat to death an unarmed Somali teenager whom they found (searching for a missing child) near their camp. It became clear that many Somalis did not welcome the United Nations forces when the body of an American soldier was dragged in celebration through the streets. Reminded of Vietnam, millions of Americans said, "Let's get out!"

Millions of Americans also cried out for stricter gun-control laws when a lone gunman shot twenty-four people riding home on a commuter train to Long Island, killing five. The National Rifle Association opposed any new laws. In an earlier cover story, *Time* described "America the Violent," and noted that violent crime had "spread into small towns and public sanctuaries."

Finally, in another cover story, *Time* revealed that 69% of Americans believed in angels.

Few things become dated as quickly as yesterday's headlines. Yet if you look at your morning paper, you will probably find fresh versions of these autumn 1993 episodes, just as those echoed many earlier events over many years. Furthermore, I propose that all these events, and others including the World Trade Center bombing and the Oklahoma City bombing, are in one respect the *same* story. The connecting link is a certain kind of personality: the *right-wing authoritarian*. By the time you finish this book, you may recognize this personality playing its role in much of your daily news, too.

Our culture maintains a popular stereotype about right-wingers and left-wingers, and the political parties they tend to join. Dave Barry put it thus:

> The Democrats seem to be basically nicer people, but they have demonstrated time and time again that they have the management skills of celery. They're the kind of people who'd stop to help you change a flat, but would somehow manage to set your car on fire. I would be reluctant to entrust them with a Cuisinart, let alone the economy. The Republicans, on the other hand, would know how to fix your tire, but they wouldn't bother to stop because they'd want to be on time for Ugly Pants Night at the country club. Also, the Republicans have a high Beady-Eyed

Self-Righteous Scary Borderline Loon Quotient, as evidenced by Phyllis Schlafly, Pat Robertson, the entire state of Utah, etc.   (Barry, 1990, p. 124).

I would bet both the Democrats and the Republicans would say, "He got us wrong, but his description of our opponents is right on." Is either rendering as true as it is funny? Are leftists really bleeding hearts with no brains? Are rightists really shallow, greedy loonies?

You can waste a lot of time arguing with people who hold these stereotypes. Everyone can cite personal experiences, lash out with "trigger words," and produce (selected) examples from history. It does not take much insight to quip stereotypes, even contradictory ones.

Some social scientists have accused right-wingers in particular of holding contradictory stereotypes (Adorno et al., 1950). But this sword cuts both ways, and people may in turn hold contradictory beliefs about right-wingers. For example, how can right-wing types be quite gullible but also suspicious to the point of paranoia? How can they strongly favor individual freedom while also wanting to "escape from freedom," letting dictators tell them what to do? Do they want to keep things the way they are, a common definition of "conservative," or want to change society a great deal?

Whether stereotypes or not, *opinions* can be dismissed as "just opinions." For example, the *New York Times* entitled its lead editorial on November 13, 1994, "Newt Gingrich, Authoritarian." House Leader Gingrich and his Republican caucus could rightly observe the editorial merely reflected someone's opinion, and in *their opinion,* the *Times*'s editorials are outrageously opinionated.

Who is right? Well, many people would despair of ever resolving such issues, but science can put opinions to a test. False ideas eventually have the ground cut from under them when subjected to scientific study. This book presents, for the first time, over one hundred studies I have done on the thinking and behavior of right-wing authoritarians. (I shall consider left-wing authoritarians, too.) I tried to make the experiments fair to all sides, giving everyone an equal chance to look good, or bad. The data fell where they naturally did. As it happened, they fell almost entirely on one side, leading to powerful conclusions that can no more be dismissed as "just opinion" than the fact that water can make you wet.

If, after reading this book, you feel, "I knew this stuff all along," then you are a lot smarter than I am. It has taken me many years to uncover the evidence that proves you right, and I was sometimes surprised by my results. But even if you have had this all figured out for a long time, you might still want to see the experimental findings that back you up.

Overall, I hope this research carries our understanding of the "psychology of fascism" far beyond the clichés of stereotype and the ethereal realm of "just opinion." We need to get at the truth. If my findings have shown me anything, they have revealed that what happened in Germany in 1933 *can* happen in North America too. Many people are already psychologically disposed to support a fascist overthrow of democracy. For example, the militias publicized after the Oklahoma City bombing bear more than a passing resemblance to the disgruntled, military-minded men whom Hitler molded into his private army of S.A. Stormtroopers for his rise to power.

It would outrage many conservatives who condemned the Oklahoma City bombing to be told they are more different in *degree* than in *kind* from the neo-Nazis out to overthrow the American government. But the evidence in this book will show the similarities.

— 1 —
Previous Research on Right-Wing Authoritarianism

By "right-wing authoritarianism" I mean the covariation of three attitudinal clusters in a person:

1. Authoritarian submission—a high degree of submission to the authorities who are perceived to be established and legitimate in the society in which one lives.

2. Authoritarian aggression—a general aggressiveness, directed against various persons, that is perceived to be sanctioned by established authorities.

3. Conventionalism—a high degree of adherence to the social conventions that are perceived to be endorsed by society and its established authorities.[1]

Elaborations on the Definition

The more precisely a scientific construct is defined, the easier one can test it, find its errors and limitations, and move on to a better model. Let me explain in some detail, therefore, what I mean by the terms in my definition of right-wing authoritarianism.[2]

By "attitudinal clusters" I mean orientations to respond in the same general way toward certain classes of stimuli (namely, the perceived established authorities, sanctioned targets, and social conventions). But an orientation to respond does not necessarily lead to a response, and few social psychologists today expect attitude measures to correlate highly with behavior regardless of the situation.

Stanley Milgram's (1974) famous experiments on obedience provide a clear and highly relevant example. Men recruited through newspaper ads were maneuvered into being the Teacher in a supposed experiment on the effects of electric shock upon learning. Although the "Learner" (a Milgram confederate) never received any shocks, the situation was masterfully convincing. The Teachers had every reason to believe they were inflicting terrible pain on the Learner soon after the experiment began. By the end of the session, if the subjects did not stop it, they could easily have believed the next shock would kill the unconscious Learner, if he was not already dead. The point of the experiment was to see when subjects would defy their local authority, the Experimenter, and shock no more.[3]

Most people are shocked themselves when they learn that in Milgram's basic experiment, almost all of the Teachers threw switches that would have inflicted great pain on the victim. And *most* of the men threw switches representing stronger and stronger shocks until they ran out of switches at 450 volts. That is, they completely obeyed the Experimenter—unwillingly to be sure, but completely, to be sure.

If you believe with me that Milgram's subjects were horrified at what was happening, their compliance in itself demonstrates the power of situations over personality. But Milgram produced an even more compelling demonstration. In two conditions of his experiment, the real subject was sandwiched between two confederates at the shocking machine as part of a "Teaching Team." When the Learner screamed he wanted to be set free from the experiment, one of the confederates quit. So did the second, soon thereafter. The Experimenter then pressured the naive subject to continue administering shocks, but only four of forty (10%) went to 450 volts. However, if the two confederates kept right on going when the Learner started screaming, as though nothing had happened, thirty-seven out of forty (92%) of the subjects who served in that condition went (with their silent partners) all the way to 450 volts.

So who is a hero, and who is jelly? It mattered almost not at all who the individuals were. Behavior in these two conditions almost completely depended on what the confederates on the Teaching Team did.

THE ROLE OF PERSONALITY

Let me catch myself before I go off the deep end. I *do* believe that in many situations it matters a great deal who the people are. Different patterns of genes make a difference. So do different patterns of socialization. After all, Milgram's subjects were in a strange environment (to put it mildly), interacting with strangers trained to say their lines whatever the subject did. Whereas we usually act in familiar settings with familiar people whose behavior we can affect. But the great lesson of social psychology has been how easily situations trump individual differences. Milgram's experiment shows us that, and a great deal else very frightening.

Right-wing authoritarianism is an individual difference variable, a personality trait if you like, developed on the premise that some people need little situational pressure to (say) submit to authority and attack others, while others require significantly more. We can find evidence of this individual difference even in Milgram's experiment. In two conditions of the initial study, the Learner sat in a separate room from the Teacher, which made it relatively easy for the Teachers to obey the Experimenter completely, as 64% did. In two other conditions, however, the Learner sat right beside the Teacher, and indeed sometimes the Teacher had to force his victim's hand down on a (supposed) shockplate to administer the punishments. That made it harder to obey the Experimenter, as you can imagine: "only" 35% proved completely obedient.

In one case, then, the situation pushed people toward obedience; but in the other, it promoted defiance. In both cases some people acted differently from the majority. They defied when it was hard to defy, or they obeyed when it was hard to obey. Who were they? Elms and Milgram (1966) found that the twenty defiant ones scored rather low on a pioneering measure of personal authoritarianism, the California Fascism Scale; whereas the twenty obedient ones, whom the Experimenter could get to shock a helpless victim sitting at their side, scored much higher.

ARE THERE REALLY FASCIST PEOPLE IN DEMOCRACIES?
But can there really be fascist people in democracies? I am afraid so. The central apprehension behind my research program, driven by twenty-five years of alarming findings now being confirmed in tragic headlines, is that a potential for the acceptance of right-wing totalitarian rule exists in countries such as Canada and the United States. This acceptance boils down to essentially an attitude, a state of mind, a willingness to see democratic institutions destroyed, which in some people may even be a desire.

Right-wing authoritarianism has thus been defined as an orientation, rather than as the terrible acts it greases the skis for, but it is still dangerous. The mood of a populace can create a climate of public opinion that promotes totalitarian movements. It can intimidate politicians, journalists, and religious leaders who might otherwise oppose repression. It can elect a dictator into office, as it did most notably in Germany in 1933. It can encourage a bold, illegal grab for power, as it did in Italy in 1922, and has violently done in so many other places since. And once the power is grabbed, who will resist? Who will love democracy enough to face the tank in Tiananmen Square, versus those who will cheer for the dictator? That is an individual difference.

By "submission" to the perceived established authorities I mean a general acceptance of their statements and actions and a general willingness to comply with their instructions without further inducement.[4]

Authoritarians believe that proper authorities should be trusted to a great extent and deserve obedience and respect. They believe that these are important virtues which children should be taught and that if children stray from these principles, parents have a duty to get them back in line. Right-wing authoritarians would ordinarily place narrow limits on people's rights to criticize authorities. They tend to assume that officials know what is best and that critics do not know what they are talking about. They view criticism of authority as divisive and destructive, motivated by sinister goals and a desire to cause trouble. Authoritarians believe, to a considerable extent, that established authorities have an inherent right to decide for themselves what they may do, including breaking the laws they make for the rest of us.

By "perceived established authorities" I mean those people in our society who are usually considered to have a general legal or moral authority over the behavior of others. One's parents (at least through childhood), religious officials, civic officers (the police, judges, heads of governments), and superiors in military service usually qualify as established authorities.

But note the modifier "perceived." Some extremists may reject normal authorities who (it seems to them) have betrayed the *real,* fundamental established authority: for example (their perception of) God's will, or the Constitution. They often believe the government has been taken over by Jews, homosexuals, feminists, Communists, and so on. Such extremists are right-wing authoritarian in this context—"superpatriots" who see themselves as upholding traditional values, but whose fear and self-righteousness hammer with such intensity that they rehearse for violence and may cross the line to violence itself. As we shall see, ordinary authoritarians stand closer to that line in the best of times than most people do. They are just not *that* afraid yet.

The ordinary authoritarians—whom this book is about—do not submit absolutely, automatically, or blindly to the usual authorities. Like anyone else, they can be conflicted about orders from above; they will not always accept orders, but they will accept them more often than others will. Similarly, officials do not all command equal degrees of respect and submission: there are "good judges" and "bad governments," "good popes" and "poor presidents." Authoritarians however, will submit to established authorities they like, and to those they do *not* like, more readily than nonauthoritarians will.

When I modify authoritarianism with the phrase "right-wing," I do not necessarily mean anything political (as in liberal versus conservative) or economic (as in socialist versus capitalist). Rather, I am using "right-wing" in a *psychological* sense of submitting to the perceived authorities in one's life (Altemeyer, 1981, p. 152), usually "the Establishment." The supporters of apartheid in pre-Mandela South Africa would be right-wing authoritarians, and so would those who praised the murderous military police in Brazil. And so would the Chinese who supported the massacre in Tiananmen Square, and the hard-liners in Russia who want to reinstate the Communist Party. Although neither the Chinese nor Russian groups are economic right-wingers, they are psychological right-wingers in their support for those they were raised to believe were the legitimate authorities.

Are there psychological left-wingers too? Yes. I shall talk about them in Chapter 9. The rest of this book concerns right-wing authoritarianism, which I often call simply "authoritarianism," because after twenty-five years, I am tired of typing out "right-wing." (I am even more tired of typing out "authoritarianism" but feel I have to give you *some* chance to know what I am talking about.)

AUTHORITARIAN AGGRESSION

By "aggression" I mean intentionally causing harm to someone. The harm can be physical injury, psychological suffering, financial loss, social isolation, or some other negative state that people usually try to avoid. Aggression is authoritarian when it is accompanied by the belief that proper authority approves it or that it will help preserve such authority.

The predisposition to such aggression does not mean that authoritarians will always act aggressively when opportunities arise. Fear of retaliation may stop them, as may the legal and social prohibitions against aggression in our culture. This is where the perception of authoritative sanction plays its role. It can *dis*inhibit the aggressive impulse.[5]

Right-wing authoritarians are predisposed to control the behavior of others through punishment. They advocate physical punishment in childhood and beyond. They deplore leniency in the courts and believe penal reform just encourages criminals to continue being lawless. They advocate capital punishment. All in all, one finds an "Old Testament harshness" in their approach to human conduct.

Anyone could become the target of authoritarian aggression, but unconventional people (including "social deviants") and conventional victims of aggression (such as certain minority groups) are attacked more readily than others. Thus we would expect right-wing authoritarianism to correlate with ethnic and racial prejudice, because such prejudice provides a conventional outlet of aggressive impulses. Authoritarians believe that certain authorities approve of this hostility, and they may believe that certain groups threaten the social order. Hence the aggressiveness in prejudice can be authoritarian.

But by no means is all prejudice thought to be linked to right-wing authoritarianism.

If social deviants and certain minority groups provide ready targets for authoritarian aggression, others can be victims as well. The authoritarian is more likely to attack a conventional person than a nonauthoritarian is, if an established authority sanctions it. This power of authority figures to direct the hostility of authoritarians against almost any target increases the danger of authoritarian aggression to all in a society.

CONVENTIONALISM

By "adherence to social conventions" I mean a strong acceptance of and commitment to the traditional social norms in one's society. Many such norms in my society are based on the common teachings of the Judeo-Christian religions. The right-wing authoritarian generally believes in "God's law" and thinks human conflict occurs because people ignore this law. Within each religion, authoritarians tend to be fundamentalists, wishing to maintain the beliefs, teachings, and services in their traditional form and resisting change. Authoritarians reject the idea that people should develop their own ideas of what is moral and immoral, since authorities have already laid down the laws.

Authoritarians' attitudes toward sex are strongly influenced by their religious principles. Traditionally sex outside marriage is basically sinful. Nudity is sinful. Thinking about sex is sinful. Homosexuality is considered a sin and a perversion. Many sexual acts, even between married partners, are perversions.

These attitudes toward sex have their parallel in conventional attitudes toward proper behavior for men and women. Authoritarians endorse the traditional family structure in which women are subservient to their husbands. They believe women should, by and large, keep to their traditional roles in society. While advocating a "decent, respectable appearance" for both sexes, they especially demand it of women. While condemning sexual transgression for both sexes, they especially condemn it when women "transgress."

Right-wing authoritarians endorse a host of other social norms. The flag and the national anthem should be venerated. They strongly believe that "our customs and national heritage are the things that have made us great" and that everyone should be made to show respect for them. People should strive to be well-behaved, properly dressed, respectable, and in general to stick to the straight and narrow. Finally, they hold these conventions to be moral as well as social imperatives. The authoritarian rejects the proposition that social customs are arbitrary and that one group's customs may be as good as another's. Other ways of doing things are wrong.

I use the term "norms" here in the normative, not the descriptive, sense. The right-wing authoritarian's conventionalism specifies how people ought to act, not how they do. The authoritarian's code is conventional because it is based on long-standing tradition and custom, not because it actually describes how most people behave today. Thus it may be that most adults in our society engage in sexual intercourse before marriage. But the fact that most people are "sinning" shows the authoritarian only that it is a sinful world.

I do not mean to imply that the authoritarian's adherence to traditional social norms has been cast in iron and cannot be changed in a lifetime. We shall see that authoritarian students today are more likely to have sex before marriage than they were in years past. But their adherence to their customs will prove more resistant to change than the nonauthoritarian's, and it is relatively more likely to be influenced by the pronouncements of the established authorities than by the behavior of peers.

Does the Trait Actually Exist?

Right-wing authoritarianism, being a covariation of social attitudes, is measured by a thirty-item Likert-type attitude scale entitled (what else?) the Right-Wing Authoritarianism (RWA) Scale. The latest version of the instrument is given in Exhibit 1.1.

Exhibit 1.1   The 1996 RWA Scale

This survey is part of an investigation of general public opinion concerning a variety of social issues. You will probably find that you *agree* with some of the statements, and *disagree* with others, to varying extents. Please indicate your reaction to each statement by blackening a bubble in SECTION 1 of the IBM sheet, according to the following scale:

Blacken the bubble labeled

   − 4 if you *very strongly disagree* with the statement.

   − 3 if you *strongly disagree* with the statement.

   − 2 if you *moderately disagree* with the statement.

   − 1 if you *slightly disagree* with the statement.

Blacken the bubble labeled

   + 1 if you *slightly agree* with the statement.

   + 2 if you *moderately agree* with the statement.

   + 3 if you *strongly agree* with the statement.

   + 4 if you *very strongly agree* with the statement.

If you feel exactly and precisely *neutral* about an item, blacken the "0" bubble.

You may find that you sometimes have different reactions to different parts of a statement. For example, you might very strongly disagree ("−4") with one idea in a statement, but slightly agree ("+1") with another idea in the same item. When this happens, please combine your reactions, and write down how you feel "on balance" (i.e., a "−3" in this example).

1. Life imprisonment is justified for certain crimes.

2. Women should have to promise to obey their husbands when they get married.

3. The established authorities in our country are usually smarter, better informed, and more competent than others are, and the people can rely upon them.

4. It is important to protect the rights of radicals and deviants in all ways.

5. Our country desperately needs a mighty leader who will do what has to be done to destroy the radical new ways and sinfulness that are ruining us.

6. Gays and lesbians are just as healthy and moral as anybody else.*

7. Our country will be great if we honor the ways of our forefathers, do what the authorities tell us to do, and get rid of the "rotten apples" who are ruining everything.

8. Atheists and others who have rebelled against the established religions are no doubt every bit as good and virtuous as those who attend church regularly.*

9. The *real* keys to the "good life" are obedience, discipline, and sticking to the straight and narrow.

10. A lot of our rules regarding modesty and sexual behavior are just customs which are not necessarily any better or holier than those which other people follow.*

11. There are many radical, immoral people in our country today, who are trying to ruin it for their own godless purposes, whom the authorities should put out of action.

12. It is always better to trust the judgment of the proper authorities in government and religion than to listen to the noisy rabble-rousers in our society who are trying to create doubt in people's minds.

13. There is absolutely nothing wrong with nudist camps.*

14. There is no "ONE right way" to live life; everybody has to create their *own* way.*

15. Our country will be destroyed someday if we do not smash the perversions eating away at our moral fiber and traditional beliefs.

16. Homosexuals and feminists should be praised for being brave enough to defy "traditional family values."*

17. The situation in our country is getting so serious, the strongest methods would be justified if they eliminated the troublemakers and got us back to our true path.

18. It may be considered old fashioned by some, but having a normal, proper appearance is still the mark of a gentleman and, especially, a lady.

19. Everyone should have their own lifestyle, religious beliefs, and sexual preferences, even if it makes them different from everyone else.*

20. A "woman's place" should be wherever she wants to be. The days when women are submissive to their husbands and social conventions belong strictly in the past.*

21. What our country really needs is a strong, determined leader who will crush evil, and take us back to our true path.

22. People should pay less attention to the Bible and the other old traditional forms of religious guidance, and instead develop their own personal standards of what is moral and immoral.*

23. The only way our country can get through the crisis ahead is to get back to our traditional values, put some tough leaders in power, and silence the troublemakers spreading bad ideas.

24. Our country *needs* free thinkers who will have the courage to defy traditional ways, even if this upsets many people.*

25. There is nothing wrong with premarital sexual intercourse.*

26. It would be best for everyone if the proper authorities censored magazines so that people could not get their hands on trashy and disgusting material.

27. It is wonderful that young people today have greater freedom to protest against things they don't like, and to make their own "rules" to govern their behavior.*

28. What our country *really* needs, instead of more "civil rights," is a good stiff dose of law and order.

29. Some of the best people in our country are those who are challenging our government, criticizing religion, and ignoring the "normal way" things are supposed to be done.*

30. Obedience and respect for authority are the most important virtues children should learn.

31. Nobody should "stick to the straight and narrow." Instead, people should break loose and try out lots of different ideas and experiences.*

32. Once our government leaders give us the "go ahead," it will be the duty of every patriotic citizen to help stomp out the rot that is poisoning our country from within.

33. We should treat protestors and radicals with open arms and open minds, since new ideas are the lifeblood of progressive change.*

34. The facts on crime, sexual immorality, and the recent public disorders all show we have to crack down harder on deviant groups and trouble-makers if we are going to save our moral standards and preserve law and order.

Note: Only items 5–34 are scored. Items are scored on a 1–9 basis. For protrait statements, " − 4" is scored as 1, and " + 4" is scored as 9. The keying is reversed for contrait items. For both kinds of items, the neutral answer ("0") is scored as 5. The lowest possible score is 30, and the highest is 270.

I have used a − 4 to + 4 response scale on the RWA Scale since 1980, rather than the usual − 3 to + 3, because experiments have shown that the former produces (marginally) higher reliability. Either a nine-point or a seven-point response scale appears to be superior to the five-point format Likert (1932) invented. A three-point response scale ("Disagree/?/Agree") seems to damage appreciably a scale's psychometric properties among populations capable of making finer distinctions (Altemeyer, 1988, pp. 39–42).

* Item is worded in the contrait direction; the right-wing authoritarian response is to disagree.

The first four items are "table-setters," intended to give the respondent some experience with the nine-point response scale and also a little familiarity with some of the content that follows. They are not scored. The test proper consists of items 5–34, which include fifteen protrait items (for example, "Obedience and respect for authority are the most important virtues children should learn"—to pick a short one) and fifteen contrait statements (such as "There is absolutely nothing wrong with nudist camps"). All items are intended to measure the extent to which someone believes in authoritarian submission, authoritarian aggression, and conventionalism. Most statements tap two, or all three, of these orientations.

The covariation of responses to the RWA Scale provides a test that the trait "exists." Since the thirty items cover many different topics, their 435 intercorrelations tend to be small. After all, how much connection can there be between believing in children's obedience and disliking nudist camps? But small as they might be on average, the correlations will gel if the model is right.

This level of interitem correlation, along with the length of the test, determines Cronbach's (1970) alpha coefficient of internal consistency. Basically, the mean interitem correlation ranged around .18, and the resulting alpha ranged around .85–.88, among the population used to develop the test—introductory psychology students at my university (Altemeyer, 1981, p. 218; Altemeyer, 1988, p. 29; hereafter the 1981 *Right-Wing Authoritarianism* will be cited as *RWA*, and the 1988 outpouring, *Enemies of Freedom*, as *EOF*). This constitutes fairly solid evidence that authoritarian submission, authoritarian aggression, and conventionalism *do* covary in that population. But do they elsewhere?

MY PREVIOUSLY REPORTED RWA SCALE ALPHAS

During 1973–74, alphas of .84 were obtained at two other Canadian universities (Alberta and Western Ontario) with the original scale. The same figure appeared at the University of North Dakota.[6] Then studies at the Universities of Alabama, Indiana, Virginia, and Wyoming and at Pennsylvania State University found alphas ranging from .85 to .89 (*RWA*, pp. 208–210, 216–218).

Two nonstudent populations were also sampled in the early days of RWA Scale research. Adult males in Winnipeg, Canada (randomly selected from voter lists and the telephone directory), produced an alpha of .85. And parents of my Manitoba students came in at .89 (*RWA*, pp. 210–211, 218).

My first book produced an avalanche of five RWA Scale studies by the time my second book appeared, seven years later. Zwillenberg (1983) found a reliability of .86 for the original scale among 503 students drawn from the University of New Haven, Brooklyn College, Columbia University, Montclair State College, the University of Georgia, Central Michigan University, the Universities of Nebraska and Denver, California State University at Fresno, and the University of California at Santa Cruz. Johann Schneider (personal communication, November 19, 1984) obtained an alpha of .94 with a translated version given to German students. Duckitt (1992) found an alpha of .93 among 212 South African students. Heaven (1984) reported an alpha of .81 among Australian students and .90 among heterogeneous adults. Lastly, Ray (1985) obtained an alpha of .89 among a random sample of Australian adults (*EOF*, pp. 13–14).

In my own research through 1987, the RWA Scale (which changes a little every year) continued to show alphas of about .88 among Manitoba students and .90 among their parents (*EOF*, p. 29). However, samples of North American lawmakers showed astounding internal consistency when answering the scale. Alphas ranged from .88 to .97 in four Canadian provincial assemblies, and from .94 to .97 in four American state legislatures (*EOF*, chapter 7).

MY OWN SUBSEQUENT STUDIES, 1989–90

In the fall of 1989 I began bothering people at various North American universities, asking if I could dip into their introductory psychology subject pools to collect some cross-validation data. Eventually I found several places that would not give *"No!"* for an answer.[7] At each site a booklet of surveys beginning with the RWA Scale was administered, usually by a graduate student. At the State University of New York at Potsdam (SUNY-Potsdam), 183 students produced an alpha of .88. At Harvard 172 students racked up a North American student record alpha of .93. Finally, alpha equaled .87 among 200 University of Pittsburgh students and .92 among 101 undergraduates at the University of Houston.

In the spring of 1989, Andre Kamenshikov administered his own translation of the RWA Scale for me to 226 students attending Moscow State University (the one in Russia, not Idaho). The alpha was .81 (Altemeyer and Kamenshikov, 1991).

OTHER RESEARCHERS' SUBSEQUENT FINDINGS

Table 1.1 presents the RWA Scale's alpha coefficients obtained lately by other researchers.[8] You can see that the test has held together well in the many populations sampled. With the exception of the Xhosa-speaking South African group (whose proficiency in English was unreported), authoritarian submission, authoritarian aggression, and conventionalism have covaried appreciably in all of the populations tested to date.

This still surprises me no end. The scale was developed among Manitoba first-year psychology students. It measures social attitudes, which would seem to be very culture-bound, and could easily be organized differently among different groups *within* a culture. So I was a little surprised to discover the test hung together as well among the parents of university students as it did among their progeny. I was even more surprised that it proved as cohesive among scattered American student samples as it had in my little neck of the woods. Then, when results started coming in from diverse American nonstudent samples, and especially when I learned of the results from overseas, I was just amazed. (I could not sit down for two days after the first Russian findings came in.)

Mind you, we have heard from only a few places. Minorities within North America and vast majorities in virtually all the countries in the world have not been studied. I fully expect the scale to fall apart here and there, and perhaps everywhere else. We have no universal trait here, I am sure. Still, we have something a little grander than I ever expected it to be.

Finally, although you perhaps have had a different experience, I have seldom found that scales have the same sparkling psychometric properties in my research that they had in their inventors' write-ups. So I have been happy to see that most researchers have obtained RWA Scale alphas as high as, and often higher than, I have gotten in my own work. Science has to be a public effort by a community of investigators struggling to discover the truth, whatever it may be. Replicability is essential to that struggle. It enables us to work

Table 1.1 Internal consistency of the RWA Scale obtained by other researchers

Investigator	Participants	Alpha
North American students		
Hunsberger (1994, p.c.)[a]	Several thousand Wilfrid Laurier U. (Can.) students	.89
Moghaddam and Vuksanovic (1990)	155 McGill U. (Can.) students	.89
Peters (1990)	239 U. of Waterloo (Can.) students in two studies	.89
Walker and Quinsey (1991)	157 Queens U. (Can.) students (and 41 nonstudents recruited through posters and employment centers)	.93
Trapnell (1992, p.c.)	924 U. of British Columbia students in two studies	.87
Colby et al. (1987)	488 U. of California at Irvine students	.89
Goldberg and Rosolack (1991)	503 Oregon college students	.88
Stone and Schultz (1992)	112 University of Maine students	.90
Stone (1994, p.c.)	108 University of Maine students	.94
Tarr and Lorr (1991)	339 students at two "eastern universities"	.86
Billings et al. (1993)	139 students, perhaps in Milwaukee	.88
Cormer (1993, p.c.)	102 Hofstra U. students	.85
Eigenberger (1994)	242 U. of Wyoming students	.87
Peterson et al. (1993)	448 U. of Michigan students in two studies	.92
Skitka and Tetlock (1993)	166 Berkeley and Southern Illinois U. students	.86
Skitka (1994, p.c.)	1,317 Southern Illinois U. students	.90
Leak and Randall (1995)	157 Creighton U. students	.87
Wasieleski (1994, p.c.)	279 U. of Alabama students	.92
Non–North American students		
Garzon (1992)	109 U. of Valencia and Castellon students (in Spanish)	.85
Edwards and Leger (1993)	215 Rhodes U. (South Africa) students (in English)	.83
	400 Xhosa-speaking Fort Hare U. students (in English)	.43
Rubinstein (1996)	708 Israeli university students (in Hebrew)	.88
	120 Palestinian university students (in Arabic)	.84

Table 1.1   (continued).

Investigator	Participants	Alpha
North American nonstudents		
Holms (1989)	183 friends of Canadian university students who did not go to university	.86
McFarland (1989a)	463 Kentucky adults	.89
Dornfest (1992, p.c.)	1,094 U. of California at Davis alumni	.93
Lykken (1994, p.c.)	3,240 members of Minnesota Twin Study and spouses	.90
Perrott (1991)	160 members of Halifax (Can.) police force	.84
Colby et al. (1992)	169 women over age sixty living in Orange County, Calif.	.92
Stober and Chance (1995, p.c.)	158 Georgia adults awaiting possible jury duty	.95
Non–North American nonstudents		
Feather (1993)	204 Adelaide (Australia) adults	.88
McFarland et al. (1990)[b]	167 Moscow and 179 Estonia citizens (translated)	.92
McFarland et al. (1994)	440 Moscow citizens (translated)	.81

a. Indicates a personal communication.
b. McFarland, Ageyev, and Abalakina (1990) studied a quota sample of Soviet citizens living in Moscow or Tallinn in the early days of *glasnost*. There has never been, to my knowledge, a North American study of the RWA Scale that tested as representative a sample.

"together"—even though we may seldom agree, never meet, or even live at the same time. It appears that, psychometrically, we have a good tool here that we can share.

Do RWA Scores Actually Correlate with Right-Wing Authoritarian Behavior?

Let's see. We have inferred that a trait exists. We have defined the trait in some detail. We have a measure of that trait, and the internal consistency of that measure supports the notion that the trait exists. But does that measure actually correlate with the kind of behavior we want to understand? Does the RWA Scale have *empirical* validity, as well as a pretty alpha? This is our second test of the measure's validity, and we shall examine it by looking at studies of authoritarian submission, authoritarian aggression, and conventionalism.

AUTHORITARIAN SUBMISSION

From its earliest days, the RWA Scale showed it could generally distinguish between people who accepted unfair and even illegal acts by government officials and those who took exception to such acts (*RWA*, pp. 189–192, 227–228). Using real occurrences of illegal wiretaps, illegal searches, denial of the right to assemble, use of *agents provocateurs*, and so on from the turbulent late 1960s and early 1970s, I found that RWA scores correlated .52 to .59 with Manitoba students' acceptance of these events. The connection among their parents equaled .54 and, among 772 American students at five scattered universities, .63.

A subsequent series of experiments revealed, as one would expect, that High RWAs (those in the top 25% of the distribution of scores in that sample, in contrast to "Lows," who similarly compose the bottom 25%)[9] showed particular indifference to government injustices directed against *unconventional* groups (*RWA*, pp. 228–232).

For a more telling connection between authoritarianism and tolerance of official malfeasance, consider the Watergate scandal. Most of over 700 American students, polled after Richard Nixon had accepted a pardon for his felonies, said they had believed the president for a very long time. In fact, many said they *still* believed Nixon was innocent. The correlations between RWA scores and this enduring trust were .48–.51. (*RWA*, pp. 224–227).[10]

Citizens in a democracy are usually protected against abuse of power by constitutional guarantees. But neither the Canadian Charter of Rights and Freedoms nor the U.S. Bill of Rights draws overall support from right-wing authoritarians.

In 1986 I asked over 500 Manitoba students to react to a (bogus) "letter to the editor" attacking the Canadian Charter. This document, it was claimed, was one of the biggest mistakes the country had ever made, causing most of our social problems because "it gives rights to everyone, no matter who he is or what he does." The students showed little overall sympathy with the ridiculous charges I invented, producing (on scales of 0–6) means of 2.46 with "how sensible" the letter seemed and only 1.22 with agreement that the Charter should be repealed. But RWA scores correlated .42 and .45 with these attitudes (*EOF*, pp. 270–271).

I repeated this study in the fall of 1990 with a sample of 235 parents of Manitoba students. While I thought the "older and wiser" parents would see the enormous danger lurking behind the bogus letter, they actually thought it was a little more "sensible" ($\bar{X}$ = 2.64) than the students had and positively *agreed* that the Charter should be abolished (4.91). Again, authoritarianism played its role, with RWA scores correlating .49 and .47 with these two sentiments.

I also did the study in February 1990, with 57 San Francisco State University students. Here the letter attacked the Bill of Rights and the U.S. Supreme Court:

> If a person stops to think about it, most of the problems we are having can be traced to the Bill of Rights—or more precisely, to the way it has been interpreted by the Supreme Court. "Freedom of speech" has been twisted to mean that pornographers can sell their filth, and that anybody can say whatever he wants, whether it's good for society or not. And "freedom of religion" has been twisted to mean children can't pray in public schools any more. And the "right to happiness" has been twisted to mean women can have abortion after abortion if they're "unhappy" being pregnant. And think how many drug pushers and criminals have gotten off scot-free because their "rights" were supposedly violated after they had robbed or killed somebody.
>
> A lot of people hoped the new Supreme Court, rid of the "Liberal Majority" which had made all these terrible rulings, would overturn them. But it's clear now that they won't. No Supreme Court can reverse the ruling of an earlier Supreme Court, so we are stuck with these interpretations as long as there is a Bill of Rights. And we will soon be destroyed as a nation because of them.
>
> So the only thing we can do, to make America the free, pure, safe Christian nation that the founding fathers intended it to be, is to repeal the Bill of Rights.

Overall, this appeal was (thankfully) rejected by the San Francisco State students. They produced a mean of 2.24 for the letter's being "sensible" and 1.82 for repeal of the Bill of Rights. But *some* of the students, especially authoritarians, resonated to this ignorant appeal to wipe out America's major defense against tyranny. RWA scores correlated .62 with judgments of sensibility and .50 with agreement for repealing the Bill of Rights.

Other researchers have also found that right-wing authoritarians have little interest in protecting human rights. Moghaddam and Vuksanovic (1990) found RWA Scale correlations of .66, .42, and .52, respectively, with McGill University students' indifference to human rights issues in Canada, the Soviet Union, and the Third World. McFarland, Ageyev, and Abalakina (1990) found, among Soviet citizens in the dying days of the USSR, RWA correlations of .71 with opposition to dissidents, .72 with sentiments that the youth should be submissive, .65 with rejection of a free press, and .74 with opposition to democracy itself.[11]

In February 1996 I repeated a study by Blass (1992b) in which I showed the first part of Milgram's (1965) film "Obedience" to my introductory psychology classes. The twelve-minute edited version ended just after the Teacher who is featured in the film delivered the 180-volt shock. I handed out forms that asked each student, among other things, "Suppose you have 100 'Responsibility Votes' to give, altogether, to the three people in this experiment, as a way of showing how much you think each person is responsible for the fact that the Learner was being given electric shocks against his will. How many of these votes would you give to the Experimenter, the Teacher, and the Learner?" The students were not asked to put their names on the forms until they were about to turn them in. To screen out those familiar with Milgram's results, I discarded all subjects (including 13 Highs and 16 Lows) who said that over 25% of Milgram's sample of 40 men would go all the way to 450 volts. Like Blass, I found the 53 High RWAs were significantly less likely than the 47 Lows to hold the authority, the Experimenter, responsible for what was happening (61.6% versus 70.7% p < .05). Instead, authoritarians tended to blame the Teacher (24.7 versus 21.2, not significant) and the Learner (13.6 versus 8.2, p < .05).

The data on authoritarian submission speak with one voice. All the studies I know show that High RWAs tend to be more submissive to established authority than most people are. They tolerate and even approve of governmental abuse of power, they are relatively willing to cast aside constitutional shields against such abuse, they are indifferent to human rights issues, and in the USSR they spoke out openly against democracy. Moreover, the relationships in all these studies have proven substantial, often rising over .50.

AUTHORITARIAN AGGRESSION

Punishment of Lawbreakers. RWA scores have often predicted the length of prison terms hypothetically imposed upon persons convicted of crimes. Among Manitoba students, the correlation for overall sentences in a ten-trial survey usually ran between .40 and .50. Follow-up questioning revealed that, compared with Lows, High RWAs believed the crimes had been more serious, and they also had more faith that punishment would change the criminals' behavior. But Highs also revealed, when answering anonymously, that they found criminals more repulsive and disgusting than Lows did, and felt personal pleasure and satisfaction at being able to punish wrongdoers (*RWA*, pp. 232–234).

Parents of Manitoba students also showed substantial correlations between authoritarianism and punitiveness in a trial situation. A correlation of .52 was obtained in a 1979 study using ten cases (*RWA*, p. 233), and .33 in a 1986 experiment using just three cases (*EOF*, p. 181).

Wylie (Wylie and Forest, 1992) mailed a booklet of surveys, including three trials, to 275 Manitobans chosen at random from voter lists. She received 75 completed returns. The sum of sentences imposed correlated .52 with RWA scores.[12]

American students show the same trends as their Manitoba counterparts. The correlation between RWA scores and sentences equaled .48 across four trials in a 1974 experiment run at five universities (*RWA*, p. 232). Three trials administered in 1990 at the Universities of Pittsburgh and Houston found correlations of .28 and .51. But David Wasieleski (personal communication,

November 2, 1994) found coefficients of only .23 and .16 with reaching guilty verdicts and length of sentence imposed by 272 University of Alabama students.

A series of cases varying the social status of the criminal produced a complex set of results in 1979. On the one hand, Highs were equally severe on the wife of an investment consultant and an unwed mother, who were found guilty of child abuse. They also punished equally an insurance salesman and a tramp drug addict convicted of bank robbery. On the other hand, they showed relative leniency toward a millionaire industrialist convicted of defrauding the government. They went easy on a police chief who beat up an accused child molester in his jail but were more punitive if told another prisoner had done the beating. Finally, they showed an even more striking double standard in sentencing an accountant and a "hippie panhandler" who got into a fight. If the evidence showed the accountant started the fight, they favored leniency. But if the evidence showed the hippie had started the fight, they laid down the law (*RWA*, pp. 234–238). (Low RWA students punished the two men equally.)

Other studies help us make sense of these seemingly contradictory findings regarding the status of criminals. RWA scores correlated *negatively* with the sentences imposed upon a police officer who beat an "uppity" protestor (*RWA*, pp. 197–199). They also correlated negatively with punishment of a U.S. Air Force officer convicted of murder. The case paralleled the My Lai massacre; the officer had led unauthorized bombing raids against Vietnamese villages suspected of supporting the enemy (*RWA*, p. 233). Similarly, High RWA American students did *not* want to punish Richard Nixon after he resigned (*RWA*, pp. 226–227). Finally, High RWAs showed another pronounced double standard in the sentencing of pro-gay versus anti-gay activists (*EOF*, pp. 112–114). If an anti-gay leader led an attack on a group of gay demonstrators, High RWAs tended to be lenient. But if it were the other way around, they became significantly more punitive. (Again, Lows punished the two assailants equally.)[13]

It appears, then, that believing in punishment as they do and enjoying dishing it out as they do, High RWAs are more likely in general to sentence wrongdoers to long prison terms. But this is not true if the wrongdoers are officials whom the authoritarian admires, or if the crime involved attacking someone Highs believe *should* be attacked (the child molester, the hippie, the uppity demonstrator, Vietnamese peasants, and gay activists). In these cases the usual positive RWA Scale correlation drops and may even become negative.

Punishment of Peers in a Learning Situation.   In 1973 I maneuvered male Manitoba students into being the Teachers in a fake learning experiment involving (supposedly) electric shock. Unlike Milgram's experiment, every time the Learner made a mistake, the Teacher *chose* which of five shocks to give. If a Teacher wanted to, he could administer "very slight shocks" every time. If someone wanted to give strong shocks each time, however, he could do that too.

Overall, the men did not zap the Learner; the mean shock chosen was 2.4, where 2 indicated slight shock and 3 equaled moderate. But some Teachers proved rather brutal, and RWA scores predicted fairly well who they would be. The correlation with shocks "delivered" was .43 (*RWA*, pp. 199–202).[14]

Prejudice.   Prejudice, the unfair *pre-judg*ing of someone, has many roots (Duckitt, 1992; Zanna and Olson, 1994). But the taproot is probably *ethnocentrism.* Since white Anglophones raised in Christian homes make up the vast majority of my Manitoba samples, I found it easy to construct an ethnocentrism scale (Exhibit 1.2) assessing their attitudes toward various in- and out-groups.

Exhibit 1.2   The Manitoba Ethnocentrism Scale

1. Arabs are too emotional, and they don't fit in well in our country.

2. Indians should keep on protesting and demonstrating until they get just treatment in our country.*

3. Certain races of people clearly do NOT have the natural intelligence and "get up and go" of the white race.

4. The Vietnamese and other Asians who have recently moved to Canada have proven themselves to be industrious citizens, and many more should be invited in.*

5. It is good to live in a country where there are so many minority groups present, such as blacks, Asians, and aboriginals.*

6. There are entirely too many people from the wrong sorts of places being admitted into Canada now.

7. As a group Indians are naturally lazy, promiscuous, and irresponsible.

8. Canada should open its doors to more immigration from Latin America.*

9. Black people as a rule are, by their nature, more violent than white people are.

10. The people from India who have recently come to Canada have mainly brought disease, ignorance, and crime with them.

11. Canada should open its doors to more immigration from the West Indies.*

12. Jews can be trusted as much as everyone else.*

13. It is a waste of time to train certain races for good jobs; they simply don't have the drive and determination it takes to learn a complicated skill.

14. The public needs to become aware of the many ways blacks in Canada suffer from prejudice.*

15. Every person we let in from overseas means either another Canadian won't be able to find a job, or another foreigner will go on welfare here.

16. Canada has much to fear from the Japanese, who are as cruel as they are ambitious.

17. There is nothing wrong with intermarriage among the races.*

18. In general, Indians have gotten *less* than they deserve from our social and anti-poverty programs.*

19. Many minorities are spoiled; if they really wanted to improve their lives, they would get jobs and get off welfare.

20. Canada should guarantee that French language rights exist all across the country.*

Note: Items are answered on a −4 to +4 basis.
* Item is worded in the contrait direction; the ethnocentric response is to disagree.

I reported in *Enemies of Freedom* (pp. 109, 183) that responses to an earlier version of this instrument correlated .30–.43 with Manitoba students' RWA scores. The version of the test shown in Exhibit 1.2, which has a mean inter-item correlation of about .30 and an alpha of about .90 among such students, produces a Pearson *r* of about .45 with their level of authoritarianism.

Parents of Manitoba students showed a correlation of .45–.48 between their RWA scores and ethnocentrism on the earlier version. On the present test, which has the same internal cohesion and alpha among parents that it has among their first derivatives, the correlation roams around .50.

Wylie included the Ethnocentrism Scale in her booklet of materials sent to the random sample of Manitoba voters (Wylie and Forest, 1992). An alpha of .93 was obtained, and RWA Scale scores correlated .54 with prejudice.

An "Americanized" version of the original scale, mentioning blacks and Hispanics more, was administered to students at three U.S. universities in 1990. Alphas fell between .85 and .90 at San Francisco State University (N = 57), the University of Pittsburgh (N = 200), and the University of

Houston ($N = 101$). Connections with students' RWA scores equaled .38, .35, and .46, respectively.

Elsewhere, McFarland, Ageyev, and Abalakina (1990) found correlations of .55 with disparagement of Jews in the Soviet Union, and .63 with hostility toward the many ethnic minorities making up the USSR at the time. Duckitt (1992) reported coefficients of .53 to .69 with a variety of anti-black measures among white South Africans.

Overall then, the evidence indicates rather solidly that right-wing authoritarians tend to be relatively ethnocentric. If you look over the range of outgroups displayed in Exhibit 1.2, you can see why I have called High RWAs "equal-opportunity bigots." Compared with others, they dislike almost every group that is different—regardless of race, creed, or color.[15]

Hostility toward Homosexuals. You would probably predict that right-wing authoritarians will also be relatively prejudiced against homosexuals. And you would be right. In fact, RWA scores may explain hostility toward gays and lesbians better than any other personality variables (*EOF,* pp. 166–177).

I have measured this hostility over the years with an Attitudes toward Homosexuals (ATH) Scale (*EOF,* p. 167). See Exhibit 1.3 for the latest version. This scale assesses condemning, vindictive, and punitive sentiments toward homosexuals in six of its items, and the opposite attitudes in the other six. In Manitoba student samples, interitem connections averaged about .45 on the original scale, and now land about .50 on the revised version, producing an alpha of about .92. Correlations with the RWA Scale used to range from .50 to .60 (*EOF,* pp. 167, 176, 181, 183). Now they generally come in over .60. Parents of Manitoba students have punched up similar results. Wylie and Forest (1992) found an ATH alpha of .91 among 75 Manitoba adults and an RWA correlation of .72.

Exhibit 1.3   The Attitudes toward Homosexuals Scale

1. I won't associate with known homosexuals if I can help it.

2. The sight of two men kissing does NOT particularly bother me.*   **

3. If two homosexuals want to get married, the law should let them.*

4. Homosexuals should be locked up to protect society.

5. Homosexuals should never be given positions of trust in caring for children.*

6. I would join an organization even though I knew it had homosexuals in its membership.*

7. In many ways, the AIDS disease currently killing homosexuals is just what they deserve.

8. I wouldn't mind being seen smiling and chatting with a known homosexual.*

9. Homosexuals have a perfect right to their lifestyle, if that's the way they want to live.*

10. Homosexuals should be forced to take whatever treatments science can come up with to make them normal.

11. People should feel sympathetic and understanding of homosexuals, who are unfairly attacked in our society.*

12. Homosexuality is "an abomination" in the sight of God.

Note: Items are answered on a -4 to $+4$ basis.
* Item is worded in the contrait direction; the rejecting response is to disagree.
** Item 2 will be replaced in the future with "Homosexuals have been treated unfairly for centuries, and should be treated today the same as everyone else."

The original version of the ATH scale was administered for me at the Universities of Pittsburgh and Houston in 1990. The alphas equaled .90 and .91, respectively, with RWA Scale associations of .57 and .71.

On a somewhat related note, Peterson, Doty, and Winter (1993) administered five items about AIDS to 278 Michigan students. All the items had significant correlations with RWA scores, running from .28 to .52. The .52 came from a statement that the "AIDS plague had been passed to decent people." Another item, demanding that everyone with AIDS be quarantined, correlated .46. A third statement, that "AIDS victims have human feelings," had an r of $-.43$.

Skitka and Tetlock (1993) however found *no* relationship between RWA scores and willingness to fund (hypothetically) AZT treatments for AIDS victims—a definite disconfirmation.[16]

Gay-Bashing. In 1991 I asked 175 Manitoba students and 337 parents to respond to the following four items about "gay-bashing": (1) Gays are despicable and disgusting, and deserve to be beaten up. (2) Such attacks are cowardly, cruel, and totally unjustified. (3) The incidents are mostly the homosexuals' fault, who insist upon meeting in public places and flaunting their perversion. (4) "Gay-bashers" are far more despicable and disgusting than gays are.

Most subjects disapproved of the crime of gay-bashing. You might expect that High RWAs, who tend to say all laws must be obeyed, would be at least as condemning as others of these assaults. But recalling the findings from the Trial cases, you might make a smarter prediction. In fact, RWA scores correlated *negatively* with condemnation of gay-bashing on all the items in both samples, the r's ranging from $-.26$ to $-.51$. RWA correlated $-.44$ with the *sum* of opposition to such assaults among the students and −.41 among the parents.

You have probably noticed that the RWA Scale connects somewhat stronger with ATH than with Ethnocentrism scores. Why should this be? Well, homosexuals provide an unconventional, socially disreputable (in the minds of some), relatively powerless minority that one can attack with (selective) biblical authority. The same was once true of Jews, blacks, women, and other groups.

Furthermore, as homosexuals have increasingly "come out," they seem to have infuriated authoritarians the way that black Americans did during the civil rights movement. "Don't these people know they should be ashamed of what they are?" and "What makes them think they have the same rights that 'decent people' do?" were heard as often in the 1980s about homosexual protest as they were in the 1960s about black protest. One expects, therefore, that as homosexuality becomes more socially acceptable in society, *some* High RWAs will lower their voices. (However, the connection in the public mind between male homosexuality and AIDS may delay this modulation.)[17]

Aggression against Women.   I have never found that RWA scores correlated with self-reported sexual assaults against women by male Manitoba introductory psychology students, who acknowledged very few such attacks.[18]

By contrast, Walker, Rowe, and Quinsey (1993) found an *r* of .18 between the RWA Scale and sexual assaults admitted on the Sexual Experiences Survey (Koss and Dinero, 1987) among 157 university students. The correlation came in at .43 among 41 *non*students recruited through posters and employment centers (Walker and Quinsey, 1991). Also, significant RWA correlations appeared in the whole sample with Malamuth's (1981) Likelihood of Forcing Sex (.18); Check et al.'s (1985) Hostility toward Women Scale (.36); and Burt's (1980) Acceptance of Interpersonal Violence Scale (.51), Adversarial Sexual Beliefs Scale (.48), and Rape Myth Acceptance Scale (.54).

These trends were replicated by Walker, Rowe, and Quinsey (1993). RWA scores correlated .35 with admitted acts of sexual aggression on the Sexual Experiences Survey among 59 students, and .37 among 75 nonstudents. High RWA men were also more likely, at .53, to report experiencing sex guilt (Mosher, 1988), which usually predicts *low* levels of sexual behavior. But sex guilt also correlated positively (.23) with sexual aggression in this study.

Other Targets.   Peterson, Doty, and Winter (1993) found RWA scores correlated .38 and .56 with sentiments that the homeless were "lazy," not "unlucky." Their University of Michigan High RWAs also considered antiabortion violence relatively justified (.21) and felt that environmentalists who disrupted businesses should be punished (.32 and .56). Leak and Randall

(1995, also personal communications in April 1994) asked their Omaha student sample simply to indicate on a 1–5 scale how hostile they were toward such targets as atheists, drug users, people on welfare, and the homeless. Small but significant RWA connections were obtained with all of these targets and most of the others named.

Posses.   In 1982 I began asking subjects just how far they would go to help the government destroy some group—a fairly direct measure of authoritarian aggression. The current version of this "Posse" measure, in this case involving the elimination of "radicals," appears in Exhibit 1.4.

Exhibit 1.4   The Posse against Radicals Scale

Suppose the Canadian government, sometime in the future, passed a law outlawing "radical" political groups in Canada. Government officials then stated that the law would only be effective if it were vigorously enforced at the local level, and appealed to every Canadian to aid in the fight against all radical political groups.

"−4" = the statement is extremely untrue of you.

"−3" = the statement is very untrue of you.

"−2" = the statement is moderately untrue of you.

"−1" = the statement is slightly untrue of you.

"0" = the statement is neither untrue of you, nor true of you.

"+1" = the statement is slightly true of you.

"+2" = the statement is moderately true of you.

"+3" = the statement is very true of you.

"+4" = the statement is extremely true of you.

1. I would approve of such a law.
2. I would tell my friends and neighbors it was a good law.
3. I would tell the police about any radicals I knew.
4. I would, if asked by the authorities, keep my "ears open" for any radical discussions, and report them to the police.
5. I would, if asked by the authorities, help hunt down and arrest radicals.
6. I would participate in attacks on radical headquarters led by proper authorities.
7. I would support the use of physical force to make radicals reveal the identity of other radicals.

8. I would support the execution of radical leaders if the government insisted it was necessary to protect Canada.

Responses to the Posse items have tended to intercorrelate about .60 on the
average, routinely producing alphas of .90 or higher.

You may be reassured to learn that most participants said they wanted
nothing to do with such pogroms. They usually answered with −4 and −3.
But whether the targets were Communists or homosexuals or religious cults
or radicals, authoritarian Manitoba students *and* parents were likely to respond with a less reassuring −2 or −1, and even to choose the "plus"
("Where do I sign up?") side of the options. The overall RWA correlations
by 1987 ranged from .42 to .52 (*EOF,* pp. 114–117, 181, 183) and have been
replicated many times since.

At San Francisco State University in 1990 RWA scores correlated .50 with
Posse-Homosexuals. Samples from the Universities of Pittsburgh and Houston
showed RWA Scale connections of .55 and .61, respectively, with Posse-
Radicals.

Leak and Randall (1995) obtained Posse reactions from 131 Creighton
University students. The targets were homosexuals, religious cults, and abor-
tionists; RWA scores correlated .38, .45, and .44, respectively, with relative
willingness to help destroy these groups.

When I discovered that High RWAs had their own "availability heuristic"
when it came to helping the government persecute certain groups, I began
searching for targets that *Low* RWAs would be willing to help "ride down."
So I dangled right-wing political parties before samples in new versions of the
Posse measure. But *High* RWAs, not Lows, proved significantly more willing
(that is, less *un*willing) to help a government destroy the Social Credit Party,
the Confederation of Regions Party, and even the mainstream Progressive
Conservative Party in Canada. Low RWAs consistently refused to join a posse
after anyone. In January 1990 I asked 300 Manitoba students in introductory
psychology how willing they would be to help persecute a certain kind of
personality:

Suppose the Canadian government, some time in the future, passed a law to
eliminate right-wing authoritarians. (Right-wing authoritarians are people who
are so submissive to authority, so authoritarian aggressive, and so conventional
that they may pose a threat to democratic rule.) Government officials stated that
the law would only be effective . . .

Perhaps because they realized the obviously self-incriminating implications,
people did not leap at this opportunity. The mean was only 15.5, out of a
possible range of 0–54. Low RWAs had no interest in helping persecute Highs,
and neither did Highs (much). But High RWAs still tended to be *more* willing

to join this posse (to destroy themselves) than anyone else was ($r = .19$; $p < .05$).

Being Mean-Spirited.   Highs' unwitting readiness to crack down on themselves pales, of course, before their hostility toward many others. In 1985 I developed a Mean-Spirited Scale (*EOF*, p. 156) to assess students' feelings about peers in high school who had made mistakes and suffered afterward (for example, had "bad trips" on drugs, or become pregnant). Had their fellow students gotten exactly what they deserved, and had the respondent gotten a secret pleasure at their suffering? In three studies of Manitoba students, RWA scores correlated .31 to .41 with such mean-spirited reactions (*EOF*, pp. 154–156, 173, 183). Leak and Randall (1995) obtained a similar correlation of .34 among Creighton students.

Summary.   With a few exceptions, the literature on authoritarian aggression says rather forcefully that High RWAs tend to be hostile when they feel their attacks are sanctioned by authority. They are highly punitive toward criminals (but show double standards when the criminals are authorities, or when the victims of crime represent groups the authoritarian wants to see suffer). High RWAs tried to shock peers more in a fake learning experiment. They also tend to be the most ethnically and racially prejudiced people in samples. They are quite hostile toward homosexuals. High RWA men may be more likely than most to assault women. Right-wing authoritarians would likely be the first to help if the government decided to wipe out some group. They tend to be mean-spirited.

Correlations with such socially sensitive admissions were generally not as high as those concerning authoritarian submission. Nevertheless, a number of relationships over .50 have appeared.

CONVENTIONALISM

The RWA Scale's connection with adherence to "proper" social conventions has been firmly established in certain religious connotations. Highs have tended to adhere to more traditional religious teachings, with all their do's and don'ts, in every religion that has been appreciably represented in nearly every sample I have studied. The correlation between authoritarianism and holding conventional religious beliefs has averaged about .50 among Manitoba students *and* parents. Wylie and Forest (1992) found a similar value of .42 among Manitoba adults.

As well, continued acceptance correlated .36 with authoritarianism at SUNY-Potsdam in 1989, and .50 at Tulane, .60 at San Francisco State University, .57 at the University of Pittsburgh, and .54 at the University of Houston in 1990.

A more detailed understanding of this endorsement in Christian populations has been available through the Christian Orthodoxy (CO) Scale (Fullerton and Hunsberger, 1982)—shown in Exhibit 1.5 with less sexist wording than the original version.[19] Most of this scale is based on the Nicene Creed, which, dating back some 1,600 years, seems to qualify as a traditional belief system. As is often true with religious measures, the CO items show tremendous levels of intercorrelation, usually averaging over .60, producing alphas of .98! (We are, after all, measuring the most thoroughly taught ideology in our society.)

Exhibit 1.5   The Revised Christian Orthodoxy Scale

1. God exists as Father, Son, and Holy Spirit.

2. Humans are *not* a special creature made in the image of God; we are simply a recent development in the process of animal evolution.*

3. Jesus Christ was the divine Son of God.

4. The Bible is the word of God given to guide humanity to grace and salvation.

5. Those who feel that God answers prayers are just deceiving themselves.*

6. It is ridiculous to believe that Jesus Christ could be both human and divine.*

7. Jesus was born of a virgin.

8. The Bible may be an important book of moral teachings, but it was no more inspired by God than were many other books in the history of humanity.*

9. The concept of God is an old superstition that is no longer needed to explain things in the modern era.*

10. Christ will return to earth someday.

11. Most of the religions in the world have miracle stories in their traditions, but there is no reason to believe any of them are true, including those found in the Bible.*

12. God hears all our prayers.

13. Jesus may have been a great ethical teacher, as other people have been in history, but he was not the divine son of God.*

14. God made man of dust in God's own image and breathed life into him.

15. Through the life, death, and resurrection of Jesus, God provided a way for the forgiveness of humanity's sins.

16. Despite what many people believe, there is no such thing as a God who is aware of our actions.*

17. Jesus was crucified, died, and was buried, but on the third day he arose from the dead.

18. In all likelihood there is no such thing as a God-given immortal soul in us that lives on after death.*

19. If there ever was such a person as Jesus of Nazareth, he is dead now and will never walk the earth again.*

20. Jesus miraculously changed real water into real wine.

21. There is a God who is concerned with everyone's actions.

22. Jesus' death on the cross, if it actually occurred, did nothing in and of itself to save humanity.*

23. There is really no reason to hold to the idea that Jesus was born of a virgin. Jesus' life showed better than anything else that he was exceptional, so why rely on old myths that don't make any sense.*

24. The Resurrection proves beyond a doubt that Jesus was the Christ or Messiah of God.

Note: Items are answered on a −4 to +4 basis.
* Item is worded in the contrait direction; the orthodox response is to disagree.

RWA scores have correlated positively with every item on this scale in all the samples I know of. That is, authoritarian Christians tend to believe *all* of these teachings more than nonauthoritarian Christians and others do. The RWA association with CO has run about .50 among Manitoba students and parents. It came in at .68 in the Tulane sample.

Similarly, Rubinstein (1996) discovered strong ties between RWA scores and orthodox religious beliefs among both Jewish and Palestinian students in Israel. Orthodox Jews scored significantly higher than did traditional Jews, who in turn placed higher than secular Jews. The same pattern appeared among the Palestinian students regarding Islam. The (eta-squared) estimates of variance shared were 37% and 50%, respectively, analogous to correlations of .61 and .71.

Leak and Randall (1995) turned up significant RWA correlations in their Creighton University sample with all eight items of a Religious Attitudes Scale composed to measure Fowler's (1981) theory of faith development (for example, "I believe totally [or almost totally] the teachings of my church"). The relationship over all eight items equaled .51. They also found RWA relationships with a measure based on Fowler's analysis of "religious maturity." In a pattern reminiscent of the connection with (Kohlberg-type) "unsophisticated" moral reasoning (*RWA*, pp. 192–196), Highs tended to endorse "stage 2" and "stage 3" statements (such as "To me, God is much like a parent, someone who rewards good actions and punishes bad ones," and "I believe that God is my faithful friend and companion who knows me deeply and totally"). The RWA–stage 2 and –stage 3 connections were .46 and .55.

Persons familiar with research on the psychology of religion, and its pain, know this is the plane where mainly reign Gordon Allport's Intrinsic Orientation and Daniel Batson's Quest Scales. Again, a number of studies have linked these scales with RWA scores, as we shall see in Chapter 6.[20]

Adherence to Traditional Sex Roles.   Several studies have found that right-wing authoritarians tend to endorse traditional sex roles. I uncovered RWA Scale correlations of .59 among 200 female Manitoba students, and .60 among 135 males, with Spence and Helmreich's (1978) Attitudes toward Women Scale in 1991. The figures for 265 mothers and 230 fathers were .59 and .52, respectively. The strongest relationships erupted with "Women should worry less about their rights and more about becoming good wives and mothers" and "A woman should not expect to go to exactly the same places or to have quite the same freedom of action as a man."

Walker and Quinsey (1991) in turn found a correlation of .78 between RWA scores and Kalin and Tilby's (1978) Sex Role Ideology Scale among their 157 student and 41 nonstudent males. This test has items such as "The husband should be regarded as the legal representative of the family group in all matters of law" and "A wife's activities in the community should complement her husband's position."

Leak and Randall (1995) similarly discovered a link of .28 among 95 Creighton females, and .44 among 42 males, with Burt's (1980) Sex-Role Stereotypes measure. Typical items state, "There is something wrong with a woman who doesn't want to marry and raise a family," and "It is better for a woman to use her feminine charm to get what she wants rather than ask for it outright." In addition, authoritarianism correlated .41 and .61, respectively, with females' and males' responses to Burt's (1980) Sexual Conservatism measure (which includes items such as "A nice woman will be offended or embarrassed by dirty jokes").

Dianne Stober and Pauline Clance (personal communication, 1995) found that RWA scores correlated .70 with a balanced twenty-item scale measuring hostile attitudes toward and a backlash against feminists (for example, "Feminism contributes to the breakdown of family values in this country"). The subjects were 158 adults waiting for possible jury duty in a Georgia city. I found a correlation of .40 among 184 Manitoba students in October 1995.

Outside North America, McFarland, Ageyev, and Abalakina (1990) found RWA scores correlated .39 with five items assessing the role of women in the Soviet Union.

Conformity to Group Norms.   In 1983 I gave the RWA Scale to a batch of Manitoba students. The following week I asked them to reanswer the test, which now included, before each item, the average answer it had received from the whole sample on the first go-around. I explained, "Many students wonder how their attitudes compare with those of others . . . You may take into account the average response printed alongside each statement, or you may ignore it completely."

Both Low and High RWAs, who were by definition equally distant from the average scores, moved a little toward the center on the retest. But the Highs shifted more than twice as much as the Lows ($p < .001$). The difference could not be explained in terms of regression toward the mean (*EOF*, pp. 310–311).

I got around to repeating this study with 243 Manitoba students in the fall of 1993, only this time I used the Attitudes toward Homosexuals Scale shown in Exhibit 1.3. Lows' mean score rose from 26.8 to 27.8 ($p < .40$). Highs—just as far from the round-one average as the Lows—dropped from 56.7 to 52.3 ($p < .001$).

This greater sensitivity to norms (in the *descriptive* sense), even on an issue such as homosexuality, can be traced to Highs' greater desire to be normal. In 1985 I asked 168 Manitoba students and 270 parents to rank "normality" and nine other values. In both samples, right-wing authoritarians tended to give normality higher marks than others did (*EOF*, pp. 311–312).

Conformity to Traditional Practices.   Emma Clapham (personal communication, October 13, 1994) administered the RWA Scale and the Attitudes toward Treatment Questionnaire to 97 direct-care staff working in English mental hospitals. She found a correlation of .64 between being authoritarian and holding "organic" (as opposed to "psychological") theories of therapy. Organic clinicians believed in "keeping discipline on the ward," "making sure the patients don't have time to think about their problems," "having a ward organized according to strict rules," and keeping nurses from ever disagreeing with doctors in front of patients.

Adherence to Social Norms of Distributive Justice.   McFarland, Ageyev, and Abalakina-Paap (1992) compared Americans' and Russians' beliefs about how the necessities of life should be distributed. They surveyed both a quota sample of 163 Muscovites in May and June 1991 and "opportunity samples" of 97 Kentucky and 182 New Mexico adults. In Russia, RWA scores correlated .36 with belief in "equality"—the official (if thoroughly abused) principle that everyone in a Communist state should get the same share of the pie. In the United States, RWA scores connected $-.36$ with endorsement of equality. Instead, American authoritarians liked "laissez-faire individualism" (.22), more the American ideal, which Russian Highs rejected ($-.34$). The authors observed that in both nations, High RWAs were likely to accept the "conventional philosophy" of the society.[21]

Scores on "Conservatism" Scales.   Tarr and Lorr (1991) administered Lorr's (sociopolitical) Conservatism Scale to 339 students in the eastern United States. This test assesses such things as support for strong armed forces and loyalty tests, and opposition to socialized medicine and limitations on the Federal Bureau of Investigation. RWA scores correlated .57 with being conservative.

They also administered Lorr's Rule Bound versus Rule Free test, which measures acceptance of the rules of society and the importance of being conventional. The link with RWA scores equaled .59.

In a promising attempt to understand conservatism, Paul Trapnell (personal communication, July 1993) gave the RWA Scale and eight-item measures of six different aspects of psychological conservatism to 722 University of British Columbia students. He found authoritarianism correlated .41 with Intrinsic Religiosity, .45 with Authority, .52 with Punitiveness, .39 with Sexual Constraint, .62 with Traditionalism, and .50 with Propriety.

Finally, David Lykken (personal communication, March 14, 1994) found a correlation of .76 between RWA scores and the Traditionalism Scale of the Multidimensional Personality Questionnaire among 1,364 twins.

Support for Political Parties.   High RWAs have shown a consistent but usually weak tendency to support right-wing, political parties. In English-speaking Canada, people who like the Progressive Conservative Party almost always score higher overall in right-wing authoritarianism than those who favor the more centrist Liberal Party. Liberals in turn usually score higher than those who side with the socialist New Democratic Party. But these relationships, found among university students from Ontario to British Columbia, found among Manitoba parents, and found in two random samples of Manitobans from voter lists, have typically been small, analogous to correlations of .20 to .30 (*RWA*, pp. 203–204, 209–211, 221–222).

Interest in politics turns out to be an important moderator here, however. A sizable number of my respondents report they have little or no interest in politics. When you set their data to the side, and look instead at just the people who say they are interested in politics, who presumably know better what the parties stand for, the RWA connections with party preference prove substantially richer (*RWA*, pp. 221–222). But one can still dig up lots of exceptions. *I am not saying all Tories are fascists!* But authoritarian people do *tend* to like the conservative parties in Canada.

Similar results have appeared in the simpler two-party American political system. Every study that has looked at party preference (to my knowledge) has found that Low RWAs *tend* to like Democrats, while the Republican Party *tends* to win the hearts of Highs (*RWA*, p. 221). Doty and Larsen (1993) even found that High RWA Michigan students responded physiologically to slides simply showing Ronald Reagan and George Bush. (They also turned on at the sight of a Mercedes-Benz.)

Several studies on other continents have found the same RWA-party pattern. Feather (1993) found authoritarian Australian adults tended (.22) to support the right-wing Liberal Party rather than the Labour Party. In Israel, Rubinstein (1996) discovered High RWA Jewish students tended to identify with the right-wing and religious parties. In turn, Palestinian Highs also tended to support "extreme right-wing parties—most of them religiously fundamentalist." The eta-squared values were 17% and 34%, respectively, analogous to correlations of .41 and .58. (The relationships are probably high in Israel because religion mixes strongly with politics there, as it increasingly does in the United States.)

The most interesting studies of right-wing authoritarianism and political affiliation, for my money, have been carried out by McFarland and his associates in the former USSR and Russia. McFarland, Ageyev, and Abalakina (1990) found that High RWAs in their samples tended to support the "distinctly conservative" Pamyat group and the Communist Party in 1989. The same authors in 1992 reported that RWA scores still predicted support for hard-line Communists (including a leader of the failed August 1991 coup). Boris Yeltsin was favored by Lows. In 1995 McFarland, Ageyev, and Djintcharadze reported that they still found RWA correlations of about .30 with support for the Communists (and Russian nationalism), and dislike for democracy, among 440 Muscovites interviewed four months before the battle at the White House in October 1993. But Lows' support for Yeltsin had dropped markedly, as his commitment to democracy appeared to weaken.

Over the course of these three studies, correlations between RWA scores and support for Communism dropped from .69 to .38. It could be that many of the High RWAs who used to back the Communists have gone over to nationalists, Czarist, religious, and anti-Semitic parties. But it could also mean that, as democratic reforms fail, the Communists are attracting a wider range of supporters and could become the major opposition.

North American Lawmakers.   In 1979 I asked Manitoba students to role-play the answers that New Democratic (NDP), Liberal, and Progressive Conservative members of the House of Commons would give to the RWA Scale (*RWA*, pp. 223–224).[22] They produced substantial differences in the predictable direction, with an eta-squared of 15% among the caucuses, corresponding to a correlation of .39.

This experiment led me to undertake four studies involving actual Canadian (provincial) lawmakers (*EOF,* pp. 242–252), which suggested the role-playing students had gotten it wrong. They had greatly *under*estimated the actual differences in authoritarianism among the various caucuses.

In the Manitoba legislature, the Tory sample mean was twice as high as that of the NDP (no Liberals sat in the Legislative Assembly at the time), with no overlap in the distributions. The point-biserial correlation was but a trifling .91. Some overlap did appear in the Ontario assembly, but the NDP-Liberal-Conservative means lined up as expected and eta-squared equaled 43%, analogous to a correlation of .66. British Columbia (then with no Liberals) resembled Manitoba, with the Social Credit caucus scoring twice as high as the NDPers, with no overlap, and the correlation a noteworthy .85. The New Brunswick House produced the familiar NDP-Liberal-Conservative order, with appreciable overlap between Liberal and Tory camps. Eta-squared proved 29%, corresponding to an *r* of .54.

The RWA correlation with left versus right caucuses across the four provinces was .87, one of the strongest findings ever obtained in the social sciences.

I then conducted four inconclusive studies of American state legislatures. In the Minnesota Senate, Republicans scored nonsignificantly higher than Democrats. The California legislature produced a sizable Democrat versus Republican correlation of .59. Not enough Mississippi Republican senators, nor Connecticut Democratic senators, responded to permit meaningful analyses.

Summary.   Many studies, approaching the issue from many angles, have found that RWA scores predict conventional behavior. Extensive connections exist with traditional religious beliefs and views of the sexes. High RWAs have also conformed more to group averages, and embraced social norms and traditional institutional practices more. They score higher on various measures of conservatism, and tend to support or belong to right-wing political parties. Some of the relationships discovered to date have been extraordinarily powerful.[23]

CONCLUSIONS REGARDING THE RWA SCALE'S EMPIRICAL VALIDITY
When it comes to connecting with behaviors that smack of authoritarian submission, authoritarian aggression, and conventionalism, the studies thus far seem to indicate that the RWA Scale has meaningful empirical validity.[24]

Mischel (1968) once observed (unfairly, I think: *RWA,* pp. 7–10) that personality tests almost never correlate above .30 with criterion behaviors. Well, nearly all of the correlations on the preceding pages came in higher than that. In fact most of the associations, across quite a range of variables, landed in the .40–.60 domain that behavioral scientists often call "strong relationships."

Furthermore, you can find correlations *over .60* on most of the pages of this review. (You will have trouble finding many psychological tests that have produced such strong relationships with such an array of variables.)

True enough, nearly all of these findings involved *other* paper-and-pencil measures, which are easier to correlate to a survey than more important behaviors such as voting or assaulting (Mischel, 1968, p. 78). Also, a lot of the connections might seem to be "catching fish in a barrel." Most notably, who can be surprised at RWA Scale relationships with religious variables, given the extent to which the RWA Scale has "found religion"—and includes religious issues in many of its items?

But a lot of the paper-and-pencil criteria represented sentiments and attitudes and inclinations and affiliations that have their own independent relevance. And anyone who thinks two measures will correlate just because they appear in the same booklet has not tried it very often.

Item Analyses.   I am sure that earlier I hid from you my pleasure at the RWA Scale's internal consistency. A relatively cohesive measure does many things for you, including protecting you from "discovering" tautological relationships. Take those fish in the barrel above. It could be that the RWA associations we discovered with religious variables merely resulted from the religion-related items on the authoritarianism measure. We would then have merely discovered that if you ask people how religious they are on one scale, and then ask them how religious they are on another measure, the two sets of answers will covary, quite amazingly. (Do not laugh. This happened with at least one measure of conservatism [*RWA*, pp. 213–214].)

However, in every instance in which I have found RWA Scale connections with acceptance of traditional beliefs, Christian Orthodoxy scores, and other measures to be discussed in Chapter 6, *all or nearly all* of the items on the RWA Scale had significant correlations with the religious variable. It was not just a trivial religion-religion hookup, although naturally the RWA Scale items touching on religion usually had stronger ties with the religious criteria. Instead we had an *authoritarian submission–authoritarian aggression–conventionalism* correlation with religion. That is, we found a connection between *right-wing authoritarianism*, the (whole) construct we are investigating, and these religious behaviors.

As well, all (or nearly all) of the RWA Scale items also significantly correlated with the Government Injustices, Trials, "electric shock," and even the general political party preference results (*RWA*, pp. 206–207), and almost every other criterion variable I have used in my research program. *Generally, the whole scale has linked up with the criterion measures of authoritarian submission, authoritarian aggression, and conventionalism in my studies.*

(Again, you will have trouble finding many other scales that have demonstrated this.)

Why Do Authoritarian Submission, Authoritarian Aggression, and Conventionalism Covary?   The network of correlations between the items on the RWA Scale and the criterion behaviors, like the correlations among the items themselves, demonstrates that authoritarian submission, authoritarian aggression, and conventionalism do covary, in many places around the world. Why should this be so?

Well, one can readily see why authoritarian submission and conventionalism would go together. Usually, established authorities promote the social conventions that make them established authorities. But why should people who submit the submission and convent the conventions also be so aggressive in the name of that authority? The simplest and most data-blessed explanation to date has built upon Bandura's social learning theory.

Bandura (1973) believes aggressive behaviors are instigated by some aversive stimulus, but acted out only if the inhibitions against aggression can be overcome. One can imagine many kinds of painful stimuli (such as guilt, anger, and envy) and disinhibitors (such as drunkenness, deindividuation, and diffusion of responsibility in a group). All of these may play their part in one act of authoritarian aggression or another. But the principal instigator and releaser appear to be fear and self-righteousness (*EOF,* pp. 124–128).

Highly submissive, highly conventional persons have invested a lot in the status quo. They perceive waves of rebellion and sin constantly shrinking their island of respectable stability, especially if they feel personally vulnerable to attack in a disintegrating, increasingly lawless society. The classic responses to strong fear, after all, are "Fight" or "Run away! Run away!"

Submissive, conventional people could be particularly likely to think they are the good guys, the righteous, God's "designated hitters," because they see themselves allied with the established, morality-deciding authorities in life. One can readily see why they might think of themselves as the "Moral Majority."

In 1985–86 I ran four "pitting experiments" to see which of many possible explanations could best account for authoritarian aggression. I measured fear with a Likert-type instrument, the Fear of a Dangerous World Scale. I assessed self-righteousness by asking subjects to evaluate someone who scored *low* on the RWA Scale. (This may seem unfair to Highs. But I had established earlier that, while Low RWAs evaluated Low and High RWA targets equally, Highs considered someone like themselves vastly superior to someone with opposing opinions.)

In these pitting experiments, which involved a sample of 346 parents as well as nearly 1,500 students, Fear of a Dangerous World correlated between

.24 and .40 with various measures of authoritarian aggression (Attitudes toward Homosexuals, Trials, Ethnocentrism, and several Posses). Self-righteousness in turn correlated .26 to .55 with these measures. More important, combining their effects explained a substantial amount of the RWA Scale's relationship with authoritarian aggression. None of the other explanations could do nearly as much (*EOF*, pp. 166–186).[25]

So anger, envy, pain, drunkenness, deindividuation, and diffusion—not to mention the greatest disinhibitor of all, safety from retaliation—may cause some acts of authoritarian aggression. But, by and large, fear puts the High RWA's finger on the trigger, and self-righteousness releases the safety.

By way of cross-validation, data on these measures were collected for me at the Universities of Pittsburgh and Houston in 1990. At both sites, Fear of a Dangerous World and Self-Righteousness explained RWA ties with Attitudes toward Homosexuals, Trials, Ethnocentrism, and Posse-Radicals as well as, or better than, they had in Manitoba.

DEMOGRAPHIC RELATIONS WITH THE RWA SCALE

Gender. I know of only one study that uncovered a gender difference in RWA scores: Rubinstein (1996). Otherwise, women have always equaled men in overall authoritarian attitudes.

Age. A number of studies have found that older adults usually score higher on the test than young adults, which could be due to cross-sectional differences or longitudinal change. I shall postpone this discussion until Chapter 3.

Education. University students differ little among themselves in educational attainment, so there is no risk that findings obtained with students have been confounded by years of schooling. On the other hand, many studies of *non*student samples have shown that authoritarians tend to be less educated. But the RWA-education relationships have almost always ranged between .20 and .30. Controlling for this connection reduces RWA-criterion coefficients very little.

Intelligence. On a related note, I have never found that RWA scores correlate with grades obtained in university courses. Also, no connection appeared with a measure of general intellectual ability, the Wonderlic Intelligence Test, among 185 Manitoba students (*RWA*, p. 325). However, Lykken (personal communication, March 14, 1994) reported that scores on the Weschler Adult Intelligence Survey correlated − .34 with RWA scores among

93 females, and −.61 among 47 males, drawn from the twins-reared-apart pool of the Minnesota Twin Study.

OTHER FINDINGS WITH THE RWA SCALE

A number of index cards still lay on the desk before me whose findings do *not* seem to bear upon the RWA Scale's construct validity. I shall briefly present them now, to clear the decks for Chapter 2.

The Environmental Movement.   Schultz and Stone (1994) found right-wing authoritarians tended *not* to be "tree-huggers," at least as measured by the twelve-item New Environmental Paradigm Scale (Dunlap and van Liere, 1978). The r among 87 students at the University of Maine equaled −.54. Peterson, Doty, and Winter (1993) in turn found positive RWA correlations among 278 Michigan students with seven statements belittling the environmental movement, but nothing significant with six others. (Three of the "no-shows" involved punishing polluters, a case where Highs' apparent dislike for the environmental movement could be offset by their general punitiveness.)

Abortion.   I doubt this will stun you, but High RWAs tend to be opposed to abortion. Some Lows do, too, depending on the circumstances, so the overall relationships have been less than majestic. For example, I asked 238 Manitoba students in 1990 to indicate how important the rights of the fetus, the mother, the father, and the rest of society were in cases of abortion, by allocating a total of 100 "votes" among these four. Nearly all of the votes were cast for the fetus and the mother, with Highs favoring the fetus ($r = .41$) and Lows favoring the mother (−.39). A replication with 491 parents brought in similar values of .37 and −.37.

Moghaddam and Vuksanovic (1990) involved 74 Montreal pro-life activists in one of their studies. The pro-lifers' mean of 220 on the RWA Scale ranks as about the highest group score ever found.

Drugs.   As with abortion, High RWAs tend to be definitely against "drugs," while Lows' attitudes depend on what drugs and circumstances you are talking about. Peterson, Doty, and Winter (1993) administered seven items about America's drug problem to 257 Michigan students. They found RWA correlations from .19 to .48, including one of .37 with desire for a "Rambo-like crusade" against drugs. Debra Cormer (personal communication, January 25, 1993) found High RWAs ($r = .24$) tended to favor workplace drug testing; but there was no relationship with self-reported illicit drug use among her Hofstra University sample.

Social Dominance.   Early in 1993 Felicia Pratto at Stanford University sent me a paper describing an admirable array of thirteen studies she and her colleagues had done toward developing a Social Dominance Orientation Scale (personal communication, January 10, 1993). This test (at the time) consisted of ten items measuring American nationalism and eighteen others assessing opposition to greater equality in the United States. (The nationalism items were subsequently dropped, and the published Social Dominance Scale consists of sixteen statements assessing attitudes toward equality: Pratto et al., 1994.)

Pratto administered the RWA Scale and these twenty-eight items to 97 San Jose State University students in April 1992, and (surprisingly) found no links between the two measures. As these students (like Leak and Randall's [1995]) had answered a very long booklet, which tends to promote careless responding, I administered the two scales to a sample of 187 Manitoba students in early March 1993. RWA correlated .38 with the sum of the (anti-)equal items (and .45 with the sum of the nationalism statements). Moreover, the (anti-) equality scores correlated much better with answers to my Ethnocentrism Scale (.71) than the RWA Scale did (.48).

The "Big Five."   Goldberg administered the RWA Scale and his 235-item measure of the "Big Five" personality factors to 503 Oregon students (Goldberg and Rosolack, 1991). RWA scores correlated −.30 with Factor V, which has been interpreted as Intellect or Openness and Culture. It also correlated .23 with Factor III, Conscientiousness, and .14 with Factor I (Surgency/Extraversion).

Professor Goldberg was kind enough to send me the 235 RWA-item correlations. Only 3 of these exceeded .30: Highs said they were not "philosophical," were "conforming," and were "non-introspective." Another 20 items had correlations in the .20s; but only (not) "introspective" and (not) "broad-minded" exceeded .24.

However, Trapnell found a much higher correlation (−.57) among 722 University of British Columbia students between the RWA Scale and "Factor V" scores obtained with a different measure of the Big Five: Costa and McCrae's Revised NEO Personality Inventory. Trapnell (personal communication, May 4, 1996) kindly sent me the RWA correlations with the 48 NEO items measuring "Openness." The highest correlation (−.50) was obtained with an item from the "Values facet" of Openness: "I believe we should look to our religious authorities for decisions on moral issues." This statement, of course, closely resembles some RWA Scale items. Of the twelve next highest correlations (all in the −.30s), five also came from the "Values facet." But some intriguing connections with the "Aesthetics facet" (e.g. "Poetry has little or no effect on me") and the "Ideas facet" (e.g. "I find philosophical arguments boring") also appeared.

Small and Nonexistent Relationships.   We are reaching the end of the trail. Some of the relationships that follow are wispy but apparently "there." Others are profoundly "significance challenged."

Feather (1993) found that Australian nonstudent Highs tended to favor rewarding "Tall Poppies"—people who had achieved a lot in life ($r = .23$).

In a series of studies involving over a thousand students, Hunsberger and his associates (for example, Hunsberger, Pratt, and Pancer, 1994) have found that RWA scores correlate about $-.20$ to $-.30$ with cognitive complexity (Baker-Brown et al., 1992).

Perrott (1991) found that Halifax police officers did not score high on the RWA Scale as a group.

I found RWA responses to be correlated $-.29$ with Humanism scores, and .30 with Normative scores on Stone's (1988) modification of Tomkin's Polarity Scale, answered by 155 Manitoba students in February 1993.

Billings, Guastello, and Rieke (1993) sought the RWA Scale's relationships with Cattell, Eber, and Tatsuoka's (1970) Sixteen Personality Factor Questionnaire. They reported only four of the sixteen correlations, ranging from .22 to .36. High RWAs were described as being low in imagination, high in conscientiousness, low in self-sufficiency, and high in closed-mindedness.

Stone and Schultz (1992), resurrecting an old California Fascism Scale (F Scale) issue, found that High RWAs performed like other subjects in a "low ego-involvement" run of the Einstellung Water Jar problems (in which subjects have to abandon a rule they have developed for solving simple mathematical problems, because it will no longer work). But Highs did significantly worse than others when the situation was more ego-involving. (See Brown, 1953.) I have since twice replicated the latter finding.

Lest you think that everything turns out "$p < .05$" in our subject pool, the RWA Scale has had nonsignificant correlations with Snyder and Gangestad's (1986) Self-Monitoring Scale, the UCLA Loneliness Scale (Russell, Peplau, and Cutrona, 1980), Rosenberg's (1965) Self-Esteem Scale, Taylor and Altman's (1966) Self-Disclosure Scale, Fenigstein, Scheier, and Buss's (1975) Self-Consciousness Scale, Ilfeld's (1976) Psychiatric Symptom Index, and an early (BIDR-6, Form 40a) version of Del Paulhus's Self-Deception and Impression Management Scales (personal communication, November 1989; Impression Management had a significant $r = .23$).

The Importance of Personality

Does the accumulated literature on right-wing authoritarianism have any larger significance for the science of psychology? It demonstrates to me, as other research programs have, that *personality counts*. I noted a few pages back that this was seriously doubted following Mischel's critique in 1968. But here we have a personality construct that connects and explains many different attitudes and behaviors—and not just theoretically, but empirically, often powerfully, and in many places around the world.

The "connecting" particularly fetches me. What links trusting Nixon during Watergate, hating homosexuals, opposing abortion, liking hospitals run in traditional ways, thinking blacks are naturally violent, blaming our social problems on the Bill of Rights, being religious, and so on? To surprisingly large degrees, authoritarianism lay beneath all of these.

To my reflexively reductionist, not–New Age, linear way of thinking, this discovery takes us a goodly stride forward. A lot of complexity has been explained by one thing. A cohesive mass of comprehension, one which social learning theory seems best able to accommodate (*EOF*, chapters 4 and 5), is accreting.

Oh, I know as a card-carrying social psychologist that personal authoritarianism will interact with situational factors. No one, I hope, expects High RWAs always to submit to authority or to betray their dislike of minorities indiscriminately. But the research indicates that in many contexts, it matters a lot how authoritarian people happen to be. It matters who we are.

Which has, at least, given me something to talk about in the "personality section" of introductory psychology besides Freud. Speaking of whom . . .

Isn't This Really Just the "Berkeley Theory"?

One can find a certain resemblance between the pioneering "Berkeley theory" of authoritarianism and mine, a connection that is entirely *un*coincidental. If you look on page 228 of *The Authoritarian Personality* (Adorno et al., 1950), you will see that the first three clusters of the Berkeley model were "Conventionalism," "Authoritarian Submission," and "Authoritarian Aggression." Six to nine *additional* clusters follow these three, depending on how you count. (Is "Destructiveness and Cynicism" one thing or two?) But we can infer that the first three clusters formed the starting point of Sanford and associates' insight into the structure of the authoritarian personality.[26]

They certainly provided the starting point for me. I never would have found anything about authoritarianism, or even gotten interested in the area, if it had not been for the Berkeley researchers (*EOF*, p. xxiii). I only noticed the covariation of authoritarian submission, authoritarian aggression, and conventionalism as a result of studying item analyses of the F Scale (*RWA*, p. 18). No F Scale, then no novice noticing nothing nowhere nohow now nor never. The Berkeley researchers discovered the covariation of "the three."

Still, the model of right-wing authoritarianism I am peddling is *not* the model of the authoritarian personality you will find in *The Authoritarian Personality* for at least five reasons.

1. The models may start off looking the same, but mine ends pretty quickly. When people say the research with the RWA Scale confirms the Berkeley theory, I wonder when it has been found that High RWAs are "cynical," or "superstitious," or have "exaggerated concerns with sexual 'goings-on' "? Those are all parts of the original model. (And they were not supported by F Scale research either.) So RWA Scale results can at best reinforce only part of the Berkeley model, because *most* of the pieces of that model are not represented on the RWA Scale.

2. While the cluster titles have the same *names* in three cases, the underlying constructs differ. Actually, one cannot easily discuss the Berkeley constructs, for the researchers said little about them. Take "authoritarian submission." It was defined as a "submissive, uncritical attitude toward idealized moral authorities of the ingroup." But what does "submissive" mean—willing to do *anything?* Does "uncritical" mean believing *anything?* Is the prefascist submissive *only* to "idealized" authorities? Are *all* authorities "idealized" by the authoritarian? Is the prefascist submissive only to "moral" authorities? Who is an "authority"? Is there only "the" in-group, and no other?

You can find some elaboration of these terms on page 231 of *The Authoritarian Personality,* but it does not answer these questions and ultimately raises more. For example, the authoritarian supposedly has "an exaggerated, all-out, emotional need to submit." How can people with such an overwhelming need walk by a police officer without throwing themselves at the officer's feet?

3. I have tried to describe in some detail what I mean by each of the terms in my definition of right-wing authoritarianism. These conceptualizations differ from the Berkeley model—as much as one can tell what that was—in several important ways. For example, Sanford and his colleagues limited authoritarian aggression to attacks on people who violate conventional values (p. 228). Therefore, shocking the Learner in Milgram's experiment would not constitute authoritarian aggression. Neither would attacks on women. By contrast, the model of right-wing authoritarianism presented at the beginning of this chapter acknowledges that the victims can be anyone—as indeed they can.

Similarly, the Berkeley theorists thought "that susceptibility to fascism is most characteristically a middle-class phenomenon" (p. 229), and so they defined conventionalism as "rigid adherence to conventional, middle-class values." My definition of right-wing authoritarianism focuses instead on the *individual's* perception of the authority-endorsed norms, which may or may not be middle class norms. (And the evidence indicates that, in North America at least, educational differences help RWA scores to be higher in the "working class" [*RWA*, p. 242]).

4. The RWA Scale may turn out to correlate with measures that seem to represent some of the Lost Elements of the Berkeley definition (such as "rigidity"). But to prove that these features are so *integral* to the authoritarian personality that they should be part of its definition, the correlations need to be very strong. They are not.[27]

To put it another way, the RWA Scale correlates with many things. If *mere association,* regardless of size, is all it takes to confirm the Berkeley theory, then we will end up with far more things that were "mistakenly omitted" from that theory than were gotten right. We will also have an enormously fragmented, uncohesive, "multifaceted," and virtually meaningless conglomeration for a construct.

5. Finally, the Berkeley model was built around Freudian theory, with its emphasis on early childhood roots of behavior, vast (and largely untestable) unconscious struggles, repressed hatreds, projected hostilities, and so on. The present approach uses none of these. So while it turns out that High RWAs do tend to be anti-Semitic, that does not mean they are prejudiced because they unconsciously hate their fathers. Thus any support of the Berkeley research would be limited and not extend at all to the actual theory presented in *The Authoritarian Personality.*

Certain findings on the preceding pages may have reminded you of the Berkeley theory. So may certain findings in the rest of this book. That is to be expected. The two research programs have looked at similar kinds of people and naturally seen some of the same things. But when someone says that the RWA Scale findings confirm the Berkeley theory, or that those findings are very reminiscent of that theory, or that this model is strikingly similar to that theory, I wonder how they ever reached that conclusion.

I am hardly saying we should close the book on psychodynamic attempts to explain authoritarianism (Hopf, 1993; Lederer, 1993; Meloen, 1993). They may turn out to be much better models than anything I, at least, can cobble together. Certainly, as we shall see in later chapters, a lot goes on (and does *not* go on) in the authoritarian mind. It is, undoubtedly, psychodynamic. But if one is to convince the scientific community with such explanations, terms will have to be well defined, constructs will have to be validly measured, hypotheses will have to be falsifiable, and so on. If the advocates of such approaches happen to be right, let us hope they can demonstrate it, so the rest of us can stop following poorer lines of inquiry.

Isn't This Really Just "Conservatism"?

Ray (1985, 1990) has several times asserted that the RWA Scale just measures conservatism (which he does not define).[28] You may have been thinking the same thing as you went through this chapter. Here again we need a clear statement of the alternative explanation before we can proceed.

As I noted in the Introduction, conservatism (and liberalism) mean many different things to different people. For example, some would say, "Conservatives are people who want everybody to obey the government." But others would say, "Conservatives are people who want no government at all." Are both kinds of people conservatives, or is neither, or only one?

That is just the first step into the quagmire. See the symposium in the September 1976 issue of *Commentary,* entitled "What Is a Liberal—Who Is a Conservative?" It contains sixty-four essays on the matter by well-informed writers from many fields. Overall, they provide sixty-four different answers.

As I shall argue in Chapter 11, I think we can explain more clearly (and powerfully) what people often mean by conservatism with right-wing authoritarianism, as defined earlier and measured by the RWA Scale. But let us consider what it would take to do it the other way around and explain our RWA findings in terms of conservatism.

From a *scientific* perspective, we should have a clear, precise, well-delineated definition of conservatism before we assert anything. If we merely wave our hand at the issue and say, "Well, everybody knows what 'conservative' means," or if we give a vague, broad definition that can cover almost anything and never be shown wrong, we are only hurting ourselves. The greatest gift of the scientific method is its ability to prove us mistaken. The more detailed the definition, the greater the chance we shall abandon wrong ideas and make progress. But the vaguer the conceptualization, the greater the chance we shall devote our lives to barking up the wrong tree.

Once a detailed, testable conceptualization of conservatism has been developed (or whatever other construct is advanced as being what right-wing authoritarianism "really" is), we have to show that it can conceptually account for all the relevant findings obtained with the RWA Scale. (There are a few new discoveries in the rest of this book that will need explaining as well.) Some of the findings appear to present large problems for a new interpretation. Why should conservatives (without spilling over into authoritarianism) be prejudiced, have so many double standards, and be so likely to hurt people in a shocking experiment?

Assuming we have a good conceptualization that can plausibly cover the field, it has to be objectively and validly measured. If the assessment is done through a psychological test, that test needs to be broad enough to cover the range of beliefs and attitudes pertinent to the underlying construct, yet cohesive enough to be essentially unidimensional. The farther we fall short on either score, the more grief we shall face further down the road. (So also shall we ultimately grieve over failure to control for response sets and various other sunken reefs in the assessment process.)

If we now have a sound conceptualization and a sound way to measure it, there remains only to demonstrate through pitting experiments its parity with the RWA Scale's breadth of relevant empirical coverage and strength of association.

We would also have to ascertain through item analyses that the validating findings with our new scale were typically attributable to the whole scale, not just a subset of obviously relevant items for one variable, another subset for another variable, and so on.

All of this should be as true of general, nonstudent populations as of our convenient introductory psychology subject pools. And if we want the construct to be relevant to other places than (say) just our country, or just North America, its parity with the RWA Scale should be established hither and yon.

If we think our new explanation is a better or "more basic" explanation, (for example, "Right-wing authoritarianism is just an aspect of conservatism"), it will not be enough to demonstrate parity with what we already have. We shall have to demonstrate overall superiority, as the RWA Scale had to do over the F Scale and other preceding measures of authoritarianism (*RWA*, chapter 4).

To summarize (and end), it requires no insight or perspicacity or ability to think of countervailing arguments, nor any evidence at all, to say, "Oh, this is really just conservatism" (or whatever else).[29] *Proving* it, however, involves substantially more. I do not mean it cannot be done. Someday, I am sure, it will be. But I suspect it requires thoughtful and determined endeavor.

—2—
Studying Authoritarianism: Research Methodology and Methodology Research

Let me congratulate you on your willingness to read the methodology chapter. These things are always deadly dull, and this will prove no exception. Either you did not know this, or you have committed some great sin and long to be punished. Or perhaps you know what it took me years to learn: the methodology section is much more important than the results.

Regrettably, one can get quite a variety of results by making enough methodological blunders. Ask me how I know. It is particularly easy to screw things up and find *nothing*. Sometimes, believe it or not, that is what a researcher hopes to find. For example, "See, my test is a good as hers; there's no significant difference in the validities." Or, "Manipulating the key variable in Theory X—a theory I frankly have little time for—had no significant effect upon the outcome." But you can also get $p < .05$ through many a methodological slip, if you are bad enough (or good enough) at it, as we shall see. So I am glad you care how the facts in the rest of this book were created. If time reveals they are misdrawn or mistaken, misshapen or miscreaten, it will be because they were misbegotten in the first place.

The RWA Scale

Most of the research presented in this book—rather like a pyramid turned upside down—is based upon the RWA Scale. So the whole thing will eventually collapse if some deep structural flaw is buried under those sturdy-looking alphas and correlation coefficients in Chapter 1. Let us take a more penetrating look at the test before investing any more in the stories that are built upon it.

ORIGINS

As I mentioned at the end of Chapter 1, the conceptualization of right-wing authoritarianism and the RWA Scale emerged from a post-crash analysis of the Berkeley model of *The Authoritarian Personality* (Adorno et al., 1950). I simply noticed that the only parts of the elaborate Berkeley model that hung together empirically were "authoritarian submission," "authoritarian aggression," and "conventionalism" (*RWA*, pp. 16–25). Over the course of eight item-testing studies conducted between 1970 and 1973, I examined many other possible elements through hundreds of different items (*RWA*, pp. 156–174, 277–297). Yet those three attitudinal clusters were still the only ones that consistently and appreciably covaried. They did so even when *contrait* items measuring their opposite sentiments were mixed into the stew.

Propelled by this dimmest of theoretical insights, I developed the construct of right-wing authoritarianism and a way to measure it. The first version of the RWA Scale (*RWA*, pp. 171–172), christened in 1973, had twenty-four items. But the momentum built up by the preceding years of testing statements produced a thirty-item version by 1979 (*RWA*, pp. 219–220).

FURTHER DEVELOPMENT

As the fury of the late 1960s and early 1970s in North America dissolved into the "1950s" of the 1980s, it became clear that some of the items on the RWA Scale were losing their zip, their social relevance. So I tested new statements almost every time I administered the scale to a group of delighted participants and was able to replace about one item per year. Usually I replaced a contrait item, for the contraits have always been the weak partners in the enterprise. The 1986 version of the RWA Scale given in *Enemies of Freedom* (pp. 22–23) had eight changes from the 1979 version mentioned above, five of them contraits.

I have continued to enjoy testing new statements, in my Adlerian fashion, and eventually found myself replacing good items simply because newer ones had better item-whole connections. I strove to keep equal the number of statements that seemingly tapped authoritarian submission, authoritarian aggression, and conventionalism—which was pretty easy to do since most items tap at least two of these. I also stifled myself when I discovered how seductively easy it was to write items about religion. They could easily have swamped the scale, and I did not want an instrument that mainly measured authoritarianism in religious contexts. Instead, I tried to make the scale better at detecting sentiments like "Let's all submit to the man-on-horseback" and "Let's stomp out the rot," because these aspects of authoritarianism worry me most.

PSYCHOMETRIC CHARACTERISTICS OF THE CURRENT SCALE

The minor successes of this item talent search have steadily jacked up the internal consistency of the RWA Scale. The mean interitem correlation for the 1990–1995 versions, used in thirty-four studies involving over 10,000 Manitoba students, has ranged from .17 to .31. The most typical values have been .22 to .25, found twenty-four times. The figures for the six parent studies I conducted between 1990 and 1995 (total $N = 2366$) varied from .23 to .27. These values mean the RWA Scale usually had an alpha of over .90 in these populations, or a signal-to-noise ratio of about 10:1 in the studies to be presented in this book.[1] That's not bad.

Does a .90 + alpha guarantee you fat relationships with other things? No. Authoritarianism may not be related to the "other things." And even if it is, improving internal consistency does *not* noticeably improve the empirical validity of a test as the alpha reaches .90.[2] It can even hurt it if the improved consistency was purchased by reducing the scope of the test.

A study I conducted in the fall of 1993 painfully illustrates this point. I gave 762 Manitoba students a booklet of surveys that began with a seventy-two-item "RWA Scale." Included were all the statements needed to produce the original twenty-four-item 1973 version of the test, the thirty-item 1986 version given in *Enemies of Freedom*, and my best scale at the time, the thirty-item 1993 version.

As expected, the older the scale, the worse the internal consistency in 1993. The mean interitem correlation was .17 for the original version, .20 for the 1986 vintage, and .22 for the latest. But the oldest scale had the *best* correlation with these students' scores on my Ethnocentrism Scale (.50). The 1986 version had the best fit with continued holding of the home religion (.47). And the 1993 RWA Scale had the best correlation only with the Attitudes toward Homosexuals Scale (.64).[3]

Happily, these results showed that it does not matter much which version of the RWA Scale you use, as far as empirical correlations go. You get about the same results with any of them, from the beginning of the series to the end—which is why in the last chapter I merrily equated the various RWA Scales that different researchers have used. Unhappily, however, the 1993 version did not have better empirical validity than the one I had in hand twenty years (and hundreds of experimental items) earlier. Why then did I go on to make a 1994 version? What madness be this?

Basically I went on because I greatly value *construct validity*. High internal consistency means the test is relatively unidimensional. It means you probably know what it really measures. It means you can not only correlate with things, you can *explain* things. You can understand. We shall soon see that tests with low internal consistency can correlate with other measures for many reasons. You may think you know what is going on, but you are likely collecting fool's gold.[4]

FACTOR ANALYSIS OF THE RWA SCALE

Factor analysis provides a statistical way of identifying underlying patterns in the responses to test items. Two different kinds of factor analysis are often distinguished (Harman, 1967; Nie, Bent, and Hull, 1970; Comrey, 1973; Goldberg and Digman, 1994). *Exploratory* factoring is used when you have little or no idea of what "components" exist in the data. *Confirmatory* factor analysis is used to test hypotheses about what factors underlie a set of results. The difference is essentially that between "I wonder what the heck is going on" and "I wonder if what I *think* is going on is going on."

Exploratory factor analysis typically uses a "principal-components" approach to identify components within the data. It extracts these components from the correlation matrix that shows the connections among all the variables, leaving 1.0s in the diagonal of that matrix. People (that is, statistical packages) usually then keep all the components extracted that have eigenvalues greater than one.[5] Because this is such a minimal standard, however, some of the components can be quite meaningless. Since you are exploring, a broad search has its advantages. But you can easily end up trying hard to make sense out of pure nonsense.

Confirmatory (or "common") factor analysis proceeds differently. It replaces the 1.0s in the diagonal of the correlation matrix with some lower number, an estimate of what each variable has in *common* with the other variables in the pile. Thus when the matrix is factored, just the common or shared variance is analyzed, which is how you can test your notion of what the items on a scale have in common.

Apparently psychologists do a lot of exploring and very little testing. Lee and Comrey (1979) surveyed five major journals and found that 67% of the factor analyses reported used a principal-components extraction *and* retained all factors with eigenvalues greater than 1.0.

Virtually none of the articles explained why this particular procedure had been followed, Lee and Comrey noted, which textbooks on factor analysis often warn must be used carefully. As these are the default options in many statistical packages, some researchers may have gone down this path simply because it was wide open, and they did not know their way about. They may have intended to *test a hypothesis* about a factor structure, but ended up making an inappropriate exploratory analysis because "most studies in the literature do it this way." A lot of editors apparently walked down this well-trod but misleading path too.

I have a definite hypothesis about the factor structure of the RWA Scale, namely, that it is essentially unidimensional.[6] So I can take advantage of common factor analysis' ability to tell me if I am wrong.

Over the years, my common factor analyses have sometimes produced just one factor on which most of the items have appreciable loadings (see *RWA*, pp. 182–188), or else two factors that correlate .40–.70 when oblique rotations are performed. (You get just one factor with good testing circumstances, or thoughtful participants, or subjects with high reading comprehension, or some other blessing.) The one factor, or two factors together, account for about 25–35% of the total variance of the RWA Scale.

To illustrate, I did common factor analyses of 456 student and 468 parent responses to the 1994 scale, using the "principal-factor analysis" procedure of the BMDP Statistical Package (Dixon, 1990).[7] I had the program insert squared multiple correlations as the estimates of communality into the diagonal of the correlation matrix and then extract factors to its heart's content. In both cases the first factor had an eigenvalue over 7.5, and the second one over 2.0. All subsequent factors had eigenvalues less than 1.0. The first two factors accounted for 34% of the test's variance among the students and 35% among the parents. I rotated them to direct oblimin criteria, with gamma = 0, and they correlated .43 among the offspring and .50 among the offspringers.

Two factors seemingly disconfirm my hypothesis that the RWA Scale measures basically one thing. But the two factors were well correlated. Furthermore, when I looked at how each item loaded on each factor, I found all the protrait items (save one) loaded higher on one factor, and all the contraits had their higher loading on the other. This basic separation of items according to the direction of their wording has appeared in every two-factor solution of the RWA Scale I have ever obtained (and on many other scales I have factored as well).

If this is *all* Greek to you, here is the upshot. Responses to the RWA Scale reflect many different things, because each item talks about something in particular and because there are many sources of measurement error. But there is a psychological connection among the test's items that accounts for about 30% of the variance the whole bunch produces. When we try to pull that 30% apart, sometimes we cannot because of the "strong force" (the cohesion among the items on this test is too strong). But when we can pull the common variance apart, the best we can do is get the protrait and contrait items into largely separate piles. These piles show that the direction of the items' wording also constitutes a force to be reckoned with. But the correlation between these two factors indicates that the RWA Scale is essentially unidimensional.[8]

RESPONDENTS' FOREKNOWLEDGE OF, OR INSIGHT INTO, THE RWA SCALE

Since I have been handing out the RWA Scale in one spot for over twenty years to successive waves of introductory psychology students, and since many students have received feedback about my research, maybe my subject pool is polluted. Perhaps lots of research participants have known what I was studying when they answered my surveys. I have always thought they eventually would, even though I get people to promise secrecy before I give them feedback.[9]

I have sometimes asked students, after they have answered the RWA Scale, what they think the test measures. I tell them it is "liberalism versus conservatism," or "opinions about morals and morality," or "opinions about our society," or "right-wing authoritarianism." (I change the order every year.)[10]

Over the years, only about 5% of the students (and their folks, in my parent studies) have given the right answer. For example, in my 1993 student studies, 8% said "liberalism versus conservatism," 33% said "morals," 55% said "opinions about society," and 4% got it right. In my own sections of introductory psychology, only 3% of over 500 students hit the nail on the head.

I have no desire to spend the rest of my life studying authoritarianism in people who know I am trying to find out how authoritarian they are. So in November 1991, I repeated a 1983 ploy (*EOF*, pp. 33–35) of offering extra experimental credits to students who could get the answer "through guessing, insight, etc." Only 10 of 220 checked right-wing authoritarianism. When they came to my office to claim their credits, I asked these students how they had gotten the answer right. Two said they had heard from previous subjects. The rest said it had been a guess, usually guided by the thought that, if credits were being given away, the right answer would be the *least* obvious one.

I used to toss "correct answerers" out of my studies. But the realization that many of them had probably just been guessing has led me to retain all, unless I know someone (such as the child of a colleague) was probably "wise." *My* guess is that even after all these years of giving feedback, and publication of my two books (which I carry to the gardening section of the university's bookstore every August, so students will not chance upon them), only about 1–2% of my samples have heard about my research.

Overall, therefore, the RWA Scale seems well disguised. People probably form opinions about what is going on while they answer the survey. But they appear to come to fairly innocent conclusions.[11]

Methodology of Manitoba Studies

PARTICIPANTS

Most of the new research reported in this book studied students taking introductory psychology at the University of Manitoba. In fact, most of the research on right-wing authoritarianism done to date in the world has been based on these students. As we saw in Chapter 1, the findings obtained with them have a good record for replication elsewhere. So besides their natural charm, large numbers, and willingness to be maneuvered into serving in seven hours of experiments (worth 7% of their grade), our students have proved to be great research subjects because they are quite ordinary. (That is why a lot of us would never go to Harvard.)

Roughly 80% of these students are in their first year of university, and about 55% are women. Their mean age is about nineteen. Most have enrolled in the Faculty of (Liberal) Arts (as opposed to, say, Science, Education, Nursing), but many aspire to major in "something practical" eventually. While the University of Manitoba serves the whole province, a solid majority of its undergraduates come from the 600,000 people who live in Winnipeg. (Whatever you have heard or imagined about Winnipeg's weather is probably true, I am delighted to say, and that is why a lot of us would never go to Stanford either.)

Introductory psychology is the most heavily enrolled course at my university (3,000 students). Most of our baccalaureates have it on their transcripts. Because of financial constraints, we pack about 200–300 students into each section of the course (a small percentage of whom are non-Canadians, whom I drop from all analyses). I teach two sections every year, which enables me to collect a lot of data on a lot of people over a long stretch of time. Unlike some schools where "intro psych" is taught in a semester, it runs all year at my university. "All year" begins right after Labor Day, with classes meeting until the beginning of December. Then the school year resumes in January, about nine hours after the Orange Bowl, and skips a week in February, and lectures end the first week in April. (That is why a lot of us would never go to any American university.)

Cross-Sectional Changes in Students' Authoritarianism over Time.   Although the items composing the RWA Scale have changed over the years, I have always included twelve of the original 1973 items in some of my autumn surveys (*RWA*, pp. 244–247; *EOF*, pp. 24–26). Scores on these "Continuing Twelve," collected by the same researcher at the same university in the same way from twenty-three successive years of incoming undergraduates, give us a fairly unique look at how the students, and perhaps society at large, have changed over time.

Figure 2.1 shows the means for the Continuing Twelve over the period 1973–1995. You can see that for quite a while the students kept showing up more and more authoritarian. *Doonesbury*'s and others' observation that "leftist radicals" disappeared during the 1980s and student bodies became more right-wing overall appears confirmed. Whatever the 1990s have brought, at least undergraduates these days appear a little less authoritarian than their older brothers and sisters were.[12]

Mean Scores on the RWA Scale among Manitoba Students.   The average score of Manitoba students on the RWA Scale used to land around the midpoint of the 30–270 range: 150 (*EOF*, p. 29). Now it falls closer to 125. Comparison of the present and earlier versions of the test shows that about 15–18 of those 25 "dropped points" resulted from the newer items on the scale. Most of the "Let's all submit to the man-on-horseback" and "Let's stomp out the rot" statements evoke less agreement than the items they replaced. The rest of the drop presumably reflects the lower authoritarianism of present students.

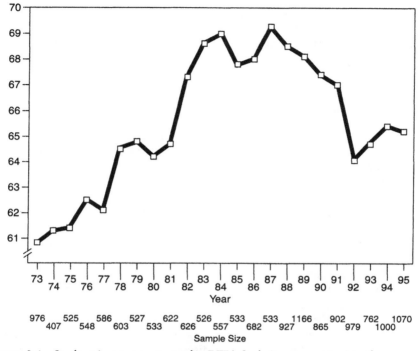

Figure 2.1   Students' responses to twelve RWA Scale items over twenty-three years

Similarly, parents' means have dropped from about 175 on the 1986 scale to about 150 today, for perhaps more complicated reasons we shall encounter in Chapter 3.[13]

PROCEDURES

You will find descriptions of the procedures I use for my surveys in my earlier books: *RWA* (pp. 177–179) and *EOF* (pp. 30–33). Only one important change has occurred in my methods over the years: my department has thoughtlessly appropriated the smallish classrooms I once used for my studies to teach courses, and I have had to pack up my booklets and scram. I now administer my surveys in lecture halls, usually during a class period.

Students tested in large numbers in cramped quarters, especially on their "own turf," tend to fill out the surveys a little more sloppily than had formerly been the case—particularly in the early morning and late afternoon. However, I am now collecting data about five times as fast as before, so I have grinned and nobly borne the change of venue.

Degrees of Anonymity. Students sometimes sign their names on an "attendance sheet" next to their booklet number. In other studies, I want the participants to be anonymous, yet still be recoverable for future experiments. I have developed a "secret number" procedure for these situations:

> You are serving in this experiment anonymously. However, I would like you to put a "secret number" of your own choosing at the top of the bubble sheet. This should be a number you will be able to recognize in a month or so as being yours—but which won't mean anything to me. Like the last four digits of your phone number, or your best friend's phone number, or your bike lock combination. So that when I come back to your class to give feedback about the purpose and results of this study, you can come up and get your own personal sheet, with your anonymous feedback on it, and not someone else's.[14]

The "Secret Survey". Every January I offer my own students an opportunity to earn an experimental credit merely for revealing their sexual experiences to me and answering any questions I care to ask about their innermost thoughts and darkest feelings (*EOF*, pp. 31–32). Accordingly, I forewarn my classes by saying something like, "On Thursday I'm going to give out my Secret Survey at the start of class, if you want to participate. It will start off asking lots of questions about your past sexual activities; and then I'm going to get intrusive."[15]

Each survey is stapled to a personal "grade-feedback sheet" with a student's name on it. This enables me to give discretely premarked answer sheets to Low and High RWAs. The students remove the identifying grade-feedback sheet and do indeed serve anonymously. But I can then compare the answers of the less authoritarian respondents with those of the highly authoritarian group on very sensitive matters.

I tell the students they do not have to answer any question they do not wish to. Then they are sent out of the classroom for about twenty minutes, to any spot they choose on campus, provided they will be alone. When they return, they put their folded answer sheets into a sealed box and sign a credit form.

Participation in this study, like all experiments at my university, is voluntary (within the context that students choose to serve in *some* seven hours of experiments to earn credits). Yet more people show up on the day of the Secret Survey than on any nontest day for the rest of the year. They are moreover extremely cooperative. Most, bless them, answer every question I ask. Some reveal they have cheated on my tests. They report things they say they have never shared with anyone else. They describe things they have done of which they are deeply ashamed.

Later in the term I give my classes a lecture summarizing the results of past Secret Surveys on sexual matters and their own overall responses. The students frequently cite this lecture as the most interesting class of the year (somehow they forget my spellbinding explanation of how the tricolor and opponent-process theories of color vision can be integrated). I have never, however, told the students about the discrete codings of Lows' and Highs' answer sheets. The only people with whom I have ever shared this "Secret of the Secret Survey" are my local Ethical Review Committee and the handful of extremely studious and trustworthy people who read the methodology chapters in my books.

Parent Surveys.   Every year I usually give some students taking introductory psychology (often my own classes) an opportunity to earn credits by involving their parents in the joyous process of blackening spaces on my bubble sheets. The students merely address a largish envelope to their folks, in which I stuff a covering letter, surveys, and bubble sheets, before sending them off.

The covering letter (see *RWA*, p. 308, for an example) explains the need to collect data from nonstudent groups and describes the payoff for the students. I assure the parents they will be answering anonymously.[16] I also try to make it easy for them to decline, revealing that their children have many opportunities to earn experimental credits on their own. The parents are given the option of returning their bubble sheets to me either through the mail or through their children. Virtually everyone chooses the latter. (Since only bubble sheets are returned, not the questions, the parents know their answers will be just an array of pencil smudges to the couriers.)

Parental love being what it is, most moms and dads come through for their offspring. For example, in October 1993 I sent out 827 surveys to parents of 443 students (of the 546 who had answered my booklet in September). Of these, 654 parents' surveys (from 340 mothers and 314 fathers of 357 students) were completed and returned.[17] Again, most people answered every question, even though the parent booklets were quite long.[18]

Methodological Issues

The rest of this chapter describes research I have conducted on some of the causes of measurement error on surveys—a topic of acquired taste. If you administer surveys, you might find one or two things worth knowing.

PREVIOUS EVIDENCE OF DIRECTION-OF-WORDING EFFECTS

As detailed earlier, many things can systematically affect scale scores besides the trait being measured. Social desirability effects (Edwards, 1957; Crowne and Marlowe, 1964) have often been demonstrated, though controversy persists about their nature (for example, Hogan and Nicholson, 1988; Edwards, 1990; Walsh, 1990).[19] Social desirability belongs to a class of "response biases" that reduce the validity of a test while beguilingly increasing its apparent internal consistency (Alliger and Williams, 1992). Such biases are pernicious test *diseases* that masquerade as symptoms of health.

Another masquerading response bias, yea-saying ("response acquiescence") has also long been suspected by researchers. Lorge (1937) observed nearly sixty years ago that people who have no opinion on an issue tend to answer "yes" or "agree" on surveys. Five years later Cronbach (1942) noted that students who guessed on an *objective* true-false achievement test tended to guess "true." Of course, other people tended to be naysayers and false-guessers.

Quite a controversy brewed up over whether response acquiescence itself could be considered a fit and proper personality trait. We shall gently steal past that battlefield. (See *RWA,* pp. 117–122, if you like to visit scenes of ancient carnage.) Instead, we shall demand proof of the more basic assertion that answers to personality tests are sometimes affected by yea-saying and naysaying. Is it true that people sometimes tend to agree with items when, given the content, they really should disagree? And do others sometimes tend to disagree with statements no matter how you word them?

If this happens, it can have calamitous yet undetected effects upon test scores. No one is going to look more "feminine" than someone yea-saying with gusto throughout a femininity scale on which all the items are written in the feminine direction. No one is going to look more "intrinsically" religious than someone yea-saying the devil out of an unbalanced intrinsic orientation scale. No one is going to look more depressed than someone joyously yea-saying on an "all-pro" depression scale, or *less* depressed than someone moodily naysaying through it. Even if people's responses are basically determined by the content of the items, these response sets could still seriously distort the scores, making some way too high and others way too low.

Furthermore, researchers noted long ago that unbalanced scales usually correlate best with *other* unbalanced scales (Hyman and Sheatsley, 1954; Campbell, Siegman, and Rees, 1967)—or indeed with anything potentially affected by yea-saying, including single-item questions. Shared acquiescence could thus create a connection between any two things, no matter what they (supposedly) measure.

So unbalanced scales can easily "work" (produce statistically significant connections with something else), whether they have much construct validity or not. In addition, direction-of-wording effects would provide gravy for this meat loaf they serve up. Like most response biases, acquiescence would raise the correlations among the items on a unidirectionally worded test, making it *look* more internally consistent than the content really is.

By the same token, yea-saying (and naysaying) would *reduce* the correlations between protrait and contrait items on balanced tests (for example, + 3 on a protrait makes you look high on the trait; +3 on a contrait makes you look the opposite). Thus balanced tests would look *less* internally consistent than the content really is. And the reduction in correlation between protrait and contrait items would tend to separate them onto different factors in a factor analysis, even if they were largely tapping the same thing.

The Case of the California Fascism Scale.   The power of yea-saying and naysaying to introduce massive amounts of error into a test's scores, while at the same time making it *look* good, can be illustrated by the California F Scale. All the items on the F Scale, like many other tests since, were phrased in the protrait direction. Would the test's characteristics change a lot, critics wondered, if you rewrote half the items in the contrait direction, thereby canceling out direction-of-wording effects on the summed test score?

Far easier said than done! It proved quite difficult to recast the content of F Scale items into anti-authoritarian sentiments (Rorer, 1965), partly because some of the original statements seem pretty bizarre.[20] When I set out to balance the F Scale in 1968, I knew a contrait had to do more than just "look right" to be a true reversal. I therefore required each reversal to have basically the same mean and standard deviation as the protrait it replaced, and to correlate with that protrait nearly as well as the protrait correlated with itself. Working with my usual speed and brilliance, I took only two years, ten studies, several thousand subjects, and over three hundred "reversal rehearsals" to find the fourteen adequate contraits I needed to balance the F Scale (*RWA*, pp. 122–132). (I learned then why research is called re-search.)

During the winter of 1970 I administered the original and freshly balanced F Scales to over a thousand students. Both versions had identical means, while the balanced version had a lower test-retest reliability (attributable to many reversals, which used "no," "not," or "never" in their wording). But the balanced version had only half the mean interitem correlation of the original (.05 versus .10), producing a significantly lower alpha (.60 versus .77). More dramatic yet, the variance of the balanced scale was only a fraction of the variance of the original test (241 versus 406). (See also Smith, 1965.)

When I partitioned those variances, I found some of the difference was attributable to the lower reliabilities of the "no-not-never" contraits. But most of the discrepancy was due to the low correlation (.09) between the sum of the fourteen contraits on the balanced scale and the sum of the remaining protraits. On the original scale, these two sets of items correlated .63! Remembering that the reversals were *known* to present essentially the same content as the originals they replaced, that correlation of .63 provided "smoking gun" evidence that the two sets of items were glued together when worded in the same direction but virtually unconnected when not. Therefore, uncontrolled direction-of-wording effects greatly contaminated the original F Scale (*RWA*, pp. 132–140). No one, to my knowledge, has ever challenged these results over the past fifteen years or shown that this conclusion is wrong.

Overall, the balanced F Scale proved a better predictor of authoritarian behavior, both in this study and in a large pitting experiment I ran in the fall of 1973 (*RWA*, pp. 140–144, 176–204). The difference was not large, but since the original scale had greater test-retest reliability, the extra variance produced by direction-of-wording effects had to be, on balance, error variance. That is, it *diminished* the scale's empirical validity.

The wound might not have been as devastating for the F Scale as it would have been for some other test, because (as you have probably been thinking all along) authoritarian subjects might be more likely than others to yea-say. (This snarl helped get the literatures on response sets, and the F Scale, thoroughly bollixed up.)[21] In this case response acquiescence might have given back some of the empirical validity it took away. But overall the message seems clear: direction-of-wording effects can lead you down the garden path if you allow them to romp about uncontrolled.

FURTHER EVIDENCE OF DIRECTION-OF-WORDING EFFECTS

Acquiescence on Balanced Scales.　Yea-saying is hard to measure on *un*-balanced scales such as the F Scale because you cannot tell if the percentage of "agrees" versus "disagrees" in the answers merely reflects the strength of the trait in that sample. But speaking just in terms of content, agreement should basically equal disagreement on properly *balanced* scales, whether the sample is high, middling, or low on the trait.

We are talking not about *which* items get agreement, and which items get disagreement, but about the *number* that get each. If we give a balanced, valid measure of "extroversion" to a group of circus clowns, they should tick off all the extrovert items, and say "not me" to all the introvert items. If we give the same measure to Trappist monks, it should be the other way around. In both cases, the number of "agrees" should basically equal the number of "disagrees."

The same should occur with less extreme groups. Say we sample university professors who enjoy lecturing. They might (1) agree with three-quarters of the extrovert items ("I enjoy being the center of attention"), but (2) disagree with the other quarter ("I will wear a red rubber nose to make people notice me"), and (3) agree with a quarter of the introvert statements ("I value moments of quiet reflection"), but (4) disagree with the remaining three quarters of the introvert items ("I wish I could live in a cave by myself"). It gets a little more complicated when we talk about *how much* people agree or disagree, but the basic equality should prevail.

Yet you often find more agreement than disagreement overall on balanced, valid psychological tests. On the RWA Scale, for example, with its long, complicated items, the breakdown is usually about 60-40. Moreover, if you give subjects a chance to correct earlier mistakes by having them reanswer the RWA Scale, compare their two sets of answers, and then decide what their final answer will be, they move about 10% of their responses from one side of the neutral point to the other—mostly from agreement to disagreement. These changes tend to occur on early items (especially the first contrait) and on longer items where confusion may have led to a yea-say (*EOF*, p. 45).

I have found that High RWAs tend to agree with items on balanced scales a little more than Low RWAs do. To illustrate, in that fall 1993 study of 762 students mentioned earlier, High RWAs agreed with 63% of the RWA Scale items, and Lows agreed with 58%. Obviously, they were not agreeing with the same statements. But Highs tended to agree with contraits more than Lows tended to agree with protraits. This result hurt the contraits, thus making the protraits more discriminating, and, along with their other advantages (see note 20), it gave them better item-whole correlations.

Respondents do not always tend to say "yes" on scales, and High RWAs do not always tend to yea-say more than Lows. My Ethnocentrism Scale provokes mostly "disagrees." When participants sense that a test measures prejudice, they may adopt an overall response set to disagree in attempting to look *un*prejudiced.

The Christian Orthodoxy Scale in turn shows almost no yea-saying or nay-saying. People usually have definite reactions to the issues raised, and some High RWAs go through the test giving +4's to every single protrait item and −4's to every single contrait (*EOF*, p. 220.) This faithfulness to content contributes to the great internal consistency of that test.

In general, the better subjects understand items, the more they have thought about the issues beforehand, the more motivated they are to give you accurate answers, and the better their reading comprehension, the less response sets will disrupt the internal consistency of balanced measures. But some people may not have thought much about the issues raised, may simply hold inconsistent ideas, and so on, which leads them to yea-say to both protrait and contrait items.

Having contraits on a test will not make people more motivated, although it probably slows down sloppy, automatic responding that continual protraits might spark. But it does let you use the invalid "agrees" from one half of the items to cancel out the invalid "agrees" from the other half, when the answers get summed. The same applies to invalid "disagrees." You *do* have to balance scales, for uncontrolled yea-saying and naysaying can produce buckets of error variance. And all the while they will lead you to believe, through inflated alphas and puffed up empirical correlations with other unbalanced measures, that things are great. The road to Measurement Hell is paved with protrait items.

EXTREMITY OF WORDING

A few people answering the RWA Scale have asked me, "Why are these statements so extreme?" Many more may have thought it, perhaps including you.

Since the items "naturally selected" themselves, from the lot I supplied for "choosing up," I do not know. I suspect that strongly phrased statements are more definite (less ambiguous), which reduces their measurement error and gives them a better chance to intercorrelate and make the team. Contraits in particular might prosper if sharply phrased, because it appears you have to whack High RWAs some (cognitively speaking) to get them to notice they disagree.[22]

I explored the effects of strong wording in September 1993 by administering the regular twelve-item Attitude toward Homosexuals Scale to half a sample of 370 students, and a "softer" version to the other half. For example, the first item ("I won't associate with known homosexuals if I can help it") became "I would prefer not to associate with known homosexuals if I can help it." The second item ("The sight of two men kissing does not particularly bother me") became "The sight of two men holding hands . . ."). And so on.

The modifications produced no change in the mean interitem correlations of the two versions, which was .55 in each case. Nor did the correlation with RWA scores differ (.65 and .64). Thus I was wrong. Extreme items did not interconnect better than milder statements. But neither does strong wording seem to hurt much.

PLACEMENT EFFECTS

Location of Items on a Scale.   The RWA Scale is almost always printed on both sides of the first sheet of my booklets. I noticed many years ago, while dutifully copying down how well each item had correlated with the rest of the test, that things got noticeably better once I turned the page over. That is, the items in the second half of the RWA Scale usually had stronger item-whole connections than those toward the front of the scale. I soon found that moving any item from the beginning of the test to the back side of the sheet raised its item-whole correlation about .06 (for example, .40 to .46). That difference may look small, but it would certainly decide which one was chosen among marginal items sitting "on the bubble." Statements at the beginning of the test seemed to suffer a "cold start" handicap; alternately, later items seemed to benefit from a "warm up" effect.

I have tried several things to "warm up" all the items before scoring them (*EOF*, pp. 42–45). For a while, as noted earlier, I had samples reanswer the entire scale. But besides being time-consuming, the procedure may have spuriously increased the internal consistency through subjects' desire to *appear* consistent after they knew what was on the whole test.

Then I simply repeated the first few items from the beginning of the test at its end. Whereupon the items always had better connections with the rest of the scale the second time around. Furthermore, as happened when the whole test was reanswered, the mean of the first protrait usually dropped (it got *less agreement* upon reexamination), and the mean of the first contrait usually rose even more (also a sign of *less agreement*).

Detailed inspection revealed that most of the changes were small (for instance, from +3 to +2), but in about 15–20% of the cases subjects leapt over the neutral point on the second go, typically disagreeing with a statement they had agreed with the first time. As you would now predict, High RWAs were more likely to vault over than others, presumably correcting an earlier yea-saying error, especially on the first contrait.

It appeared therefore that giving subjects a second chance at early items, especially contraits, helped them overcome response set tendencies. Perhaps they better understood what the statements meant after answering the whole test (Tourangeau and Rasinski, 1988), or perhaps the intervening items— especially the contraits—caused subjects to "process deeper" and more carefully (Krosnick, 1991).

But I still feared that the *re*administration of the first few items allowed subjects to appear more consistent with the rest of the scale than they truly were. So in 1991 I readopted the tactic I had started with nearly twenty years earlier (*RWA*, p. 322), leading off with some nonscored "table-setters," including an anti-authoritarian statement. The test itself followed, with no repeats.

Since some items have to come before others on a scale (at least, I have not yet found a way around this), I have tried to raise the internal consistency of the RWA Scale fair and square by putting the best items first. That is, I lead off with the protraits and contraits whose item-whole correlations generally lead the pack. These apparently least ambiguous, most "trait-representing" statements best communicate what I mean by the collected items on the test. Accordingly, good old item 5 in Exhibit 1.1 is my best protrait. And item 6, that especially vulnerable first contrait, is my best interconnecting anti-RWA item.

Location of Scales within a Booklet.   I also noticed many years ago that the position of a scale within a test booklet affects its internal consistency (*RWA*, p. 326). Generally, once again, the leadoff spot suffers most. But coming at the end of my longish booklets can hurt too.

I began to understand this flip-flop of the Serial Position curve when I examined the connection between the internal consistency of scales and the speed with which individuals finished the experiment. Comparing speeders (the first 25% of a sample to turn in their booklets) with slowpokes (the last 25%), I found that the speeders generally showed less consistency than the slowpokes on the first scale, but that the slowpokes did poorer on the last.

You will likely see why if you watch a class of students answer a long battery of tests. Speeders, who include not only the lickety-split information processors, but also those simply trying to get out of the room as soon as possible, start ripping their way through the booklet—often while you are still giving the instructions. (It is easy to spot them when they turn over the first page.) But they seem to slow down somewhat toward the end, seeing they otherwise will finish *way too quickly,* and not wanting to be the first to carry their materials to the front of the room. (You will sometimes see them going over their last answers again, waiting for someone else to play Moses and lead the exodus. Once someone does, a clutch of fleeing followers will usually come forward.)

The slowpokes, by contrast, spend too much time on the first tasks, perhaps because they are answering defensively. Then, when the speeders start splitting, and especially when the slowpokes notice the room is emptying and the period is drawing to a close, they start sprinting madly to the finish line.

Fast answering in either case means less thinking, more confusion, more yea-saying, more careless "bubbling," more error, and less internal consistency.

EFFECTS OF "SETTING FACTORS"

I have noticed several "setting factors" that affect the care with which students answer surveys. For example, I have already mentioned that students answer more sloppily when serving in large, packed rooms (in which they might naturally feel less responsible than when in smaller, more "individualized" circumstances). Alphas will also slip a bit when subjects are tested in their classrooms at a regular meeting time, rather than outside class on my turf. And students find my surveys as engrossing in the early morning and late afternoon as they find my lectures at such hours. They also get careless, at any hour, after answering for fifty to sixty minutes. Similarly, two other influences have appeared regularly in my studies: students' prior experience as participants, and their degree of anonymity.

Prior Experience.   The relationship between prior experience and internal consistency parallels the Yerkes-Dodson curve. Alphas are lowest at the beginning of the year (yet another "cold start" effect), highest toward the middle (October to February), and then low again at the end of March.

The reasons for this seem rather straightforward. One's first psychology experiment may be fairly arousing ("Oh my God! What are they going to find out about me?"), especially if it catches you in your first month at university. Students may accordingly answer somewhat defensively, with a weather eye cocked toward social desirability. But they discover that, whatever an experimenter may find out, it does not affect their lives. So they lighten up and answer more spontaneously. By the end of the year, with five or six studies behind them, students may see experiments strictly as a "I'll blacken some bubbles, you give me the credit" exchange. Also, at the end of the course your net is likely to fill with undermotivated subjects who missed the earlier studies and are now just trying to pass the course.

Degree of Anonymity.   I first noted the effect of anonymity in a 1974 experiment (*RWA,* p. 244) that found students who served anonymously answered with less internal consistency than did those who put their names and booklet numbers on an attendance sheet for "administrative purposes." The latter group in turn proved less consistent than students who put their names right on the booklets. These findings have been replicated several times (see *RWA,* p. 326).

If you suspect students care less, and become careless when they know their answers cannot be linked to them, I agree with you. But I have always been leery of the way internal consistency sparkles when subjects put their names directly on the materials; social desirability motivations and a wish to *look* consistent might be pumped up too much. So I have usually employed the attendance-sheet ploy. (Yet another vote for the Golden Mean.)

Sometimes, however, a study requires that subjects be anonymous, or else you might as well not do it. I understand that alphas will suffer some. Having students put down a secret number, with the expectation that they will get personalized feedback later, does not improve their consistency.

Summary of Setting Effects on Internal Consistency.   Being otherwise preoccupied, I have not yet run the necessary $3 \times 2 \times 2 \times 2 \times 3 \times 3$ experiment required to study the interactive effects of (1) place in booklet, (2) number of persons being tested, (3) location (in own class or not), (4) time of day, (5) time of year, and (6) anonymity of subjects. (You can do this experiment if you wish. I give it to you. Just be sure to have at least 100 subjects in each cell or, better yet, 200, to get reasonably stable readings of alpha.) But I do not believe these factors pile up independently; and even if they do, recall that none of this has much effect on empirical validity.

I *do* have a pretty solid feeling for whether, all things considered, the situation in which I run a given study will help or hurt the scales. If you want to maximize the internal consistency of your key measure, but only fairly and squarely, you should probably place it in the middle of your booklet, run subjects in groups of 25 or 50 rather than 250, in "your" room, not "theirs," in the late morning or early afternoon, in the middle of the term, and have the participants sign attendance sheets. It might make your alpha .85 instead of .80.

But you may have noticed that I myself put my most important measure at the *beginning* of my booklets, run subjects in *large* numbers, usually in *their* classrooms, *whenever* the class meets, usually in September when it almost always is their *first* experiment; moreover, I frequently have them serve *anonymously*. At the end of a chapter on methodology, you might well say, "If this be methodological sophistication, give me ignorance any day."

Nevertheless, can you see why this increases the chances that other researchers will find as high or higher alphas for the RWA Scale than I do, and the chances that my RWA Scale findings will be replicated elsewhere?[23]

—3—
The Personal Origins of Right-Wing Authoritarianism

A good and proper personality theory explains how people get the way they are. So how come some of us turn out very right-wing authoritarian, most of us become average, and some of us end up very *un*authoritarian?

It says in my lecture notes (so it must be true) that behavior results from the interaction of the usual suspects: the genes that created us, and the environment that surrounds them. But because I store my lectures in a different compartment of my brain (teaching department) than I use to conjure up studies (research department), I have managed for many years to ignore the possibility that authoritarianism could have genetic roots.

Genetic Origins

THE MINNESOTA TWIN STUDY

Environmentally oriented researchers like me have lately been jabbed with a pointed stick by the Minnesota Twin Study (Tellegen et al., 1988; Bouchard et al., 1990; Lykken et al., 1990; Waller et al., 1990). This research team has done a remarkable job locating and recruiting for study monozygotic (identical) twins and dizygotic (fraternal) ("sororital"?) twins, tracking down all the multiple births in Minnesota between 1936 and 1955.

In addition, they have located from around the world over fifty pairs of identical twins reared apart. While the members of these monozygotic twins raised apart (MZ-apart twins) would probably not have been raised in starkly different environments, the researchers determined that most of them had been separated soon after birth. None of them had contact during their formative years, and most of them had no contact for most of their lives.

By comparing these MZ-apart twins with monozygotic twins who had grown up together, Bouchard and his colleagues (1990) calculated that about 70% of the variance in intelligence was inherited. Evidence for genetic roots of intelligence had appeared in many earlier studies (Bouchard and McGue, 1981), but not at this magnitude. Growing up in the same home seemed to have almost no effect.

More astounding yet, the Minnesota team uncovered evidence of strong genetic causes for many personality dimensions (Tellegen et al., 1988). Again, precedents existed. Evidence had been accumulating for some time that schizophrenia, manic-depression, and other serious mental illnesses had genetic precursors that put their unlucky inheritors at risk. But the Minnesota data indicated that "ordinary" personality variables, which psychologists had long assumed were almost entirely controlled by environment, appeared to have genetic sources as well, sources that made the environment definitely "second string" by comparison. What sort of ordinary personality dimensions? They cited achievement orientation, social closeness, and alienation, and traditionalism, and religiousness . . . Jab! Jab! Jab!

I first learned of the Minnesota Twin Study while watching the *NBC Nightly News* in 1986. The presentation was sensational: all these identical twins who had been raised apart had been tracked down and discovered to have lived very similar lives. Two had been given the name Jim, for instance, married (and divorced) women named Linda, then married a Betty, and so on. Since I lecture in introductory psychology on the misinterpretation of coincidence, I was thoroughly turned off.

Then, in late December 1986, I read a *New York Times* News Service article by Daniel Goleman based on a paper the Minnesota team had submitted for publication in the *Journal of Personality and Social Psychology*. (Newspapers do not ordinarily pick up scientific papers that have just been *submitted* to a journal.) The news story stated at one point, "Among traits found most strongly determined by heredity were leadership and, surprisingly, traditionalism or obedience to authority." The part about leadership harkened back to Aristotle's view that a few of us are born for greatness, while most of us are born to be followers. Which social psychology texts had long treated the same way a wolf treats a bush he wants to use as a territorial marker. And as for submission to authority (not to mention "territory"), give me a break.

Looking back, I can see that I was blocking out another part of the teaching department. in my cerebral cortex. It says in my *social* psychology lecture notes that most animal societies have well-established dominance systems. "Alpha" animals usually dominate everyone else, who submit to them and all others above them in the pecking order. The behaviors that determine dominance versus submission in a pair of animals were linked long ago by Delgato (1963a, 1963b, 1964, 1965) to parts of the limbic system in the brain, whose operation could be genetically influenced. Indeed, dominance is purposely bred in some species. So the notion that authoritarian submission among humans could be inherited, to some extent, would not seem as preposterous to a geneticist or a gamecock breeder as it would to a psychologist who paid no attention to his own lectures.

MINNESOTA STUDIES OF SOCIAL ATTITUDES

In December 1988 the anticipated article on genetic determinants of "ordinary" personality traits appeared in the *Journal of Personality and Social Psychology* (Tellegen et al., 1988), based on a design other researchers could only lust after. In the study 217 pairs of identical twins reared together had answered Tellegen's Multidimensional Personality Questionnaire (MPQ) between 1970 and 1984, as had 114 pairs of fraternal twins raised together. Another 44 pairs of monozygotic twins reared apart, and 27 dizygotic twins reared apart, also completed this test between 1979 and 1986. The twins reared together were substantially younger (twenty-two years on the average) than those reared apart (with a mean of forty-one years). And 4 (15%) of the fraternal-apart pairs were of different sex (which would introduce a new variable in comparison with identical twins). But these were, on the whole, unprecedented samples.

The MPQ consists of eleven "primary personality dimensions" such as Well-Being, Social Potency, Achievement, Social Closeness, and Traditionalism. The last one, upon which my attention was riveted, is measured by eighteen items. Most (twelve) of these items are protraits and somewhat resemble the "conventionalism" sentiments on the RWA Scale (for example, "I very much dislike it when someone breaks accepted rules of good conduct"). Only three of the items are contraits ("More censorship of books and movies is a violation of free speech and should be abolished"). The other three items use a "forced choice" format ("I would prefer to see: (A) Stricter observance of the Sabbath, (B) Greater freedom in regard to divorce").

The Traditionalism Scale reportedly has an alpha reliability of about .90 (mistakenly given as .49 in table 4 of Bouchard et al., 1990). I do not know the evidence for its empirical validity, but that is not directly the issue here.

When Tellegen and his colleagues compared the similarity within sets of twins in each of their four samples, across *all eleven* MPQ scales, they found the median "personality-resemblance" correlation among the identicals raised together was .52, while that for their fraternals raised together equaled .23. Among the twins raised separately, the median level of personality resemblance was .49 for those who had identical genes and .21 for those who did not. Identical twins turned out quite similar, compared with fraternal twins. Being raised in the same home seemed to have almost no effect for either kind of twins.

However, the figures for just the Traditionalism Scale showed much *less* genetic influence. For the large samples of twins reared together, the correlation was .50 for monozygotes and .47 for dizygotes. For the twins reared apart, the values showed a little more spread, .53 for the former and .39 for the latter. If you just look at the identical twins (.50 versus .53), it appears "it's all in the genes." But if you notice how similar the fraternal twins are to the identical ones, genetic *identity* makes little difference. Using the formula for heritability in twins, $h^2 = 2 \ (R_{MZ} - R_{DZ})$ (Falconer, 1960, cited by Tellegen et al., 1988)—which provides the *upper limit* of heritability (Falconer, 1960, p. 185)[1]—you get only 6% heritability for the twins reared together and 28% heritability for the twins reared apart (some of whom were not of the same sex). Genes may call the tune on most of the MPQ scales, but the evidence for Traditionalism was underwhelming.

HERITABILITY OF RELIGIOUS VARIABLES

A paper by Waller and associates (1990) presented more solid evidence for the genetic determination of variables presumably related to right-wing authoritarianism. Pairs of monozygotics reared apart, and (same-sexed) dizygotics reared apart answered five scales that measured religious values, attitudes, and interests, such as the Religious Values Scale developed by Allport, Vernon, and Lindzey (1960). Religious attitudes were assessed with twelve Minnesota Multiphasic Personality Inventory items that Wiggins (1966) believed measured religious fundamentalism. Two measures of occupational interest in religion were included: nine items from the Strong-Campbell Vocational Interests Inventory and four items assembled by some of the authors. A five-item scale from the latter source, measuring interest in religious leisure time activities, rounded out the package. Large samples of monozygotic and dizygotic twins reared together also answered the last two "home-grown" measures.

These instruments had internal consistency reliabilities varying from .82 to .93 and intercorrelated from .40 to .77. Both sets of results probably benefited from the general protrait direction-of-wording found in the measures.

Looking just at the data from the twins reared apart, the five measures all suggested a powerful genetic factor. The monozygotic correlations varied from .39 to .59; those of the dizygotic twins, from −.22 to .20. When the data from the twins reared together were dealt in, some evidence for environmental influence appeared, especially on the measure of leisure time interest in religion. A model-fitting procedure indicated that about 50% of the variance in scores on the five measures was genetically influenced, which is 50% more than almost anyone would have suspected.

MINNESOTA TWIN STUDIES USING THE RWA SCALE

Toward the end of 1988, David Lykken wrote me a nice letter in which he shared his concerns over right-wing authoritarianism in North America. He suggested that the prime source of variance in RWA scores would prove to be genetic, as he believed was the case for traditionalism. Lykken proposed that fraternal twins could turn out similar on something like the MPQ's Traditionalism Scale because their parents had chosen each other partly according to how traditional they were ("assortive mating"). When they reproduced, they tended to pass on similar genes for traditionalism to their offspring, including any dizygotic twins that might turn up. He wanted to give the RWA Scale to some of the twins in the Minnesota Registry to see how genetically determined its scores would be.

I have some hesitation about the assortive mating explanation. Why did it not show up on the other MPQ dimensions? And would it not have to be very powerful to bring fraternal twins so close to the level of similarity found in persons who had *identical* genes? But I could easily believe women and men mated assortively when it came to authoritarianism, although it might not be the first topic to come up in the moonlight. Husbands' and wives' RWA scores correlate about .60 in my parent studies (although they had been married long enough simply to have *become* more similar). Moreover, who wouldn't want to have his scale administered to this incredible sample?

Lykken's first study was completed by May 1990 (Lykken, personal communication, May 14, 1990). He sent the RWA Scale to about half of the twins in the Minnesota Twin Registry and obtained scores from 177 pairs of monozygotic twins, and 145 pairs of dizygotic twins, all raised together. (You know what I mean.) The results were broken down by gender. The correlation between RWA scores of male identical twins was .67, while that for females was .73. The values for male and female dizygotic twins were .55 and .71, respectively (Lykken, personal communication, March 14, 1994).

These data basically looked like the Traditionalism Scale results to me. There was not much difference between identical and fraternal twins, and therefore hardly any evidence for genetic determinants of authoritarianism.

However, this conclusion was completely contradicted by a subsequent study, conducted by Thomas Bouchard with his samples of twins reared apart (Lykken, personal communication, March 14, 1994). These data (sensibly *not* broken down by gender since the samples were so small) produced a correlation of .62 between the RWA scores of 44 pairs of identical twins reared apart, and a nonsignificant $-.18$ among 22 pairs of fraternal twins reared apart. Comparing these two coefficients, I would say that genes rule. (And then some: $h^2 = 160\%$, which is an upper limit with a vengeance!.) But where is the assortive mating effect for the dizygotic twins?

Then in 1993 the Minnesota team sent the RWA Scale to the twins reared together who had not been sampled in 1990. They got back answers from 241 monozygotic and 154 dizygotic pairs. A big genetic difference appeared among the males: .57 versus .04 for the two kinds of twins. Among the females, the difference was smaller but still appreciable: .63 versus .43 (Lykken, personal communication, March 14, 1994).

Lykken combined the results of the two twins-reared-together studies and got male correlations of .61 for the monozygotes and .39 for the dizygotes. For females, the numbers were .68 and .55. Combining the genders gives you something like .65 and .50 (using the z-transformations needed for averaging correlations). That translates into an upper limit of heritability of about 30%, so genes for fascism may exist. If, however, you just consider the twins-reared-apart study, it is all heredity and then some.

I am blithely assuming some things in this discourse that you are probably screaming no one should assume. You might well ask, "Don't identical twins also grow up in more similar *environments* than fraternal twins do, since people are more likely to treat them the same?" And don't children placed for adoption tend to get placed in similar homes, especially if the adoption agency is religious? And are not any conclusions about the power of genes over environment suspect because of the "narrow" range of environments involved? I agree all these need to be considered. The Minnesota team has discussed them (though not always in the context of social attitudes), and you can find their responses in the publications previously cited. But you might also take a look at the give-and-take on pages 191–192 of the April 1991 issue of *Science* (volume 252) and Horgan, 1993.

My conclusion at this point is that the twin data confuse me. The problem is not the monozygotic twins. They rack up correlations in the .60s quite regularly, whether they grew up together or not. But the dizygotic twins blur the picture enormously, for their correlations wander all over the place.

THE MANITOBA ADOPTION DATA

Twin studies potentially give the cleanest answer to nature-nurture questions short of actual DNA connections to behavior. Studies of the similarity of adopted children to their biological and adoptive kin offer another approach, but one that can be easily contaminated by such things as the extent to which the child had contact with the gene-givers. If we wish to test the hypothesis that a trait is *entirely* controlled by DNA, however, as Bouchard's twins-reared-apart study of RWA indicated, we do not have to worry about such contaminants. Compared with children raised by their biological parents, adopted children should not particularly resemble their adoptive parents at all.

I have ascertained the correlation between parents' and students' RWA scores many times, and it usually lands around .40 (*EOF,* p. 64). The vast majority of these parents fill out my surveys for their own gene-carriers. (A sociobiologist would say that is *why* they fill out the surveys.) But some adoptive parents also appear in my samples.

In the fall of 1993, 1994, and 1995 I ascertained in various ways if students answering my booklets had been adopted. Sometimes their parents told me at the end of a parent's booklet. Sometimes the students themselves told me and I discreetly involved their parents in the study. (I did not want either students or parents to know I was studying adoption situations.)

I now have RWA scores on 75 adoptive parents (35 mothers and 40 fathers) of 44 students. The mother-child correlation equals .61, and that for fathers and their adopted children is .50. Overall, the parental average equals .55, which is both statistically significant and embarrassingly higher than the .40 I usually get across generations with biological connections. These numbers do *not* support the notion of fascism genes and instead direct our attention to environmental influences.

Environmental Origins

THE "CORN PONE" THEORY

Since right-wing authoritarianism consists of a set of attitudes, we must begin our search for any environmental roots of authoritarianism with the dominant theory of opinion formation, which is, of course, Mark Twain's "Corn Pone" theory. Like most psychological explanations, it was based on an earlier theory, in this case credited to a slave named Jerry, who preached mock sermons to the young Samuel Clemens from atop a woodpile. Jerry's explanation of the origin of social attitudes can be summarized in one sentence (which, as far as we know, was also the complete statement of the theory): "You tell me where a man gets his corn pone, and I'll tell you what his 'pinions is" (Twain, n.d., p. 1400).

Since we all start out getting our corn pone at home, the obvious prediction of this theory (and later, less parsimonious ones) would be that we learn our RWA attitudes from our parents. Yet while this prediction would appear valid for young children, you do not have to hear many adolescents slam doors— or remember the ones we slammed—to realize that the final product is sometimes not a perfect copy.

My own research with the RWA Scale establishes the following family feud by the time the students enter university. The parents want their children to have virtually the same RWA Scale attitudes they do. The children know it. The parents believe that they have largely succeeded, that their children *are* scaled-down versions of themselves. But they misperceive, for the fit between their own and their children's RWA scores, as we saw earlier, averages only about .40 (*EOF*, pp. 63–64). That boils down to about .02 per year of serving up the corn pone to a twenty-year-old. (If the .40 all came with the DNA, of course, the rate of return on our socialization efforts crumbles to .00. Maybe that's why we resist genetic explanations so.)

OTHER POTENTIAL INFLUENCES THAT ARE NOT

That being the case, you might next think that university students have been more powerfully and more recently influenced by their peer group. But in the fall of 1984 I obtained the RWA scores of the best friends of 206 introductory psychology students, which correlated only .31 with the students' scores (*EOF*, pp. 71–73). Since friends are more likely to shape each other's opinions *mutually* (whereas my children will tell you that kids have almost no influence over their parents' attitudes), that .31 is worth only about .16 when it comes to explaining where the students' attitudes came from.

Students' RWA scores are correlated with their reports of how much the family religion was emphasized as they were growing up. Correlations with a ten-item Religious Emphasis Scale (*EOF*, pp. 205–206), which asks such things as how often one went to church and prayed before meals, run about .35 with RWA. Another ten-item scale (*EOF*, pp. 203–204), which asks more authoritarian-oriented questions about the child's religious training (about submission to church authorities, fear of God, and so on), correlates about .40. But both of these relationships blow away when you partial out the parents' RWA scores, which we need to do since parents usually determine religious practices in the home.

Well then, let's start a trend and blame authoritarianism on schools and the media. But when I asked university students to go through the RWA Scale and indicate, item by item, what effect their educations had on their attitudes, the basic answer was "None." They gave the same answer for the news, except that they thought crime stories made them slightly more authoritarian aggressive (*EOF*, pp. 66–71).

EFFECTS OF EXPERIENCES

I did not get very far explaining how the environment had shaped students' authoritarianism until I developed a questionnaire measure of the students' *experiences in life* with authorities, social conventions, dissenters, physical punishment, religion, and the other matters brought up on the RWA Scale. Four item-development studies during 1982–1984 eventually produced a twenty-four-statement Experiences Scale, which students were instructed to answer in terms of what had actually happened, *not* in terms of what their opinions were (*EOF*, pp. 343–349). The first item, for example, reads: "It has been my experience that physical punishment is an effective way to make people behave. (Have you received physical punishment or known others who did? If not, blacken the '0' bubble. If so, to what extent did it make you and/or others behave as intended?)" The second states: "I have known people with 'poor manners' who really did not care whether people thought they were respectable or not, and they seemed basically as good and pleasant as everybody else. (Have you personally known persons with poor manners, who did not care if they were behaving respectably or not? If *not,* blacken the '0' bubble. If so, did they seem basically as good and pleasant as everybody else?)" These two items are intended to tap experiences that would presumably shape attitudes toward authoritarian aggression and conventionalism. Other items looked for seminal experiences regarding authoritarian submission. For example, "The authorities and officials I have trusted in my life, at home, in school, et cetera have always treated me honestly and fairly. (Has that been your experience?)"

Because the content of the Experiences Scale parallels that of the RWA Scale, I went to some length to dissociate the two tests in subjects' minds. Typically, I would administer one scale, and another experimenter would give out the other several weeks later, in different settings, in supposedly different experiments. Still, the correlation between the two measures always turned up around .70 (*EOF,* pp. 73–86). *We can therefore predict rather well how authoritarian a university student will be if we merely know his or her answers to the Experiences Scale.*

Cross-Replications.   These studies were performed with Manitoba students and reported in Altemeyer, 1988. On October 24, 1989, David Hansen administered the RWA Scale for me to 183 SUNY-Potsdam students. Sixteen days later I visited his campus and gave out the Experiences Scale to 143 of these same participants. The surveys were printed on different size and color paper and answered on different bubble sheets, and no connection was made between the two studies by either experimenter. Yet the scores on the two scales correlated .71.

McFarland, Ageyev, and Abalakina (1990) had Western Kentucky University students administer the RWA Scale and the Experiences Scale (in the same booklet) to 124 adults. The two scores correlated .78.

Interpretation.   I do not think for a second that we have experiences in life independent of all that has happened before. I believe that parents, peers, religion, schools, the media, and *previous* experiences help shape how we will encounter authorities, physical punishment, persons with poor manners, and so on, *and* how we will interpret those encounters. But life can still surprise us. We can be treated unfairly by authorities and know it; we can learn firsthand, from the back of a hand, that physical punishment often does not "work"; experiences with unconventional people can crash through our preconceptions.

A good example of the last was provided in a September 1985 study of the origin of students' attitudes toward homosexuals (*EOF,* pp. 166–170; see also p. 88). Most students indicated they had never known a homosexual. Those who did know one indicated that before this encounter they had rather negative attitudes toward gays and lesbians. Now they proved significantly more accepting than most people. This was even true of High RWAs. A few Highs met homosexuals and came away disliking homosexuals as much as ever. But most Highs, despite all their stereotypes and fears, became more tolerant and less prejudiced as a result.

The trouble is, most High RWAs had never (knowingly) met a homosexual. Nor, they said, had they gotten to know any dissenters or "unpatriotic" or nonreligious people either. They had had no close contact with nontraditional families. They had not taken advantage of the greater freedom young people have to explore and experiment. They had not broken rules, smoked things they should not smoke, or read verboten magazines under the covers by flashlight. They had not learned that their parents did not always know what was best for them, in their era with its new problems and angst. They had not had rebellious ideas or done unconventional things, and they were not friends with those who did.

All of these things, by the evidence (*EOF*, pp. 82–83, 88–89; McFarland, Ageyev, and Abalakina, 1990), tend to make adolescents *less* authoritarian. And Highs had taken a pass. So they remained highly authoritarian through adolescence, while most of their classmates became less so.

A SOCIAL LEARNING MODEL OF AUTHORITARIAN DEVELOPMENT

Integrating what we know so far, our best present model of how people become authoritarian, or nonauthoritarian, again proceeds from Bandura's (1977) social learning theory. This theory, like others, states that attitudes are shaped by the reinforcements and punishments administered by parents and others as we grow up. It allows that the joys and pains we get from our own experiences will be important, and that self-regulatory, self-evaluative cognitive processes ("I am a fair person"; "I believe in the truth") can reinforce as much as corn pone can. It also states that we will learn as much or more from observing *others* as we will from the personal blessings and batterings bestowed by the Law of Effect.

Direct Teachings.   When we are young, we probably learn a lot about authoritarianism from direct teaching. *Obedience* is a key concept, and a battleground, for a two-year old, and parents do not usually hold seminars on civil disobedience with preschoolers. Indeed, in many families obedience remains a bottom-line condition for staying in the family home through adolescence, and beyond. Parents also teach their children to beware of certain threats, such as child molesters and kidnappers. We know from the accounts of both students and parents that as children, High RWA students were taught greater *fear* of these and many other "dangerous people" than others were (*EOF*, pp. 145–147). The child is directly taught, as well, social *conventions* about dressing and undressing, eating and evacuating, playing and praying, speaking and sleeping—virtually everything he or she does from morning to night. "And sit up straight while reading this!"

Imitation.   Other determined socializers, such as day-care staff, older siblings, grandparents, and Sunday school teachers usually reinforce the parents' attempts to reform the little barbarian in their midst. But besides making direct attempts at shaping, all these older, powerful figures can serve as models whom the child might imitate. Modeling appears to be an important channel of communication when it comes to authoritarian attitudes about society. Both students and parents agree that, with certain exceptions, the parents made only slight to moderate attempts to shape directly the attitudes measured by the RWA Scale (*EOF*, p. 100). Children therefore probably acquire a lot of their stereotypes from overhearing their elders talk. Television also provides many models, and out-groups.

Early Authoritarianism.   We have no "kiddie version" of the RWA Scale, but if such a thing were possible, I believe we would find that children in elementary school are pretty authoritarian. They would believe they *should* obey the authorities in their world and *should* follow the rules (Piaget, 1965). We might even find some vestiges of authoritarian aggression (but nothing like *The Lord of the Flies*). However, right-wing authoritarianism, as I have defined it, probably does not begin coalescing into a personality trait until adolescence. Children's cognitive abilities are simply too limited at younger ages to grasp the issues and connect them.

As they begin the long transition to adulthood, their growing cognitive powers, their awareness of the wider world, and especially their *experiences* in that world can play havoc with the concepts and conditioned emotional responses they picked up in childhood. As they struggle to figure things out for themselves, their understanding increases and their attitudes become more organized—including their beliefs about authoritarian submission, authoritarian aggression, and conventionalism.

Unlike the Berkeley theory, which traced adult authoritarianism back to events in early childhood, this model says adolescence provides the real crucible. By the time people emerge from it, they have better-organized, more "adult" levels of understanding. As we saw in Chapter 1, the interitem correlation of introductory psychology students on the RWA Scale, and that of their friends from high school who did not go on to university (Holms, 1989), rival that of their parents.

An Illustrative Tale of Two Citizens.   What particularly makes some people Highs, and others Lows, according to this social learning explanation?

Let's take two twelfth-grade public high school students, whom I usually name "Hugh" and "Lou," standing at their lockers at the beginning of another wonderful school day. Hugh grew up in a family that stressed dominance and obedience to authority. There is no presumption that his parents were brutes, just that he was taught in hundreds of ways to be "mindful" and "respectful" and "dutiful" within rather narrow tolerances. When he stepped over the line, he was punished, perhaps physically.

Hugh likely comes from a "traditional" family, with predictable gender roles and a pattern of social dominance. He probably was given a religious upbringing, and the family religion was very likely emphasized throughout his youth. The religion itself may have stressed submission to authorities, hostility toward "sinners," and strict observance of a firm moral code. And Hugh would have learned early on that the Truth was already known, so his job was not to find it but to memorize it.

Hugh would likely have been taught to identify with his family, his religion, an ethnic group if he had one, and his country. His parents also emphasized to him that the world harbored dangerous people. He has known for a long time who the "enemies," the "perverts," the "bad guys" are. His friends, his movies, his magazines, his clothes would likely have to meet parental approval, to make sure these did not contradict what had been taught in the home.

In other words, Hugh has been tied to a short leash that has kept him traveling in a relatively small, tight circle. (His parents wish it could be tighter; they would rather he go to a religious high school with others of his faith, one with the "right kind" of teachers.) This "within-group" factor has strongly influenced his "between-groups" interactions, in the jargon of statistics. He has had very few of the *experiences* in life that could change him, make him less submissive, less hostile toward the out-groups, less narrow-minded.

But Hugh does not mind the short leash. He believes that trustworthy authority, safety, and righteousness lie within his tight circle, while danger, evil, and damnation prey without. His friends, who gather around him before the bell rings, agree. (I know Hugh well; I was, in many particulars, Hugh.)

Slamming her locker shut down the hall is Lou, who is *not* one of Hugh's friends and who is—from the sound of it—going to give her teachers a hard time today. She comes from a family much less traditional, much more egalitarian than most. Lou had to obey when she was younger, but her parents—who probably had more formal education than Hugh's—understood and even felt gratified when she showed some independence. She was rarely, if ever, spanked.

Lou's parents did *not* teach her that authority was always right. Precious little "rendering unto Caesar" occurred around her dinner table. Rather than accept dominance and competition as givens in life, she likely has been taught values of equality and cooperation. Furthermore, Lou may not have been raised in any religion, and if she was, it was not particularly emphasized—maybe because the religion itself did not insist on emphasis and strict devotion.

Lou was not raised with well-defined in-groups, nor was she taught that "different" people were probably dangerous and evil. Her parents may, in fact, have nurtured her awareness of social injustice and human diversity. She has probably traveled more, and seen more of the world, than Hugh. She has also increasingly chosen her own friends, clothes, "looks," activities, and (eventually) curfews, while her parents lie awake at 2:00 A.M. afraid the phone will ring. But disaster has not struck. Lou's experiences, her explorations, her experiments have proved largely benign and fulfilling.

Unlike Hugh, Lou did not learn from her mother and father that Truth was in the bag, or in a book. Instead, it was hers to discover. Her parents offered her guidance, but basically she had to question and decide things for herself. If Lou were to become very different from her folks—say, in religion—her parents might become upset, but not nearly as upset as Hugh's parents would be if he did the same.

As she joins *her* circle of friends before the bell rings, they have their morning gripe session and then talk about going to university next September. If Lou and Hugh go to my university and take introductory psychology, bet on Lou to score pretty low on the RWA Scale, and Hugh to be a definite High.

The Moderates.   Lou and Hugh represent unusual cases, in which the circumstances of their respective pasts reinforced one another and pushed in one direction. Around them on the extremes of the RWA Scale distribution lie many others who got there by somewhat different routes. And between the extremes in a sample of 500 students we would find hundreds of others with hundreds of different backgrounds.

Most parents, for example, are not as restrictive as Hugh's but also not as white-knuckled permissive as Lou's. In-groups may have been identified, but less strenuously than they were in Hugh's family. But not many families deliberately jack up the children's social consciousness, as Lou's did. Unconventional behaviors and strange friends from different backgrounds are moderately accepted but hardly welcomed. Religion is present, but it does not dominate daily life. And so on.

On balance, the Moderates' *experiences* in adolescence made them less authoritarian than they had been earlier. They had gotten into disputes with their parents, teachers, the police, and came away feeling they had been unfairly treated. They had spotted hypocrisy in pews and privilege. They had enjoyed the independence a driver's license brought. They had met some different people and been "broadened." They had broken rules and had a good time.

But some broke the rules and got pregnant, or totaled the car, or got ensnared in a vicious drug habit. And some students grew up with a High RWA father and a Low RWA mother. Some had only one parent. Some effectively had none, and grew up on their own. There was probably a different family situation in every house on your block when you were growing up, and all the kids had their own set of experiences in life. Throw in possible genetic factors, and that is where the distribution of RWA scores comes from.

A SLIGHT DIGRESSION: GROUP COHESIVENESS

Let us recapture the image of those little knots of Hugh's friends and Lou's friends waiting for the homeroom bell. We would expect each cluster to have fairly homogeneous attitudes, would we not? We have known since the famous research of Newcomb (1961) that "birds of a feather flock together." That is how people consensually validate their opinions and create their social realities. But would we not also predict that the birds in Hugh's group will have to have more similar plumage than those in Lou's group? Because Hugh has been taught to travel in those "tight circles," will he not mind "difference" more?

I am not saying that Lou would welcome Hugh into her group. Respecting other people's choices does not mean you agree with them, want to spend your time with those people, or even like them. Lou will still feel most comfortable with those like herself, just as you and I do. But I do not think she would build fences around her friendships quite as high as Hugh would.

John Duckitt (1989) has proposed that right-wing authoritarianism is based on a need to identify with important groups. In 1990 he sent me a scale that he thought might measure his construct (Exhibit 3.1). I included these twenty-two items, joyously balanced against yea-saying, in a booklet administered to 422 Manitoba students in the fall of 1990. Their mean interitem correlation was .15, producing an alpha of .81. Summed scores connected .49 with the RWA Scale (which was in the right direction) and correlated a little *better* with attitudes toward Indians, Pakistanis, and Quebecois than the RWA Scale did.

Exhibit 3.1   Duckitt's Group Cohesiveness Scale

1. Our society cannot afford disunity in these difficult times.

2. Diversity in culture and lifestyle must be encouraged in any healthy society.*

3. It is absolutely vital that all true Canadians forget their differences to form a truly united and cohesive nation.

4. If our country is to survive and prosper, it is crucial that we Canadians submerge our differences and succeed in forging a common spirit, purpose, and identity.

5. Differing and even conflicting opinions and even ideologies are absolutely essential for a truly democratic Canadian society.*

6. One of the greatest problems confronting Canadians today is our failure to develop a true unity of purpose and dedication to a common Canadian heritage.

7. It is essential that we encourage rather than stifle dissent.*

8. Nationalism is the last refuge of the scoundrel.*

9. At all costs Canadians must begin to dedicate themselves to the creation of a strong and real sense of national identity.

10. Appeals to national unity and cohesion can easily lead to the oppression of minorities and the stifling of dissent.*

11. It is unlikely that Canada will survive in the long run unless we can bring ourselves to forget our petty differences and disagreements, and pull together as a single united people.

12. In the long run our cultural and ideological differences will make us a healthier, more creative, and stronger society.*

13. Those who would like to push Canadians into a common national identity are ultimately the enemies of liberty.*

14. If we could only create a truly united Canadian people, there will be no difficulty or danger we could not overcome.

15. The greatest asset of our society is our diversity.*

16. If we Canadians cannot achieve total agreement on our national goals, we will never overcome the difficulties confronting us.

17. People who continually emphasize the need for unity will ultimately stifle creativity and impoverish our society.*

18. The most important task for Canadians today is that of developing a strong national identity.

19. Independent thinking and the readiness to be different and express one's individuality are signs of a strong and healthy society.*

20. Unity means strength, and a strong united nation is absolutely essential for progress and prosperity.

21. Most of all our society needs creative and freethinking people who have the courage not to conform to old fashioned ways and traditions even if this upsets many people.*

22. What we need most of all in this country is a single-minded dedication to the task of creating a truly united Canadian nation without petty squabbling and disagreements.

Note: Items are answered on a −4 to +4 basis.
* Item is worded in the contrait direction; the cohesive response is to disagree.

These results encouraged me to try to improve the Group Cohesiveness Scale, for which Professor Duckitt may understandably not be thankful and should not be held responsible. I thought the original set was too nation-oriented to reflect a *general* personality trait. So I tried to broaden its scope to include other groups, developing (over five studies involving 1,175 students and 337 parents) such items as:

For any group to succeed, all its members have to give it their complete loyalty.

If you are a true member of a group, you will support it when it's wrong, not criticize it like some outsider.

Anyone who works for a company owes it loyalty and "team spirit" against outsiders.

People who belong to the same religion should NOT stick together as much as possible. [contrait]

People can easily lose their individuality in groups that stress "being a good, loyal member." [contrait]

Members of a family do NOT need to be loyal to each other in all things. [contrait]

Broadening the content of the scale naturally weakened its internal consistency. My best revised Group Cohesiveness Scale, twenty-six items answered by 252 students in October 1992, had a mean interitem correlation of .13 and an alpha of .80. It correlated .52 with the RWA Scale. But its relationship with scores on my Ethnocentrism Scale came in at only .23, whereas the RWA scale correlated .43 with Ethnocentrism. Cohesiveness also did not correlate as well with continued acceptance of the home religion (.21 versus .44), nor differentiate political party preference as well.[2]

We can conclude that right-wing authoritarians, as we would expect from their background of tight circles, believe in group cohesiveness, group loyalty, group identification, unity before "outsiders," and so on. Slogans such as "America: Love it or leave it" and "My country, right or wrong" would come easily from them. But to the extent that I have been able to operationalize

John Duckitt's interesting construct, authoritarianism does not appear to be *basically* caused by a need for group identification.

EFFECTS OF HIGHER EDUCATION

Getting back to our developmental model of right-wing authoritarianism, we have gotten people to university and found we could explain their RWA scores at that point rather well in terms of their backgrounds and the experiences they had in life. What happens to them now? Does development stop once they have answered the RWA Scale in introductory psychology?

Probably not. The social learning model underlying our explanation does *not* hold that personality is cast in iron at some particular age, and thereafter only chipped away at the edges. As long as new learning can occur, new role models can emerge, new circumstances can pop up out of the blue, and new experiences can give us thrills or a poke in the eye, our social attitudes can change.

The attitudes of some university students can be walloped by——university. And not just because their marvelous professors expose them to a wider range of ideas. As well, they encounter a wider range of peers at a school whose catchment area is the world. Furthermore, if higher education usually lowers RWA scores, it should particularly lower those of High RWAs, since they have been traveling in those tight circles up to this point and have more to learn from the new experiences.

A longitudinal study conducted between September 1982 and May 1986 confirmed all this (*EOF,* pp. 91–95). RWA scores were obtained from 26 liberal arts majors (excluding psychology), 32 commerce majors, and 18 nursing students who were about to graduate. All had filled out the RWA Scale when they first entered university nearly four years earlier. Lo and behold, their authoritarianism had dropped significantly over the interval in all programs, about 11% overall, with the liberal arts students dropping more than the others. Freshman *High* RWAs dropped more than twice as much over the years as the freshman Lows did. So they, and our society, were well served by their university experience.

LIFE AFTER UNIVERSITY: THE FIRST ALUMNI STUDY

Well then, does change stop once we stop going to school? The evidence again says "No." In May 1986, at the same time I was contacting those graduating seniors, I also mailed solicitous letters and a one-page survey to 160 Manitoba alumni who had answered the RWA Scale *twelve* years earlier, in the fall of 1974 (*EOF,* pp. 95–99).[3] Reminded of this highlight of their undergraduate career, 90 (of however many I reached) completed the test again and told me a little about themselves. Most of them (58) had gone on to some form of postgraduate education, with the whole sample averaging 17.6 years of formal schooling. Their mean age was 30.3 years, most were (65) or had been (6) married, and 48 had children. Their first-borns averaged 3.5 years of age.

What do we expect here? Since these folks went to school a lot, their RWA scores should have been at least 10% lower than they were as freshmen. And overall, their authoritarianism *had* dropped over the intervening twelve years, but only about 5%. Maybe their teachers in the mid-1970s were not so hot. Or could their authoritarianism have gone down "a lot" at university but then rebounded. What could have caused this?

I did not have to look far. The participants *without* children—nearly half the sample—had RWA scores 9% lower than they had had at age 18. The ones with kids (who had had the same levels of authoritarianism as introductory psychology students as those who remained childless, and just as much education) were virtually back where they had started. They had "fully recovered" from the beneficial effects of their university experience. And their children were still tots! My RWA score shot up about 20 points, along with my blood pressure, while our children were ricocheting through adolescence.

FURTHER EVIDENCE: THE SECOND ALUMNI STUDY

On May 2, 1994, I repeated this alumni study, sending out surveys to 138 Manitoba graduates who had served in a study I ran in September 1976— nearly eighteen years earlier.[4] Three of these were returned by the postal service as undeliverable. By June 7, when I mailed the feedback letters, I had received completed surveys from 87 alumni. This response rate of 64% slightly bettered that obtained in the first alumni study. As in 1986, one of the alumni exercised an option to remove the survey number from the questionnaire, reducing the sample available for longitudinal analysis to 86.

The survey consisted of two table-setters and the same twenty-eight-item RWA Scale that had evolved from the 1976 experiment—answered now as then on a −3 to +3 basis. Then I asked for various bits of demographic information, including the ages of any reproductive gambles. I further inquired (on a −2 to +2 scale) how religious they were now, in beliefs and in practices, compared to when they had entered university. I asked each alumnus to chart broadly, on a graph I provided, how "liberal or conservative" their attitudes on the surveyed (RWA) issues had been at various ages, starting at 18. The questionnaire ended with a request for an explanation of any big changes on their graphs.

Sample Characteristics.   Forty-five of the respondents were females, 41 males. Their mean age was 36.1 years, with the solid majority being either 35 or 36. Their mean level of education was 17.9 years, comparable to the first alumni study's 17.6. Seven of them had never been married. Six others had been married and now were divorced. The other 73 were married, almost all of them for the first time. The seven unmarried alumni had no children, and so did 17 other respondents. The other 62 had children, 43 of them having two. The children ranged in age from six months to 16 years. The oldest child averaged 7.7 years. Only three of these alumni had teenagers.

These 86 alumni cannot be considered representative of any larger group, not even of my university's graduates. They went to school for a long time, they allowed the alumni office to keep in touch with them, *and* they answered my request. Most of them still lived in Winnipeg, and all but 8 still lived in Canada. As a group they are Canadian urban professionals, married with children.

Most of them were born in 1958, were just reaching adolescence when the 1960s turned into the 1970s, and entered university as the class of 1980. There they served in a crummy old psychology experiment for which they received no meaningful feedback, and whose results sat in a file drawer for 18 years while they lived the second half of their lives. Until one day out of the blue, the crummy old psychologist asked them to serve science once again.

Results.   The intercorrelation of responses to the twenty-eight RWA Scale items averaged .22, yielding an alpha of .89 on this go around—a little higher than that obtained in 1976. But individual scores proved much less stable, the "eighteen-year test-retest reliability" being .59. (The 1986 "twelve-year test-retest reliability" had been .62.) Many people had changed a great deal.

Transposing the means to equivalence with a thirty-item test answered on a -4 to $+4$ basis, the 86 alumni had a mean score of 153.5 in 1976, and a significantly *lower* mean of 140.0 in 1994. The 24 alumni who were *not* parents (who had gone to school for 18.0 years on average) showed a significant drop of 28.3 points, from 158.9 to 130.6 (or 18%). The 62 alumni who had experienced the bliss of 2:00 A.M. feedings, tooth eruption, and the Terrible Twos, who had 17.8 years of education, also showed a drop, of 7.8 points, from 151.3 to 143.5 (or 5%), which also was significant ($t = 2.06$; $p < .05$). (But the drop among the nonparents was significantly larger.)

Not everyone dropped, naturally. One person shot up 57 points. But 9 others *fell* more than that, including 4 parents. One parent, a rather high 172 at age 18, now scored a very low 64.

As before, people who were relatively authoritarian at age 18 changed the most; initial RWA scores correlated .47 with the amount of subsequent drop. Females and males dropped equally. I had thought that the *longer* parents had been stepping on Lego pieces in their bare feet, the higher their RWA scores would have rebounded. But the correlation equaled only .11 (which is not statistically significant).

The alumni had some insight into what had happened to them, and why. They almost always thought their years at university had been liberalizing.

But most of them (47) thought their present responses to the items would be more "conservative" than they had been as introductory psychology students, whereas actually the solid majority of them (61) scored lower on the RWA Scale. (Eleven thought their attitudes had not changed, 20 thought they would be more liberal now, and 8 did not answer the question.) The parents did not sense how powerfully those little bundles of joy had apparently changed their attitudes. Only 18 of the 62 moms and dads mentioned parenthood as one of the factors that had affected them, and only 5 of these listed it first. Other answers that appeared often ("Life experiences," "More responsibility," "Getting realistic," and "Changes in society") undoubtedly referred to raising children in some cases, but also potentially to other things.[5]

Discussion.   Basically, the results confirm the first alumni study. Higher education apparently lowered the authoritarianism of most of these people, especially the Highs who began to experience the wider world (as some of them noted in their comments). The alumni who remained childless stayed low after finishing their educations—a period of many years now, during which they grew older and wealthier, advanced in their careers, and probably acquired a mortgage. These and the other things that are *supposed* to make us more conservative as we grow older could *not* have had much of an impact upon these people's authoritarianism, for they still fall substantially below their freshman RWA level.

But those who became parents apparently bounced back up. In this study, unlike the one in 1986, the parents did not quite rebound to their freshman levels (despite being parents longer than their 1986 counterparts). But they nevertheless ended up close to their initial scores.

I am struck by the considerable changes that occurred in the *second* half of many of these lives. The data hardly confirm Freudian notions that adult personality is set by the age of six. The "formative years" seem to extend to age thirty-six at least!

Finally, I am also impressed by the direction of the change. Because of the large amounts of university experience these people had, their RWA scores dropped a lot. Parenthood ratcheted these scores back up, but even the parents remained significantly less authoritarian than they were as young adults. Although this may disappear once the children hit adolescence, I find it remarkable that these "thirty-somethings" were still less authoritarian than they had been at age eighteen. (Remember the warning, "Never trust anyone *over* thirty"?) We do not, it seems, inevitably grow more conservative as we grow older.

FURTHER CAUSES OF CHANGES IN ADULT AUTHORITARIANISM:
SOCIETAL CHANGES

Some of the alumni parents just discussed said that "changes in society" had affected their attitudes. They could well be right. Evidence indicates that major social events can shift our level of authoritarianism at any point in our adult lives. As the winds of crisis blow, we can become less authoritarian than before, or more so.

As an example, the items on the first version of the RWA Scale could only become relatively unglued over time because they had been strongly bonded in the first place—probably by the civil rights movement, the war in Vietnam, and Watergate. These social upheavals had split American society down to its family roots, polarizing opinions and creating a New Left that challenged the wisdom and integrity of the Establishment and its authorities. Their open talk of revolution accompanied by the battles in the street caused many others to recoil away from them, toward the real winner of the 1968 Democratic national convention in Chicago, Richard Nixon.

The RWA Scale was first used at the end of this era, and its continuous employment at my university ever since lets us see how levels of student authoritarianism have changed over the years. We saw in Figure 2.1 that scores on the Continuing Twelve rose fairly steadily from 1973 until 1987. Then they started a gradual decline that has gotten us, by 1995, essentially back to the levels of the late 1970s and early 1980s. *How* did these changes take place, and *why?*

How? The *rise* occurred basically because the low end of the RWA Scale distribution (in absolute terms) wilted and died. ("Where have all the flowers gone?") At the same time, the number of "slightly" and "moderately" High RWA students increased (*EOF,* pp. 24–27). ("Gone to business school, every one.") Table 3.1 updates this breakdown of the Continuing Twelve scores. One can see that the pendulum is swinging back, that more Lows and fewer Highs are showing up each year.

Why? Well, Lows probably waned in the first place because the societal issues that nurtured their development in the late 1960s and early 1970s largely disappeared. The civil rights movement drifted to the back pages of newspapers, the war in Vietnam ended, Nixon resigned. But why then did so many young people Velcro themselves onto Ronald Reagan, Brian Mulroney, and Margaret Thatcher? They may have concluded that "conservatives" had the answers liberals lacked.

Why the *drop* then? We are getting some of the children of the flower children now. If you had a child in 1970, he or she would have entered university in 1988 or later. But also some *young* people may have decided that the conservatives do not have the answers and it's time to give the liberals a try. If the times they are a-changing (again), people entering adulthood could be a-changing too.

SOCIETAL THREAT AND SHIFTS IN ADULT AUTHORITARIANISM

A number of writers have presented archival evidence that when American society experiences high levels of social threat, authoritarianism increases

Table 3.1   Distribution of summed scores of Continuing Twelve items among students, 1973–1995

Year	N	Very Low (%)	Moderately low (%)	Slightly low (%)	Slightly high (%)	Moderately high (%)	Very high (%)
1973	976	3.5	11.2	30.9	40.2	13.2	1.0
1979	527	1.3	6.5	31.3	43.8	16.0	1.1
1985	533	0.2	2.8	22.5	51.2	22.0	1.3
1991	902	0.6	3.9	25.9	52.4	16.9	0.3
1995	1070	0.7	5.9	27.2	46.9	18.1	1.2

Note: When RWA Scale items were answered on a −3 to +3 basis (from 1973 through 1979), "very low RWA" meant scores on these twelve items ranged from 12 to 24, "moderately low" from 25 to 36, "slightly low" from 37 to 48, "slightly high" from 49 to 60, "moderately high" from 61 to 72, and "very high" from 73 to 84. When a nine-point (−4 to +4) response scale was adopted for the RWA Scale in 1980, the categories above were redefined as 12–28, 29–44, 45–60, 61–76, 77–92, and 93–108, respectively.

within its people. Economic disaster such as the Great Depression seemed to boost conversion to "authoritarian religions" (Sales, 1972) and elevate authoritarian submission, authoritarian aggression, and other elements of the Berkeley model of the authoritarian personality (Sales, 1973). Periods of high inflation, strikes, and terrorist bombings can also threaten society. Doty, Peterson, and Winter (1991) took these and other indicators into account and found archival evidence of an overall rise in the many traits of "Berkeley authoritarianism" during the relatively threatening years 1983–1987.

Archival evidence convinces me less than laboratory experiments.[6] But we cannot run laboratory experiments on societies, and the conclusion that social threat leads to increases in right-wing authoritarianism is buttressed by many chilling historical examples, most notably what happened in Germany in the early 1930s. I have tried to study the factors involved in such cases through role-playing experiments conducted in the mid-1980s.

This role-playing convinces one even less than archival studies do, because I was asking participants to *imagine* how they would feel under various circumstances in the future (*EOF*, pp. 289–310). People sitting in a quiet testing situation almost certainly underestimate how disturbed they would get if their world actually came crashing down around their ears. But we might still learn something by comparing "imaginings" from one situation to another.

First, as a control condition, university students who had already completed the RWA Scale were asked to reanswer the test, imagining they were twenty years older, well off, and the parents of teen-aged children. Overall, they imagined they would become a little more authoritarian as a result.

Then, in another condition, I also threw in economic turmoil in Canada twenty years ahead accompanied by a violent *left*-wing upheaval. Students' role-played RWA scores shot up nearly three times as much as the control groups had.

But when I presented a scenario involving economic turmoil and a violent *right*-wing coup within the government that seemed about to destroy democracy, students did *not* react by becoming *less* right-wing authoritarian. Instead, their RWA scores did not differ significantly from the Controls'.

I repeated the experiment with a sample of parents and got the same overall results: a violent left-wing threat produced a significant rise in projected authoritarianism. But a violent right-wing threat did *not* reduce RWA.

The violent left-wing threat to democracy in these rosy futures involved street violence and urban riots aimed at toppling the government, whereas the right-wing threat came from the government itself, from the top down. How would people react to a violent right-wing movement dedicated to overthrowing the government through violence in the streets? I wrote a "Brownshirts" scenario about an extremist right-wing group that was battling the police in the streets, trying to destroy their political opponents by force, and urging that their leader be given dictatorial power.

Students (and parents) reacted to this scenario by becoming significantly *more* authoritarian, probably hoping the government would crush the extremists. Thus people seem spring-loaded to become more right-wing authoritarian when there is trouble in the streets. But that is exactly the direction an authoritarian leader would want them to go. (If you put these two violent right-wing scenarios together, you have a generally faithful rendering of how the Nazis seized power in Germany. A lot of street violence between the Communists and the Nazis led to electoral victory for the latter. The Nazis portrayed themselves as the defenders of law and order even though Hitler had tried to overthrow the government by force himself, earlier, and his Stormtroopers were causing most of the violence. Once installed as chancellor at the head of a minority government, Hitler seized dictatorial power "temporarily" from the top following the Reichstag fire, to the cheers and relief of millions. The role-players in my experiments appear to have "reacted" in the same way that masses of Germans did in the early 1930s.)

Back to the future. I next determined that *non*violent left-wing protest movements did not raise RWA scores nearly as much as violent left-wing protests did. My nonviolent movement was forceful. It held "widespread but peaceful demonstrations" involving large "well-controlled protest marches." Speakers at rallies severely criticized the government, but the audience listened politely to government spokespersons. Many demonstrators carried out acts of civil disobedience, forcing the authorities to arrest them. But the protests were always peaceful, and the role-playing subjects recoiled little.

Finally, I discovered that if a government brutally repressed nonviolent left-wing protestors, participants indicated they would become significantly *less* authoritarian. If inducing left-wing protestors to become violent is the "Nixon trap," inducing a government to use violence against nonviolent protestors can be called the "Gandhi trap."

I should note that in the many scenarios in which I found the role-players became *more* authoritarian, the High RWA subjects did not go up all that much. (They already believed the world teetered on the edge of chaos.) Instead, the Moderate and Low RWA students jumped up the most. Perhaps they would only become more authoritarian *temporarily*. But "temporarily" was all Hitler needed to seize power and eventually plunge the world into the most murderous war of all time.[7]

A Summing Up

What causes personal authoritarianism? It may be genetically determined to some extent. But while a plausible theoretical case for DNA roots can be advanced, the evidence for genetic factors is presently inconsistent and unconvincing.

We can predict introductory psychology students' RWA scores rather accurately if we know whether they have had certain *experiences* in life. The critical period for the development of adult authoritarianism, in terms of these experiences, is probably adolescence.

But we also have evidence that authoritarianism can shift back and forth during adulthood. Higher education usually lowers it, especially among High RWAs. It appears that getting older, per se, does *not* cause RWA scores to climb. But becoming parents likely will. We know that levels of right-wing authoritarianism in university students change periodically over time, perhaps even cyclically, arguably in reaction to the events of the preceding era.

Finally, it seems likely that violent societal threats affect the level of authoritarianism within a country. But people appear much more likely to head for the high end of the RWA Scale during such times than for the low end, no matter who is threatening democracy.

— 4 —
The Cognitive Behavior of Authoritarians

In this chapter we shall consider five related lines of evidence about how right-wing authoritarians think and make decisions. All of these cognitive tendencies can be deduced from what we already know about the authoritarian. In particular, they follow fairly directly from authoritarian submission itself and the way High RWAs are often brought up.

Compared with others, authoritarians have not spent much time examining evidence, thinking critically, reaching independent conclusions, and seeing whether their conclusions mesh with the other things they believe. Instead, they have largely accepted what they were told by the authorities in their lives, which leaves them with time for other things, but which also leaves them underpracticed in thinking for themselves. We shall see how this deficiency puts authoritarians themselves at risk, as well as the society in which High RWAs properly have as much right as anyone else to say what our policies should be, and who shall lead us.

The relationships uncovered in this chapter are not large. But by the time you finish it, you may feel you understand authoritarians—and maybe even some recent history—better.

Ability to Make Correct Inferences

We shall begin this exploration in the summer of 1989 in a jury room in the most northwest corner of the mainland United States: Port Angeles, Washington. Within, a group of men and women are trying to break a deadlock over a criminal case, and one of them, a Ph.D. student in psychology named Mary Wegmann, cannot believe what she is hearing. Certain members of the jury, she thinks, have an amazing tendency to misremember evidence and to make erroneous inferences. As she listens to the arguments going to and fro, it seems to her that the people who cannot remember the trial evidence correctly, and who are leaping to the wrong conclusions, are authoritarians.

Mary Wegmann's inference, in turn, could have been the wrongest in the room. But she was in a position to put it to a test, as she had hit upon her dissertation topic while performing her civic duty.

Dr. Wegmann (1992) (to take the suspense out of the personal story) solicited volunteers from the student body at Peninsula College and from the recent jury pool in Clallam County, Washington, for a study of "ability of the general public to recall conflicting opinions." Volunteers were screened by telephone for perceptual handicaps and reading difficulties and then given an appointment at a computer lab on the college campus. There they were helped to feel comfortable working at a terminal, and tested to make sure their reading comprehension and short-term memory were adequate for the experiment. Then they spent an hour or more, at their own pace, answering the RWA Scale via the computer and learning about the "conflicting opinions."

The fifty students and twenty-nine jurors who participated read a pair of pro and con essays on socialized medicine on the monitor screen for as long as they wanted. Afterward, they answered questions, also on screen, about each essay. They did the same for a pair of essays on corporal punishment in schools. Then they *listened* to ten minutes of a *McNeil/Lehrer News Hour* report on a school segregation court ruling, in which two lawyers debated the merits of the outcome. The subjects then answered questions about what they had heard. Finally, they answered Watson and Glasser's (1980) Critical Thinking Appraisal Test via the computer.

In both samples, High RWAs had more trouble accurately remembering the material they had just read (r's of $-.37$ for students, $-.46$ for jurors) and heard ($r = -.36$, $-.15$), and making correct inferences on the critical reasoning test ($r = -.42$ and $-.49$). For each sample, RWA correlated $-.47$ with *overall* ability to remember and reason properly, which is what Mary Wegmann had noticed in the heat of a deadlocked jury.

These results surprised me because I had never discovered Highs to differ from Lows in "intellectual" skills. In the fall of 1980 I had found no RWA correlation with students' performance on the Wonderlic Intelligence Test— a group-administered "twelve-minute dash" through the usual IQ fields of vocabulary, comprehension, and so on. I also had established several times that High RWAs did as well in introductory psychology as others. At one point I had also given out abstract-reasoning tests to my students, such as "If some A are B, and no B are C, is it true that no A can be C?" (Nope.) I found that most of them did not have a clue; they thought almost everything was true. So Mary Wegmann's findings intrigued me.

I was particularly interested in the results of the "inferences test," because I thought people accustomed to agreeing with authorities would be weak at drawing their own conclusions. So in 1991 and 1992 I gave the correct-inferences test Wegmann had used to over 800 students. Both times I found Highs did significantly worse on it than others. The relationships came in somewhat smaller than those Wegmann had found, but in my experiments subjects could look back in their booklets at the evidence under discussion whereas in Wegmann's study that information had been replaced on the computer screen. (And Highs still had trouble making correct inferences.) In both experiments, High RWAs particularly had trouble recognizing decidedly *false* inferences.

I do not mean to imply that right-wing authoritarians believe everything is true. They carry quite a list of "false teachings" and rejected ideologies in their heads. But they usually learned which ideas are bad in the same way they learned which ones are good—from the authorities in their lives. Highs therefore have more trouble identifying falsehoods on their own because they are not as prepared to think critically. They learned to yea-say instead, and "agree" usually leaps to their tongue faster than "disagree"—as we saw in Chapter 2. So if an inference *is* true, they will have a good chance at "getting it right." But should it be false, they often will not notice.

Suppose, then, a vicious, outlandishly false rumor spreads through a community. Suppose an unfair stereotype circulates through a society. Suppose someone tells a Big Lie. Who will be inclined to believe these things, right off the bat, *before we even consider the content* of the rumor, stereotype, and lie?

Agreement with Contradictory Ideas

To the extent that we copy other people's opinions, rather than critically evaluate them and decide for ourselves, we can end up believing a lot of contradictory ideas. Our heads can become depositories for slogans, conventional wisdom, "well-established facts," things that "They say . . ." and religious quotations, each kept in its own compartment (like my teaching department and research department), and pulled out as the situation demands. These beliefs can be antithetical, but as long as our thinking remains highly compartmentalized, we shall probably not notice.

One can cite many examples of compartmentalized thinking in Highs. In the United States, High RWAs would be particularly offended at any suggestion that children stop saying the Pledge of Allegiance in school. I suspect that, if they had their way, we would say it right after we sang the "Star Spangled Banner" at every football, basketball, and baseball game—and then again during the seventh-inning-stretch, just in case we had forgotten what we stood for while we were standing. But curiously, two of the things we stand for are stated in the conclusion of the pledge: "with liberty and justice for all." No matter how many times Highs say the Pledge of Allegiance, with hands over hearts and heads bowed, they seldom seem to connect those words with the rest of their thinking.

American Highs have been mightily offended by the Supreme Court ruling against prayer in public schools. In Canada children used to recite the Lord's Prayer routinely at the beginning of the school day, until it was challenged in the courts. The case aroused the fury of those who believe in school prayer. These people probably have read the Bible a great deal, but they seem to have missed that Jesus himself was against public prayer, saying we should go into a closet and shut the door when we say the Lord's Prayer (Matthew 6:5–13)— the very prayer Highs wanted said aloud in public schools. (Right-wing authoritarians also have a pronounced double standard about teaching religion in public school, as we shall see in the next chapter.)

You can find many compartmentalized religious ideas in Highs' thinking, starting with the statement they will often make that every word in the Bible is literally true—even the passages that contradict one another on the same page. (For instance, how many animals of each kind did Noah take into the ark? Compare Genesis 6:19 with Genesis 7:2.) But the writings they compartmentalize the most appear, ironically, in the Gospels, which contain many hard to accept "soft" teachings.

In March 1985, I asked students what they thought of Jesus' admonition during the Sermon on the Mount, "Do not judge, that you may not be judged. For with what judgment you judge, you shall be judged" (Matthew 7:1). I also asked about Jesus' resolution of the proposed stoning of the adulteress: "Let he who is without sin among you be the first to cast a stone at her."

Twenty Christian Highs said we should take the teachings literally. Twenty-seven other Christian Highs said we *should* judge and punish others, but none of them explained how they reconciled this view with Jesus' teachings. Apparently, they "believed" both (contradictory) things. But the kicker came when I looked at various measures of authoritarian aggression I had gathered from these students. No matter what they *said* they believed, both these groups of Highs were quick with the stones on the Attitudes toward Homosexuals Scale, the Ethnocentrism Scale, and Posse-Homosexuals (*EOF*, pp. 222–224).

FURTHER STUDIES

I encountered blatant self-contradiction in the thinking of High RWAs by accident in the fall of 1988 when I tried to develop a Social-Justice Attitude Scale. I asked 393 students to respond to twelve statements about why some people are rich and others are poor. As is my wont, I wrote six items that said, essentially, people get what they deserve in life, while the other six said that some unfortunate people get treated very unfairly. Unfortunately for me, the responses to the set of items showed little interitem consistency, so the Social Justice Scale never had a chance. (It was not my first "Little Scale That Couldn't.")

When I picked through the psychometric rubble, I found that the twelve items held together quite nicely among the Low RWAs, who typically said, (1) people do *not* always get what they deserve, and (2) some people *are* treated very unfairly. The problems arose among the Highs, who typically said, (1) people *do* get what they deserve in life, and (2) some people *are* treated very unfairly. To be specific, High RWAs tended to agree with such items as "If poor people really wanted to, they could 'pull themselves up by their bootstraps' " *and* "A person can have lots of drive and determination, but still *not* get very far in life because of discrimination against their sex or race."

If you are one of the heroes who read the methodology chapter of this book, you know that we again have here the bane of poor, honest test developers: High RWAs' tendency to yea-say. But yea-saying does not flow just from confusion or apathy. It can also come from a tendency to "think out of both sides of our heads." The authoritarian with compartmentalized thinking can piously agree that life treats many unfairly and yet also believe that everyone in America has equal opportunity. Highs will say, "racial prejudice does exist. I am against it. I am not myself prejudiced. Why some of my best friends . . ." But they will also say, "Everybody knows 'those people' have chosen to live that way. Otherwise they wouldn't."

FURTHER STUDIES OF SELF-CONTRADICTION

Wondering if Highs would "think with a forked brain" on other issues, I asked 238 students in February 1990 to respond to ten pairs of statements adapted from Tomkins's (1965) Polarity Scale. Each pair supposedly represented opposite opinions on some issue. For example: "If human beings were really honest with each other, there would be a lot more anger and hostility in the world," versus "If human beings were really honest with each other, there would be a lot more sympathy and friendship in the world."

Students trudging through my booklet first encountered ten of Tomkins's statements at the bottom of a page, which they answered on the usual -4 to $+4$ basis. When they turned the page over, they encountered the "opposites," in somewhat different order, at the top of the back side. (See Exhibit 4.1).

Exhibit 4.1   Ten Contradictory Pairs of Items

1. If human beings were really honest with each other, there would be a lot more anger and hostility in the world.

2. A government should allow total freedom of expression, even if it threatens law and order.

3. If an individual breaks the law, it is NOT always to society's advantage that he be punished.

4. Human beings should be treated with respect only when they deserve respect.

5. Children should be taught to strictly obey their parents, even though they may not always feel like it.

6. Fear can make the bravest man tremble. We should not condemn failure of nerve.

7. Reason and objective facts are the chief means by which human beings make great discoveries.

8. The trouble with democracy is that it usually represents the will of all the people, instead of just the best people.

9. The most important duty of any government is the maintenance of law and order.

10. Parents should first of all be gentle and tender with their children.

[Page is turned over.]

11. If an individual breaks the law, he should be punished for the good of society.

12. If human beings were really honest with each other, there would be a lot more sympathy and friendship in the world.

13. A government should only allow freedom of expression so long as it does not threaten law and order.

14. Faith, not reason, is the chief means by which human beings make great discoveries.

15. All human beings should be treated with respect at all times.

16. Children should be encouraged to express themselves and seek their own ways, even though parents may not always like it.

17. Cowardice is despicable and in a soldier should be severely punished.

18. The trouble with democracy is that it seldom represents the will of the people.

19. Parents should first of all be firm and uncompromising with their children; spare the rod and spoil the child.

20. The most important duty of any government is to promote the welfare of *all* the people.

I found, not surprisingly, a lot of consistent answering. Some people have at least as much internal consistency as some psychological tests do. And others probably noticed they were covering the same ground again, checked back, and got their act together. But I also found considerable inconsistency, as people often agreed with both a statement and its opposite. Lows gave yea-yea responses 114 times, and Highs did 174 times ($p < .05$). (Lows had a nonsignificant tendency to "nay-nay" more than Highs did, 60–47.)

I repeated this experiment with 211 students the following month and got nearly identical results. Lows showed more consistent answering overall than Highs. They again had a nonsignificant tendency to "nay-nay" more than Highs, while Highs proved significantly more likely than Lows to agree with both parts of a seemingly contradictory pair.

In September 1990 I administered eight contradictory pairs to 466 students. Most of the pairs came from the previous studies, but I also dealt in a few of my own, such as "When it comes to love, men and women with opposite points of view are attracted to each other ('opposites attract')," versus " 'Birds of a feather flock together' when it comes to love." The results proved essentially the same: Low RWAs answered "nay-nay" slightly more than High RWAs did, while Highs gave "yea-yea" responses significantly more than Lows did. The same thing happened among 235 parents tested the next month.

So High RWAs contradict themselves more often than Lows, and apparently do not notice it, even when the contradiction occurs within a minute or so. They appear to examine ideas less than most people do. You do not get the feeling they have considered many notions and just "squeezed" them. Instead they seem to be, like Sancho Panza, suckers for slogans and sayings.

As I always say, "It takes one to know one." So how come I do not realize my own compartmentalized thinking? Well, we do not come equipped with self-diagnostic programs. We often need others to point out the inconsistencies in our thoughts. I get such loving help all the time, sometimes prefaced with "You sexist pig!" as I try to unlearn a lifetime of gender conditioning. Oddly, women tend to correct my sexist statements more than my male-bonded buddies do. For some reason, people who think as I do tend *not* to notice the inconsistencies in my beliefs. But that is probably another reason why High RWAs do not realize how compartmentalized and contradictory their ideas are, for (compared to others) they tend to surround themselves more exclusively with people who agree with them.

What Is "Our Most Serious Problem"?

Authoritarians' shortfalls at critical thinking and tendencies to yea-say also surface if you ask them if some particular social problem is our most serious problem. I first discovered this in January 1990 when I asked 300 students if they thought "the 'drug problem,' and the crime it causes, are the *most* serious problems in our country today." I found that 74% of the Highs, compared with 44% of the Lows, said drugs were problem number one ($p < .001$).

I was not knocked off my horse by the news that Highs considered the drug problem more serious than Lows did. But I was surprised that, three-quarters of the Highs thought it, of all our social ills, was our *most* serious problem. Yet when I asked 238 other students the following month if they thought "the destruction of the family" was our most serious problem, 84% of the Highs wrote "Yes," compared with 38% of the Lows ($p < .001$).

So which one constitutes our most serious problem, drugs or the destruction of the family? They may be related to some extent, but they are not the same thing. Furthermore, when I asked 209 students the following fall if they thought the loss of religion and commitment to God represented the most serious problem afflicting our society, 72% of the Highs said "Yes," compared with 3% of the Lows ($p < .001$). Thus *several* different things are all "our *most* serious problem," in the not altogether reflective minds of right-wing authoritarians.

Perhaps Lows would also overreact if we highlighted their concerns. Indeed, when I asked 211 students in March 1990 if "the destruction of the environment" was our most serious problem, 66% of the Lows agreed. But so did 60% of the Highs ($p > .50$). And when the following fall I polled 213 others on whether "the destruction of individual freedom" was our greatest problem, only 44% of the Lows said "Yes," as did 25% of the Highs ($p > .20$). In January 1991 I tried "poverty"; 35% of the Lows, and 34% of the Highs, agreed it was our most serious problem ($p > .50$).

In summary, when I proposed to university students that something was our biggest problem, Low RWAs usually disagreed—even when I mentioned issues Lows are particularly concerned about. And High RWAs agreed nearly as much as Lows that problems *on the Low RWA agenda* were our biggest trouble. When I lobbed issues from the Highs' own agenda before them, most of them said this, that, and the next thing were all "our most serious problem." When it came to the danger of the drug problem, etcetera, most Highs found it hard to "Just say 'No.'"

Well so what? What is so bad about Highs being a little sloppy in their use of terms? Well, it is more serious than that; the "biggest problem" data speak to more than just imprecision in the authoritarian mind. High RWAs stand about ten steps closer to the panic button than the rest of the population. They see the world as a more dangerous place than most others do, with civilization on the verge of collapse and the world of Mad Max looming just beyond. As we saw earlier, their parents taught them the world was dangerous, and the resulting fear drives a lot of their aggression. Ask the militias training in the woods.

Look back at the RWA Scale items in Chapter 1. Notice how many talk about our imminent *ruin,* about *perversions eating away* at society, about *the situation in our country getting so serious,* about *the rot that is poisoning us.* Such items have always drawn solid agreement from Highs, regardless of how turbulent or placid the times. Problems have come and gone over the past twenty-five years; some things have gotten steadily worse, but other things have gotten steadily better. (Anybody remember 1968?) But the "cry havoc" items have continuously struck a chord in the authoritarian psyche, because authoritarians always perceive society as going to hell in a hand basket. Like the people in River City, "we have Trouble, Trouble, Trouble with a capital T."

High RWAs, accordingly, can be easily frightened, which makes them vulnerable to precisely the kind of overstated, emotional, and dangerous assertions a demagogue would make. So how hard would it be for a sufficiently unscrupulous, power hungry, *real* agitator to turn authoritarians' general anti-Semitism into the Nuremberg Laws? Or for a washed-up, unprincipled senator from Wisconsin to turn Cold War fears into a life-crushing, four-year witch hunt? Or to get Highs to join a "posse" after any vulnerable group today?

I do not mean, in pointing out this latent threat, to move *you* three paces closer to the panic button. High RWAs have been around for a long time, and cooler heads have usually prevailed. But as long as authoritarians do not think much about what they hear, and believe "X is our biggest problem, where X is a variable," and are vulnerable to fear-arousing bombast, they are prone to stampede. And once stampedes start, you either get out of the way, join them, or get trampled.

Biases in Judging "Sufficient Evidence"

Let me repeat: High RWAs do not believe *everything* they hear. They will reject out of hand "dangerous ideas" from "bad sources." But they show a hefty double standard when testing for truth: evidence for disagreeable conclusions is scrutinized more critically than evidence supporting what the authoritarian wants to believe.

I studied this propensity in 466 of my students at the beginning of September 1990 by asking for reactions to the twenty statements in Exhibit 4.2 (shown with correlation to RWA scores in parentheses). Take the first item. Do you agree that "the fact that airplane crashes sometimes occur when the pilots' biorhythms are at a low point proves biorhythms affect our lives?" I hope not. If biorhythms affected *nothing,* you would still find coincidental times when planes crashed and the pilots' biorhythms had been "low" (just as there are days when planes crash and graduate students are caught up in their work—although these are much rarer).

Exhibit 4.2   The Sufficient Evidence Test

1. The fact that airplane crashes sometimes occur when the pilots' bio-rhythms are at a low point proves biorhythms affect our lives.* (−.12**)

2. There is no way to test the theory that crystals can restore harmony to a person's "spiritual energy," since you *cannot* objectively measure such a thing. (−.05)

3. Skeptics *cannot* explain all the thousands of UFO sightings that have occurred, so there must be something visiting our planet from somewhere else.* (.13**)

4. Even if tarot card readers, fortune tellers, palm readers and "prophets" can tell you things about the past and future that turn out to be true, it does *not* mean these people have any magic or supernatural powers. (−.09**)

5. Just because sensational crimes sometimes occur on nights when there is a full moon, that does *not* prove the full moon has mysterious powers over us. (−.03)

6. The fact that some people make up wild stories, and fake footprints of "Bigfoot" proves that there is *no* such thing as "Sasquatch" or "Bigfoot."* (−.14**)

7. So many people have had dreams about something that later came true, our dreams must be some form of ESP.* (−.04)

8. Just because many religions in the world have legends about a big flood, that does *not* prove the story of Noah in the Bible is true. (−.45**)

9. The explanation that ESP cannot work if there are skeptics present satisfactorily explains why it is hard to demonstrate ESP in scientific experiments.* (−.11**)

10. The fact that the pyramids are very large and precisely built, and that there are ancient lines in the Peruvian desert that resemble an airport, does *not* prove the earth was visited by "ancient astronauts" from other worlds years ago. (.02)

11. So many people sincerely believe they have memories from earlier lives, there must be something to reincarnation.* (.07)

12. The accounts of many people who nearly died, who say they traveled through a dark tunnel toward an all-loving Being of Light, proves the teachings of Christianity are true.* (−.36**)

13. The fact that archaeologists have discovered a fallen wall at the site of ancient Jericho does *not* prove the story in the Bible about Joshua and the horns. (−.48**)

14. Even if most of the people in the world claimed to have seen a ghost, it would *not* prove there is such a thing as a spirit world. (−.07)

15. So many people have been caught cheating while "communicating with the dead," "bending spoons with mind power," "reading minds"—it proves there is *no* such thing as ESP.* (−.11**)

16. Just because many planes and ships have disappeared in the "Bermuda Triangle" over the years, that does *not* prove there are any mysterious forces operating there. (−.05)

17. If someone shows some ESP ability on one occasion, but cannot ever show it again, it *still* proves beyond a doubt that ESP exists.* (−.06)

18. The fact that the Shroud of Turin was scientifically shown to have been made in the Middle Ages indicates it is a fake, *not* a miraculous impression made by God. (−.24**)

19. Whenever science cannot explain something mysterious, it shows there are supernatural and spiritual forces at work in the world.* (−.17**)

20. Astrology should be doubted because no one has explained yet *how* the position of planets in the sky can affect us. (−.07)

Note: Items are answered on a −4 to +4 basis.

* Indicates the item is considered false, so the right answer would be to disagree. Keying is reversed for these items. A high score over all twenty items therefore indicates high critical reasoning ability.

** Indicates the correlation with RWA scores was statistically significant ($p < .05$ by a two-tailed test; $N = 466$). A negative correlation means High RWAs showed *less* reasoning ability.

To *prove* that biorhythms affect pilots' performance, we need (as a start) data for plane crashes for all the days: "high biorhythm" days, "medium" days, and "bad hair" days. So I think one should disagree strongly with item 1.

Yet I wholeheartedly agree with item 2's hesitation about "crystal power." Since we cannot measure immaterial energy, we are going to have trouble testing a crystal's ability to harmonize such energies. (Please do not write me that *your* crystal works.)

As indicated in Exhibit 4.2, I think half of the items on my Sufficient Evidence Test of critical thinking ability are true, and the other half are false. Deeper thinkers may want to pick a fight over some of my calls, but I did try to balance the summed scores against yea-saying.

Overall, my brand new university students did not blow me away with their critical thinking. Summed scores could go from 20 to 180, and someone who did not have a clue and simply guessed would score about 100. The mean among my classes equaled 107.4, and responses to the items usually averaged about 0 on the −4 to +4 format (or, in other words, "Huh?").

When I correlated the students' RWA scores with their reactions to each of these items, I mostly found very small relationships. High RWAs usually did worse than others, but seldom by much. They were only slightly more seduced by the biorhythm "proof," they did not particularly believe in "crystal power," and they were *more* skeptical than most about UFOs, as well as tarot card readers, full moons, and Bigfoot.

But when it came to "evidence" connected to Highs' religious beliefs, their critical thinking took a hike. They might have been as skeptical as others about ghosts, the Bermuda Triangle and ESP, but to their minds common legends about a big flood *proved* the story of Noah. If one finds a fallen wall at Jericho, that proves Joshua's horns brought it down. "Near-death experiences" prove the teachings of Christianity. And scientific analysis be damned, High RWAs *know* the Shroud of Turin was miraculously created by God.

I included six of the items in Exhibit 4.2 in a booklet answered a few months later by 491 parents. Again, Highs showed minor vulnerabilities to believing that our dreams are a form of ESP and that the full moon has mysterious powers over us. They did not buy the UFO trip any more than Lows did. But they were impressed by the "evidence" for Noah's ark ($r = -.38$), Joshua's horns ($-.31$), and the Being of Light ($-.28$).

Standing back a bit, you could say that Highs' tendency to disengage critical thinking when considering religion is the predictable outcome of being rewarded all their lives for placing faith over reason. I would not dispute this. But I also think the tendency extends beyond religion and has deeper roots, namely, authoritarian submission. Highs' further reliance on social reinforcement for their beliefs ("consensual validation") rather than on thinking for themselves, makes them vulnerable to mistaken judgments in many fields, which leads us to this chapter's final topic.[1]

A Special Vulnerability to the Fundamental Attribution Error

The Fundamental Attribution Error (Ross, 1977) describes a common mistake people make when analyzing others' behavior. Simply put, we tend to overexplain others' actions in terms of their personalities, and underexplain their doings in terms of situational factors. (We similarly give ourselves personal credit when analyzing our own wonderfulness, and blame our shortcomings on other people and bad luck.)

Authoritarians' beliefs that poor people are too lazy to improve their lives looks like the Fundamental Attribution Error. So does Highs' self-righteousness. In addition, their tendency to accept inadequate evidence, if it leads to cherished conclusions, suggests they will be particularly likely to make the Fundamental Attribution Error when people say things authoritarians want to hear.

HOMOSEXUAL RIGHTS

In the fall of 1990, in a study patterned after the first Fundamental Attribution Error experiment (Jones and Harris, 1967), I asked the same 466 students who answered my Sufficient Evidence Test to guess someone's true attitude toward homosexual rights. They had to make their inference from a short essay allegedly written for an exam. I told half the subjects the writer had *chosen* the "point of view" of the essay. The other half were told that the professor in the course had *assigned* that point of view. What was the point of view? In each condition, half the students read a pro–homosexual-rights essay, while the others read an anti–homosexual-rights essay.

Imagine you are one of my participants, and it so happens you have drawn a booklet containing the "Choice, Pro–Homosexual Rights" arrangement. You read:

> As part of a final exam in a philosophy course at this university last year, the students were assigned to write a short essay supporting EITHER of the following principles:
>
> EITHER that homosexuals should have *no* restrictions on their lives in this country, compared with the rest of the population;
>
> OR that homosexuals should have *some* restrictions on their lives in this country, compared with the rest of the population.
>
> Each student was allowed to *choose* which principle to argue for. One of the students in the course wrote the following essay:

> Homosexuals are every bit as good as everybody else, and have the right, under the Charter, to be treated equally. They work as hard as everybody else, are usually more creative, and make quiet, responsible neighbors. Fear of homosexuals is largely based upon stereotypes. In most places in the world being "gay" is *not* a bad thing. So there are many reasons why homosexuals should have the same rights to where they live and work that others do.

> What would you say is this student's *own, personal attitude* toward homosexuals? (Please mark the scale below with an "X.")

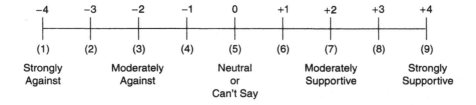

Knowing the situation the essay writer was in, you have several possibilities to consider when estimating his or her real opinion, don't you? Perhaps the essay writer believed the prof would grade "pro-homosexual" essays higher. Perhaps this philosophy student felt he or she could demonstrate debating skills better on that side of the issue. Perhaps the student knew that side of the debate better. Perhaps the student personally believed what he or she wrote. So the "right answer" is probably either 0 or "plus Something" on the scale above.

While you, my dedicated participant, are trying to figure this out, the person to your immediate left is going through the same procedure. Only this judge was told an essay writer chose to write the following, quite different essay:

> Homosexuals can never ask that they be treated like ordinary people. They have an unnatural life style, one that disgusts many and goes against the laws of nature. People always react against somebody who breaks the natural law. Besides, "gay" men are particularly liable to get AIDS, and nobody wants to be around somebody who has a fatal disease. So there are all kinds of reasons why homosexuals should not have the same rights to where they live and work that normal people do.

What did *this* philosophy student really think? Again, you can approach the matter from several angles, but the sensible answer is probably 0 or "minus Something."

The "Choice" conditions in a Fundamental Attribution Error experiment such as this serve as control groups for the real focus of attention: What will subjects infer if they are told the philosophy student *had* to express a certain point of view? That's the task that the person sitting to your right has gotten by the luck of the booklet distribution. His version states:

> Last year a professor at this university taught a philosophy course in which he tried to teach his students how to *make strong arguments for any side of an issue, no matter what their personal feelings might be.*
>
> He then told his students he was going to ask them a question, on the final exam, about homosexuality. He said he was going to *assign* them to write an essay on "gay rights."
>
> When the students got their exams, they found they HAD to write a short essay arguing strongly for the principle "Homosexuals should have *no* restrictions on their lives in this country, compared with the rest of the population."
>
> One of the students in this course wrote the following essay.

The pro–homosexual-rights essay followed.

And finally, the person sitting two seats away from you (in either direction), got the "Assigned, Anti–Homosexual Rights" version of the task in this "2 × 2" experiment.

Now when you get an essay built around an assigned point of view, written as part of an exam in which students are trying to show how forcefully they can argue for *anything,* what can you say about the student's personal opinion on the issue? Zilch. So if you are asked what the essay writer really believed, you would have to say 0, right? But people often do not say 0. Instead they ignore the situational constraints on the essay writer, which in this case were very powerful, and say the essay reveals something about the writer's personal feelings. They thus make the Fundamental Attribution Error (FAE).

My *real* subjects in the "Assigned" conditions made the FAE about equally for each essay—which amazes you the first time you see it. But here we are wondering how right-wing authoritarianism figures into the story, so I analyzed the results separately for Lows and Highs (making the study a "2 × 2 × 2"). The ANOVA found, naturally, a strong main effect for the Position of the essays, a significant Choice by Position interaction, and a significant triple interaction ($F = 17.9$, $p < .05$) that represents the object of the hunt. (Or, in English, the position of the essayist on homosexual rights obviously made a difference, and that difference was affected by whether the position was chosen or forced. But the judges' own authoritarianism affected their judgments too.)

Here are the means for the Low and High RWA students who answered the four versions of the task.

Condition	Low RWAs		High RWAs	
	N	Mean	N	Mean
Choice, Pro–Homosexual Rights (Control)	32	8.16	21	7.86
Assigned, Pro–Homosexual Rights	18	5.39	24	6.63
Choice, Anti–Homosexual Rights (Control)	20	2.20	32	2.16
Assigned, Anti–Homosexual Rights	33	3.24	24	2.25

Let us do this step by step. Thirty-two Lows happened to get an essay that a philosophy student had allegedly *chosen* to write from a pro–homosexual rights viewpoint. What was the essayist's real opinion? You can see that, on a 1–9 scale, the 32 Lows inferred such a student would be strongly pro-homosexual (mean = 8.16). Eighteen other Lows got the same essay, but with the understanding that the point of view had been *assigned* to the writer. What was the writer's personal point of view then? These 18 Lows sensibly said, "Beats me." Their mean equaled 5.39, a shift of only .39 from 5.0 (the "Neutral or Can't Say" midpoint).

Given that this same essay produced a shift of (8.16 − 5.00 =) 3.16 units in the (control) "Choice" condition among Lows, we can therefore calculate the Fundamental Attribution Error in the "Assigned" condition in terms of its percentage of the control group shift; that is, 0.39 divided by 3.16, or just 12%. However you cut it, Low RWAs reading the pro-homosexual essay made very little attribution error.

How did *High* RWAs react who read the same pro-homosexual essay? The 21 Highs in the (control) "Choice" condition also inferred that the writer was revealing strong personal feelings (7.86). But when 24 other Highs were told the essay's point of view had been assigned by the teacher, they *still* thought the writer was rather pro-homosexual (6.63).

Let us calculate our "FAE ratio" again, which allows us to take into account the effects of the essay per se upon High RWAs. We get (6.63 − 5.00 =) 1.63 for the "Assigned" condition, which is divided by the result for the (control) "Choice" condition (7.86 − 5.00 =) 2.86. That gives a 57% Fundamental Attribution Error, a much bigger error than the Lows made on the pro-homosexual essay.

We might guess that Lows in turn would show some attribution error on the *anti*-homosexual essay. And they did, as you can see. Their mean in the "Assigned" condition was (5.00 − 3.24 =) 1.76 units away from the sensible "Can't say" neutral point. The Lows who read the "Choice" version ended up (5.00 − 2.20 =) 2.80 units away from neutral. So 1.76 divided by 2.80 equals a 63% FAE. But High RWAs still made a bigger one: 2.75 divided by 2.84, a 97% FAE.

What do all these numbers boil down to? Simply this: compared to Lows, High RWAs tended to ignore the fact that the essayist in the "Assigned" condition *had* to express the point of view assigned. They thought the essayist really meant it. They particularly thought the essayist was sincere when writing an anti-homosexual argument. This of course is what most High RWAs would write themselves.

Now I shall reveal a guilt-edged secret. This September 1990 study was my *third* run of this experiment. The first two runs, done in 1989 with smaller samples and slightly different wordings, produced somewhat conflicting results. The first study indicated Highs not only overbelieved assigned anti-homosexual essays, they also *under*believed assigned pro-homosexual ones. This result suggested enormous interpretive bias on the parts of Highs and set my imagination on fire. ("Why, they twist everything to suit themselves!") But when I repeated the study, the results proved much less spectacular, essentially like those from the third experiment described above.

Combining these three experiments ($N = 1001$), the various Fundamental Attribution Errors average out (weighted means) as follows:

	Low RWAs	High RWAs
Pro-Homosexual Essay	36%	57%
Anti-Homosexual Essay	66%	103%

To put it simply, Highs made more attribution errors than Lows, *especially when they tended to agree with the message*. Indeed, Lows were somewhat restrained when they read an agreeable essay they knew had been forced onto the writer (a 36% FAE). Authoritarians, by contrast, completely accepted the essayist's sincerity (103%!), even though they had been told that the writer was simply trying to demonstrate on an exam the ability to argue well. Is this not amazing?

POLITICAL PLATFORMS

The results above suggest that High RWAs will be particularly vulnerable to an insincere communicator who tells them what they want to hear. This observation fits with earlier findings in this chapter, notably those concerning Highs' disengagement of critical thinking when they like the conclusion. In the present context, High RWAs might often fail to take into account the situational pressures that could lead a communicator to say whatever is necessary to manipulate them. So they will be "suckered" more often by "cons," and by "pols," too.

I tested this hypothesis with another 2 × 2 × 2 experiment, also run three times during 1989–90. Instead of making inferences about the beliefs of someone writing an exam, these subjects (654 other students and 235 parents) were asked to evaluate a speech by a politician running for mayor. "Law and order," allegedly, had become the central issue in the campaign.

In the "Speaker *High* Choice" conditions, the students were told that a candidate knew from polls that half the electorate favored a tough law-and-order stand that would crack down on criminals; the other half of the electorate favored a "community-improvement" approach that would go after the origins of crime.[2] Thus in this situation, a candidate who came out strongly for one or the other could be seen as probably giving a personal position.

In the "Speaker *Low* Choice" conditions, the polls showed overwhelming (90%) support for one of these approaches. A candidate who then came out strongly in favor of the position favored by the voters could thus be seen as merely saying what he or she knew 90% of the electorate wanted to hear, revealing nothing about his or her personal beliefs. (I did not run a third condition in which a politician came out strongly *against* the inclination of 90% of the voters, even though this happens at least three or four times every hundred years.)

Each student received only one speech and one scenario of the circumstances behind it. Half the students read a "Dirty Harry" speech:

> I am a very firm believer in law and order. I believe that crime is getting so bad in our city, a decent person takes his life in his hands just walking down the streets now. We need more police, and if I'm elected they're going to get my full

support in cleaning out the drug dealers, break-in gangs, bank robbers, rapists, and all the other criminals who are ruining our city. Furthermore, as mayor I'm going to do everything I can to make sure that thieves and dope-heads and murderers get sent to prison for a long, long time, and not get sent back to us on "day parole" after they have only been in jail a short time.

The other speech advocated improving the communities where crime was rampant:

I am a very firm believer in Community Improvement. I strongly believe the only way to stop crime is to stop producing criminals in our slums. We've got to improve the lives of our poor. We've got to give them good job training, and then good jobs at good wages once they're trained. We have to build good housing in our community for people with low incomes. We have to get the poor involved in shaping their futures. And most of all, we have to change the attitudes of those people in our city who believe that white people are better than brown, yellow, or black people. Crime is caused by the system, and we've got to change the system.

After reading the scenario and speech, students judged the candidate's *real* opinion about how to fight crime on a nine-point scale that ran from "Strongly Pro Community Development" to "Strongly Pro Law and Order." Again, a midpoint of 0 represented "Neutral or Can't Say." We would expect the "Speaker High Choice" condition to give a better idea of the candidate's true position, and we would look for the Fundamental Attribution Error in the "Speaker Low Choice" condition.

This experiment did not produce as much attribution error as the homosexual-rights studies. (Do *you* believe politicians who courageously come out in agreement with strong public opinion?) But the pattern of the FAE below will look familiar.

	Low RWAs	High RWAs
Pro Community Improvement	17%	36%
Pro Law and Order	51%	73%

Authoritarians again made more attribution errors in both cases. Unlike Lows, who were particularly suspicious of someone they knew had strong political reasons for telling them what they wanted to hear, Highs were astoundingly gullible. They basically ignored the politician's knowledge of the 90% poll and believed the law-and-order candidate was sincere.

So let us say, if you don't mind, that you are a crooked, unscrupulous person who wants to win high public office. You will say whatever you have to say to get elected. Which block of voters are you going to target (besides the moderates of course), the Low RWAs or the High RWAs?

The choice is easy, is it not? Advocating a Low RWA position will alienate the Highs and not necessarily win the more critically inclined Lows. But Highs do not wonder much about the sincerity of someone who tells them what they want to hear. So their votes are yours if you just *say* the right things about law and order, the flag, patriotism, abortion, tax cuts, and so on. Then comes the dessert: even if it comes to light someday that you *are* "a crook," or sold arms to Iran, we know the High RWAs who supported you all along will still believe in you for a long time, come what may. Do you think Low RWAs would trust you no matter what?

Right-wing authoritarians' incredible credulity encourages manipulators to take stands that will be popular with them. I am *not* saying all conservative politicians are beady-eyed, scum-covered Machiavellians. But we can see why such politicians would tend to head to the political right. High RWA voters are such an easy sell, they attract the unscrupulous. And because their votes can be locked up simply by advocating their causes, *their* issues are more likely to set the political agenda in a country.

I have also found that Highs make a strong fundamental attribution error when judging assigned essays on whether the Bible is the word of God. They also were more likely to trust a television evangelist who conducted a poll to find out what kind of revival meeting would maximize financial contributions, and then staged the most lucrative kind of program. So Highs probably fall for deceptive exploiters in religion as well.

EXPLANATION AND OBSERVATION

Why do authoritarians so often ignore situational factors when a communicator tells them what they want to hear? I think it basically goes back to authoritarian submission and those "tight circles" we considered earlier. High RWAs generally have not determined for themselves what is true and false, to the extent that others have. Instead they are more likely to absorb the teachings of the authorities in their lives. They subsequently maintain their beliefs against challenges by limiting their experiences, and surrounding themselves with sources of information that will tell them they are right—including like-minded people.

Compared with others, Highs rely a lot on consensual validation to maintain their views. They develop a noticeable "us-them" outlook on information sources that springs automatically from their general ethnocentrism.[3] Who are "us"? They are people who believe what we, "the good people," believe. So people who say what authoritarians want to hear are welcomed, rather uncritically, because they bring a treasured gift to Highs: confirmation. But this easy access to the in-group—which I think betrays how *un*certain High RWAs sometimes really are of their beliefs—makes them vulnerable to deceivers who know what song to sing.

All of this explains the conflicting stereotypes of right-wingers' gullibility and right-wingers' paranoia, which I raised in the Introduction. You can expect to see *both* behaviors in High RWAs, because of their underlying ethnocentrism. People from the "us" circle will be trusted, in some instances far more than they should be. Someone *professing* the right religious beliefs, for example, will often get Highs to open their hearts and their pocketbooks. But people from the "them" camp will usually be *dis*trusted more than is warranted, sometimes to the point of paranoia, which ranges from believing Communists are poisoning everyone through fluoridation to "knowing" the government is about to swoop down, confiscate your guns, and march you off to a concentration camp. Highs' relative inability to discover the truth on their own forces them to rely more upon inadequate social criteria that lead to both Type I and Type II errors (missing the truth and cherishing falsehoods).

A Caution

Let me summarize this chapter with the observation that right-wing authoritarians have not caught some mysterious disease from outer space that affects their cognitive processes but leaves the rest of humanity untouched. They are not "them" while the rest of the world is "us." Instead, I think they have just gotten an extra helping of some very common human weaknesses.

A lot of people have trouble making the right inferences from evidence, especially when it comes to seeing what is wrongly concluded. Witness advertising copy. (Or, in Chapter 10, witness how horribly *Low* RWAs fall for a Big Lie.) Also, people tend to yea-say in general; Highs just do it more than most. In addition, all minds probably have compartments holding contradictory ideas. And Highs are hardly the only self-righteous people running around; we all seem vulnerable to a self-serving bias.

Similarly, almost everyone can be shaken by fear of "our biggest problem" and various crises, as we saw at the end of Chapter 3. Lows believe in biorhythms and ESP almost as much as Highs do. Who among us does not scrutinize evidence supporting disagreeable conclusions more than evidence for what we want to believe? If Lows and Moderates did not also make the Fundamental Attribution Error, it would not be called the *Fundamental* Attribution Error. Almost everyone uses consensual validation to shore up personal beliefs. And each one of us is probably ethnocentric in many ways.

If you are a Low RWA, Highs just show you what you would be like if you were "somewhat different," not if you were "completely different."

But the evidence *does* indicate that right-wing authoritarians tend to lead the league in these human foibles, and because of that they put themselves—and potentially all of society—at extra risk.

They also occupy first place when it comes to other, more "psychodynamic" failings, as the next chapter reveals.

—5—
Inconsistency and Blindness in the Authoritarian Mind

We shall now focus on more "psychodynamic" matters as we continue our explorations of authoritarians' cognitive processes. Most of what lies ahead in this chapter follows rather directly from what we have already observed, notably the compartmentalization that High RWAs do especially well. But we shall consider more serious contradictions and blindnesses than before—inconsistencies that people would probably find threatening if they realized them, and thus often do *not* realize. We shall again cover five related lines of evidence, as we journey deeper into the twists and turns of the authoritarian mind.

Double Standards

Double standards reveal something truly insidious in our thinking. You can see this in the way we react when we get caught with one. "Defensiveness" shoots right off the scale. I myself desperately try to find some way to slip off the hook, usually by developing some convenient rationale, *after the fact,* that justifies what I did. Have you ever found yourself similarly scrambling for plausible explanations to save face?

I think we dread being skewered on our double standards for several very painful reasons. First, they show how unfair we can be. Second, they show our unfairness hides behind a facade of "principle." We are therefore hypocrites to boot. And third, because our double standards sometimes come as a surprise to us when we get caught, we see that the person we have been fooling best is ourself.

We often do not realize our double standards because we compartmentalize our thinking, keeping matters that ought to be connected unconnected. Since High RWAs compartmentalize their thinking a lot, we can expect them to have lots of double standards. Thus we saw in Chapter 1 several criminal-sentencing experiments that uncovered bad faith in right-wing authoritarians' attitudes toward justice. Recall how High RWAs punished a prisoner who beat up another prisoner more than they punished a police chief who did the same thing. They punished a hippie who started a fight with an accountant more than the accountant if the roles were reversed. And they sentenced a gay activist who led an attack on opponents more than an anti-gay activist who did the same in a flip-flop situation.

I uncovered another double standard in a 1978 study in which students were asked to judge the seriousness of an unfair election practice (*RWA*, p. 323). Half the subjects were told a New Democratic government had discretely threatened Conservative Party supporters if they contributed to a Conservative campaign. The others got the reverse story. Low RWAs condemned both acts of intimidation, equally. Highs proved less concerned overall about official wrongdoing, and were significantly more condemning of a New Democratic government putting the screws to its political opponents than of a Conservative government doing the same.

I also found many High RWA double standards when it comes to gender roles. They were much more likely to say, on Spence and Helmreich's (1978) Attitudes toward Women Scale, that swearing, drinking, and telling dirty stories are less objectionable when men do them, that the father should have greater authority in raising children, that men should aim for careers and women should aim for housekeeping, and so on. (See Chapter 1.)

RELIGIOUS INDOCTRINATION IN PUBLIC SCHOOLS

I have since completed double-standard studies on several additional topics. The first concerns religious indoctrination in public schools. This study was suggested by an earlier experiment (*EOF*, pp. 278–281) in which I asked people what they would do if a law were passed requiring the strenuous teaching of Christianity in public schools, aimed at getting all students to accept Jesus Christ as their personal savior. I was stunned when nearly half of the 43 Highs said they approved. I thought more would see the inherent unfairness of such a practice to non-Christians, and to Christians with different views as well.

In September 1991, 483 students answered a booklet containing one of two versions of the religion in public schools issue. One version read:

Suppose a law were passed requiring the strenuous teaching of religion in public schools. Beginning in kindergarten, all children would be taught to believe in God, pray together in school several times each day, memorize the Ten Com-

mandments and other parts of the Bible, learn the principles of Christian morality, and eventually be encouraged to accept Jesus Christ as their personal savior.
How would you react to such a law?
0 = I think this would be a *bad* law; minority rights should be respected, and no particular religion should be taught in public, tax-supported schools.
1 = I think this would be a *good* law; the majority in a country has a right to have its religion taught in its public, tax-supported schools.

Only 3 of 61 Low RWA students (5%) thought this would be a good law; in contrast, 27 of 56 Highs (48%) supported the idea ($p < .01$).
The other half of my sample got a transplanted version of the issue.

Suppose you were living in a modern Arab democracy, whose constitution stated there could be NO state religion—even though the vast majority of the people were Muslims. Then a fundamentalist Islamic movement was elected to power, and passed a law requiring the strenuous teaching of religion in public schools. Beginning in kindergarten, all children would be taught to believe in Allah, pray together facing Mecca several times each day, memorize important parts of the Koran, learn the principles of Islamic morality, and eventually be encouraged to declare their allegiance to Muhammad and become a Muslim.
How would you react to such a law?

The same two response options were provided. Again, only a few (4 of 59, or 7%) of the Lows approved of such an idea. But *this time* Highs were also opposed (3 of 55, or 5%)—significantly less supportive than the 48% endorsement rate Highs gave to Christian indoctrination in Canada.
I repeated this experiment the next month with another 309 students, only this time the foreign situation involved Israel. Accordingly, following the election of a "fundamentalistic Hebrew party,"

all children would be taught to believe in the Jewish God, Jehovah, they would engage in Jewish religious ritual several times each day in school, memorize important parts of the Talmud, learn the principles of Jewish morality, and eventually be encouraged to declare their allegiance to the Jewish faith and become a Jew.

In this study none of 28 Lows favored a law stressing Christian training in Canadian public schools; most Highs (24 of 39; 62%), however, supported a Christian indoctrination law. When the issue was transplanted to Israel, only 1 Low out of 43 (2%) indicated approval, as did only 7 out of 35 Highs (20%). The latter percentage was again significantly lower than the 62% Highs totaled in the Christian condition.
The same month I included the Christian-Islam experiment in a booklet answered by 337 *parents*. Lows again showed almost no support (less than 10% in both cases) for teaching either religion in public schools. However, 16 of 40 Highs (40%) approved of using the public schools in Canada to indoctrinate students in Christianity. But only 10 of 46 other Highs (22%)

said it would be right for Islam to be similarly promoted in an Arab country, again significantly lower than the 40% obtained among Highs in the Christianity in Canada condition.

All three studies showed that Lows very consistently believed in minority rights when it comes to promoting a religion in public schools. However, a sizable percentage (40–62%) of the High RWAs thought the *majority* had a right to have their religion, Christianity, forced upon everyone attending public school in Canada. But they disagreed that an Islamic or Jewish majority in another country had such a right. In those cases, they overwhelmingly said that *minority* rights should be respected.

In other words, Highs often support majority rights when they compose the majority but support minority rights when in the minority. Obviously, they believe in neither. While High RWAs think of themselves as being driven by high principles, in reality they often snatch their "principles" off the shelf, after the fact, to justify getting what they want. Many Highs can speak out of both sides of their mouth on an issue, and perhaps never notice they are doing so.

As another example, High RWA groups can be expected to cry "fascism" and "totalitarianism"—of all things—when their attempts to propagate such views as creationism and denial of the Holocaust are resisted. But we know from their responses to the RWA Scale and the Government Injustices measure that they would censor others much more, if they had the chance.

SEPARATIST RIGHTS

For some time, a separatist movement in Quebec has tried to remove La Belle Province from the confederation of Canada. Separatists cite a long list of grievances against the rest of the country, but more basically, they want to preserve Quebec's distinct Francophone culture. Many Quebecois want to form their own nation. Do they have the right to leave the rest of us, if most of them want to?

Out on the western prairies where I live, people tend to think Quebec has gotten far more than its fair share of the benefits of Canadian nationhood. Federal policies encouraging or requiring bilingualism, enacted to assuage the Francophone minority in Canada, have created great resentment. An attempt in 1992 to accommodate Quebec's unique status, and address other problems, through constitutional reform failed miserably when a national referendum was rejected by voters from one ocean to the other to the other.

A balanced eighteen-item Attitudes toward Quebec Scale (alpha .90), answered by those 337 parents mentioned above, found most respondents agreeing with statements such as "The French in Quebec are selfish, spoiled, and greedy" and "The French in Quebec have been taking advantage of the rest of the country for years, and they still aren't satisfied." RWA scores correlated (only) .35 with negative attitudes toward Quebec Francophones, lower than we usually find for a measure tapping ethnocentrism. (Many Lows in Manitoba also resent Quebec.)

Are people in my part of Canada so fed up they are ready to hold the door open so Quebec can leave? No. In the fall of 1993 I gave 183 Manitoba students the following description of the situation.

> New France, an area of North America along the St. Lawrence River, had had its own culture, traditions, schools, laws, religion and language for many years until 1759, when it was forced to become part of British North America after the battle of the Plains of Abraham. The people of Quebec never said they wanted to become part of Canada, and for many years an independence movement sought to make Quebec independent. But also, during the years it has been part of Canada, it became an important part of the nation's economy and political structure. Many national facilities and assets were placed there. Soon, the people of Quebec will vote on whether to dissolve their ties with the rest of Canada and become an independent, sovereign state.
>
> Does Quebec have the *right* to withdraw from the rest of Canada, if a majority of the people living there vote to do so?
>
> _____ No. Quebec could separate only if the rest of the country also agreed to its separation. It has been part of the nation too long, and is too interconnected economically and politically, to be able to quit on its own.
>
> _____ Yes. The region was forced to become part of Canada in the first place. And the most important consideration has to be, what do the people want? A people have an inherent right to be independent, if they wish to be.

Among the 49 Lows, 26 (53%) said "Yes." Among the 45 Highs, only 9 (20%) thought Quebec had a right to separate on its own ($p < .001$). Another 187 students got the same question in a different context.

> Ukraine, an area of eastern Europe, had had its own culture, traditions, schools, laws, religion and language for many years until 1764, when it was forced to become part of the Russian state by Catherine the Great. The people of Ukraine never said they wanted to become part of Russia, and for many years an independence movement sought to make Ukraine independent. But also, during those years while it was part of Russia, it became an important part of the nation's economy and political structure. Many national facilities and assets were placed there. Last year, the majority of people living in Ukraine voted, in a free election, to dissolve their ties with the rest of the USSR and become an independent, sovereign state.
>
> Did Ukraine have the *right* to withdraw from the rest of the Soviet Union, once a majority of the people living there voted to do so?
>
> _____ No. Ukraine could separate only if the rest of the country also agreed . . .
>
> _____ Yes. The region was forced to become part of Russia in the first place . . .

In this case, 41 of the 44 answering Lows (93%) said "Yes," as did 42 of the 46 Highs (91%).

Both Lows and Highs therefore showed a significant double standard about the rights of Quebec and Ukraine to separate, although High RWAs showed a much bigger one.

If you are about to say, "Well, the two cases are not comparable. Canada is a democracy, whereas the Soviet Union was a dictatorship," or "Ottawa never tried to starve the population of Quebec to death the way Stalin did Ukrainians," or so on—I agree with you. But such differences, it turns out, have little to do with the double standard shown above.

In October 1993 Canadians went to the polls to elect a new federal government. Quebec voters elected separatists in almost all their ridings. But some federalists, pledged to keeping Quebec part of Canada, were elected in Montreal, Quebec's largest city. That allowed me to give half of a post-election student sample (total $N = 269$) the Quebec-Canada issue presented above. But the other half got a yet more Balkanized possibility.

> Montreal and its surrounding cosmopolitan area ("Greater Montreal") are presently part of both Quebec and Canada. In the recent federal election, most of Quebec voted for the Parti Quebecois, which says its goal is to separate the province from the rest of Canada to form its own nation. But Montreal ridings elected a lot of Liberals, who ran as federalists committed to keeping Quebec a part of Canada. Soon, the people of Quebec will vote on whether to dissolve their ties with the rest of Canada and become an independent, sovereign state. SUPPOSE most Quebecois vote to separate, but the people around Montreal to the Ontario border vote to stay part of Canada.
>
> Does Greater Montreal have the *right* to withdraw from the rest of Quebec, if Quebec separates and becomes its own nation?
>
> _____ No. Greater Montreal could only separate if the rest of Quebec agreed to its separation. It has been part of Quebec too long, and is too interconnected economically and politically, to be able to quit on its own. *The wishes of the people living around Montreal cannot be the most important consideration.*
>
> _____ Yes. A people have an inherent right to decide what country they want to be. *The wishes of the people living in greater Montreal have to be the most important consideration.*

Again, about half of the 30 participating Lows (47%) said Quebec had a right to separate from Canada. In this sample, so did 38% of the 40 Highs. But a solid majority of both groups said Montreal had a right to separate from Quebec. In the case of the 37 Lows involved, 65% said "Yes" (which was not significantly different from the 47% produced by Lows in the Quebec Separation condition: $z = 1.49; p > .10$). Of the 27 Highs who answered the

Montreal question, 67% said "Yes," which *was* significantly different from the 38% chalked up by the Highs considering the separation of Quebec from Canada ($z = 2.34; p < .03$).

So what was sauce for the goose was not always sauce for the gander. To double-check this result, I repeated the experiment with another 245 students. This time 44% of 34 Lows said "Oui" to Quebec separation from Canada, and an overwhelming 81% of 27 other Lows said Montreal had a right to leave Quebec ($z = 2.97; p < .01$). Among the Highs, only 14% of 35 said "Yes" to Quebec's rights, compared with 68% of 28 Highs, who said "Yes" to Montreals' ($z = 4.35; p < .001$).

The three experiments on Quebec's right to separate can thus be summarized as follows. Both Low RWA and High RWA Manitoba students show a double standard toward a people's right to form their own nation. On the one hand, most of them think Quebec has no right to separate from the rest of Canada on its own (although the vote among the Lows was nearly a saw-off). On the other hand both groups think, by large majorities, that Ukraine did have that right to leave the Soviet Union, and that Montreal would have the same right to leave Quebec.

The double standard regarding Montreal versus Quebec particularly strikes me, for many of my subjects seemingly believe Montrealers do not have the right, *as Quebecers,* to leave the nation of Canada if they wish to; but they do have the right, as *Montrealers,* to leave Quebec if it becomes a nation. (Interestingly, separatists in Quebec have adopted precisely the opposite double standard: Quebec has a right to leave Canada, but Montrealers do not have a right to leave Quebec.)

In all the studies, Highs showed greater double standards than Lows did.

A DOUBLE STANDARD IN LOWS TOO?

Low RWAs *could* have shown double standards as easily as Highs in the three criminal assault cases, the unfair election practices case, and the Quebec separation experiments. But they were hardly placed in jeopardy in the Christian-Islam-Judaism schooling studies. Lows do not endorse teaching religion in the public schools in their own society, so they can hardly look hypocritical opposing it in another country.

To "catch" Lows being more hypocritical than Highs, you have to turn the tables and put them in conflict over something they believe in. I have been searching for a situation that would do this. For a while, I thought I had found it in the environmental movement.

In September 1992 I asked 176 students to respond to the following "economy versus environment" dilemma, which was based on an actual case in our part of Canada.

Company X is a large, multinational corporation that operates several pulp mills in Northwestern Ontario. Environmentalists have charged, for many years, that these plants routinely dump tons of bleach and other pollutants into rivers in the area, and into Lake of the Woods. The Ontario government is considering forcing the company to modernize its plants over a five-year period, to make them less polluting. But the company says it cannot afford the changes "for the foreseeable future," and will close the plants rather than meet "such unreasonable standards."

Would you have the government *insist* upon imposing the new environmental standards?

0 = No. If the company closes the plants, the entire region will become economically depressed.

1 = Yes. Companies cannot be allowed to go on destroying the environment while they make money.

I gave this description to half the sample, who served as a control group. The others got the same information, plus one additional detail.

Imagine that you work for Company X in a management position. If the company closes the plants, you will lose your job. Imagine also that your family depends heavily upon your income, and that it will probably prove difficult to find another job.

Would you have the government *insist* . . .

I expected High RWAs to be less concerned than Lows about the environment. So I did not expect the "you'll lose your job" manipulation to affect Highs as much as Lows. Instead, the Lows were on the spot in this experiment. Would they put their income where their mouth was, when *their* jobs were at stake in an environmental controversy?

The answer was no. Of the 23 Lows who answered the control version of the case, 22 (96%) wanted the government to insist upon the tough environmental standards. Another 20 Lows answered the "you'll lose your job" version, and significantly fewer of them (75%) wanted the government to stick to its guns ($z = 1.95$, $p < .05$ by a one-tailed test). The values for the Highs were 69% and 76%, respectively.

I then sought to replicate the finding, as I almost always do, using 370 students in September 1993. This time 84% of the Lows in *both* conditions said, "Enforce the standards." The *Highs* showed more sensitivity to losing their jobs (78% versus 67%, but $z > .30$). I tried again, and again, and again, with samples of 245 and 269 students in November 1993 and 468 parents in October 1994. I never found another statistically significant difference for Lows, or for Highs.[1]

SOME CONCLUDING OBSERVATIONS ABOUT DOUBLE STANDARDS

The administration of justice, abuse of political power, gender roles, the separation of church and state, a people's right to self-governance—on all these matters, right-wing authoritarians have been found to maintain notable double standards. While I am not proposing that High RWAs have double standards about everything, they do appear to have more than their share, on quite a variety of topics. I think we can call it a feature of their thinking.

If we look back at the findings in this section, we can see afterimages of some of our earlier discoveries about authoritarians. For example, we saw in the attribution error research that they do not reflect much about other people's ideas. Well, here we see that they do not appear to reflect much upon their *own* ideas either. In particular, High RWAs do not seem to challenge their own thinking, to get outside themselves and ask, "Wait a minute. If it's all right for Montreal to leave Quebec, why is it wrong for Quebec to leave Canada?" It is easy to see why they do not. Highs were not raised to criticize the in-group. And who is at the center of their in-group?

Similarly, High RWAs do not seem to consider matters from perspectives other than their own, or mentally reverse situations. They do not appear to wonder, when they belong to the majority, "Suppose I were in the minority. How would I feel if the schools were trying to make my kid believe in some other religion?" Or, "Would I say the same thing if the Conservatives were trying the same kind of intimidation?" So their thinking seems more ad hoc, more one-compartment-at-a-time, than Lows' thinking does. Lows in turn show more interconnectedness, consistency, and fairness. Authoritarians are not as reflective, as systematic, as careful, or as principled as they themselves want to be. But again, they likely received little training in making their own decisions and evaluating things for themselves.

Impressions of American and Soviet Behavior: RWA Images in a Mirror

Let us return to those golden days of yesteryear, to the Cold War, when every dawn presented the possibility of global nuclear destruction.

In 1961, Urie Bronfenbrenner reported how he had been struck, during a visit to the Soviet Union, by the extent to which American and Russian citizens saw the world in opposite ways. Americans generally believed that the Russians were the aggressors on the world scene, that the Soviet government exploited and deluded the Russian people, that the Soviets could not be trusted, and so on. Bronfenbrenner said that the Russians he met felt the same way about the United States government.

Together the two sets of perceptions formed a mirror image—probably distorted and undoubtedly dangerous. This "good guy–bad guy" dichotomy was apparently as stable a feature of the Cold War, on both sides of the Iron Curtain, as it was among the Rattlers and Eagles in the famous Robbers' Cave Experiment (Sherif et al., 1961).[2]

The intensity of these feelings, on the American side at least, was driven home in a study of the double standards found among a group of California undergraduates (Oskamp, 1965). These students thought it all right that the United States had established rocket bases close to the borders of Russia, that America had carried out blockades, that it had intervened in civil wars in Third World countries, and so on. The same actions by the Soviet Union, however, were roundly condemned.

Care to venture a guess about what sort of student was most likely to show such double standards? We do not know. Oskamp did not measure authoritarianism. But one of the nicest things about science is that you can redo an experiment to see if various interpretations are wrong. One of the nicest things about *Glasnost* was that by 1988 you could dream of doing it on both sides of the conflict.

THE SOVIET STUDY

In the fall of 1988, I asked an undergraduate acquaintance majoring in sociology at Moscow State University, Andre Kamenshikov, if someone on his faculty would be interested in administering a forty-four-item survey to a student sample. Several months later, after Andre had translated the items himself, he received permission to collect the data on his own.

The questionnaire began with the RWA Scale, whose printed instructions described it (as usual) as a survey of public opinion. About a sixth of the items had to be modified to meet Russian circumstances (as was also done by McFarland, Ageyev, and Abalakina, 1990). For example, a contrait statement about freedom of speech allowing people to advocate overthrowing the government was changed to say Soviet people must have the right to criticize the Communist Party and demand its resignation from power. Similarly, a statement that atheists are as moral as regular churchgoers was modified to say that people who fight the present order are as good as those who defend this order. The "established authorities" were identified as the traditional, pre-Gorbachev Communist officials.

Two items, dealing specifically with Gorbachev's recent reforms, followed the thirty RWA Scale items:

31. The Soviet Union will be a much better country if the policies of *glasnost* and *perestroika* prevail.
32. *Perestroika* and *glasnost* are changing society too fast and too intensely; the changes must be limited and much slower.

The next twelve items measured opinions about the Soviet and American governments. Two mirror-image versions of this scale were distributed in the sample, though each subject received just one of the forms. The first item on form A, for example, read: "The Soviet Union has the right to intervene militarily when one of its neighbors shows signs of becoming allied with the United States." The same item on form B went: "The United States has the right to intervene militarily when one of its neighbors shows signs of becoming allied with the Soviet Union." Both forms of the survey contained three items favorable, and three items unfavorable, to the USSR and to the United States (see Exhibit 5.1). Like the rest of the questionnaire, each was answered on the usual −4 to +4 basis. The survey ended with a few demographic questions about gender, academic program, and so on.

Exhibit 5.1   "Form A" of the Mirror-Image Scale

33. The Soviet Union has the right to intervene militarily when one of its neighbors shows signs of becoming allied with the United States.

34. The only reason the United States keeps building nuclear weapons is to defend itself from the Soviet Union.

35. When it comes right down to it, Soviet government leaders just want peace and freedom for all the people of the world.

36. American peace and disarmament proposals are not propaganda ploys, but sincere efforts to bring about world peace.

37. When the United States sends foreign aid to foreign countries, its real goal is to dominate and control those countries.

38. Most other countries tend to see the United States as diabolical and evil.

39. If the Soviet Union knew it could do so without being hurt itself, it would probably launch a nuclear attack against the United States.

40. When the Soviet Union intervenes militarily in another country, it really does not care what's good for the people there, but only about its own interests.

41. The government of the Soviet Union tells its people the truth about its actions and goals abroad.

42. When the United States does something nice, such as helping trapped whales, it really doesn't do it for the publicity, but because it genuinely cares.

43. The American government is only pretending to be trying to end injustice in the United States.

44. The leaders of the Soviet Union are basically aggressive, warlike people.

Note: On form B, the proper names were reversed: "Soviet Union" became "United States," "American" became "Soviet," and vice-versa.

Most of the students Andre Kamenshikov tested were recruited in the spring of 1989 during a meeting of a "college orientation" course, and a law course at Moscow State University. He appeared before class began and announced he was a sociology student conducting an opinion survey under the auspices of a social research laboratory known on campus. He said the completely anonymous survey covered general opinions about society, and Soviet-American relations, and would take about fifteen minutes to complete. Altogether he distributed about 250 surveys in these classes, of which 160 were completed and returned at the end of the period (during which the students were supposed to be listening to a lecture).

To improve this return rate, and to round out his sample of Moscow State undergraduates, Andre set up a table in the halls of other classroom buildings, where about 90% of the passing students he randomly buttonholed completed the questionnaire then and there.

Altogether 236 sets of answers were collected, of which 10 had to be discarded because of incomplete responses. The largest contingents among the 226 remaining participants were 68 philosophy, 58 physics, 37 law and 26 history majors. Their mean age was 20.6 years, and on the average they had completed 1.8 years at university. Most (62%) were males, and nearly all were ethnic Russians.

THE AMERICAN STUDIES

In October 1989, nearly all the students enrolled in the introductory psychology course at Harvard (N = 172) answered the same survey. The forty-four items were administered in class by a graduate student, Gregg Solomon, who said he was collecting data on social attitudes and Soviet-American relations.

The same month, 183 introductory psychology students at SUNY-Potsdam served in an experiment outside class time conducted by Dr. David Hanson. Their booklet began with the RWA Scale and continued with one of the two versions of the mirror-image task.

In late January 1990, I administered a booklet of surveys, with the help of a graduate student, Paul Frankel, to 57 Tulane university introductory psychology students. This study also took place outside class time and began the same way as the SUNY-Potsdam experiment.

RESULTS

Moscow State University.   As reported in Chapter 1, the RWA Scale had a low alpha (.81) among the Moscow State sample. (It was answered in less than ideal conditions, and McFarland et al.'s [1990] translation is likely superior.) As also reported earlier, the mean RWA score was quite low. Predictably, these students very strongly endorsed Gorbachev's reforms on items 31 and 32.

The means of the 226 Russian answers to the mirror-image questions are presented in Table 5.1. There it can be seen, for example, that the 111 students who answered form A of the survey disagreed fairly strongly with the notion that the Soviet Union has the right to intervene militarily in its neighbors' affairs. It can also be seen that the 115 students who answered form B objected just as strongly, but not more so, to the notion that the United States has such a right. That is, there is no evidence of a double standard in these answers.

But possible nationalistic biases can be found in some of the other items. The Soviet students were inclined to blame both superpowers for the nuclear arms race, but especially the United States (item 34). They also thought that Soviet leaders were more interested in peace and freedom around the world than American leaders were (item 35) and that Soviet peace and disarmament proposals were more sincere (item 36). They doubted either country would launch a surprise nuclear attack against the other, but they still thought the United States was more likely to do such a thing than the Soviet Union was (item 39). And they doubted either government cared much about the people whose countries it invaded, especially the U.S. government (item 40).

Nevertheless, these Russian students thought that the world tended to see the Soviet Union as more diabolical and evil than the United States (item 38), that while neither set of leaders was truthful with its people, the Soviet government was less truthful than the American one (item 41), and that the Soviet Union was less likely than the Americans to act altruistically "because it really cares" (item 42). Finally, these Moscow State students were equally cynical about the motives behind American and Soviet foreign aid (item 37), felt the two governments were equally committed to trying to end injustice in their respective countries (item 43), and perceived neither set of leaders as "basically aggressive and warlike" (item 44).

Overall then, one can find some evidence of a nationalistic orientation in these answers. But just as often there was none, or a seemingly reversed one.

Such were the results for the *overall* sample. Now, to the point: did the more authoritarian Moscow State students favor the Soviet point of view more than their Low RWA classmates did? A net pro-USSR "image" score was calculated for each student by summing all the opinions about the Soviet Union (scored in the direction of a favorable opinion) and subtracting the corresponding sum for the items concerning the United States. In short, how favorable were they to the USSR, compared to the United States? The mean of this image score equaled 5.24 over the twelve items. RWA scores correlated .46 with the students' tendency to view their country as good and America as bad.

American Universities.   As can also be seen in Table 5.1, Harvard students produced only four significant differences in their answers to the different versions of the mirror-image items, with three favoring the United States. Their mean pro-USA Image score barely registered at 1.64, indicating these students had almost no "USA! USA!" orientation. (They also scored low on the RWA Scale, lower than any American student sample before or since.) But relatively authoritarian Harvard undergraduates still tended to be the most nationalistic: the RWA-image correlation came in at .38.

SUNY-Potsdam students showed significant differences in their perceptions of the two countries on five of the twelve items, all favoring the United States. Their mean image score of 5.87 similarly revealed a stronger tendency to see the United States as the good guys and the Soviets as the bad guys than was found at Harvard. Again, Highs tended especially to see the world this way: $r = .40$.

Despite the small sample at Tulane, six of their perceptions of the two nations proved significantly different, and their image score (11.12) strongly favored the United States. Once more, High RWAs were particularly likely to see their country in a good light and their opponent as evil ($r = .47$). (You will notice a fifth column in Table 5.1, reporting the results of a mysterious, even more nationalistic Group X. It will be unmasked in a later chapter.)

DISCUSSION

Much has apparently changed since Urie Bronfenbrenner's visit to the Soviet Union during the depths of the Cold War. The Moscow State students showed little nationalism in their attitudes toward the Soviet and American governments. This relatively balanced view coincides with the low authoritarianism of these reform-minded students. Learning to distrust the traditional regime apparently brought with it a distrust of that regime's depiction of "the enemy." The same could be said for the very Low RWAs at Harvard. But the Cold War was still hot elsewhere in the United States, as doubtless it was elsewhere in the Soviet Union at the time.

Who formed the front ranks of the Cold War warriors, on *both* sides? Which Russians tended to believe their country had a right to intervene in their neighbors' affairs that the United States did not have? Which Americans tended to think they were building nuclear weapons only because of the Russian threat? Which Russians thought their leaders truly wanted peace and freedom around the world while the American leaders did not? Which Americans believed their government invaded other countries because it cared about the people living there? Which Russians believed the United States would launch a surprise nuclear attack if it could get away with it? You will not be surprised by the answer, in all cases: largely the right-wing authoritarians.

So here is an apparent truth that most authoritarians could probably never accept. *If they had grown up to be the kind of person they are, only in the*

Table 5.1 Mean responses to the mirror-image items

Scale: 1 Very Strongly Disagree · 2 · 3 Moderately Disagree · 4 · 5 Neutral · 6 · 7 Moderately Agree · 8 · 9 Very Strongly Agree

		Moscow State	Harvard	SUNY-Potsdam	Tulane	Group X
33A.	USSR can invade neighbors	2.33	2.39 *	2.84 *	3.29	2.18 *
33B.	USA can invade neighbors	2.30	3.85	4.51	4.28	3.32
34A.	USA forced into arms race	2.89 *	4.32 ⊛	4.87	4.54	4.05
34B.	USSR forced into arms race	4.10 *	4.95	4.92	4.38	3.44 *
35A.	USSR wants world peace	6.42 *	4.23	4.78	3.93 *	3.67 *
35B.	USA wants world peace	4.76	4.24	4.78	5.28	5.92
36A.	USA peace proposals sincere	5.87 *	5.21	5.30	6.11	6.41 *
36B.	USSR peace proposals sincere	7.08	5.59	5.31	5.72	5.27
37A.	USA foreign aid insincere	5.96	5.14	4.54	4.00 *	4.07 *
37B.	USSR foreign aid insincere	5.89	5.65	4.92	5.24	6.56
38A.	Others think USA is evil	4.06 ⊛	4.74	4.73	3.32 *	4.72 ⊛
38B.	Others think USSR is evil	4.68	4.42	5.23 *	5.55 *	3.92

39A. USSR would sneak attack USA	2.52 *	3.77	4.21 *	4.50 *	3.61 *
39B. USA would sneak attack USSR	4.28	3.35	3.67	3.14	2.42
40A. USSR invades others for self	5.96 *	6.29 *	5.80 *	6.14 *	6.36 *
40B. USA invades others for self	6.96	5.73	4.30	4.55	4.10
41A. USSR gov't. tells the truth	3.95 ⊛	2.79	3.19	2.32	2.51
41B. USA gov't. tells the truth	4.54	3.38 *	3.58	3.69 *	4.22 *
42A. USA genuinely altruistic	6.71 ⊛	5.06	5.61	5.61	5.75
42B. USSR genuinely altruistic	6.24	5.18	5.34	5.59	5.37
43A. USA not ending injustices	4.58	3.90	3.75 *	3.46	3.57 *
43B. USSR not ending injustices	4.93	3.92	4.29	3.41	4.36
44A. USSR leaders are warlike	2.97	2.97	3.70	3.68	3.75 *
44B. USA leaders are warlike	3.30	3.41	3.56	3.21	2.69
Net nationalistic image	5.24	1.64	5.87	11.12	14.22

*Indicates $p < .05$ by a two-tailed t-test.
⊛Indicates the significant difference is in the anti-nationalistic direction.

enemy country, they would hate the people they now love, and despise the ideas they now say they would die for. If American High RWAs had grown up instead to be Russian High RWAs, would they see Communism as a great evil? No. We know in fact that Russian High RWAs tend to see capitalism as a great evil (McFarland, Ageyev, and Abalakina, 1990). To put it simply, authoritarians believe what their authorities tell them. The script of who is good and who is bad starts off with blanks. The proper names are dutifully filled in as socialization proceeds, and not examined much afterward.

McFarland, Ageyev, and Abalakina (1990) helped us see how much High RWAs in the United States and Russia have in common, besides their acceptance of the established authorities and conventions in their country. They tend to be the most prejudiced members of their societies. Are American Highs anti-Semitic? Yes, and so are Russian Highs. American Highs do not like "foreigners"? Hey, neither do their Russian counterparts. Do American Highs want to keep women barefoot and pregnant and in the kitchen? How about that, so do Russian Highs. American Highs long for the "good old days" when things were "normal." Russian Highs would drink a toast to them too. American Highs do not really want democracy, and—funniest thing—neither do Russian right-wing authoritarians.

With all these things in common, why then do they hate each other? They were raised to and, after all, they *are* authoritarians, just as the fundamentalist Jews and fundamentalist Arabs studied by Rubinstein (1996) in Israel are. Such people, with their fear and their self-righteousness, tend to drive and perpetuate the conflict between groups. But if you are in the front rank on one side, glaring at your hated enemy in the first rank across the way, you are really looking at a mirror. He is you.[3]

THE WORLD'S FUTURE ACCORDING TO LOW RWAS AND ACCORDING TO HIGHS: THE GLOBAL CHANGE GAME

What would the world be like if everyone were a Low RWA? What would happen instead if everyone were a High? We shall never know, of course. But on two nights in October 1994, I took a look at the possibilities of these impossibilities in a three-hour simulation of the earth's future entitled the Global Change Game.

This sophisticated simulation, designed to raise environmental awareness, takes place on a large map of the world laid out on a gymnasium floor or other large space. The 65 or so participants are randomly assigned to one of ten regions on the planet: North America, Latin America, Europe, the Commonwealth of Independent States (CIS), Africa, the Middle East, India, Southeast Asia, China, and the Pacific Rim. Most players represent approximately 100 million people. The disparity of only a few players standing in the wide open spaces of North America, while 9 others form a huddled mass in India and 12 players are squeezed into China is pointed out to the participants by the game facilitators, 8 other students who designed and run the simulation.[4]

The regions begin the game with realistic assets and problems. North America, Europe, and the Pacific Rim are well off. India and especially Africa are in dire straits. Food supply, medical facility, and employment-opportunity tokens are distributed to each region according to their actual holdings in the real world. So are armies. North America, the CIS, and Europe have massive nuclear-weapons capabilities. Environmental conundrums of one sort or another plague all the regions.

The "Elites."   At the beginning of the simulation, out of the blue, the facilitators ask for a leader to "emerge" in each region: "Whoever is going to be the leader of your region, stand up." These "Elites" are then taken aside and given coats, ties, and hats to wear. They are also told that they will control the finances of their region, and can secretly divert some of their team's assets into personal wealth (by buying chocolate dollars wrapped in gold paper). A "prize" (a book on the environment, it turns out) will be awarded at the end of the game to the Elite who has the greatest personal wealth, they learn.

The Elites stand only for themselves (not 100 million people) and are the only players who may travel freely around the world. They thus become the negotiators for their regions, consulting with their team as they wish. Besides contacting one another, they can visit the Game Bank to buy farms, factories, armies, and so on, and arrange loans. They can also make announcements to the "world" ("China has coal for sale") on an overhead projector.

The rest of the team in each region usually must sit in place on the map, where they do the real work of the group, thinking up solutions to their region's problems. The Elites may hunker down to this too. But they can instead spend most of their time consorting with other Elites.

The Play's the Thing.   The game is complex and challenging and has struck knowledgeable people as surprisingly realistic. Latin America, for instance, must focus on economic development while bearing in mind problems of deforestation, water pollution, desertification, and population control. When a team has developed a proposal, one of the facilitators will question it at length, trying to make sure the plan is feasible and sustainable. The facilitator can reward good proposals and also punish regions with famine, strife, and pestilence if they have terribly abused the environment.

The fourth horseman of the apocalypse, war, may also gallop across the globe. Whenever one region invades another, the team with the most army tokens wins and thereby acquires some of the territory and assets of the loser.

However, the two combatants' army tokens cancel each other and are lost to both sides (along with the wealth it took to create them). So a "3-to-2" war would leave the victor with just one army, and the loser with none. In addition, the loser suffers civilian deaths. But the victor can control the conquered territory only by stationing an army there.

A nuclear war kills the entire population of the earth. As the game starts, the three superpowers are asked if they want to relinquish their nuclear weapons.

The simulation begins in 1990, with the earth's population set at 5.5 billion. A large clock marks the passage of the years, to 2030, when the game ends. A census of population, poverty levels, pollution, and income is taken every ten years, based upon complicated formulas. Added population in each region is represented by stuffed animals.

The facilitators point out, at the beginning of the game, that 3.4 billion of the earth's population lack at least one of the "necessities of life" (food, health care, or employment). Players who do not have food, health care, and employment at any census point are given a black arm band. Anyone who receives three such arm bands "dies." Regions can declare some of their population "refugees," but if no one accepts the refugees, they drown in the ocean.

A global environmental crisis is programmed to occur about an hour into the game. One of the facilitators has been mysteriously stamping the hands of some players at random with a red symbol. The facilitators announce that the stamped players have skin cancer, caused by the depletion of the planet's ozone layer. A chart is shown on the projector, revealing that European and North American pollutants are largely causing the problem. But people all over the globe are endangered. If the problem is not dealt with, they and more will die.

This description does not do justice to the complexity possible in the Global Change Game, which has been played in schools across Canada. Although the simulation is designed to heighten environmental awareness, this heightening largely occurs in the debriefing at the end of the game, after the players have created the future.

The Low RWA Game.   What kind of future did 67 Low RWAs create on October 18, 1994?[5] Well, even though women slightly outnumbered men in the room (on both nights), seven of the ten people who made themselves Elites were men.

When the superpowers were asked to stand if they wanted to keep their nuclear weapons, the North Americans rose almost instantly. About five seconds later, after some quick exchanges, the Europeans also stood up. After further hesitation, the CIS followed. So nuclear disarmament went by the board.

As soon as the simulation began, the Pacific Rim Elite called for a global summit on "the island paradise of Tasmania." There the Elites agreed to meet again whenever big problems arose.

Regions set to work on their individual problems. Swords were converted into plowshares, as the number of armies in the world dropped. No wars occurred during the simulation, and no threats of war were ever made (although the North American Elite proposed the idea to his compatriots, I later discovered).

When the ozone-layer crisis occurred, a global summit was held and 15 "world bucks" were contributed in total from around the globe to buy enough "scrubbers" to reduce CFC emissions and replenish the ozone layer.

Other examples of international cooperation occurred, but the problems of the Third World mounted steadily and black arm bands began to drape like leaves over Africa and India. Europe gave some aid, but North America was conspicuously unconcerned. (The North American players literally turned their backs on the endangered players.) When a global summit was called to deal with the problem, the North American Elite did not attend until two other Elites came over and got him. He then stood outside the gathered circle and gave nothing.

India threw 100 million people (a teddy bear) into the ocean as refugees, which no one accepted. By the end of the game, Africa had lost 300 million people to starvation and disease. Casualties during the Low RWA game therefore totaled 400 million.

The Lows did not focus on population growth, and by the end the earth held 8.7 billion people. But the participants were able to provide food, health facilities, and jobs for almost all of this increased population. The Lows pulled off this remarkable feat by a considerable amount of interregional cooperation, by demilitarizing, by developing sustainable economic programs, and because their Elites diverted only 9 world bucks to their personal wealth. But the "fat" regions still remained much better off than the rest. The North American Elite diverted the most wealth into his own pockets.

The High RWA Game.   The next evening, 68 High RWAs showed up for their turn.[6] Things proceeded rather differently from the start. All ten of the Elites were males. When it came time to retain nuclear weapons, all three superpowers stood up quickly (although only the Elites arose, whereas among the Lows the whole team had stood). And the game had barely begun when the Elite from the Middle East announced an oil shortage that doubled the price of oil. This failed to produce a cartel, however, as other oil-producing regions undercut the higher price.

Next, the CIS began buying armies. It had eight by the year 2006 and invaded North America, which had smaller conventional forces. North America retaliated with nuclear weapons, and a holocaust ensued.

When this happens in the Global Change Game, the facilitators turn out all the lights. They explain the probable consequences of a radioactive atmosphere and nuclear winter. The total human population of the earth (7.4 billion by that point) was declared dead, along with almost all other forms of life.

Then the staff gave the players a second chance, turning the clock back to the situation in 2004. Regions went back to solving their problems. But no team gave up its nuclear weapons.

Soon the CIS attacked China (which had no nuclear weapons, an example of the bullying described in note 3), destroying eight armies, killing 400 million Chinese and occupying a large part of the country. The Middle East Elite convened a "United Nations" (UN) for the Elites to discuss future crises.

At this point the ozone-layer crisis was announced. No one called for a UN meeting, however. Eventually Europe announced it had reduced its CFC emissions and stated on the overhead projector, "If you are not stupid, you'll do the same." Europe also loaned poor countries money to cut their emissions.

By the 2020 census the earth's population was in serious trouble, with poverty spreading unchecked in the underdeveloped nations. The Middle East Elite then talked the Elites of Africa and India into joining a "New Confederacy" with him as its leader. These Elites agreed without consulting their teams and gave the Middle East Elite all their resources. They then spent the rest of the game essentially following him around as he alternately threatened and cajoled others. He quickly bought armies, in response to which the CIS and China—recently at war—formed the "Alliance." Each conglomerate threatened to attack the other, and the CIS promised to use its nuclear weapons if war ensued. But the Middle East Elite successfully argued that would be suicidal, and got what he wanted: a stand-off with a superpower. He then proposed on the overhead a "World Government," to replace the UN, but no one showed any interest.

In the meantime poverty got worse and worse, particularly in the New Confederacy. Another Elite called for a world summit, to deal with the black arm bands swamping Africa and Asia, and drew a crowd of one.

By the time the game ended, 1.7 billion people had died from starvation and disease—nearly all of them in the Third World. Including the 400 million who died in war, the total deaths in the High RWA world reached 2.1 billion. The world was less crowded (6.7 billion) than in the Low RWA run, but Highs achieved population control through starvation, disease, and war. (We should recall the minor fact that *everyone* died earlier from the nuclear war—a new version of zero population growth.)

The High world ended in disaster because the High Elites seldom cooperated but instead tried to dominate one another from the start. Most cooperative acts, such as forming alliances, were still in service to competitive goals.

Highs also spent large parts of their resources on armies, and while they tried intensely to develop economic wealth, they proved insensitive to long-range environmental concerns. For example, one region decided to increase vastly its forest industry. A facilitator warned that converting much of its country-side to a single species of tree would make the ecosystem vulnerable. The team responded, "Let's do it anyway. Lumber is very profitable."

The High Elites also devoted over twice as much (22 world bucks) to their personal fortunes as the Low Elites did. Had they been less greedy, they could have saved hundreds of millions of their own people. Want to guess who ended up the richest person on the planet? You're right.

Observations.   All of the game facilitators knew that the exercise was be-ing used for a psychology experiment on these two nights, and two of them knew exactly what variable was being manipulated. But no one knew who was showing up on what night (although the two "in the know" had a good idea, from the guys' haircuts, that the second night featured the High RWAs).

Nevertheless, most of the outcomes reported above arose entirely from the players themselves, not from interactions with the facilitators, who had no influence over who became Elites, how the regions interacted, and whether war broke out.

In this context, I asked the facilitators what they had noticed about the two groups. Here are the three most agreed-upon observations.

1. Big gender differences were evident between the two runs. Women played a much more active role on the first night. On the second, when the players were asked to make themselves Elites, many of the women were ob-served to have lowered their eyes, "as if afraid someone would pick them if they made eye contact." (I also noticed that, in those situations in the second game when there were not enough stuffed animals to "die" in a region, women almost always ended up with three black arm bands. Men lived in these regions too, but somehow the women mainly perished. The High RWA males "grabbed all the seats in the lifeboats.")

2. The players on the first night were observed to have grasped the inter-regional phase of the game much better. While still driven by self-interest, many regions saw that their interests were best promoted by solving problems with others, sometimes on a planet-wide basis. The Low Elites also used the overhead projector much more often to make announcements to *everyone,* whereas the High Elites did most of their communicating in private huddles. There were more world summits on the first night than in any previous run of the Global Change Game.

3. The Elites on the second night "haggled" much more with the facilita-tors, and one another, than the Elites on the first night did, over costs of farms

and factories, interest rates on loans, and so on. They were better "hagglers" too, the game organizers thought.

Conclusions.   Obviously, I do not think these results generalize willy-nilly to the real world. The players were about nineteen years old, knew that the situation was a game, knew that no one would really die in their wars or from starvation or skin cancer, and knew that it was a psychology experiment. Also, whatever its sophistication, the Global Change Game cannot be nearly as complicated as the global change game being played in the real world every day.

Still, I would be surprised if you did not note similarities between how these two groups of people acted, when the future of the world was in their hands, and the past history of the world. You may also have noticed the many points at which the results of this experiment connect with other differences we have discovered between Low and High RWAs. And finally you may, with me, greatly prefer the world that the Lows created over that which the Highs burned to a cinder and, upon restarting, filled with corpses.[7]

Highs' Blindness to Themselves

Do High RWAs realize their shortcomings? Well, does anyone? But maybe Highs have more blind spots than most people do. Take authoritarian aggression. Would Highs relatively willing to join a posse after right-wing authoritarians realize that they are themselves right-wing authoritarians? One can doubt it.

I have tried in a number of ways to see if Highs know how aggressive they are (*EOF,* pp. 186–190). For example, in 1984 I described my "shocking" experiment to a student sample, and asked them to predict how much shock they would give *relative to others serving in the study.* Highs thought they would give lower than average shocks, whereas in the real experiment Highs did just the opposite.

I asked another group of students, after they had completed the Attitudes toward Homosexuals Scale, how hostile they thought they were compared with the rest of the sample. High RWAs recognized their comparative hostility in that case, to some extent. But their estimates still fell significantly short of the actual difference.

I have several times asked participants who had just answered my Ethnocentrism Scale to indicate how prejudiced they thought they would be compared with the rest of the sample. Consistently, most High RWAs (answering anonymously) thought they would land in the "Average" or "Unprejudiced" ranges.

Finally, several times after describing the RWA Scale and its major correlates in feedback sessions to classes, I have asked the students to guess (anonymously) their place in the room's RWA distribution (*EOF*, pp. 312–317). High RWAs usually thought they would be average. Only a few of them correctly realized they had scored in the top quartile. So Highs almost never grasp, when they hear about authoritarianism, that they are hearing about themselves. (So if you and I think we are *not* Highs, that means diddly.)

DO AUTHORITARIANS REALLY NOT REALIZE?

If Highs base these judgments upon comparisons with the people they know, they could indeed be average in that circle, not realizing how aggressive and authoritarian the circle itself is. But the fact that authoritarians admit to more of their hostility toward homosexuals suggests that they also twitch to the social acceptability of their feelings.

High RWAs may sometimes "know better" than the answers they give us. But they may not tell the truth when personally identifiable because they do not want to admit it to others. And they also *may* not tell the truth, even when answering anonymously, because they do not want to admit it to themselves.

No one can say what someone else realizes and does not realize. I know of at least one major belief, however, that most High RWAs practically shout, but that some of them admit they actually doubt, deep down inside. I am talking about belief in God.

You can unplug such admissions by asking people to respond through their "Hidden Observers"—a technique Hilgard (1973, 1977) invented to see if deeply hypnotized subjects really felt no pain while their arms were immersed in ice water. When asked this way, his subjects revealed much more pain than they otherwise admitted. Hilgard considered the Hidden Observer a subconscious process that knows the real truth. I saw it as a way to allow people, hypnotized or not, to admit things they could not admit otherwise: *they* do not spill the beans; the Hidden Observer does.

When you ask High RWAs in a regular survey format if they believe in God, most of them will fill in the $+4$ bubble on a -4 to $+4$ scale, and some will create a $+5$ bubble in the margin because $+4$ just does not say it strongly enough. But I have found that about 25% of my Highs will say, on the Secret Survey through their Hidden Observers, that they have secret doubts about God's existence that *they have never revealed to anyone before* (*EOF*, pp. 152–153). And they have had these secret doubts for many years. This revelation still astonishes me.

Thus many High RWAs, raised all their lives to profess belief in God, and still under considerable pressure to "bear witness," believe much less than they dare let on. But they have never revealed this. It takes a very special set of circumstances for them to speak the truth. But are there still other things about themselves that they cannot admit, even in these special circumstances?

THE "NAME YOUR AWFUL FAULTS" STUDY

In January 1988, I gave my students' Hidden Observers a new task on the Secret Survey. It was based upon Shakespeare (1604).[8] I started off reminding them of the lecture on hypnosis.

> I'm sure you recall the evidence about the "Hidden Observer" from Hilgard's research on hypnosis. Suppose there is a "Hidden Observer" system in you, which realizes fully things you would consciously deny. The Hidden Observer only reveals itself when it is safe to do so, and when directly spoken to.
> This next question is not really for "you," but for the Hidden Observer.
> Name two or three things which your person is very reluctant to admit about herself/himself, and maybe would never admit to herself/himself, but which are still true.

Lines for three such admissions followed on the sheet. While some of the responses were fairly shallow ("He smokes too much") or silly ("She likes bubble gum"), many of them seemed to drip with pain, and some were chilling. As usual, the Secret Survey sheets were coded for Low and High RWAs (see Chapter 2). Overall, the 95 Lows wrote down 1.87 ugly faults, and the 101 Highs, 1.29 ($p < .01$). The lower output from Highs was mainly due to 42 students who did not write down anything (42%, compared with 20% of the Lows).

A little later on the Secret Survey I asked,

> If you gave no answer to the Hidden Observer question above, was it because___
>
> _____ I cannot think of anything to say.
>
> _____ I can think of things to put down, but it is too embarrassing, frightening, etc. to admit them.

Nearly all (36) of the 42 Highs, and 15 of the 19 nonresponding Lows, checked the first alternative. They could not think of anything that they were very reluctant to admit to themselves.

I repeated the experiment the following year. Only this time I tried to "prime" retrieval processes by first asking the students to write down "the nicest thing you ever did in your life." But this approach had no effect on the results: 88 Lows mentioned 1.92 faults on the average, and 76 Highs wrote down 1.45 ($p < .05$). Again, more Highs (30%) than Lows (18%) gave no answer to the question, and almost all said later there simply was nothing to put down.

Now when people claim complete self-honesty while stating that they have no faults they are reluctant to admit to themselves, we cannot say they are lying. But we can at least raise an eyebrow, Spock-like. Such people would seem to be very unusual. Are some people *completely* open to their faults?

If all of us do have some ugly truths about ourselves we would just as soon ignore, then one ugly truth about these nonresponders, right off the top, is that they are *not* as honest with themselves as they say they are. They are defensive about their self-knowledge and defensive about their defensiveness. In this situation, with the Secret Survey and the availability of the Hidden Observer to do the ratting, I would say such doubly defensive people were not trying to deceive others but attempting to maintain an exaggerated self-image (an old High RWA habit). For it turns out that, far from being completely open to themselves, High RWAs have a notable tendency to *avoid* unpleasant truths.

The "Learn about Your Faults" Studies

LOW SELF-ESTEEM

This study is not based on Shakespeare. You may find a passing similarity to Shelley (1818), however.

In March 1989 I visited two sections of introductory psychology, ostensibly to reveal the purpose and results of a booklet of surveys administered the previous fall using the attendance-sheet system. Being a somewhat untruthful person on this occasion (at least initially), I told the students I had been studying self-esteem. I reminded them of a self-esteem scale they had completed in the booklet and then went on to give a glowing, highly exaggerated account of the scale's predictive validity. Students who scored high on this test, I declared, were likely to do well at university, be more popular with others, have successful careers, and be good parents. People who scored low in self-esteem were more likely to drop out of university, be unsuccessful at love and marriage, and not get the kinds of jobs they wanted.

All this took about ten minutes. Then I told the class that as part of the feedback process, I was going to give each student his or her score on the test. I laid alphabetized piles of sheets around the front of the room, and told the students to come get theirs. The students found their sheet contained a frequency distribution graph of hundreds of alleged self-esteem scores. When the class was reseated, I told all to tear their names from the upper right corner of the sheets, supposedly to prevent any possible linkage with the score about to be revealed. Actually, I wanted the subjects to be anonymous, and know it, later when I used the sheets for a behavioral measure of defensive avoidance.

I then told all how to find their self-esteem scores on their sheets: "Almost everyone's score is 'a hundred and something.' Look very carefully in the upper left corner of your sheet. I have written the first digit of your score there; it's very small, and probably a '1.' Now look carefully at the lower left corner; I wrote the second digit of your score there. Now look at the lower right corner; it has the last digit." I used the blackboard to illustrate how a middling score of 150 would be encoded on the sheet, to make sure all got their correct scores—well, "correct" in the sense of being the score I wanted them to think they had gotten. For I had randomly given half the students scores of 182, 183, or 184, which placed them in the top 15% of the self-esteem frequency distribution before them. The other students got scores of 122, 123, or 124, which—you guessed it.

Smiles appeared here and there; other faces went blank. I told the students to tear the remaining corners off the feedback sheet and asked if there were any questions. No hands went up. So, gathering my things, I announced that I had written an "easy-read" summary of the studies I had mentioned earlier, studies that proved the self-esteem scale was valid. I would send copies of this summary to the next class meeting, if anyone was interested, but I needed an idea of how many to print. So I asked the students simply to write "Yes" at the top of the feedback sheet if they wanted a copy, or "No" if not, and then fold the paper several times and pass it to the aisle.

I collected the sheets, which had been discretely premarked for Low and High RWAs and "feedback scores." These sheets would now tell me how many Lows and how many Highs, after getting good or bad news about their personalities from a psychological test, wanted to see the evidence for the test's validity.

Immediately after I had collected all the sheets, I came clean. I announced the self-esteem scores were entirely bogus, and demonstrated this by asking all who had gotten 122, 123, 124, 182, 183, or 184 to raise their hands. After the laughing, hissing, and booing died down, I told them everything: RWA Scale, defensive avoidance, the works. Swearing them to secrecy, I promised to report the results of the experiment at their next class meeting. This I did, completely; honest.

Finally, I made the point before leaving that while psychological tests some-times can assess *groups* of people validly, no scale can make foolproof indi-vidual diagnoses. If they had been buoyed or deflated by their fake self-esteem score, I hoped that would inoculate them against someday putting too much credence in any such test result. I would like to think this insight made the experience worthwhile for the students. (But that may just be a further ex-ample of a motivated self-delusion.)

Altogether 42 Low RWA students received high self-esteem scores, and 67% of them asked for a copy of the "evidence for validity." Another 41 Lows received low self-esteem scores, and 63% of them wanted to see the evidence.[9] Among High RWA students, 48 received good news about their self-esteem, with all its stated implications for a grand, happy life, and 73% of them wanted to see the validity summary. But only 47% of the 51 Highs who were told they had low self-esteem wanted to see evidence for the scale's validity ($p < .01$).

In a nutshell, the two groups of Low RWAs showed practically no difference in their desire to see the summary of the literature on the self-esteem scale. I can easily imagine their different motivations. Those told they were great might have been after the thrills. Those told they had crummy self-esteem might have wanted to review the literature for themselves, and perhaps dump all over it. But the latter did *not* particularly flee from an unpleasant truth. By contrast, over half of the authoritarians given the same bad news "ran away, ran away." So much for being completely willing to deal with their shortcomings.

HIGH PREJUDICE

I next wondered if Highs would directly tell me they flat out did not want to receive bad news about themselves. Beginning in 1992, I frequently inserted the following question at the end of my Ethnocentrism Scale, when students had answered it anonymously. "Suppose, for the sake of argument, that you are *less* accepting, *less* tolerant and *more* prejudiced against minority groups than are most of the other students serving in this experiment. Would you want to find this out, say by having the Experimenter bring individual sheets to your class, showing each student privately his/her prejudice score compared with the rest of the class?"

In 1992–93 I asked this question of 493 students serving anonymously in three different studies. Of the 115 Lows, 76% said yes, they wanted to know if it turned out they were more prejudiced than most. But only 55% of the 123 Highs wanted to know ($p < .001$).

But perhaps Highs simply care less about the results of such scales. So in 1993–94 I asked half the sample in three studies (total $N = 906$) the question above, while the other half were asked, "Suppose, for the sake of argument, you are *more* accepting, *more* tolerant, and *less* prejudiced . . ."

The results in the "Suppose you're *more* prejudiced" condition closely resembled those of the previous year: 76% of 112 Lows said "Yes," compared to 56% of 115 Highs ($p < .001$). But when the proposition became "Suppose you're *less* prejudiced," 71% of 112 Lows and 74% of 120 Highs wanted to be told. Fewer Highs were willing to find out bad things about themselves than wanted to find out good things ($p < .001$). If you think everyone acts that way, the Lows did not. They wanted to know if it turned out they were relatively prejudiced.[10]

To summarize, then, while authoritarians tend to insist they are quite honest with themselves, and ready to admit any failing, the evidence indicates the contrary. The self-esteem experiment showed that many Highs wanted to avoid dealing with personally distressing feedback. They did not even want to examine the evidence to see if they *had* a reason to be worried. Instead one can easily imagine that, had they not been dehoaxed, many Highs would just have put their "low self-esteem" scores in a mental box and locked it tight. The "Suppose you're prejudiced" studies go a step farther and show that many Highs have so much trouble dealing with unpleasant personal truths, they would keep from learning them. Highs usually think they are average in prejudice or even unprejudiced. But if they are wrong, many prefer to stay prejudiced rather than try to change.

Thus, far from fearlessly facing their failures, Highs seem to run away from them. But as long as Highs screen out, paper over, and erase their shortcomings, they will find it hard to overcome them—which leads us to our last topic.

Cognitive Consistency and Guilt in the Authoritarian Mind

Authoritarian minds challenge our theories of cognitive consistency. For High RWAs, with all their inconsistencies, double standards, and blind spots make a mockery of the notion that people will feel "dissonance" or "imbalance" if their ideas do not fit together properly. Consistency theories will burn out their escape clauses on authoritarians. How many times can they say, "*not enough* dissonance was created," or "this particular imbalance was 'not noticed,' " or "on this occasion the person *ignored* this incongruity."

We *could* dismiss this theoretically dissonant fact with a little name calling: "Authoritarians are sick, mentally 'unbalanced.' Our consistency theories were designed to explain normal behavior, not pathology." But this will not stick. Some right-wing authoritarians have clearly been mentally ill; but most Highs get along well enough in life. They can become successful lawyers and doctors and professors and scientists and managers and presidents of the United States. You will probably find yourself working for one, someday.

I do not mean that the inconsistency of the authoritarian mind defies understanding. It just twists and turns and stops abruptly and sometimes simply skips town. It requires a deeper understanding than we need for more consistent minds. But once you get it, things make sense, loose ends tie together, and you can see why High RWAs act the way they do, why they are so vulnerable, why they are so hostile.

Guilt provides a good example of the nonobvious twists in Highs' thinking. At one time I thought it, not fear, might be the major instigator of authoritarian aggression (*EOF*, pp. 124–126). I thought High RWAs might, out of guilt about their own sins, attack "sinners" to convince others, and themselves, how holy they were. For Highs *do* sin a lot, by their lights. First of all, they have demanding moral standards in some ways. For example, nowadays most people consider masturbation normal and not sinful—but not most Highs. Just thinking about sex can count as a sin. In an era when the "F word" has become nearly all the parts of speech, many Highs still sin in their own minds when they say "dammit." Even white lies are verboten, much less the lies some psychologists tell.

Besides stumbling over their high standards, authoritarians also trip over the common do's and don'ts of morality. I have several times given students an opportunity to cheat on exams, to keep quiet about favorable mistakes in determining their grades, and to get experimental credits dishonestly (*EOF*, pp. 147–151). I have always found that Highs do these things as much as everyone else. So authoritarians could be carrying a lot of heavy guilt trips around in their minds, aversive stimuli that (I thought) could lead them to strike out at others when occasions permitted.

I tested this hypothesis in a January 1987 Secret Survey by asking the Hidden Observers, "Does this person have *secret* guilts about things (s)he has done wrong, which very few persons (or even no one) know about, but which trouble her/him and make her/him wish (s)he had never done these bad things?" Unfortunately for my theory, 108 Highs reported significantly *less* secret guilt (mean = 2.19 on a 0–6 scale) than did 101 Lows (2.76).

Once again, the great thing about the scientific method is that it will tell you when you are wrong, and I undeniably was. I began to peer deeper into the authoritarian mind, asking my next batch of Secret Survey respondents, "Is there something you do to get over the guilt, to 'forgive yourself,' when you have done something morally wrong?" Immediately afterward, I asked these students to indicate how completely forgiven they felt, on a 0–6 scale, when they had done whatever they did to relieve their guilt.

Let me ask *you*. What do you do to quiet your conscience? Apologize to wounded parties? Be extra nice to some third party? Just plain party-party-party? How cleansed do you feel afterwards? Tippy top, like new?

Highs and Lows mentioned all these things and more, and said these erased some of their guilt. But High RWAs had another, very effective guilt-reduction program that Lows almost never mentioned: they asked God for forgiveness. And boy did that take away the stain, they reported (*EOF*, pp. 189–190).

I objectified this open-ended inquiry with the following item on the subsequent January 1989 Secret Survey. (The numbers in parentheses show how many Highs checked the alternative. Those in brackets show the Lows' answers.)

People sometimes do things they know are morally wrong. When you do such things, which one of the items on the list below are you *most likely* to do to get over the guilt, to "forgive yourself" for what you did?

_____ Go out and do something nice for someone else. (4) [8]

_____ Ask God for forgiveness by prayer, going to Confession, or some other religious act. (37) [6]

_____ Rationalize the bad act. Tell myself it was not so bad, that I had no choice, etc. (13) [21]

_____ Talk to someone close, such as a best friend or parent, about what I did. (19) [32]

_____ Get very busy with some assignment or job to take my mind off it. (3) [8]

_____ Other: Namely _____ (2) [9]

You can see that Highs and Lows handle guilt in somewhat different ways. Highs are less likely to talk with someone about the bad thing they did, and they are less likely to say they rationalize it. Instead they mainly deal with guilt religiously.

Again, it works better than anything else. On the next question, I asked subjects to indicate "How completely forgiven do you feel, when you have done this?" on a 0–6 scale. Highs felt significantly more forgiven than Lows (means of 3.61 and 2.87, respectively), entirely because of the efficacy of prayer and confession.

Ultimately, then, all of this makes sense: religious training probably gives you more grounds for considering yourself a "sinner," but it also gives you a way of getting rid of your sins that nonbelievers lack: divine forgiveness. The feeling of being cleansed by God's mercy explains why Highs carry less guilt than others. They have put their sins behind them. So when some nosy psychologist self-righteously studying self-righteousness asks, "How good are you?" Highs will not be dragging around residual feelings of guilt.

But while the reward of having guilt removed helps keep the authoritarian religious, wiping the slate clean so easily probably undermines the desire to improve; hence the deeds may well be repeated. And the resulting self-righteousness plays a major role in authoritarian aggression. It disinhibits aggressive impulses. Though it may seem terribly *inconsistent* that feeling forgiven leads to attacking others, it makes sense when you put together the pieces of the authoritarian mind.

"So What's Your Point?"

In the last chapter we saw that right-wing authoritarians tend to be especially good at some common cognitive failings. In this chapter we have seen how these shortcomings, and the cognitive operations they are based upon such as compartmentalization, lead Highs to serious inconsistencies and personal blindness. We saw that authoritarians not only believe contradictory ideas, but also endorse contradictory principles. High RWAs use so many double standards that their behavior shows relatively little fairness and integrity.

They may present themselves as highly principled people, but their principles shift quickly to justify whatever they happen to want—a shift they probably never notice.

Similarly, the mirror-image studies of American-Soviet perceptions show that the High RWAs on both sides of the Cold War were most likely to believe their government's portrayal of the conflict. Right-wing authoritarians tended to be the Cold War warriors, distrusting and threatening each other, bitterly opposed to the other's system. Yet High RWAs on both sides could easily have been in the front ranks on the other side, had they grown up to be the same kind of person in the other country.

When given a chance to control the earth's future in a sophisticated global simulation, Lows cooperated a great deal and solved many of the problems that arose—although some selfishness and ethnocentrism appeared. Highs, by contrast, completely destroyed the planet in a nuclear holocaust and, when given a second chance, still engaged in destructive domination strategies. High RWA leaders also stole more from their peoples to accumulate personal wealth.

Delving into authoritarians' awareness of themselves, we found many "official denials" that anything was amiss. There was virtually nothing about themselves Highs were unwilling to face and deal with, according to them. Yet when we told some High RWAs they were low in self-esteem, and that this had serious implications for their future, a lot of authoritarians fled from the news, not even checking to see if it was correct. And many Highs told us, point blank, that if it turned out they were more prejudiced than average, they did not want to be told. They would rather go on being prejudiced than learn the truth.

Finally, we saw that for all the wrongdoing in their lives, Highs carry around little guilt because they erase their sins so thoroughly through their religion. That *self-righteousness* plays a major role in their authoritarian aggression.

In closing, we should observe once again that in comparing the behavior of Highs with Lows in these experiments, we have usually found differences of degree, not of kind. Many right-wing authoritarians appear seriously low on integrity, self-understanding, and resolve to make themselves better. But who can claim to be filled to the brim?

—6—
Authoritarianism and Religion

Today is May 10, 1994. I finished working on Chapter 5 yesterday, and decided I would wait a while before starting Chapter 6. Partly because the first surveys from the May 1994 Alumni Study are coming in. You already know from Chapter 3 what they show, but to me today they are just "many happy returns" in my mailbox at school. But I also called a halt to writing because I did not know how to begin this chapter. I have written on authoritarianism and religion several times, and always gotten off on the wrong foot with some people, I think. Then I read one of the alumni answers this morning, and "Voila!"

The answers came from a thirty-six-year-old woman. Looking back in my dusty piles of computer printouts from 1976, I found that she said—half her lifetime ago—that she had been raised a Mennonite and that she "completely" accepted the teachings of her faith then. She scored high on the RWA Scale at the time.

On my 1994 survey she indicated she was now "much more" religious than when she was eighteen, both in terms of beliefs and practices. This boggles the mind right away, because devout Mennonites can hardly get "much more" religious in the usual sense. But she also indicated, on my "plot your social attitudes over the years" chart, that she had gotten steadily more liberal over time. She explained: "My religious beliefs have evolved a lot. I am more aware of myself. I have tried to overcome my prejudices. I try to be like Jesus every day, understanding and accepting and helping others, condemning no one, seeing in myself the bad things I see in others." Perhaps not coincidentally, her RWA score had dropped a great deal over the years.

I am myself at age fifty-six "much *less*" religious than I was at eighteen, but I do not believe I am "against religion," as people sometimes assume. I would not mind finding that religious people are the best, the most honest, the most caring, the most selfless, and the fairest people, the ones with the most integrity. It would be great to discover big fat *negative* correlations between being religious and being ethnocentric and hostile and narrow-minded. (For one thing, we would have something that works against prejudice.) I would shout out big *positive* correlations, if they existed, between being religious and championing human rights, equality, and democracy as easily as I can admire Albert Schweitzer, Mahatma Gandhi, Martin Luther King, Jr., and Bishop Tutu.

Religion does seem to make people better in various ways. Those committed to religion spend more time working among the poor as tutors, relief workers, and campaigners for social justice, and give more to charity, than uncommitted people do (Myers, 1993, pp. 529–531). The trouble is, we do not often find such heartening relationships when we do other studies. Instead we usually uncover no relationship, no evidence suggesting religion has improved people. Or else, it may have made them *worse.*

So I was glad to have this testimonial from the alumni study, because *one can clearly be religious in different ways.* Indeed, many Lows in my samples are Christian and religious, but in different ways from most Highs. This chapter will describe some research Bruce Hunsberger of Wilfrid Laurier University and I have been doing on identifying and measuring these different ways. But first let us review the findings concerning authoritarianism and religion, and religion and prejudice.

Findings on Authoritarianism and Religiousness

As mentioned in Chapter 1, RWA scores have correlated with acceptance of the home religion in *all* the faiths appreciably represented in my samples. Among Christians, one finds strong relationships with endorsement of the traditional beliefs of the Nicene Creed, as measured by the Christian Orthodoxy Scale. These findings do not surprise me. After all, a lot of the items on the RWA Scale mention religion and traditional religious values.

Those religion-mentioning items would not be on the RWA Scale, however, if they did not correlate highly with the "man-on-horseback" and "stomp out the rot" sentiments. I know from many item analyses that religious RWA statements predict many kinds of authoritarian aggression and other disturbing features of right-wing authoritarianism.

The continued acceptance of traditional religious beliefs appears to have more to do with having a personality rich in authoritarian submission, authoritarian aggression, and conventionalism, than with beliefs per se. As was true of the U.S.-USSR comparisons, and as Rubinstein (1996) found among

Jews and Palestinians in Israel, the beliefs themselves can be anything. Authoritarians just absorb whatever beliefs their authorities teach.

I should explain here what I mean by "traditional religion." Besides strong endorsement of the Christian Orthodoxy Scale, authoritarian students and parents who served in a 1984 study said they attended church more often than most, prayed more than most, and believed more fervently that God would judge each person after death, taking some into heaven while condemning others to hell. They believed in Satan and relied on their religion to help control their own evil impulses. They also thought it was more important to believe in the "right religion" than to be a good person (EOF, pp. 205–219). Leak and Randall (1995) replicated most of these relationships (all that were tested), and also found that High RWAs tended to say they were "deeply religious in the traditional (and spiritual) way."

So authoritarians tend to be religious. Studies also indicate that certain kinds of religious training probably help create authoritarian personalities. As mentioned in Chapter 3, students who reported their religion had stressed obeying heavenly and earthly rules, taught them to fear the wrath of God, tried to influence almost everything they did, and so on, tended to become highly authoritarian (EOF, pp. 203–205). Religion may merely have been one of the ways High RWA parents transferred their authoritarianism to their children. But some religions did these things much more than others, and they tended to have the most authoritarian members. (Partialling out socioeconomic status and education makes little difference.)

We should also realize that religions provide much of the encouragement for staying in those tight circles featured in authoritarian development and maintenance. Many faiths want their young people to attend church-related schools and then try to limit their contact with "outsiders" beyond the classroom as well. The Group Cohesiveness Scale showed High RWAs believe members of the same religion should "stick together as much as possible." Such practices and beliefs advance the ethnocentrism so prominent in Highs.

Furthermore, many religions promote a "memorize the Truth" rather than "find the truth" approach that stunts the development of critical reasoning and produces compartmentalized thinking. We have seen several unfortunate results of this stunting in religious contexts in the last two chapters: after years of being trained to put faith ahead of reason, authoritarians suspended critical thinking over such things as the fallen wall at Jericho. They were quite vulnerable to the Fundamental Attribution Error regarding the Bible and the television evangelist's revival meeting. They used double standards over promoting religion in public schools.

I can add more evidence of how High RWAs compartmentalize and think uncritically when it comes to their religious beliefs. Recall from Chapter 4 that in March 1985 many of my students gave their reactions to Jesus' teachings about judging not and not being the first to cast stones. However Highs interpreted these teachings, they went right on judging and throwing stones in other parts of the booklet (*EOF,* pp. 222–224).

After they finished this task, I asked the students to imagine how they would react if future archaeological discoveries cast the gravest doubt that Jesus had ever existed (*EOF,* pp. 224–226). Specifically, they were to suppose that excavations uncovered ancient parchments that predated the time of Jesus, telling the story of Attis, a legendary Greek figure, born of Zeus and a virgin, who began a three-year public ministry at the age of thirty. These scrolls contained most of the parables, miracle stories, and teachings of the Gospels, including the death, resurrection, and ascension of Attis. Scholars examined the scrolls, pronounced them genuine, and concluded that the story of Jesus of Nazareth was concocted by a reform movement within Judaism, based largely on the legend of Attis.

What effect would such a development have on High RWA Christians? Of the 60 in my sample, 10 would not answer the question. Of the remaining 50, only 7 said this evidence would definitely affect their faith. Some hedged, and 28 (most of those who answered) said this discovery would have no effect whatsoever on their beliefs. Basically, this reaction reminds me of how Highs responded when they got bad news about their self-esteem and possible bad news about their level of prejudice: "Batten down the hatches, and run away."[1]

In conclusion, we can say authoritarianism tends to make people religious in the traditional sense, and certain kinds of religious training tend to make people authoritarian. One often finds religious elements in authoritarian thinking.[2] For yet another example, recall how easily religious beliefs enable High RWAs to erase their guilt, thereby probably facilitating their authoritarian aggression.

Findings on Religiousness and Prejudice: A Critique

An appreciable research literature has accumulated on the connection between religiousness and prejudice, and one finding dominates all. If one takes church membership as the criterion for being religious, then as Gorsuch and Aleshire (1974) observed in their influential review, "the results are clear and consistent. Church members are more prejudiced than those who have never joined a church. All the studies found the same relationship, which was statistically significant when tested" (p. 283).

THE PROPOSED ROLE OF RELIGIOUS ACTIVITY

Given this powerful conclusion, researchers have tried to find a subset of church members who are as *un*prejudiced as those who belong to no church. Gorsuch and Aleshire (1974) pointed out, for example, that many people say they belong to a church but do not attend it. If these people are highly prejudiced, they will give religion a bad name in studies that just examine membership.

A simple linear model proposes that *inactive* members of a religion—usually assessed by church attendance—will be *more* prejudiced than active members. A curvilinear model (such as Allport and Ross, 1967; Spilka, Hood, and Gorsuch, 1985) holds instead that prejudice initially goes up as activity increases, but at some point starts going down. Both models end up predicting that very active church members will be *un*prejudiced. While few people are so active, they counter the argument that churches create prejudice, since such people go to church more than anyone else.

Gorsuch and Aleshire (1974) undertook the thankless job of combing the (not always well-detailed) literature on religious activity and prejudice, and gave the results of twenty-seven such studies in table 4 of their article. Testing for a curvilinear relationship, they classified subjects as Low, Moderate, or High attenders whenever they could. They concluded the relationship was curvilinear: "The marginal church members manifested more prejudice than either the nonactive or the most active members . . . There seems to have been little difference in degree of prejudice between the highly religious and the nonreligious" (p. 285).

You should note the mixing of apples and oranges in that quotation: the "nonactive" and the "nonreligious." The former belong to a church, but seldom can be found in it. The latter do *not* belong to a church, and we know from many studies that they tend to be relatively unprejudiced. One must keep the nonreligious on the sidelines when determining the effects of activity *within* religion—which is the subject of Gorsuch and Aleshire's conclusion about the curvilinear relationship. Unfortunately, only twelve of the twenty-seven studies investigated just church members (for example, "327 Catholic students"). The other fifteen, dealing with such samples as "736 community residents," would have included some completely unaffiliated subjects. The low prejudice of the unaffiliated could have pulled down the mean of the "low attenders," creating an illusion of a curvilinear relationship within religions.

If you look at those appropriate twelve studies, you find only *one* that produced a significant up-and-down curvilinear relationship (Hoge and Carroll, 1973). In contrast Rosenblum (1958) found Lows and Moderates were *both* significantly more prejudiced than High attenders. The remaining ten studies involve "two-point" comparisons that can say nothing about curvilinear trends. Five of these were significant in the predicted direction, four were nonsignificant (or not known to be significant), and one was significant in the "wrong" direction.

If this nonetheless impresses you—or if you want to include all twenty-seven studies and "Confound the confounded confounding!"—you should note that the criteria Gorsuch and Aleshire used to classify participants as Low, Moderate, or High in activity were rather strangely laid out (p. 302). Low attenders were those who went to church "usually less than once a quarter." Moderates went "usually several times a year to once a week." Highs went "usually at least once a week."

Do you see that the criterion for the Moderates overlaps that of both the Lows and the Highs? In particular, the frequent category of people who say they go to church once a week could be called "Moderate" in one study and "High" in another. Since the Moderates play a critical role in establishing a curvilinear relationship, this very permeable membrane surrounding their definition makes me squirm in my chair.[3] So I cannot agree it has been shown that very active church members are as unprejudiced as *nonmembers,* or that the curvilinear relationship has been demonstrated among church members.[4]

If the latter is someday supported, can a drop in prejudice between Moderate and High attenders be used without qualification to argue that "churches do not cause prejudice"? What about the rise between Lows and Moderates? And could you not simply say that the majority of church members should either become very active, *or* stop going altogether, if they want to be less prejudiced?

Finally, I suspect that if parenting, schooling, and the media can affect prejudice, so can churches, for good or evil. How *active* you are in your church may have little to do with how prejudiced you are, compared to *what your church teaches,* directly and indirectly, about authoritarianism and ethnocentrism.

THE PROPOSED ROLE OF INTRINSIC AND EXTRINSIC ORIENTATION

Gordon Allport (1966) offered a different subset of religious people who would prove as unprejudiced as those who belong to no church. He thought they would have an "intrinsic" orientation to their religion, one that "regards faith as a supreme value in its own right. It is oriented toward a unification of being, takes seriously the commandment of brotherhood, and strives to transcend all self-centered needs. Dogma is tempered with humility, and in keeping with the Biblical injunction the possessor withholds judgment until the day of the harvest. A religious sentiment of this sort floods the whole life with motivation and meaning." In contrast, an "extrinsic" orientation is "strictly utilitarian; useful for the self in granting safety, social standing, solace and endorsement for one's chosen way of life" (p. 455). Allport thought "Intrinsics" would prove less prejudiced than "Extrinsics," who were at the opposite end of a continuum.

Does this make sense, given Allport's description of an intrinsic orientation? Certainly it does, as far as "taking brotherhood seriously." Tempering dogma and withholding judgment would probably reduce prejudice too. But the other elements do not seem to lead necessarily to low prejudice. Taking your faith as a supreme value, one that unifies your being, transcends all self-centered needs, and fills your life, could equally apply to following a fascist leader. So again, I think it matters a great deal what the religion stands for. An intrinsic orientation will lower prejudice most if tolerance and "sisterhood" are strongly featured in the religion's actual teaching.

In an influential study, Allport and Ross (1967) tested the prediction that Intrinsics would be less prejudiced than Extrinsics. Students from Allport's graduate seminar administered, to 309 church*goers,* measures of intrinsic and extrinsic orientations and several prejudice scales. Foremost among the last was an unpublished Social Problems Questionnaire containing twelve items about blacks, ten statements about Jews, and ten other statements. These prejudice measures were at least somewhat balanced against response sets.

Intrinsic orientation was measured by nine items (Exhibit 6.1), and extrinsic orientation was tapped by eleven statements such as "The church is most important as a place to formulate good social relationships" and "The purpose of my prayer is to secure a happy and peaceful life." The Intrinsic and Extrinsic items were not presented in the article but instead filed with the American Documentation Institute. Most researchers have subsequently used the slightly revised version Batson and Ventis published in 1982 (p. 145).

Exhibit 6.1   The Intrinsic Religious Orientation Scale

1. It is important for me to spend periods of time in private religious thought and meditation.

2. If not prevented by unavoidable circumstances, I attend church.

3. I try hard to carry my religion over into all my other dealings in life.

4. The prayers I say when I am alone carry as much meaning and personal emotion as those said by me during services.

5. Quite often I have been keenly aware of the presence of God or the Divine Being.

6. I read literature about my faith (or church).

7. If I were to join a church group I would prefer to join a Bible study group rather than a social fellowship.

8. My religious beliefs are what really lie behind my whole approach to life.

9. Religion is especially important to me because it answers many questions about the meaning of life.

Note: This wording was adopted by Batson and Ventis, 1982, p. 145, so that all items could be answered on a nine-point Likert scale.

Where did these scales come from? They were constructed in Allport's graduate seminar in 1963, a time when Allport reportedly held "intrinsic" to mean "truly devout"—a meaning he later dropped (Feagin, 1964).[5] As I look them over, I am struck by how poorly the Intrinsic items cover the construct Allport described in 1966. Four of the items (3, 5, 8, and 9) do ask whether religion unifies the whole being or floods the whole life. But there is nothing about faith being a supreme value, nothing about taking brotherhood seriously, nothing about tempering dogma with humility, and nothing about withholding judgment. Instead, one finds items about meditation, attending church, reading about your faith, praying alone, and preferring a Bible study group over a social club. Are these *related* to religion? Of course. Do they measure personal "devotion"? Yes. Do they measure what Allport (1966) said was an intrinsic orientation? I seriously doubt it.

The Intrinsic Scale not only wandered far from its construct (or vice versa), it also fell into a deep hole because *all the items were worded in the protrait direction!* This was also true of the Extrinsic Scale.[6] As we saw in Chapter 2, unidirectional wording can seriously compromise a test. How would you know whether results obtained with these scales reflect respondents' religious orientation or just yea-saying and its psychometric and personality fellow travelers? This problem appeared immediately in Allport and Ross's own study.

See if this looks familiar. Allport and Ross expected Intrinsic scores to correlate highly and negatively with Extrinsic scores. That was the whole premise. But they only correlated − .21[7] The reason was quickly discovered. "Subjects who endorse extrinsically worded items do not necessarily reject those worded intrinsically, or vice versa . . . Many subjects are provokingly inconsistent. They persist in endorsing any or all items that to them seem favorable to religion in any sense . . . [They are] indiscriminately pro religious" (p. 437).

Furthermore, the Intrinsic and Extrinsic Scales did not correlate the way they were supposed to with prejudice. Extrinsic scores correlated .21 to .32 with the subscales of the Social Problems Questionnaire. The Intrinsic scores had approximately the same correlations. (You have to infer this, because while Allport and Ross presented the prejudice correlations for the Extrinsic Scale, they never told their readers how the Intrinsic Scale did. They just presented correlations for the two scales combined. But the results for the *combined* scores, .18 to .26, were similar to those for the Extrinsic Scale alone.)

They could have fixed the scales by developing enough anti-religious items ("I get very little out of my religion") to control for response sets. Then they would have been able to see how much indiscriminately pro-religious responding actually occurred, as opposed to yea-saying. But they tried a different fix, and simply set aside subjects who double-agreed a lot. They accordingly called people highly intrinsic only if they basically agreed with the Intrinsic items *and* disagreed with the Extrinsic ones. Similarly, "extrinsics" had to agree with the Extrinsic items and disagree with the Intrinsic ones. Those who largely agreed with both were cast into the "indiscriminately pro-religious" category. About 100 subjects ended up in each of the three piles.

After this sorting, Intrinsics scored 28.7 on the "anti-Negro" scale, Extrinsics scored 33.0 on the same scale, and Indiscriminants scored 36.0 ($p < .001$). Similar results were found in the "anti-Jewish" and "anti-Other" data. And *that* was the evidence Allport and Ross (1967) put forth as demonstrating that intrinsically oriented people are less prejudiced than extrinsically oriented people, and that indiscriminately pro-religious people are the most prejudiced of all.

However, when you start shoveling the yea-sayers out of the Intrinsic and Extrinsic Scale piles, you are largely removing "you know whom" from the test of those scales' validity. Allport and Ross showed only that when you set the more prejudiced people aside, you can find the difference you said was there in the whole sample. But how can one justify this procedure in a study designed to explain prejudice? When you look at *all* the data, they disconfirm the explanation.

Did researchers shy away from using the Intrinsic and Extrinsic Scales because (1) they plainly failed to measure what they were supposed to measure; (2) they plainly failed to show what they were supposed to show; and (3) they suffered from the same problem that had compromised all the F Scale studies since 1950? Well, did researchers shy away from using the F Scale?

Today the Intrinsic and Extrinsic Orientation Scales have a sizable literature that some investigators swear by, but that I feel one can safely ignore. I have seen this show before; the ending is fairly predictable (see Kirkpatrick and Hood, 1990).[8]

In summary, I think the nine Intrinsic items—response sets aside—assess in various ways the importance of one's religion, in a nonsocial sense. But again, that is not what Allport meant by an intrinsic orientation. And even if the test *did* measure being committed to the essential, inherent, core de la core message in a faith, that will not necessarily make one less prejudiced. If the central message of Christianity is "love your neighbor as yourself," there is not a drop of that on the Intrinsic Scale.[9] Instead the scale goes off in other directions. But one can meditate and read about one's faith and go to church and prefer a Bible study group and pray well alone and say religion lies behind one's whole approach to life—and still be a High RWA. In fact, the Intrinsic and RWA Scales correlate about .40 (*EOF*, pp. 214–219).

Finally, you will sometimes find research summaries that state extrinsic people are more prejudiced than intrinsic people, and therefore intrinsic people are not prejudiced. I am sure you see the problem with that reasoning.

C. Daniel Batson has proposed a more "existential" dimension to help us understand the connection between religiousness and prejudice: religion as *quest* (Batson and Ventis, 1982). This axis, in Batson's theory, spurts off at right angles from two other orthogonal dimensions—"Religion as an end" and "Religion as a means"—that correspond to Allport's intrinsic and extrinsic orientations.

The Quest dimension concerns the degree to which the individual "seeks to face religious issues such as personal mortality or meaning in life in all their complexity, yet resists clear-cut, pat answers. An individual who approaches religion in this way recognized that he or she does not know, and probably never will know, the final truth about such matters. Still the questions are deemed important and, however tentative and subject to change, answers are sought" (Batson and Burris, 1994).

Batson (1976) developed a six-item scale, the "Interaction" or "Quest" Scale, to measure this construct. However . . . you guessed it: All the items were written in the pro-quest direction. For example, "It might be said that I value my religious doubts and uncertainties" and "God wasn't very important to me until I began to ask questions about the meaning of my own life." So we have our recurrent problem of not knowing how much Quest Scale scores represent "questing" and how much they reflect nefarious response sets.

Batson expects people high in Quest, with their open-mindedness and willingness to search for complex truths, to be *less* prejudiced than those who score low in Quest. That is, he expects negative Quest-prejudice correlations. To a certain extent, that has been found.

Batson, Schoenrade, and Ventis (1993) summarized seven studies that pursued the Quest-prejudice relationship. Most involved the usual administration of surveys, but we shall also encounter two covert behavioral measures for which Batson has a particular gift.

Snook and Gorsuch (1985) administered the Quest Scale and a social distance survey measuring discrimination against nonwhites to 94 Afrikaner and 135 English students in South Africa. Quest scores correlated $-.21$ with maintaining large distances among the Afrikaners and $-.17$ among the English participants. Both coefficients attained statistical significance.

Griffin, Gorsuch, and Davis (1987) gave out surveys at Seventh-Day Adventist churches on St. Croix in the Virgin Islands. Besides containing the Quest Scale, the booklets asked opinions on nine cases in which one could deny basic constitutional and human rights to Rastafarians—a religious and political movement Adventists disliked. Quest scores did *not* predict discrimination against the Rastafarians ($-.08$; $N = 190$).

Ponton and Gorsuch (1988) obtained usable social-distance data from 275 students (nearly all of them women) at the University of Venezuela at Caracas.

The students indicated how close they were willing to get to eight target groups. Quest scores did *not* produce a significant relationship with discrimination.

McFarland (1989b) gave the Quest Scale and short measures of attitudes toward homosexuals, women, blacks, and Communists to 247 students at Western Kentucky University. Analyzing just the data from white Christians who indicated their religion was important to them (N = 173), he found that Quest scores correlated − .31 with dislike for homosexuals, − .19 for negative attitudes toward women, − .13 with anti-black sentiments, and − .26 with hostility toward Communists. All coefficients reached statistical significance.

Last among the survey studies, McFarland (1990) collected essentially the same information from 470 active adult Christians in Kentucky and Tennessee through student pollsters. The correlations were − .18, − .09 (not significant), − .12, and − .27, respectively, following the order in the paragraph above.

In the covert behavioral studies, Batson, Naifeh, and Pate (1978) asked 51 white undergraduates with at least a moderate interest in religion to indicate how much they would like to have a chat with each of two interviewers, one of whom was black, the other white. Quest scores had *no* relationship with preference for a particular interviewer. (However, they correlated − .34 with the survey measure of racial prejudice used by Allport and Ross, 1967.)

And finally, Batson et al. (1986) found Quest scores predicted ($r = - .45$) white students' reluctance to watch a movie with a black person, provided the avoidance could be disguised as a dislike for the movie.

Overall, the quest construct has considerable promise as a "moderator variable" for separating nonprejudiced from prejudiced religious people. But when you see such inconsistency in the data, it often means the numbers are almost buzzing with measurement error. I would opine that the construct needs to be measured better. The scale should be balanced against response sets and have its internal consistency boosted. In the studies reported above, the alpha of the scale varied from .18 (yes!), to .69. This is like fastening big lead weights to a brick and telling it to swim.

McFarland (1989b) added four items to the Quest Scale (including one contrait), increasing its alpha from .49 to .70, and moving the prejudice correlations from the range of − .13 to − .31, up to the range of − .24 to − .40. Similar improvements were obtained in McFarland 1990.

Batson and Schoenrade (1991) recently increased the Quest Scale to twelve items, including two contraits. The only study I know that related this new measure to prejudice was done by Leak and Randall (1995), who found it correlated − .19 with Posse-Homosexuals, − .18 with Posse-Cults, and − .25 with Posse-Abortionists. (It also correlated only .02 with summed hostility scores toward atheists, makers of pornography, drug users, and others.) All these results are still difficult to interpret because of the seriously unbalanced direction of wording.

THE ROLE OF RELIGIOUS FUNDAMENTALISM

When Bruce Hunsberger and I considered the issue of religiousness and prejudice, we focused on the role religious fundamentalism might play in promoting ethnocentrism. Others had played this hunch before us. Most notably, McFarland (1989b) had included a six-item (all protraits) Fundamentalism Scale in his booklet and obtained prejudice correlations (.19 to .44) comparable to those he got with his ten-item version of the Quest Scale. He did not, however, define "fundamentalism" beyond noting its similarity or equivalence to "orthodoxy." And his measure focused on Christian issues ("It is very important for true Christians to believe that the Bible is the infallible Word of God").[10]

We conceived of fundamentalism as being, not so much a set of religious beliefs, as an attitude toward those beliefs, held by a certain kind of personality. And we thought you could find this "fundamentalist attitude," and the accompanying personality, in many religions. In other words, when newspapers referred to fundamentalist Christians trying to take over the Republican Party, or fundamentalist Jews and fundamentalist Muslims both trying to destroy the peace process in Palestine, or fundamentalist Hindus attacking a mosque in India, the groups may have been wearing different kinds of clothes but they were all cut from the same cloth. They were right-wing authoritarians.

But what is religious fundamentalism? We (1992, p. 118) defined it as:

> the belief that there is one set of religious teachings that clearly contains the fundamental, basic, intrinsic, essential, inerrant truth about humanity and deity; that this essential truth is fundamentally opposed by forces of evil which must be vigorously fought; that this truth must be followed today according to the fundamental, unchangeable practices of the past; and that those who believe and follow these fundamental teachings have a special relationship with the deity.

We saw a difference between orthodoxy and fundamentalism. Orthodoxy refers to accepting the *beliefs* of a religion, as assessed by (say) the Christian Orthodoxy Scale (Exhibit 1.5): Do you believe Jesus was the son of God? Do you believe Jesus rose from the dead? Do you believe you have an immortal soul? We have found CO Scale scores to be *un*correlated with prejudice.

Fundamentalism, by contrast, refers to the *attitude* that your religion's beliefs (whatever they are) encompass the fundamental, complete truth about fundamental forces of good and evil and fundamental practices based on a fundamental, special relationship with God (speaking fundamentally).

We expected fundamentalists to be orthodox, of course, but we did not expect all who hold the tenets of their religion to be fundamentalists. You can believe what your religion teaches, and still acknowledge that the beliefs of other peoples may prove just as valid as yours. In that difference we thought we might find the connection with prejudice that we had not found with our measure of Christian Orthodoxy. Fundamentalists in many religions, as we conceived them, would be more ethnocentric than those who were "merely" orthodox in beliefs.

The Religious Fundamentalism Scale.   Professor Hunsberger and I composed twenty-eight items, half protrait, half contrait, to measure the conceptualization given above. In the autumn of 1990, over 500 Wilfrid Laurier University students and 235 Manitoba parents responded to these items. As is often true of religion scales, interitem correlations proved high, and a balanced twenty-item Religious Fundamentalism Scale (Exhibit 6.2) appeared almost effortlessly.

Exhibit 6.2   The Religious Fundamentalism Scale

1. God has given mankind a complete, unfailing guide to happiness and salvation, which must be totally followed.

2. *All* of the religions in the world have flaws and wrong teachings.*

3. Of all the people on this earth, one group has a special relationship with God because it believes the most in his revealed truths and tries the hardest to follow his laws.

4. The long-established traditions in religion show the best way to honor and serve God, and should never be compromised.

5. Religion must admit all its past failings, and adapt to modern life if it is to benefit humanity.*

6. When you get right down to it, there are only two kinds of people in the world: the Righteous, who will be rewarded by God; and the rest who will not.

7. Different religions and philosophies have different versions of the truth, and may be equally right in their own way.*

8. The basic cause of evil in the world is Satan, who is still constantly and ferociously fighting against God.

9. It is more important to be a good person than to believe in God and the right religion.*

10. No one religion is especially close to God, nor does God favor any particular group of believers.*

11. God will punish most severely those who abandon his true religion.

12. No single book of religious writings contains all the important truths about life.*

13. It is silly to think people can be divided into "the Good" and "the Evil." Everyone does some good, and some bad things.*

14. God's true followers must remember that he requires them to *constantly* fight Satan and Satan's allies on this earth.

15. Parents should encourage their children to study all religions without bias, then make up their own minds about what to believe.*

16. There *is* a religion on this earth that teaches, without error, God's truth.

17. "Satan" is just the name people give to their own bad impulses. There really is *no such thing* as a diabolical "Prince of Darkness" who tempts us.*

18. Whenever science and sacred scripture conflict, science must be wrong.

19. There is *no* body of teachings, or set of scriptures, which is completely without error.*

20. To lead the best, most meaningful life, one must belong to the one, true religion.

Note: Items are answered on a −4 to +4 basis.

* Item is worded in the contrait direction; the fundamentalist response is to disagree.

The February 1991 Parent Study.   This scale was answered by 491 Manitoba parents in February 1991, along with many other measures: the RWA Scale, a pool of twenty-four Quest items, the Attitudes toward Homosexuals Scale (Exhibit 1.3), the Manitoba Ethnocentrism Scale (Exhibit 1.2), the Posse-Radicals measure (Exhibit 1.4), and a three-case version of the Trials measure in which the subject passes sentence on a dope pusher, a pornographer, and someone who spit on a provincial premier. The booklet closed by asking the respondent's gender, age, educational attainment, home religion, present religion, and the frequency of church attendance and scripture reading outside church.

The measures of ethnocentrism and reactions to homosexuals served as indices of prejudice similar to those used previously in this literature. We also included the Posse-Radicals and Trials measures to test our underlying notion that religious fundamentalists would be, not just prejudiced against certain minorities, but *authoritarian aggressive* in general.

Results.   Focusing just on the Religious Fundamentalism Scale, it had a mean interitem correlation of .37 and an alpha of .92 among these 491 parents. It correlated .68 with the RWA Scale, appreciably higher than the .50 we usually find between Christian Orthodoxy and RWA among parents. Fundamentalism further correlated .30 with prejudices against aboriginals, Jews, blacks, Vietnamese, and other groups mentioned on the Ethnocentrism Scale,[11] .41 with hostility toward homosexuals, .34 with Posse scores, and .23

with the Trials measure ($p < .05$ in all cases). The Fundamentalism Scale also connected .65 with church attendance and .51 with scripture reading. Controlling for education, which correlated $-.20$ with Fundamentalism, reduced all of these associations a little, but all remained statistically significant.

Item analyses revealed that Fundamentalism scores correlated significantly with all of the RWA Scale items, all but three of the twenty Ethnocentrism items, all of the ATH items, all of the Posse items, and each of the trial sentences. So religious fundamentalists did not score high on the RWA Scale just because of tautological relationships with the "religion" items on the latter. They gave more authoritarian answers to *all* of the items. And fundamentalists proved prejudiced against nearly all the minorities that were mentioned, not just one or two. They not only said they did not want to associate with homosexuals, they also said (more often than others), "homosexuals should be locked up to protect society" and "the AIDS disease currently killing homosexuals is just what they deserve." They indicated that if the government decided to eradicate "radicals," they would be less reluctant than most to tell officials about any radicals they knew, help hunt them down, and approve of torturing and killing them.

These *item* correlations typically landed in the .20s and .30s, as single-item relationships frequently do. But they appeared almost everywhere.

So if you want to know who the *non*prejudiced Christians are, I think you can say, for a start, the *non*fundamentalist ones, in general.[12] To illustrate, 81 of the 491 parents in this study said they had no religious affiliation. These "nonaffiliated" subjects pulled down lower scores on the prejudice and other authoritarian aggression measures than any Christian denomination (Altemeyer and Hunsberger, 1992, table 3)—reaffirming the old "powerful conclusion" about nonaffiliates being relatively unprejudiced. Their means equaled 76.8 on the Ethnocentrism Scale, 49.1 on ATH, 16.2 on Posse-Radicals, and 28.0 on Trials.

Now let us look at differences within Christianity. If you take the 374 parents who said they were Christians, and study just those who placed in the bottom quartile of the Religious Fundamentalism Scale distribution ("*Non*-fundamentalist Christians," $N = 94$), you find their mean Ethnocentrism score was 77.8, and they had means of 47.8 on ATH, 16.5 on Posse, and 28.8 on Trials. These scores are all comparable to the nonaffiliates' and are significantly different from the means of the "Fundamentalist Christians" (those in the top quartile), which equaled 90.1, 65.2, 23.2, and 40.3, respectively.

So if the question has been, can you find a subset of church members who are *un*prejudiced as those who belong to no church?—the answer appears to be, at last: "Yes. Those who score low in religious fundamentalism."

One can easily overgeneralize this conclusion. On the one hand, many people scored high on the Religious Fundamentalism Scale and did *not* look at all like bigots heading for a lynching. And some nonfundamentalists *did* look like bigots. Such off-quadrant cases loom large in the data because, after all, the correlations between fundamentalism and authoritarian aggression were usually small potatoes. They matter only because (1) they are not huge and negative; (2) they are not even negative, but positive; and (3) they are statistically significant.

If you want big relationships, I can provide a variable that correlated better with Fundamentalism (.68), Ethnocentrism (.53), ATH (.64), Posse (.51), and Trials (.33) than any of these correlated with anything else. This variable would pop up first in any multiple regression analysis trying to find out "what is really going on here?" And you know what it is: RWA scores. Fundamentalism correlated with prejudice because fundamentalists tended to be right-wing authoritarians. If you partial out the effect of mutual relationships with RWA scores, all of the connections between religious fundamentalism and authoritarian aggression become essentially zero. Do it the other way, and the RWA-aggression correlations are just nicked.

Fundamentalism can therefore usually be viewed as a religious manifestation of right-wing authoritarianism. It correlates better with RWA scores than any other religious variable I know of, certainly better than Christian Orthodoxy does. It is the way authoritarians tend to react to the religious impulse. One can find a few secular High RWAs to be sure, and some religious authoritarians do *not* score high on the Fundamentalism Scale. But religious fundamentalists, as we have defined and measured the term, provide way more than their "fair share" of the right-wing authoritarians, and the most prejudiced people in our society.

They provide more for three reasons, I think, that go back to the beginning of this chapter. First, certain denominations tend to emphasize an authoritarian outlook and produce High RWA adults (Altemeyer and Hunsberger, 1992, table 3). Second, authoritarians will be attracted to the absolutism of the fundamentalist outlook. (If you have not been trained in *searching* for the truth, what could be better than a ready-made "completely right, infallible faith"?) Finally, authoritarians will resonate to the ethnocentrism of fundamentalist belief that *their* religion is the true religion, and all others are inferior.[13]

Authoritarianism, Fundamentalism, and Prejudice in Non-Christian Samples

Is all this true just of Christianity? Or do fundamentalists in many religions tend to be the most authoritarian and prejudiced?

In the summer of 1992, Bruce Hunsberger and I mailed surveys to people in Toronto, Canada, whom we judged, on the basis of their last names, were likely to have been raised as Hindus, Jews, or Muslims (Hunsberger, 1995).[14]

The covering letter, printed on university stationery, said the recipient's name had been randomly selected from a directory of Toronto residents for an *anonymous* study like a Gallup poll, strictly for scientific purposes. We were supposedly contacting fifty people, and a $2 bill was enclosed as a token payment. Since a number of names had been taken from the same page in the directory (the letter said), a relative might also have been contacted. The recipient was asked not to discuss the matter with any acquaintance before giving his or her own opinions.

You will note we made no mention of religious or ethnic background. We wanted people to answer as "randomly selected residents of Toronto," not as Hindus, Jews, or Muslims, so they would not shape their answers to represent their minority group "properly." We could have gathered larger samples and tested them more efficiently through temple and mosque associations. But such studies seem seriously compromised to us, compared to those with a smaller N but cleaner interpretation.

THE HINDU SAMPLE

I mailed surveys to 75 persons named Goyal, Gupta, Mehta, Pandey, Pandya, Patel or Sharma in the Toronto telephone directory. Seven of these were returned by Canada Post as "undeliverable." Of the remaining 68, 21 (31%) returned completed questionnaires. All 21 indicated, on a demographic section at the end of the survey, that they had been raised as Hindus. I also got 2 more Hindu participants from a mailing intended for Muslims (what do I know?), for a total of 23.

The 23 respondents averaged 39.4 years in age and 15.2 years of education. At the end of the survey they indicated they attended "church" 2.4 times per month and read scripture outside "church" 2.5 times per week. Eighteen (78%) were males.

THE JEWISH SAMPLE

Bruce Hunsberger mailed surveys to 75 persons having one of nineteen different surnames (Abrams, Bernstein, Goldberg, Katz, Rubinstein, Shapiro, and so on). Twenty surveys were returned as undeliverable or unanswered, so Bruce (having been thoroughly drilled in recycling) mailed them to new "Abramses," "Bernsteins," and others. In the end he received 37 completed surveys from the 95 people he tried to reach (39%). Of these, 32 said they had been raised in Judaism.

The Jewish sample proved 43.6 years old on the average and had 16.3 years of education. They attended "church" an average of 1.0 times per month and almost never read scripture otherwise (0.1 times per week). Seventeen of these 32 respondents were females.

THE MUSLIM SAMPLE

We actually tried this one *first,* and since I did it, it got screwed up. I sent out surveys to 75 persons named Ahmad, Ahmed, Ahsan, Abdullah, Hamidid, Hussain, or Mohammed. But 44 were eventually returned by Canada Post, mostly because the address from the phone book proved to be an apartment building, and I had not specified apartment numbers in the addresses. I read-dressed 42 of these, using a Toronto municipal directory then and thereafter to get apartment numbers. Ten of these also bounced back, mainly because the person had moved. If all of the letters not returned actually got to someone, I contacted 63 persons. Ultimately, 24 responded (35%), but 2 had been raised Hindu and 1 a Coptic Orthodox, leaving a Muslim sample of 21.

These 21 persons averaged 41.2 years old and had 14.9 years of education. They attended "church" 2.1 times per month and read scripture elsewhere 2.9 times per week—about as much as the Hindu sample did. Like the Hindu respondents, most (18 of 21, or 86%) were males.

SAMPLE NONREPRESENTATIVENESS

It should be obvious that these small samples are not representative of even their own families, much less the sizable Hindu, Jewish, and Muslim communities in Toronto, much less the world. A considerable self-selection factor for education clearly operated, as well as a pronounced gender bias in two of the groups. I would also bet (though we did not collect information on this, for fear it would jeopardize participation) that many of the respondents were raised and educated outside Canada. Their levels of church attendance and scripture reading also indicate considerable secularism, compared to what you would probably find in India, Israel, and Saudi Arabia.

So all we have here are *some* people who were raised in the Hindu, Jewish, or Muslim religions, who now live in Toronto, Canada, and who kindly answered an "opinion survey" that landed in their mailbox from out of town one day.

THE SURVEYS

In all cases the survey began with the RWA Scale, followed by the Religious Fundamentalism and Attitudes toward Homosexuals Scales. The demographic information ended our nosiness.

We used the ATH Scale as our measure of prejudice because the Manitoba Ethnocentrism Scale was developed to measure "white" prejudice, and specifically mentions "people from India," Jews, and Arabs. In contrast, homosexuals are a minority group common to all the cultures involved.

RESULTS

Scale Performance.   The RWA Scale "bombed out" among the Hindu and Muslim samples, attaining alphas of only .70 and .79, respectively. The length of the statements and unfamiliar referents may have caused problems for some participants. The alpha among the Jewish respondents equaled .92.

The Religious Fundamentalism Scale, in comparison, was answered with exemplary consistency by both Hindu (.91) and Muslim (.94) samples. The alpha among the Jewish participants equaled .85.

The Attitudes toward Homosexuals Scale had its troubles in the Muslim sample (alpha = .74). Its alpha came in at .85 in the other two groups.

We should recognize that when sample sizes soar no higher than 32, some fairly bizarre psychometric indices can turn up. But a low alpha is a low alpha, and we did *not* measure some of our variables nearly as crisply and powerfully as we wanted to.

Means.   Compared with my usual, mostly Christian, parent samples, the Hindu participants proved rather authoritarian (175.2), about equally fundamentalist (84.5), and somewhat more hostile toward homosexuals (67.6). Jews in turn scored very low (110.8, 48.3, and 30.8) on all measures. The Muslim sample was also rather authoritarian (171.5), very fundamentalist (112.3), and very hostile toward homosexuals (75.5).

Despite the tiny samples, the Jewish scores were significantly lower than the other groups' averages on all measures, and the Hindus' Fundamentalism Scale mean was significantly lower than the Muslims'. (But remember these samples are not necessarily representative of any larger group. One can imagine many covarying differences in these samples, such as gender and length of time spent in Canada, that could be working beneath the surface here. This study was *not* conceived to find, and cannot find, if brand X is nicer than brand Y.)

Intercorrelations.   What the study *was* designed to do was to see if fundamentalists within each non-Christian religion also tended to be authoritarian and relatively prejudiced. Among the respondents raised as Hindus, Religious Fundamentalism scores correlated .47 with RWA responses and .52 with (hostile) attitudes toward homosexuals. RWA correlated .57 with ATH. The corresponding coefficients for those raised in Judaism were .67, .42, and .45, and for those raised in Islam, .60, .65, and .74. All these values attained statistical significance.

Discussion.   This study was undertaken to answer two questions. First, would the Religious Fundamentalism Scale "hold together" in non-Christian samples, or does it just measure Christian fundamentalism? It *could* have fallen apart completely in any of these samples, but with alphas ranging from .85 to .94, it clearly remained cohesive. Despite the considerable differences in beliefs, the same system of *attitudes toward religious beliefs* existed and varied among these Hindus, Jews, and Muslims as existed and varied among our Christian samples. Fundamentalists, as identified by the Religious Fundamentalism Scale, had the same relatively ethnocentric attitudes—"We are God's special people," "Ours is the only real truth,"—in all these diverse samples.

The second question was, *if* the fundamentalism measure proved applicable to a group, would the fundamentalists in that religion also tend to be the most right-wing authoritarian and prejudiced members? Again, the answer *could* have been "No" in any and all cases. But clearly again, the data always said "Yes." The correlations did not necessarily rise as high as those obtained among the Manitoba parents, but they were nonetheless sizable.

Furthermore, the same ultimate conclusion obtains: fundamentalist Hindus, Jews, and Muslims in these samples tended to be the most prejudiced against homosexuals because, more basically, they tended to be the most authoritarian members of their groups. Partial out the binding RWA Scale effects, and nothing remains. Fundamentalism appears to be the religious manifestation of authoritarianism in all these different groups we have studied.

As interesting and consistent as these results are, I should "get real" here. Altogether there are well over a billion Hindus, Muslims, and Jews in the world. Roughly 99.9999% of them did not serve in this study. (In nearly every case, I must confess, we did not even try to reach them.) The risk of overgeneralization is great. Furthermore, one can think of other religions (such as Buddhism) in which the Religious Fundamentalism Scale will very likely collapse.

But we seem to be standing at the gates of a simple, compelling, unifying understanding of many things here, and all interested parties are invited to jump in and join us in the test. We did not exhaust the subject pool.

Summary

We began this chapter wishing religion made people better and noted that it can but also that it can make them worse. We saw that right-wing authoritarianism and traditional religiousness help produce each other. We then took up the much researched issue of whether religiously affiliated people tend to be *more* prejudiced than those who are unaffiliated. The answer has been such a loud, persistent "Yes" that investigators moved on some time ago to searching for some subset of religious people who are as unprejudiced as the nonaffiliated. It has been suggested that the very active, the "intrinsically" religious, and the religiously "questing" fit the bill. I have found it hard to agree with those conclusions, based on present findings.

We did find evidence, however, that affiliated people low in religious fundamentalism comprise the "lost tribe" of unprejudiced religious types. To put it the other way, fundamentalism is positively associated with prejudice and other forms of authoritarian aggression. It appears to be the religious manifestation of right-wing authoritarianism. We saw this in several large Christian samples, and also in small (supremely unrepresentative) groups of Hindus, Jews, and Muslims.

It should be noted that many religious people score moderate or low on the RWA Scale, not high. These respondents tend *not* to be fundamentalist. They seem more seeking, more including, less dogmatic—our next topic, save one.

But, first, if you do not mind, we are going to examine university students' sexual behavior, which often occurs despite their religious training.

—7—
Sex and the Single Authoritarian

You have probably found all of the preceding chapters, especially the one on research methodology, so compelling that you have only stopped reading this book over the past two days to deal with biological imperatives. Not so this time, I fear. Few people will be attracted to a chapter that promises to reveal the complete, raw sexual goings-on of your average university stud muffin, and the incredibly passionate "college coeds" you find advertising in the Personals column. You will probably have to gulp down lots of caffeine just to keep your head from pitching forward into this book over the next hour. And if you are a student whose teacher assigned this chapter for the next test (tomorrow, right?), your prof was simply following a very old rule you learn in graduate school: Always Assign the Dullest Chapter. So even though you have no personal interest in the topic, since you long ago rose to the higher planes of human existence—TRY TO STAY AWAKE!

I have written this chapter for two reasons. First, the sexual behavior of authoritarian and nonauthoritarian university students commands interest in its own right. I am reliably informed that students in the 1990s still think about sex and even occasionally do something about it. If you think sex plays a role in human endeavor, you might be interested in the role it plays in the endeavors of High and Low RWAs. You may be surprised.

Second, the data may be interesting to those who do not care a hoot about authoritarianism, but who have a dispassionate, scientific interest in how much fornication is going on now. I know this has been studied many times. You cannot have a respectable fight with your toddler at a grocery store checkout these days, without being distracted by at least four magazines proclaiming the latest sex polls. But as David Myers (1992, p. 12) has pointed out, these polls are often poorly done and almost certainly give a distorted account of what is really going on. Shere Hite's (1989) popular *Women and Love* was based on responses from 4,500 women, which impresses one initially. But the sample was drawn exclusively from members of women's organizations, and less than 5% of the surveys mailed out were completed and returned. So Hite's report that 70% of the respondents who had been married at least five years were having affairs does not necessarily apply to your Aunt Bertha and Uncle Harry. Ask them, if you do not believe me.

Even scientifically drawn, representative samples can suffer from appreciable self-selection bias, because for some unfathomable reason people will not always reveal the details of their sexual behavior to strangers. High RWAs especially will not (*RWA*, p. 327), and so I developed the Secret Survey for use with my own introductory psychology students. Because of the secrecy afforded by this testing procedure (see Chapter 2), and also I think because of the rather self-revelatory way I teach, I have gotten close to 100% response rates, year after year, to questions about sex on the Secret Survey. For example, the first time I used it (in January 1984), 7 of 326 students (2%) declined to answer a question about their virginity status. The last time I used it (in January 1995), 1 of 422 (<1%) did not answer the same question. The "no responses" have never gone above 3%.[1]

Another fairly unique feature of the Secret Survey studies, compared with other sex surveys, arises from my methodological and personal fixedness. I have accumulated data in the exact same way on the sexual behavior of the same kind of university students in the same place over the past twelve years. The results give us a good look at how things have changed over time, at least in my neighborhood.

Nevertheless, I would not want to pass these results off as the answer to a sex surveyor's (or voyeur's) dreams. While I have tried to minimize the circumstances that would lead to denial or exaggeration, I do not know that the students have told me the truth. These are university students, not necessarily representative of everybody their age, much less everybody young and unmarried in Manitoba, much less everybody living in North America. But I do recommend the technique, if you want to broaden the data base I am about to present. If nothing else, it will help you get to know the members of your local ethical review committee a lot better.

Sexual Activity

The first sexual question asked on the Secret Survey has always been "Are you a virgin?" While I was taught, from an early age, that this was a yes-or-no proposition, I have given my students six possible answers:

Yes, without qualification. (53) [20]

Yes, but I don't want to be. (4) [10]

Yes, but I have engaged in advanced sex acts (for example, oral-genital sex) as a way of having "sexual relations" without having intercourse. (15) [22]

No, but I am married/was married. (19) [6]

No, but it was against my will. (3) [3]

No. (73) [91]

(No Response) (4) [3]

The numbers in parentheses represent the answers the 171 females serving in my first Secret Survey gave in 1984. Those in brackets show the breakdown of the 155 participating males. If we set aside the married subjects, rape victims, and nonresponders from the sample, we can see that 50% (72 of 145) of the female students back then were virgins, and 36% (52 of 143) of the males were ($p < .05$).

The respective frequencies for the 1995 Secret Survey were: for females, 45, 3, 21, 3, 3, 154; and for males, 28, 24, 25, 4, 0, 111. So the percentage of virgins, with the same exclusions as above, has fallen to 31% (69 of 223) for the females, but stayed essentially unchanged 41% (77 of 188) for the males.

Figure 7.1 presents these percentages for each of the years I collected Secret Survey data. (I did not teach introductory psychology in 1986–87, nor in 1990–91.) You can see that virginity has become *rarer* in women than in men among these samples since 1989. You can also see that about a third of the students who appear before me these days in introductory psychology are still virgins halfway through their freshman year. (This surprises the students when I give them the results; they usually think virginity is rarer.) Most of the female virgins want to be virgins and have not "fooled around" much. Most of the male virgins either wish they were not or have engaged in advanced sexual acts, but not intercourse.

Figure 7.2 shows the percentage of High RWA students, by gender, who said they were virgins in each of my secret surveys. Figure 7.3 gives the same breakdown for Lows. (Note that the Y-axis in Figure 7.3 basically starts where the Y-axis in Figure 7.2 ends. We are dealing with two different ranges of behavior here.)

Several features jump out at me as I look at each figure and compare them.

1. As you would predict, High RWAs are more likely to be virgins than Lows, for both women and men.

2. That being understood, both Low and High RWA *females* are less likely to be virgins now than they were when I started collecting these data. Low

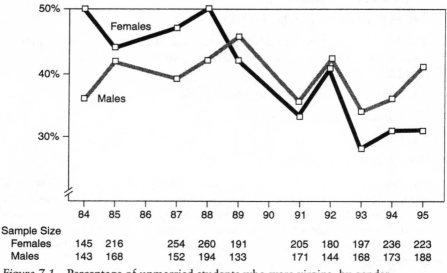

Figure 7.1   Percentage of unmarried students who were virgins, by gender

RWA females never did seem to place much value on virginity per se, and today a solid majority of them report they are nonvirgins. But the biggest change in Figures 7.2 and 7.3 has occurred among the *High RWA* women. Once intent on "saving themselves for marriage," most High women have *not* been virgins in five of the last six years.

3. In comparison with the women, male students have shown rather stable rates of virginity. High males have almost always been in the 40–60% range and until recently were *less* likely to be virgins than High females. Low males have varied even less, usually landing in the 30–40% bracket and usually *more* likely to be virgins than Low RWA women . . . although not particularly happy about it.

4. As Figure 7.1 depicted, the double standard about male and female virginity has disappeared in this population during the run of these studies. This has not just happened among the Low RWAs, but also the Highs.

I asked the virgins who completed the Secret Survey in January 1996 why they had remained virgins. Only 22% (mainly Highs) cited religious reasons. Another 16% reported they were saving themselves for marriage (but not because of their religious beliefs). The most common answer (27%) was they were waiting for a sufficiently serious love relationship, the "right person." Some 11% were ready and willing but had "not had the opportunity." "Being scared" and fear of pregnancy and sexually transmitted diseases rounded out the responses.

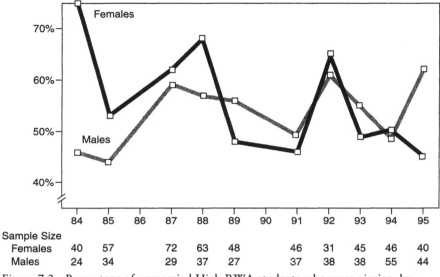

Sample Size	84	85	86	87	88	89	90	91	92	93	94	95
Females	40	57		72	63	48		46	31	45	46	40
Males	24	34		29	37	27		37	38	38	55	44

Figure 7.2 Percentage of unmarried High RWA students who were virgins, by gender

CIRCUMSTANCES OF FIRST INTERCOURSE

In January 1987 I asked my students to describe the circumstances of their first act of intercourse, in the sense of whether they wanted it to happen, or were they manipulated into it (by pressure of some kind, use of alcohol, and so on). Males usually said they basically wanted to have sex on that first occasion, whereas the females generally had more mixed feelings and sometimes had been manipulated into the act. Of 149 female nonvirgins, 21 said or strongly implied that their first act of intercourse had been a rape.[2] Many more indicated they had not been 100% in agreement with having sex.

Two years later I asked the nonvirgins to indicate, on a 0–4 scale, "To what extent did you *want* to have intercourse that first time?" The mean answer among males was 2.86, while that among females was significantly lower, 2.26. Of 114 nonvirgin females, 6 answered "0," ("Not at all") and 24 answered with a "1" ("A little"). Another 27 responded "2" ("Moderately"), 48 said "3" ("Strongly"), and 9 said "4" ("Intensely"). The corresponding figures for 73 nonvirgin males responding were 3, 4, 11, 37, and 18. I would say at least 30 of the women, and 7 of the men were forced or manipulated into having their first acts of intercourse against their wills.

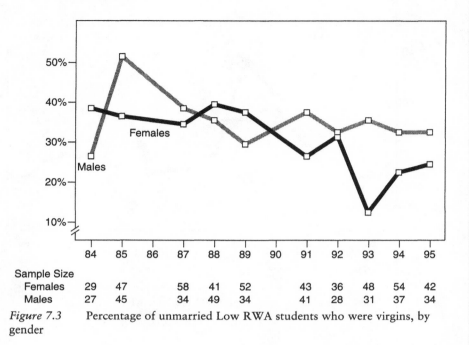

Sample Size	84	85	86	87	88	89	90	91	92	93	94	95
Females	29	47		58	41	52		43	36	48	54	42
Males	27	45		34	49	34		41	28	31	37	34

Figure 7.3   Percentage of unmarried Low RWA students who were virgins, by gender

AGE OF FIRST INTERCOURSE

In 1987 I also asked my nonvirginal students how old they had been at the time of first intercourse. For females the answers ranged from 8 to 22, with a *mean* of 16.5 years. The range among males was 12 to 21, with a mean of 17.1 years. Low RWAs tended to begin intercourse a little sooner than High RWAs (Low females averaged 16.4, High females 16.6; Low males began at 16.8, and High males at 17.4). Many females probably had their first intercourse with slightly older males.

The age of first intercourse has dropped steadily since 1987. In 1995, the female mean was 15.8 years, and that for the males was 16.2. Most (69%) of the unmarried women in my class in January 1995 were not virgins, and most of the nonvirgins had begun having sex *before* their sixteenth birthday. Ditto for the males, but they had started a little later on the average.

In terms of RWA scores, an interesting change has appeared in the data recently. High RWA female nonvirgins used to start having intercourse later than Low women. But in both 1994 and 1995 High nonvirgins had started sooner (means of 15.6 and 15.4, versus 16.3 and 15.8, respectively; $p < .05$ overall). *Male* High nonvirgins had also "caught up" with their Low counterpoints, both groups having their first act of intercourse at about 16.6 years of age. Overall, authoritarian students who become sexually active are now starting as soon as nonauthoritarians, or sooner.

NUMBER OF ACTS OF INTERCOURSE
In January 1987 I asked my students who had "lost" their virginity how many times, approximately, they had had intercourse. The answers (excluding the marrieds and rape victims) ranged from "once" to "over a thousand." (One of my students explained she had been a prostitute for nearly three years.) Because a few "high scoring" individuals can create a quite misleading mean, I shall report these central tendencies in terms of the median, which was 30 for the males, and 50 for the females.[3]

One additional fact leapt out from the data: females were much more likely to have had *many* acts of intercourse than males. Of the 135 women, 51 had copulated over 100 times, compared with only 18 of 93 men. Of the 93 nonvirgin guys, 31 could still keep track on their fingers.[4]

The numbers can get somewhat misleading when we sort out the Low and High RWA students' *medians,* because the small samples of nonvirgins, by authoritarianism, by gender, are fairly discontinuous. (The median could come just before, or just after, a gap in the array.) Bearing that in mind, the median for the Low nonvirgin males equaled 40, and that for the High non-virgin males was 16. Both the Low and High RWA nonvirgin females had had a median of 50 of acts of intercourse. (But remember we are excluding the virgins, whose ranks contained more Highs than Lows.)

I collected "How many times?" data from my nonvirgins in every Secret Survey thereafter. The results, given in Figure 7.4, instantly reveal three things:

1. The female nonvirgins always had engaged in more sex than the males.

2. Males in the mid 1990s were copulating a little more than their older brothers did in the late 1980s, the median going from 30 to 45. Fewer of the fellows are able to keep track with their fingers now.

3. But the women are having a lot more intercourse now (from 50 to about 85).

So, not only are female students less likely to be virgins today than male students, they have also copulated about twice as much as the guys. (It causes some anguish among the fellows in my classes when I reveal this fact in the feedback lecture on the Secret Survey.) *Part* of the reason is that women get a head start, beginning sex at an earlier age than men.

In terms of RWA scores, in 1995 the median value for Low males was 65 acts of intercourse, while that for High males was 45. Both Low and High

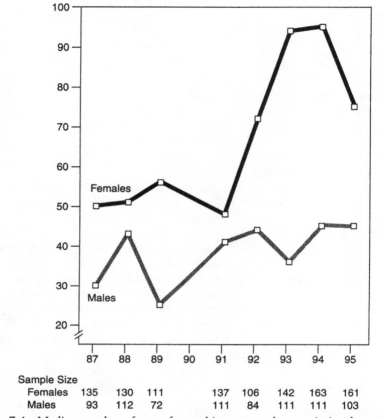

Figure 7.4   Median number of acts of sexual intercourse by nonvirgins, by gender

females had had more sexual experience than their counterparts, with medians of 70 and 85, respectively.

NUMBER OF PARTNERS

Got a picture of sex in the nineties on my campus? "Orgy-Porgy"? "Manitoba Women Don't Say No"? No way!

As I reported in *Enemies of Freedom* (p. 163), I asked my January 1985 students, "With how many partners have you engaged in sexual intercourse?"[5] Excluding the large number of virgins in that sample, the females' answers ranged from 1 to 31, and the males' from 1 to 50 (presumably an estimate). Medians again appeared to be the sensible measure of central tendency and worked out to 2.3 for the female and 3.1 for the male nonvirgins. While a few people (12 out of 139 women, and 18 out of 103 men) were into double digits on their "scorecards," the modal answer was just "one" partner.

If we look at RWA scores, the median landed at 2.3 for the Low females, and at 2.0 for the High women. Low males had had more sexual partners than High males, with medians of 4.3 versus 1.9, respectively.

These numbers have dropped some over the years, perhaps because of fear of AIDS. In 1995, the female median equaled 1.7 partners, compared to the males' 2.7. No noticeable difference appeared between Lows and Highs.

So if you were thinking everybody is increasingly doing it with everybody else up here in the North True and Free, the data say "no!" Most of the *sexually active* students had had sex with only one or two persons by the midpoint of their first year at university in 1995. (And counting the virgins, most of my students, year after year, had had sex with either zero or one person.)[6]

INTERPRETATION

Are more first-year students on my campus sexually active now than used to be true? Yes, increasingly so. Do they start younger? Yes, apparently. Do they do it more often? Yes, increasingly so. But do they do it with more people? No. Many students are "doing the deed" at a rate that a lot of guys in my generation could only dream about, but usually in stable relationships, not in one-night stands.

Thus females have reached parity with males in most sex categories, and dramatically exceeded them in number of acts of intercourse, not because they have become "looser," but because they have, through greater inclination or ability, formed more long-term, stable relationships than males of the same age. As they (and some of the men) often put it when filling out my "cold, clinical" survey, sex is very much part of the love they experience with someone else. "Coupling" after all is coupling, and it can be the only time two people get close, or just part of a continual and deeply enriching closeness.

High RWA women are increasingly making this accommodation, catching and even surpassing Low RWA women in many aspects of sexual behavior. But authoritarian men remain relatively inactive. They are more likely than anyone else in the 1990s to be virgins, and those who are *not* virgins have had less sexual experience than anyone else. Partly this happens for religious reasons, which High RWA women have increasingly discounted. But it may also result from a difficulty authoritarian males have finding women who will form long-term relationships with them. High RWA men have more "old-fashioned" attitudes about sex roles and male dominance than any other segment of my samples. There are not many women left on my campus who buy into that, which helps explain authoritarian men's hostility toward feminists.

Other Issues

BIRTH CONTROL

In January 1988 I asked my students, "If you are *not* a virgin, how often do you use some kind of birth control device?" I provided a 0–100% scale for their responses. Males said they (and their partner) practiced birth control 65.7% of the time, while females reported using a device significantly more often, 83.8%.

In January 1992, I pursued the issue again, asking, "If you are *not* a virgin, *for the past year*, what *percent* of the time when you engaged in sexual intercourse, did you use some reasonably trustworthy way of preventing pregnancy? (That is, the 'pill,' an IUD or diaphragm with spermicidal foam, or a condom?)" This time males reported an average of 79.2%, and females 86.6% ($p > .20$). Thus students usually took precautions against pregnancy: 66% of the females and 60% of the males reported using such birth control devices 100% of the time. The seven females and twelve males I found who never, or almost never, practiced birth control usually had low levels of sexual activity (for example, "two partners, one time with each"). But one female reported she had had sex 130 times with her boyfriend and they had never used any protection. Another woman said she had had sex 50 times with ten different men, and practiced birth control only 10% of the time. Then there was the guy who had had intercourse 200 times with forty different partners, and another who figured he was "close to 1,000" with "about thirty-five" women, who had never taken any precautions against impregnation.

I also asked about *condom* use in 1992: "If you are *not* a virgin, what *percent* of the time during the past year when you engaged in sexual intercourse, did you use a condom to prevent AIDS or some other STD [sexually transmitted disease]?" Males reported a condom had been used 39.0% of the time, and females 34.8%. Since a lot of intercourse occurs in long term relationships, where the tendency might more naturally be to rely on birth control pills to prevent pregnancy, and each other's integrity to prevent sexually transmitted diseases, I would say the AIDS-awareness campaigns appear to have had a beneficial impact. Still, the people we met in the last paragraph who had had many sexual partners, and had done nothing even about birth control, are walking Centers for Disease Uncontrol.

"ARE WE HAVING FUN YET?"

In 1985 I asked my Secret Survey respondents, "In general, how much have you enjoyed the sexual activity you have engaged in thus far in your life?"

Responses, given on a 0–4 scale, averaged 2.85 for both male and female nonvirgins (close to "Very Much," the modal response for both genders). So I think we are onto an important new finding here: university students usually find sex enjoyable.

Ten years later I got up the gumption to ask for details. I asked my students to tell me, on a −4 to +4 basis (which translated to the usual 1–9 format), how much they enjoyed fourteen sexual acts, *If* they had experienced them. The acts are shown in Table 7.1, along with the means of the answers given by the 223 females and 188 males. (The number of responses for each act varied considerably: nearly everyone had "necked," but only about half said they had done number 14.)

Table 7.1 Mean evaluations of various sex acts, 1–9 scale

Women	Men	Act
8.4	7.8	1. "Necking"—Lots of embraces and kisses on the face, neck.
7.8	8.0	2. "Petting"—The male strokes the female's breasts.
7.0	7.8	3. "Genital touching"—*Your* touching, stroking the other person's genitalia with your hand.
7.8	8.2	4. "Genital touching"—Having *your* genitalia touched, stroked by the other person's hand.
Oral sex		
6.2	6.8	5. *Your* giving oral stimulation to the other person's genitalia, but *not* to orgasm.
5.5	7.2	6. *Your* giving oral stimulation to the other person's genitalia, producing an orgasm.
7.0	7.1	7. *Being* orally stimulated by the other person, but *not* to orgasm.
7.5	8.1	8. *Being* orally stimulated by the other person, producing an orgasm for you.
6.7	7.3	9. *Mutual* simultaneous oral-genital stimulation, as foreplay, but *not* to the point of orgasm.
6.9	7.8	10. *Mutual* simultaneous oral-genital stimulation to the point of orgasm for one or both.
Positions for sexual intercourse		
8.0	7.4	11. "Standard"—Female lying on her back, male on top, facing each other.
7.8	7.9	12. Male on his back, female on top, facing each other.
6.4	7.7	13. Male behind female, who is kneeling or standing.
6.7	6.6	14. Male behind female, both lying on their sides.

The first thing that struck me about the results, continuing the theme above, was how positively nearly all the acts were evaluated. Means over 7.0 on a 1–9 scale mean that people often answered with a +3 or +4 (which translate into an 8 or a 9)—a strong endorsement. All the acts got positive ratings (greater than 5.0) overall.

The second thing that struck me was how little difference showed up between the women and the men. (I am probably betraying the bias of my era here.) Still, differences appeared. Women did not like giving oral stimulation to orgasm (5.5) nearly as much as men liked doing it (7.2), or especially as much as men liked receiving it (8.1). Women did not like intercourse with the man behind them (6.4) as much as the men did (7.7). But you can see that all the other differences in the means came in less than 1.0.

I hasten to add that these high numbers do not mean that the students enjoy these sex acts so much they are willing to do them whenever with whomever. For the vast majority of them, these experiences took place in the context of a love relationship, and not necessarily every time one lover wanted them to.

WHAT ISN'T FUN

Given this astonishing news that young people find sex enjoyable, it seemed prudent to ask for the other side of the story. In 1993 I asked, "What things about 'sexual behavior' (from meeting someone to as-far-as-things-go) cause you anxiety? What things about sex do you dislike?" First of all, 21 of 201 females and 23 of 172 males said, essentially, "Nothing. It's great!" Another 26 females and 29 males gave no answer, sometimes saying they had had *no* sexual experiences. But the rest, since I asked, did have one or two (or three or four) things about sex they did not like.

Here is the Top Ten list for women, with the frequency of being mentioned given in parentheses.[7]

10. Anal intercourse. (8)

9. Rape. Usually, fear of rape, although three of the women who mentioned this said they had been raped. (10)

8. First meeting. Just getting to know someone. Overcoming shyness. (12)

7. Pregnancy. (14)

6. Sexually transmitted diseases. (16)

5. Oral sex. Usually, having to perform it on men. (16)

4. Selfish lovers. Not being fully aroused before intercourse. Or, "He has his orgasm and I'm left hanging." (16)

3. Feeling "used." "It turns out he was in love with you for one night." "Liars." "Men who do not like to cuddle afterwards. It was just sex to them." (17)

2. Being seen naked. Some women thought their bodies "unbeautiful" and wanted the lights out. (18)

1. Being pressured. "Guys trying to intimidate you by really 'hitting on you' intensely." "Men practically dragging you into bed because they bought you a drink and you danced with them." "My boyfriend saying we are through if I do not do certain things." (21)

Got that? Just what you thought? Then what did the men say?

10. Women Who Sleep Around. Some guys said they disliked "easy women." (7)

9. Teasers. (The term was usually prefixed with reference to a distinguishing feature of the male anatomy.) (7)

8. Commitment. "I don't like having to lie around with the woman after I'm done." "I hate it when they want you to spend the night with them afterwards." (8)

7. Condoms. (9)

6. Not satisfying the woman. "I don't know if my partner is fully pleased." "You have to please the woman, and I wonder if I do." (10)

5. Sexually transmitted diseases. (10)

4. Pregnancy. (11)

3. First meeting. Knowing what to say. Overcoming shyness. (14).

2. Having to be the "aggressor." "The guy takes the chance. The women get to say 'No.' " "I find it hard to put the 'moves' on a girl." "*You* have to figure out how far you can go, you always have to take the next step." (15)

1. Sexual performance. "You have to impress the woman with your stud-manship, or else you're dead." "Worrying about my performance throws off my concentration." "Men can't 'perform forever.' " Also, anxieties over impotence or penis size. (16)

What do you notice about the two lists? Well, women and men have *some* common anxieties: shyness, pregnancy, and sexually transmitted diseases. But basically, they look like people with very different orientations. (Another breakthrough!) Want to know how many men said they were afraid of being seen naked? Zero. Want to know how many women worried about being able to satisfy their partner? One. How many guys do you think wrote, "Those darn women, all they want is a quick roll in the hay, and then you never see them again"? (Actually, two lodged such complaints, but only two.) How many women do you think objected to having to take almost all of the sexual initiatives? Zero. How many men worried about being pressured to "come across" after a date, or being raped? Zero. How many women complained about guys expecting an emotional commitment "just because we had sex"? Ditto.

Let us recall the first finding: students generally found their sexual experiences quite rewarding. But for some men and women, sometimes, although they cohabit on the same planet, and even in the same bed, they live in two different worlds.

DIFFICULT DECISIONS WOMEN FACE

A number of the men who complained about guys having to be "the aggressor" went on to say things like "The woman gets to reject the man when he tries, but the man never gets to reject the woman." They probably did not consider all the times male students reject female students out of hand on the grounds of appearance. The traditional sexual game has therefore pressured women to make themselves sexually attractive, to create that interest. While this will usually "work," it also reinforces women being judged as sexual objects, as "meat," instead of being seen in terms of their intelligence, personality, and character. Young women, especially if their consciousness has been raised, thus have to decide whether they will present themselves as sexual objects. I wondered how many of them willingly did so these days.

In 1992 I intrusively asked the women answering the Secret Survey, "How often have you, *in the last year,* dressed so that you would be sexually attractive to males, in the sense of making men think, 'What a sexy body!' " Of 195 respondents, 31 (14%) said "Never." The other 86% said they had done so at least once. The median value was about two dozen times over the past year. About 5% said something like "All the time," or "Every day I can."

By 1996 it finally occurred to me that my question might have been unfair to these women because (1) they might have been dressing sexily for a lover—which is not the same thing as trying to make men in general think "what a sexy body"; and (2) I had not asked men the same question. So I asked my January 1996 Secret Survey takers how often in an average month they dressed to be sexually attractive to the opposite sex in general, and then "to someone in particular." I got essentially the same answer to both questions, an average of 6.0 times per month from the women for "men in general," and 6.9 times for someone special. Interestingly the males' means were nearly the same: 6.6 and 5.5.

A second part of the traditional sexual game holds that a woman should not *easily* agree to sexual intercourse when she is willing. To do so could mark her as a "tramp" in her own mind, and in the opinion of the man busily trying (he thinks) to seduce her. So women might feel pressured to say "No" for a while when they are agreeable to sex, even though this undermines the "No means No!" defense against date rape.

In my 1992 survey, I asked my female students, "How often have you said 'No' to a 'proposition' (an attempt at sexual intercourse) when you actually felt 'Yes,' but wanted the male to keep trying so he would not think you were 'easy'?" Seventy of the women said they had done so at least once. While this amounts to only 36% of 195 women who answered the question, it represents 57% of the nonvirgin females.

I asked this question again in my 1996 Secret Survey, of all my students. Of 173 responding women, 43% said they had said "No" at least once when they meant "yes." These 74 women represented 65% of the nonvirgin females.[8] Again surprisingly, 28% of the 125 responding men said they had done the same thing.

MISCELLANEOUS SEXUAL BEHAVIORS

Masturbation.   In January 1994 I asked yet another bland, matter-of-fact question: "Approximately how many times during an ordinary month do you masturbate (i.e. touch your genitalia to produce great pleasure, and perhaps orgasm)?" The answers ranged from zero to twenty for the females, with 61% saying "never." The median value for the other 39% was about four times per month. Masturbation proved more common among the males, with a range of zero to thirty, 33% saying "never," and the median among the rest being about eight times per month.

Sexual Fantasies.   In January 1995 I asked my students how often they had "fantasies in which you are having serious sexual contact with another person (i.e. beyond hugging and kissing)?" Almost everyone said they had such fantasies *sometimes*. The median rate for females was "about every other day." Males had them more often, their median being "about once or twice per day."

I also asked these students who the "other person" in their sexual fantasy usually was. The most common answer checked by the women (105 of 216, or 49%) was their present boyfriend. The men had no such runaway favorite: 29% said the "other person" was an "acquaintance or casual friend"; 24% checked "someone I see, but don't know"; and 19% said they fantasized about their present girlfriend.

Emboldened, I ended the 1996 Secret Survey with the most intrusive question I think I have ever cast. I asked my students to tell me in detail about their favorite sexual fantasy, and over 90% gave me at least an outline of such. As for setting, both men and women preferred a tropical beach over any other location. (Understandable among Winnipegers in January!) As for attire, most fantasies started with the participants dressed ordinarily. Males were more likely than females to skip the preliminaries. Whom were they with? Nearly half (47%) of the women made love with their present boyfriend in their favorite fantasy. The men were again all over the place. The most common choice was a rather indiscriminate "some attractive female" (20%), followed by a "supermodel" or TV star (19%), and a friend (17%). "Present girlfriend" came in fourth (16%), just a breath ahead of "an acquaintance" (15%). Only 6% of the women had multiple partners in their fantasies, and they were as likely to be another woman as another man. But 22% of the men had multiple partners, and all the extras were women.

The fantasies, after much ado, almost always ended in sexual intercourse. The students gave many answers to the question "what is the best, the most satisfying part of this fantasy for you?" But the women most often cited being loved and desired (17%), being held and cuddled (17%), and the love and intimacy of the moment (14%). The most common answers among the men were the sex itself (22%), having sex with more than one woman (15%), and seeing women naked (10%). Since we are talking about one's favorite, self-generated fantasy, I think these answers indicate what women and men want most from sex.

Fantasies of "Others" during Sexual Intercourse. (Warning: Skip to the next topic if you are feeling insecure in a sexual relationship.) In 1993 I probed another highly personal area: "If you are not a virgin, do you sometimes fantasize, while having intercourse, that you are having sex with someone else? If 'Yes,' with whom? (Don't name names, please. But rather something general like 'movie star,' 'person on the bus,' 'old flame,' 'complete stranger,' etc.)." Twenty-eight percent of the female nonvirgins, and 36% of the males said "Yes." Want to guess what the most common fantasy was? (This could really test your peace of mind.) "Making it" with an old flame, for both males and females. But while the second most frequent choice for male students was having sex with a movie star or "Miss January," the females mentioned making love with a complete stranger second most often.

Cheating on a Lover. (Maybe you had better skip this one too, if you are not 100% sure of your partner.) In both 1993 and 1994 I inquired of my students: "Have you ever 'cheated' on a boyfriend/girlfriend? That is, willingly engaged in sexual behavior (oral-genital stimulation or intercourse) with one person while you were 'committed' to someone else? If 'yes,' how often?" In 1993, 27% of the women said they had cheated, and in 1994, 29% said they had. The figures for the men were 28% and 33%, respectively. (If you prefer a more depressing outlook, set aside the virgins, who obviously have done little sexual cheating, and the overall numbers boil down to 45% of the male and 39% of the female nonvirgins.) "Cheaters" cheated anywhere from one to sixty times, but the median for both sexes was about twice.

Who cheats? The best predictor was provided (obviously) by the answer to an earlier question on the survey about how many sexual partners the person had had. Most students had had zero or one partner, and only two of these had ever cheated (by the definition I provided). The more sexual partners a person had had, the more likely some of these sex acts had involved a betrayal of a relationship. Two-thirds of the students with over three sexual partners had cheated at least once. Among those (few) with over eight partners, nearly 80% had cheated.

Use of a Prostitute.   In 1987 I asked my 157 male students, "Have you ever had sexual intercourse or oral-genital sex with a prostitute?" Only one of the men said he had.

Incidence of Homosexual Behavior.   In 1984 I inquired, "Have you ever willingly participated in a homosexual act?" Ninety-six percent of the students said "No."

ASSAULT IN A SEXUAL CONTEXT

Rape: Male Admissions.   I have twice asked my male students, on Secret Surveys, if they have ever forced a woman to have sexual relations with them. In 1984, the question was worded, "Have you ever forced a woman to perform sexual acts with you?" The responses, and frequency of response (in parentheses), follow.

Yes. It was a clear case of rape. (3)

Yes and no; she said "no" but I didn't believe she meant it. (7)

Yes and no; I manipulated her into a situation where she was likely to agree even if she really didn't want to (e.g. through alcohol, drugs, social pressure). (26)

No. I've never done anything like this. (110)

You can see that only a few men admitted to rape. But overall about 20% of them said they had made a determined effort to obtain sex *somehow* even though the woman had said she did not want to. (Note: 3 + 7 + 26 = 36 25% of 146, but some men checked several categories.)

In 1992 I asked my 155 male students a more detailed series of questions about their aggressive sexual behavior from age fourteen on. I found that:

1. Forty-four percent of the respondents admitted they had at least once "engaged in sex play with a female (fondling, kissing, or petting, but not intercourse) when she did not want to by *overwhelming her with continual arguments and pressure.*"

2. Twenty percent of the respondents admitted they had at least once "engaged in sexual intercourse with a female when she did not want to by *overwhelming her with continual arguments and pressure.*"

3. Thirty-four percent said they had at least once gotten a woman to agree to having sexual intercourse, when she did not want to, "by flattering her, or by telling her you cared about her more than you really did."

4. Thirty percent said they had gotten the woman to agree "by taking her to a situation (a 'romantic spot' perhaps, or a 'make-out party') where you thought she could be talked into it."

5. Eleven percent of the men said they had "attempted sexual intercourse with a female (got on top of her, attempted to insert penis) when she didn't want to by *giving her alcohol or drugs*—but intercourse did not occur." Nine percent (sometimes the same students) said they had also tried this and succeeded.

6. Five percent of the sample said they had simply used physical force on at least one occasion to rape a woman.

Overall, most of the men (55%) said they had tried, at least once, to have sexual contact with a woman in one of these ways.

Rape: Female Accounts. In 1989 I asked my female students a series of questions about date rape, prefacing them with the following description:

"Date rape" has been in the news lately. "Date rape" clearly occurs when a man insists on sexual intercourse during a date, and physically forces himself onto the woman. Another kind of "date rape," according to some people, occurs when a man on a date manipulates a woman into intercourse by telling her he won't see her again otherwise, or by getting her drunk, or by psychologically pressuring her with guilt ("You owe it to me"), inferiority ("What's wrong with you?"), etc.

Of the 205 women in the sample, about one in four (48) said they had fought off attempted forcible rapes while on dates. Twelve (with some overlap) said they had *not* been able to fight off an attacker and had been raped. About a third (64) said a date had at least once tried to manipulate them, nonphysically, into having sex with them when they did not want to, but it had not worked. Twenty-eight reported that such attempts *had* led to unwanted intercourse.

I gave the nearly 200 women in my 1992 Secret Survey more detailed questions about being forced or manipulated into having intercourse, corresponding to the questions (described above) I had asked the men in that study. Nineteen percent of the women said they had been "talked into" sex "by the male *overwhelming you with continual arguments and pressure.*" Twenty-seven percent said they had been duped by male flattery, or a guy telling them he cared for them more than he really did. Seventeen percent said they had been maneuvered into agreeing after being taken to a "romantic spot" or a "make-out party." Twenty-one percent said alcohol or drugs had led them to intercourse they did not want. Thirteen percent said they had been physically forced into intercourse.

Overall, 84 of the women (42% of the females in the sample, 68% of the nonvirgins) had had intercourse at least once under these conditions.

If you check back a bit to see the males' answers to these questions, you will find the numbers generally correspond. Overall, men believe their flattery and "romantic spots" work a little better than the women think. And the women attribute their "agreement" to alcohol or other drugs much more than the men would say. But the biggest difference involves outright physical rape: appreciably more women (13%) said they had been forcibly raped than men (5%) admitted to having committed this felony. But if you were to add in the "She said no, but I knew she meant yes" incidents—which I did not ask about in this study—the gap would probably close. Some men doubtless do not admit to the rapes they have committed.

SEXUAL HARASSMENT

I also asked the women in this 1992 Secret Survey four questions about sexual harassment. Most (116 of 196, or 58%) said they had been "accidentally" touched in a sexual place ("a sneaky sexual touching") during the past year, and 65 (33%) said they had been openly sexually touched against their will. Seventy-eight (40%) reported being told explicit sexual stories by a male that made them feel uncomfortable, and 134 (68%) said they had been pestered for "innocent" sexual favors (a kiss, an embrace, close dancing) during the past year.

Altogether 166 (83% of the females in the sample) had been sexually harassed in some way during the past year.

SEXUAL ABUSE DURING CHILDHOOD

In January 1987 I asked my students if they had been sexually abused while they were children: "Were you ever sexually abused (e.g., being sexually fondled, sexually kissed, or more advanced sexual acts) by an older relative, teacher, etc.? If so, how often? *If* you are *completely* willing, would you describe the circumstances involved? How old were you? Who was it?" Forty-nine of 275 females (18%) said they had been abused, along with 2 of 157 males (1%). Virtually everyone gave descriptions of the circumstances surrounding the attacks. A couple of the incidents, I would say, would not count as childhood sexual abuse (for instance, getting pinched while traveling in Italy)—but only a couple. Most of the assaults occurred *before* the women reached adolescence, the youngest being five. While uncles and fathers were the most frequent perpetrators, the range of assailants staggers one: brother, cousin, grandfather, grandfather's friend, brother's friend, father's friend, mother's boyfriend, babysitter, neighbor, "older man," "man I babysat for," "old friend of the family," strangers.

Let us put some faces to these grim statistics. Imagine you teach introductory psychology, and the next time you are in class, you draw a little mental box around the eight women sitting nearest the center of the room. They are probably smiling and chatting, eager to hear more about Pavlov's dogs. But if your students are like mine, then probably:

Seven of the eight have been sexually harassed during the past year.

Three or four of them have been manipulated into having unwanted sex.

Two of them have had to fight off a rapist by this point in their lives.

One of them *has* been forcibly raped.

One of them was sexually abused as a young child.

Want to know who does such things to your students? Well, some of them may also be sitting before you.

I hasten to add that if your students are like mine, most of them come from two-parent, middle-class families and lived in nice neighborhoods. Do you imagine that things are better for those who grew up in worse circumstances?

Attitudes about Sexual Issues

As you probably noticed, I spent most of the 1992 Secret Survey digging at the facts of sex, rape, and sexual manipulation. But I also got in a little plain old attitude measurement, asking the students for their opinions on the ten gender-related issues shown in Exhibit 7.1. Responses were given on the usual −4 to +4 (that is, 1–9) basis. Means for the 200 women in the sample are given in the parentheses following each item; those for the 155 men are given in brackets. The sexes had predictable, significantly different opinions on all of the items, except number 5.

Exhibit 7.1   The Ten Attitude Items Used in the 1992 Secret Survey

1. The thought of two women making love to each other is disgusting. (6.85) [4.40]

2. Women attack men just as often as men attack women—only the newspapers don't make such a big deal out of it. (3.67) [4.09]

3. Wife abuse is one of our most serious problems. (7.25) [6.49]

4. Men today are being unfairly bad-mouthed and attacked by the media as aggressive brutes who supposedly are always attacking women and children. (4.86) [5.57]

5. Men sexually molest children far more often than women do. (6.11) [6.01]

6. No man should take advantage of a woman who is naive and gullible. (8.12) [6.31]

7. Homosexual men are more likely to molest children than heterosexual men are. (3.03) [4.38]

8. Basically, sexual relations between a man and a woman depend upon power: the man tries to control the woman so he can get what he wants; the woman tries to use sex to control the man. (3.40) [4.38]

9. The thought of two men making love to each other is disgusting. (6.89) [7.58]

10. Even if a woman is sexily dressed, that does not give a man the right to assume she wants to have sex. (8.35) [6.66]

Note: Items are answered on a −4 to +4 basis. Female means ($N = 200$) are given in parentheses. Male means ($N = 155$) are given in brackets.

You can see that the biggest gender gaps occurred on items 1, 6, 7, and 10. I find item 1 interesting, for if you compare it with item 9, you can clearly see the double standard men have about homosexuality (which is also evident in "skin magazines"). Guys tend to shout "Yuck" at the mention of male homosexuality, but they think female homosexuality kind of "neat." Women have moderately negative personal reactions toward both kinds of homosexual acts.

In two of the other cases of large gender differences (items 6 and 10), the males have moderate opinions on issues females feel very strongly about. Women almost unanimously "very strongly agreed" that men should not take advantage of a woman who is naive and gullible, and that men should not assume that a sexily dressed woman wants to have sex.

The other large difference (item 7) indicates women understand better than

men that heterosexual, not homosexual, men do almost all of the child mo-
lesting in our society. Females, of course, are their usual victims.

Finally, I would also point out the difference in opinion on item 8. While
my female students basically rejected the "power" analysis of sexual relations,
men were more likely to see sex as a matter of "who controls whom."

Connections with Right-Wing Authoritarianism

You have probably noticed that this narrative has zipped right along for the
past few pages because we were not pausing at each milepost to see if High
RWAs differed from Lows. We did not pause because, for the most part, no
differences appeared, or else the ones that did were small. For example, High
RWA women were *less* likely than Lows to say they had ever dressed to turn
men on. They were also *more* likely to say "No" when they were agreeable
to sex, to show a guy they were not "easy." But while we might have predicted
both results, the correlations proved less than .20.

A few notable connections did turn up. Females who had been sexually
abused as children were more likely to end up as Lows than Highs. I have
attributed this result to the effect of personally experiencing extremely untrustworthy "authorities" (*EOF*, p. 103). Lows said they masturbated somewhat more than Highs said they did. Highs were more likely to find both
female and male homosexuality disgusting, and to think that homosexual men
were more likely to molest children than heterosexual men were (r's of .37,
.46, and .40, respectively). The *mean* score of the High RWA males on the
item about male homosexuality being disgusting equaled 8.83, (where the
maximum possible is 9.00).

But High RWA nonvirgins were as likely to practice birth control, and to
use condoms, as were Low RWA nonvirgins. High RWA women were as
likely as Low women to have been sexually harassed and sexually assaulted
as adults. Low RWA men were as likely as High RWA men to do the assaulting. Sexually active Highs were as likely to fantasize about "old flames" during intercourse as Lows were, and as likely to cheat on a committed relationship.

So like our earlier analysis of virginity, age of first intercourse, number of
acts of copulation, and number of partners, whatever differences may have
once existed between nonauthoritarian and authoritarian students have
largely disappeared.

Let me pause over that for a moment to make two observations. First, Highs
used to condemn premarital sex out of hand and used to think sex outside
marriage a great sin. They disagreed for years with the RWA Scale item,
"There is nothing wrong with premarital sex." But now they usually agree

with it, especially the female Highs. I am sure they were taught differently in home and church, but the sexual revolution has spread among them too.

It would be nice if this "slipping" led authoritarians to become more tolerant of others, to drink a little longer from the cup of human kindness and understanding. But Highs still feel they are morally superior to almost everyone else. How is this done? What's the trick to becoming "immoral" and still thinking yourself "very moral"?

I think we can find the answers in Chapters 4 and 5. Highs have a proven capacity to compartmentalize their thinking, to believe contradictory things, to adopt double standards, to shift their principles to justify what they want, and to avoid unpleasant insights into themselves. I suspect all of us tailor-fit the cloak of righteousness to our own behavior, and Highs can be at least as good at that as anyone else.

As my second point about the "sameness" of Lows and Highs in much of these data, I note that Low RWA males acted as badly as other males. They proved as likely to attack and manipulate women, to cheat, to think men are being "bad-mouthed" by the media today, and to think a sexily dressed woman is inviting intercourse. In other contexts, Low males (like Low females) have shown greater fairness, integrity, and sympathy than others have. But when it comes to sex, the data indicate that Low RWA men often do not think with their brains.[9]

Summary

This chapter presented the results of eleven Secret Surveys I conducted on the sexual behavior of my own introductory psychology students from 1984 to 1995. These studies were blessed by a very high level of participants' participation and apparent willingness to reveal very private matters.

We first saw evidence that male students have not become more sexually active over these years but that female students have. In fact, they are as sexually experienced as males now, if not more so, among both Low *and* High RWAs. The age of first intercourse has dropped over time, and the number of acts of intercourse has risen, especially among the women. But the number of sexual partners has remained rather stable and small. Most of the sex that is happening in this population seemingly happens within long-term relationships. Many students are still virgins.

Students usually practiced birth control all of the time, and used condoms somewhat often to prevent sexually transmitted diseases. To the surprise of no one, they find sex enjoyable, but they also have some anxieties and dislikes about it. Females and males tended to have different lists in that regard. Most women said they sometimes dressed to make men see them as sexual objects. But men were just as likely to dress sexily. Some women revealed they have said "No" to a man's proposition for sexual intercourse, when they intended to agree, just so they would not appear "easy." So also did some men.

Most men masturbated, about twice a week. Most women did not; those who did, did so about once a week. About a third of the sexually active students admitted that they sometimes fantasize about making love with person X while they were doing so with person Y. A slightly smaller percentage admitted to having had sex with someone else while committed to person Y. Those who have had "many" sexual partners proved most likely to cheat on a lover.

Students described their sexual fantasies. Women were more likely to imagine themselves with their boyfriends and get satisfaction from being desired and held. Males did not often think about their girlfriends, and more often enjoyed fantasizing about sex itself and multiple partners.

Most of my male students revealed they had at least once tried to have sexual contact with a woman (though not necessarily intercourse) through manipulation or force. Nearly all the women said they had been sexually harassed, many of them had been manipulated into having unwanted intercourse, a lot had had to fight off a rapist, and about one in eight had been raped. A similar number were sexually abused as children.

As you would predict, males and females have different attitudes toward sexual matters in many respects.

— 8 —
Dogmatism

The social sciences made two massive attempts to understand "authoritarianism" from the 1940s into the 1970s. The first effort, ignited by the "Berkeley researchers," came to be based largely on the California F Scale. The second effort was set off by Milton Rokeach's *The Open and Closed Mind* (1960) and built on his Dogmatism (D) Scale.

How massive were these undertakings? By 1974, David Hanson could list 533 doctoral dissertations on these subjects—a considerable output at that time. Unfortunately, the F Scale and its underlying conceptualizations had so many defects—touched upon at the end of Chapter 1—that ultimately the first effort became ensnared in a tangle of methodological knots and inconsistent findings (*RWA*, pp. 18–80). And if you scan through the *Psychological Abstracts* for the 1980s and 1990s, you will find that the second effort has also been largely abandoned. Whatever happened to dogmatism?

Milton Rokeach's Theory of Dogmatism

In a sense, Rokeach's theory had its origins in a penetrating criticism of *The Authoritarian Personality* by Shils (1954). The Berkeley researchers, Shils observed, seemed to believe that people who scored low on the F Scale would be "complete democrats." Presumably, democrats *would* score low on a valid measure of prefascist personality. However, so too would Communists, who also strongly opposed fascism. But Communists submitted to their own authorities and were not "complete democrats" by any stretch of the imagination. So Shils proposed that an authoritarian also anchors the left end of the political spectrum, counterbalancing the one on the right. Thus started the quest to find the "authoritarian on the left," a beleaguered crusade we shall join for these next two chapters.

Rokeach (1960, p. 11) used *The Authoritarian Personality* as a major point of departure, but he took Shils's criticism one step further. "If our interest is in the scientific study of authoritarianism, we should proceed from right authoritarianism not to a re-focus on left authoritarianism but to the general properties held in common by all forms of authoritarianism" (p. 14). Thus Rokeach set out to study "general authoritarianism," unassociated with any particular ideology, by examining the *structure* of a person's ideas, the belief system, independent of its content.

BELIEF SYSTEMS

Rokeach's own belief system provided that belief systems could be described in terms of three major "dimensions": (I) What a person believes and does not believe; (II) How central or peripheral each belief is; and (III) How broad the time perspective of the beliefs is.

This simple model quickly became more complicated. A dimension had "properties." With regard to the first dimension, for example, Rokeach held that people vary in the degree to which their beliefs and disbeliefs are (A) isolated, (B) differentiated, and (C) comprehensive. These properties in turn could have several "aspects." Isolation (I-A above) could appear (1) in the existence of logically contradictory beliefs; (2) in the accentuation of differences and minimization of similarities; (3) in the perception of irrelevance where relevance seems obvious; and (4) in the denial of contradiction.

The resulting model, in all its complexity, cannot be said to have been guided by a particular theory in psychology (as the Berkeley model was by psychoanalytic theory), or developed from mindless, grind-'em-out item-testing experiments (the way my model of right-wing authoritarianism was inferred). Instead, it mainly flowed from Rokeach's own thinking about ideologies. To be sure, that thinking was influenced by Kurt Lewin (Rokeach, 1960, p. 29). And Rokeach paid attention to the results of his item-development studies. For example, a spread of items tapping "Paranoid Outlook on Life" was dropped from the final version of the Dogmatism Scale because it did not cut the psychometric mustard (pp. 76–77). But the theory of the "open and closed mind" came essentially from the open mind of one person, as did the instrument for measuring it.

THE DOGMATISM SCALE

Representing the Theory.   Unfortunately, the forty-item scale Rokeach settled on to measure his theory seriously underrepresented most of that theory. The "Belief-Disbelief" dimension was represented by only four items, as was the "Time Perspective" axis. So what did the other thirty-two items do? They tapped the "Central-Peripheral" dimension. Thus from the start, the scale gave short shrift to most of the construct Rokeach *described,* and would hence lack construct validity.

Unidirectional Wording.   Rokeach began writing dogmatism items in 1951, under the influence of Adorno et al. (1950). Indeed, the instructions for the Dogmatism Scale, along with a strange six-point response format that had no "neutral," were taken straight from *The Authoritarian Personality.* Regrettably, he also tested only protrait items, despite well-known warnings about response sets from Lorge (1937), Cronbach (1946), and even Likert (1932). By the time lightning struck the F Scale in the form of Hyman and Sheatsley's (1954) devastating critique of the Berkeley methodology, Rokeach had already produced the final version of the Dogmatism Scale. All of its items were worded in the protrait direction. Thus no one would look as "closed-minded" as someone who agreed with everything, and no one would look as "open-minded" as someone who disagreed with everything. "What is wrong with this picture?"

As far as I know, Rokeach never concluded he had made a mistake.[1] In 1963 he responded to an accumulation of "reversal studies" that showed people often agreed *both* with protrait authoritarian items and with contrait versions of the same idea.[2] He offered three explanations of these findings. Maybe it was due to response bias. But it *could* be that subjects consciously lied sometimes. Or it *could* be that some people, through compartmentalized thinking, actually believed both of the contradictory ideas.

One will have some difficulty testing the second explanation, but as you know from Chapter 4, evidence now supports the third—at least among High RWAs. But as we also saw, in Chapter 2, the first explanation has been directly confirmed. A whole lot of yea-saying and naysaying can go on when people answer scales—and aren't you sick of hearing about it by now?

Psychometric Properties of the Dogmatism Scale.   Rokeach chose the D Scale from eighty-seven statements he wrote to tap the many elements of his model. The final version (which we saw shortchanged almost all of the model) contains "quite a strange collection of items that cover a lot of territory and appear on the surface to be unrelated to each other" (Rokeach, 1960, p. 90). For example:

The United States and Russia have just about nothing in common.

Man on his own is a helpless and miserable creature.

While I don't like to admit this even to myself, my secret ambition is to become a great man, like Einstein, or Beethoven, or Shakespeare.

Unfortunately, the items seemed largely unrelated to each other because they *were*.[3] Mean interitem correlations on the test averaged about .10, less even than the .13 that typically popped up on the F Scale. Response sets could easily produce most of that .10.[4]

Let us suppose the *content-based* level of interitem correlation among the forty Dogmatism items actually averages about .05. That would produce a "true" (content-based) alpha reliability of about .67, or a signal-to-noise ratio of 2:1. This slight internal consistency then gets undercut by the error-producing response sets. We can therefore predict right off the bat, before any of those hundreds of dissertation projects was approved, that *the D Scale is going to have a very hard time measuring anything reliably.* With so much noise in the data, relationships—apart from those created by good old response sets—were likely to be small and fly-by-night. In a nutshell, that is what happened to dogmatism.

VALIDITY OF THE DOGMATISM SCALE AS A MEASURE OF NONIDEOLOGICAL AUTHORITARIANISM

The inconsistency appeared in Rokeach's own "validating" studies. For example, Catholics at Michigan State scored significantly higher on the D Scale than Protestants or nonbelievers, but not so in two New York City colleges, where no group scored higher than the other (Rokeach, 1960, pp. 109–115). Rokeach also found that people selected by students in his graduate seminar for being very open-minded, or very closed-minded, scored quite differently on the D Scale. But people selected by professors did *not* (pp. 102–108). (We shall close our minds to the interpretation that becoming a prof makes one an insensitive clod.)

Much more troubling, Rokeach's own experiments raised large doubts that he had succeeded in his primary goal of measuring belief systems independent of ideology. He had developed another forty-item test that measured social opinions, the Opinionation Scale. Half of the items tapped contemporary left-wing ideas (for instance, "It's just plain stupid to say it was Franklin Roosevelt who got us into the war"), while the other half tapped right-wing sentiment ("It's simply incredible that anyone should believe socialized medicine will actually solve our health problems"). Rokeach expected that ardent left-wingers would score just as high on the D Scale as ardent right-wingers. But they did not; D Scale scores almost always correlated better with right-wing Opinionation scores (p. 124).

More telling yet, Dogmatism correlated higher still with the *total* Opinionation scores (how many times someone agreed with both left-wing and right-wing statements, or disagreed with both). (Déjà vu, anyone, from Chapters 2, 4, and 6?) This fact shows how much response sets were likely trumping item content.

Similarly, the strongest D Scale correlations Rokeach found (about .65; p. 121) appeared with the F Scale. This finding and the Opinionation data led Rokeach to theorize that right-wingers might turn out to be more dogmatic than left-wingers after all (pp. 126–129). His conclusion may or may not be true; stay tuned to this station. But one can offer a much simpler reason why the unidirectionally worded D Scale should correlate so nicely with the unidirectionally worded F Scale. Furthermore, the conclusion about which extreme on the political scene marches to the more dogmatic drum was contradicted by data Rokeach himself collected in England from 135 students representing the spectrum from Communists to Conservatives. The former scored a little *higher* than the latter; but none of the differences among the five parties represented in the sample attained statistical significance (p. 114).

I think that if you read *The Open and Closed Mind* with an open and critical mind, seeking a reasonably clean line of D Scale evidence supporting the basic premise of the work, you cannot find it. Instead, *in*consistency rules, as we would expect given the basic weakness of the instrument upon which all the research depended. With such an unpromising beginning, set against the background of disillusionment in the 1960s with the identically flawed F Scale, one can wonder how the D Scale became such a heavily used psychological test.

VACCHIANO, STRAUSS, AND HOCHMAN'S (1969) REVIEW
One reason researchers continued to use the Dogmatism Scale may have been the impression that, despite all the odds against it, the test magically "worked." That is, despite its massive shortcomings in construct validity and construction, it produced relationships with relevant or interesting variables. "It correlates with things, so it must be valid after all!" One review in particular fostered this impression, arguably the most important critique ever made of the Dogmatism Scale's literature: Vacchiano, Strauss, and Hochman's 1969 paper in the *Psychological Bulletin*.

The first thing the review focused on, appropriately, was the D Scale's validity as a measure of generalized authoritarianism free of ideological connections. It then went on to other topics such as perceptual processes and rigidity in problem solving. I shall only cover the first topic here, since the others have less relevance. (But the evidence on nearly all of the rest is "just as convincing.")

Plant, 1960.   Vacchiano Strauss, and Hochman stated first that a study by Plant (1960) "substantiated Rokeach's contention that the Dogmatism Scale is a better measure of general authoritarianism than the F Scale" (p. 261; all quotes from the review are taken from this page). Plant gave the Berkeley Fascism and Ethnocentrism Scales, along with the D Scale (so, the D, E, and

F Scales) to 2,350 first-year students at San Jose State College. He did not present any reliability data on these tests; indeed, the entire report takes up but one page. But he did find, as Rokeach had found in English samples, that the F Scale correlated a little higher with Ethnocentrism (about .68) than the D Scale did (about .59). This result supposedly showed that the D Scale was a better measure of general authoritarianism.

First of all, notice that the argument here amounts to "Less is better." The D Scale allegedly measures general authoritarianism better because it does not correlate as well with ethnocentrism as the F Scale does. But that does not show the D Scale measures anything better. Second, the D Scale may have done a little poorer job simply because it is a more disjointed, psychometrically weaker instrument ("Worse is better"?). Third, the F Scale was built from the ground up to correlate with the Ethnocentrism Scale. Items that did not correlate with prejudice were dropped from the F Scale item pool. If the Dogmatism Scale can do almost as well, without sending its potential statements through such a sieve, it could be argued that Plant's data indicate that the domain of the D Scale is really *more* related to ethnocentrism than "fascist authoritarianism" is. Fourth, the *strongest* correlations in the study existed between the F and D Scales, about .72, which nearly equals the usual level of reliability of the two tests. So the D Scale can hardly be measuring something substantially different from the F Scale. And finally, since the Ethnocentrism Scale also consists entirely of protrait items, we have a pretty good idea of what mostly bound these *three* scales together. We do not know what the relationship among these constructs would be if response sets were controlled, except that they would be much, much lower (Campbell, Siegman, and Rees, 1967; *RWA*, pp. 26–35).

Hanson, 1968.   The Vacchiano, Strauss, and Hochman review next cited a study by Hanson (1968), which they said demonstrated that the D Scale "taps general authoritarianism, whereas the F Scale taps only right authoritarianism." Hanson's study was his master's thesis, which was certainly more ambitious than mine. He administered a booklet to 301 introductory sociology and public affairs students at Syracuse University. The booklet contained the forty Dogmatism items interspersed with eighty items from a revision of Stern's Stereopathy-Acquiescence Scales (Stern, Stein, and Bloom, 1956). These scales have both "authoritarianism items" (such as "There would be no juvenile delinquents if parents would just insist on strict obedience from their children") and "reversals" ("Most censorship of books or movies is a violation of free speech and should be abolished"). Half of these eighty items were categorically worded (that is, "*no* juvenile delinquents"), while more qualified wording appeared in the others ("*most* censorship").

Hanson envisioned nine "Types" of respondents. For example, someone who *rejected both* kinds of authoritarianism items (categorical and qualified) and *both* kinds of reversals—a real "naysayer"—was labeled "Rational." (No, I do not know why.) Someone who rejected both kinds of authoritarianism items and the categorical reversals, but agreed with the qualified reversals was termed a "Qualified Nonauthoritarian." A third type, rejecting both kinds of authoritarianism items but accepting both kinds of reversals was called a "Nonauthoritarian." Two similar "Authoritarians" and a variety of "Qualifieds" and "Irrationals" were also anticipated.

Hanson, in a move that may remind many of us of our own master's theses, formulated eight hypotheses (some of them having five or six separate predictions) about the level of dogmatism he would find among the various Types. Whereupon Nature cruelly struck. Half of his subjects could not be classified as being *any* of the Types, and of the 151 who could be classified, most (59) were Rationals (who rejected everything). Among the rest, combined nonauthoritarians heavily outnumbered combined authoritarians, 64 to 9. These two groups did not significantly differ in Dogmatism scores.

If you consider the Stereopathy-Acquiescence items as a measure of "rightist" authoritarianism, and overlook the difficulty in finding a significant difference with only 9 "authoritarians" from an original sample of 301, this study indicates that rightist authoritarianism is unconnected with dogmatism. But Hanson also found that, *over the whole sample,* dogmatism correlated higher with authoritarianism items than with nonauthoritarianism items. He observed, "It would appear then that, to some extent at least, there is an inherent relationship between authoritarianism of the right and dogmatism" (p. 94). Vacchiano, Strauss, and Hochman told their readers of only the first finding and never mentioned the way the $N = 9$ loaded the dice in favor of the null hypothesis of no relationship.

Finally, I do not know why the *Psychological Bulletin* reviewers implied that Hanson's study pitted the D and F Scales. Only seven of the eighty Stereopathy-Acquiescence items came from the F Scale.

Kerlinger and Rokeach's (1966) Factor Analysis.   The reviewers next cited a factor analysis of the F and D Scales' statements performed by Kerlinger and Rokeach (1966) as further evidence that the D Scale measures "general authoritarianism." In an admirable attempt to broaden the usual sample, Kerlinger and Rokeach gave the two tests to over 1,200 students in Louisiana, Michigan, and New York. These responses were subjected to a (confirmatory, hypothesis-testing) principal axes solution. The number of factors extracted was *not* reported, but the ten most powerful ones were retained and subjected to Equamax orthogonal rotation, and then oblique Promax rotation. Items with loadings of at least .25 on a factor were examined to judge the nature of the factor.

It is worth noting that, even with *ten* factors and a pretty generous inclusion criterion of .25, nearly half the items on each of the scales failed to "load significantly" on *anything*. That, like the low levels of interitem correlation, indicates just how very disjointed and rambling ("multifaceted") both tests are.

When Kerlinger and Rokeach examined their ten first-order factors, five of them were basically loaded with D Scale items, and three were basically loaded with F Scale items. The correlations among the ten obliquely rotated factors were then themselves factor analyzed, and the three resulting *second*-order factors were graphically rotated into an orthogonal structure. Four of the five first-order "D Factors" had their highest loadings on the first second-order factor, while the three first-order "F Factors" had their highest loadings on either the second or the third second-order factors. (Isn't this fun?) Thus the two scales seemed to have independent underlying factor structures—despite their high correlation with each other.

As I indicated in Chapter 2, however, factor analysis is much less the deus ex machina than some researchers suppose. Investigators have so many decisions to make at various stages of the process that the results can often be swished one way or the other, as this study illustrates. One of the biggest ambiguities involves the "number of factors retained problem." Why did Kerlinger and Rokeach retain *ten* of however many factors they initially extracted?

They said that initially they used "Humphrey's Rule" (Fructer, 1954, pp. 79–80) to determine how many factors should be retained. Doing so gave them eight factors. But they could get only *one* second-order factor out of these eight. (Which meant the two tests did *not* have different underlying factor structures.) So they increased the number of factors retained to ten, which gave them the results described above. But to my mind, you are manufacturing "findings" at this point, not discovering them. What would you get with nine first-order factors, or eleven, or fifteen? Was ten the number that most gave the authors what they hypothesized would be there?

I would not be surprised if some factor analysis showed that the F and D Scale items did, after sufficient mashing in a computer, load on different factors. The tests appear different in many ways. (For one thing, the D Scale statements strike me as being less zany overall than the F Scale items.) But that would still not prove that the D Scale measures "a generalized authoritarianism independent of a particular ideological content." It would just show it measures something forcibly different. And Kerlinger and Rokeach's factor analysis, I submit, makes a very weak case for even that.

Barker's (1963) Studies.   Next Vacchiano, Strauss, and Hochman stated that "Barker (1963) also demonstrated that dogmatism was independent of political ideology but was related to a sense of commitment to a particular position on the political spectrum."

Barker reported two studies. The first had 160 *graduate* students in the New York City area—most of them in *psychology* or education—answer a battery of surveys. Included were the D Scale, a version of the F Scale, and the Berkeley Political-Economic Conservatism (PEC) Scale (a fourteen-item survey consisting of nine "liberal" items and five "conservative" ones).

Neither the reliability of these tests, nor the correlations among them were presented. Instead the sample was divided into Low and High Dogmatics at the mean. Each of these 80-person splits was further subdivided by PEC scores into three groups: 30 "leftists" (*below the mean* on PEC), 20 "middle of the roaders" (*"within* the semi-interquartile range on PEC"), and 30 "rightists" (above the PEC mean).[5]

Barker then compared the scores of these six subgroups on other tests in the battery. For example, Dogmatic Leftists did not score significantly higher on measures of "intolerance of ambiguity," "anti-intraception," and "censorship" than did Dogmatic Middlers or Dogmatic Rightists. This was interpreted as evidence that dogmatism was independent of political ideology. This interpretation may be true, but it would be more convincing if (1) we knew the measures of these traits were reliable and valid (it is easy to find "no differences" with poor tests); (2) we knew what role the subject categorization had played in this finding; and (3) these data had come from a less test-sophisticated sample.

Barker's second study, however, got to the core of the matter. He administered the D Scale (along with other measures) to nearly all of the members of "leftist" and "rightist" groups at Ohio State University and to some unaffiliated students. The rightists scored *significantly higher* in Dogmatism than both the unorganized students and the leftists. Somehow the 1969 *Psychological Bulletin* review ignored this finding and said, "Barker (1963) also demonstrated that dogmatism was independent of a particular ideological content."

Direnzo's (1967) Study of Italian Lawmakers.   Finally, the *Psychological Bulletin* reviewers cited an interesting study of Italian legislators by DiRenzo (1967), saying it supported "the Barker finding" about dogmatism and a sense of commitment "in that active politicians were found to be generally more dogmatic than nonactive members of their own party."

DiRenzo administered ten of the D Scale items during confidential interviews with 129 of the 596 members of the Italian Chamber of Deputies.[6] He interviewed nearly all the members of the minor parties, and 20% of the major parties (for example, Christian Democrats, Socialists, Communists). He also had 25 freshmen at the University of Rome each ask the same questions of 20 people of their choice, according to an (unspecified) quota sampling procedure. The politicians *did* score much higher overall on whatever the ten items measure. But the two sets of data were collected in very different ways.

Are you per chance wondering how the different caucuses scored? Good question, absolutely central to the issue, and one which Vacchiano, Strauss, and Hochman somehow decided not to report. The Communists and the Socialists had, by far, the lowest scores. The right-wing Monarchists and the Neo-Fascists landed at the top of the distribution ($F = 4.37$; $p < .01$). This result also contradicts the review's conclusion that the D Scale measures general authoritarianism independent of ideology. But *Psychology Bulletin* readers would never have known it.

The five studies we have covered in these past few pages, which Vacchiano, Strauss, and Hochman covered in two paragraphs, address the basic premise underlying the Dogmatism Scale. *None* of them supports that premise, and *most* flatly contradict it, suggesting instead a D Scale–"rightist" link. So also do most of the other studies that the reviewers considered under different headings or that have appeared since: Bailes and Guller (1970), Direnzo (1968, 1971, 1986), Granberg and Corrigan (1972), Karabenick and Wilson (1969), Knutson (1974), McCarthy and Johnson (1962), Schwendiman, Larsen, and Cope (1970), Smithers and Lobley (1978), Thompson and Michel (1972).[7]

Conclusion.   Nearly all of the studies bearing on the matter found either *no* D Scale relationship with the variables of interest or some kind of connection with right-wing sentiment. That, we might recall, is what Rokeach (1960) himself found at the very beginning.

Conservatives may prove more dogmatic than liberals eventually, but the occasional D Scale findings we have seen do not prove this. It could instead merely be that conservatives tend to yea-say more than most people do, or that liberals tend to naysay. Indeed, you may recall the evidence from Chapter 2 that right-wing authoritarians *do* tend to yea-say more.

In conclusion, you may also recall that it was apparent from the beginning that the Dogmatism Scale lacked construct validity. *If* the complicated model of "general authoritarianism" that Rokeach proposed did have merit, the scale he developed to measure it failed its assignment. Furthermore, the interitem correlations were much too low to be measuring *any* important "belief system." Yet many researchers invested their time and energy in the Dogmatism Scale, quite possibly encouraged by a glowing review in a prestigious journal, believing that the scale "worked." Well, did it? Did it turn out to be "valid after all"? Will other scales wandering down the same road today do any better in the long run?

An Alternate Conceptualization of Dogmatism

Unlike Rokeach, I find it hard to merge authoritarianism and dogmatism. For me the concepts cover different domains that may overlap somewhat but are still worth distinguishing.

The big, hernia-inducing dictionaries give a rather common definition of dogmatism. *Webster's Unabridged Third International Dictionary,* for example, states as its first meaning: "A positiveness in assertion in matters of opinion; a statement of a view or belief as if it were an established fact." The 1989 edition of the *Oxford English Dictionary* begins in similar fashion: "Positive assertion of dogma or opinion; dogmatizing; positiveness in assertion of opinion."

The core element here, I submit, is unjustified certainty. All of us who have ever been shown to be wrong when we were certain we were right—marriage helps you keep track of these—were therefore "dogmatic" in this dictionary sense, though quite understandably, I am sure. But I think that *psychologically,* dogmatism also means you will seldom if ever accept that you *are* wrong.

Dogmatism is relatively unchangeable, unjustified certainty. It is conviction beyond the reach of evidence to the contrary. It is, as Rokeach said, closed-mindedness.

ELABORATIONS ON THE DEFINITION

As usual, we are dealing with *relative,* not absolute, differences in behavior. A person need not be totally unyielding to be dogmatic compared with others. Furthermore, a lot depends on the comparison group. Pope John XXIII, who called the Second Vatican Council in 1962, was arguably the least dogmatic pontiff in hundreds of years. But he still might come across as rather fixed in his ways if he is in heaven now, shooting the breeze with Socrates.

When I say "unchangeable," I mean sticking to your beliefs no matter what. If I am 100% certain that there is no such place as heaven, and that Socrates was *not* a man, and then I die and (in passing) glimpse Socrates in heaven corrupting the youth with his questions, and I *still* refuse to believe, that is "unchangeable."

You do not run into many people whose entire span of beliefs seem unchangeable. Usually we are firmer about some "central" things than the rest. You could get me to change my introductory lectures on intelligence pretty easily—although I am getting tired of reworking them. But you would have trouble getting me to believe intelligence has had little to do with our ascen-dance as a species.

This brings us to "unjustified." We often do not know what is true and false, and occasionally "crackpot" ideas turn out to be right. (What seems sillier, on the face of it, than the notion that the sun does not go around the earth?) Also, one person's "dogmatism" can be sensible resistance to malarkey in another person's mind. Suppose a study disconfirmed one of your most cherished beliefs. If you do not drop your beliefs immediately, are you dog-matic? I think not. But if a literature of experiments accumulates, testing the proposition from many perspectives and in many ways, and they all say, "You are *wrong*" and still you do not budge, then you are likely dogmatic.

We often cannot say whether other people's certainty is justified. But we can measure how open they are to the possibility they might be wrong. And we can see how they react to disconfirming evidence.

Finally, what is "certainty"? In probabilistic terms, it means being confident beyond the .0000001 level. Most people, blissfully lacking the training that causes scientists to think in such terms, are "certain" of their beliefs when they stop examining them, when they take them as "givens," when they reject new ideas out of hand because such do not fit with the old. While we are certainly more certain of certain certainties than we are of others, some people seem a lot surer of a lot more than others do. When one cannot experience, with the King of Siam, "times I almost think I am not sure of what I absolutely know," no matter what the contradictory evidence, we are dealing with dog-matism.

BEING NONDOGMATIC

People can be, correspondingly, *non*dogmatic in several ways. You can believe in little or nothing, even to the point of refusing to take slight stands. You can have a great many opinions but little certainly, changing with the wind. You can have many opinions about which you feel certain and still be non-dogmatic if you are receptive to disconfirming evidence. You could, *in prin-ciple,* hold your opinions with unassailable certainty and not be dogmatic *if* your opinions are justified. Many people seem to opt for this position. How many folks have you met who thought their opinions were unjustified? But people believe in too many contradictory things for all to be right, their cer-tainty notwithstanding. So that can be a pretty slippery slope on which to take your firm stands. (I am not saying there is no truth or falseness; rather, we have a spotted record at telling the difference. Is being certain an indicator of being right?)

DOGMATISM AND AUTHORITARIANISM

Dogmatism, defined as relatively unchangeable, unjustified certainty, *can* fol-low from submission to an authority. The authority may be "established" (the president, the Politburo, the pope), or "revolutionary" (Karl Marx or Mao Tse-tsung for some North American Communists I have known), "intellectual" (Freud or Skinner for some psychologists I have known), and maybe nonintellectual authorities as well (are there Yogi Berra dogmatists?). But some people can also develop their opinions from their own experiences in life, without regard to any outside authority, and be dogmatic. So you do not have to be authoritarian to be dogmatic. I also suspect some right-wing authoritarians are not dogmatic at all, and hence able to change. Being one of these does not automatically imply being the other.

However, I would expect High RWAs to be generally more dogmatic than Lows, because of the different ways "Hugh" and "Lou" (see Chapter 3) have formed their ideas. Hugh did not develop as many ideas on his own as Lou did; instead, he got them from "the authorities in his neighborhood." He believes what he has been told to believe, on the strength of authority. Is the authority likely to be wrong, in Hugh's mind? I don't think so. So will he likely be sure that what he believes is correct, the rock of the ages, the absolute truth, compared with Lou? Yep. In fact, I think that if you have not figured things out much for yourself, you are almost forced to become dogmatic, because otherwise you are helpless against opposing opinions with evidence on their side.

It probably goes without saying that we can be dogmatic about many different kinds of opinions: religious (the original connotation of *dogma*tism), societal, interpersonal, (dare I say it?) scientific, how we do our jobs, how we raise our children. But I think the dogmatism most worth studying, and potentially the most harmful, occurs in the areas of an individual's life that are seen as the most crucial and important. I hope to focus on those.

It probably should *not* go without saying that I am treating dogmatism as a personality variable. "Dogmatic people" generally holds their opinions with unchangeable, unjustified certainty, compared with others. That does not mean all of their opinions are held thus; it does not mean they will never change their minds; it does not mean situational pressures cannot crumple their dogmatic shell. It does not mean they will prove "inflexible" in everything they do. I should also add that ultimately people's certainty, like their opinions themselves, are private acts to which we have no direct access. As usual, we have to rely on such things as self-reports. Toward which end, you see, I have developed this scale . . .

THE DEVELOPMENT OF THE DOG SCALE

I began writing items to measure this conceptualization of dogmatism in the fall of 1992. To avoid asking, over and over again, "How unassailably certain are you that your opinions are correct?" I also tried to tap some things that seemed to be corollaries to believing you have Truth pinned to the mat. For example, do all honest, clear-thinking people agree with you? Is doubt destructive, and will open-mindedness only lead you astray? Do you see everything with clarity, and does everything "fit into place"? Could your opinions possible change in the future? And most important, could anything change your mind?

I have named the test that measures these sentiments the Doggone Old Gnu Scale for measuring dogmatism (the "DOG" Scale, however you abbreviate it). (Why should subatomic physicists have all the fun?)

The October 1992 Study: Like the Religious Fundamentalism measure, the DOG Scale came together almost effortlessly. (If I sound smug, I get my comeuppance in the next chapter.) A hired graduate student administered a batch of twelve protrait and twelve contrait items I had composed to 160 of my introductory psychology students at the end of October 1992. A resulting fourteen-item balanced scale had a mean interitem correlation of .22 and an alpha of .79.

A revised twenty-four-item pool, administered to 144 other students from my classes the next week under the same disguise, produced a twenty-item scale with mean interitem correlation of .31 and an alpha of .90. It was just like falling off a log. Subsequent tinkering in two further studies using 197 and 212 students from other classes produced the DOG Scale shown in Exhibit 8.1, which had the same stout psychometric properties as that in the first twenty-item scale.

Exhibit 8.1   The DOG Scale

   X. I may be wrong about some of the little things in life, but I am quite certain I am right about all the BIG issues.

   Y. Someday I will probably think that many of my present ideas were wrong.

   1. Anyone who is honestly and truly seeking the truth will end up believing what I believe.

   2. There are so many things we have not discovered yet, nobody should be absolutely certain his beliefs are rights.*

   3. The things I believe in are so completely true, I could never doubt them.

   4. I have never discovered a system of beliefs that explains everything to my satisfaction.*

   5. It is best to be open to all possibilities, and ready to reevaluate all your beliefs.*

   6. My opinions are right, and will stand the test of time.

   7. Flexibility is a real virtue in thinking, since you may well be wrong.*

8. My opinions and beliefs fit together perfectly to make a crystal-clear "picture" of things.

9. There are no discoveries or facts that could possibly make me change my mind about the things that matter most in life.

10. I am a long way from reaching final conclusions about the central issues in life.*

11. The person who is absolutely certain she has the truth will probably never find it.*

12. I am absolutely certain that my ideas about the fundamental issues in life are correct.

13. The people who disagree with me may well turn out to be right.*

14. I am so sure I am right about the important things in life, there is no evidence that could convince me otherwise.

15. If you are "open-minded" about the most important things in life, you will probably reach the wrong conclusions.

16. Twenty years from now, some of my opinions about the important things in life will probably have changed.*

17. "Flexibility in thinking" is another name for being "wishy-washy."

18. No one knows all the essential truths about the central issues in life.*

19. Someday I will probably realize my present ideas about the BIG issues are wrong.*

20. People who disagree with me are just plain wrong, and often evil as well.

Note: The first two statements ("X" and "Y") are not scored. They give the respondent a little familiarity with the content to follow, but may be omitted. Items are answered on a −4 to +4 basis.

* Item is worded in the contrait direction; the dogmatic response is to disagree.

I hope you agree with me, as you examine the DOG items, that they do not refer to any particular field of thought or opinion. The statements apply to whatever someone takes to be the "important things" in life, the "central issues," and so on. Because of this focus on the "biggies," I do not propose that DOG scores will measure "rigidity" in smaller issues (such as the dispute over "You say 'Tomato,' and I say 'Tomato' "). But the DOG Scale was not hard-wired to make religious people, ardent socialists, environmentalists, or any group in particular look particularly dogmatic.

Nevertheless, in the four item development studies mentioned above, scores on the mock DOG scales correlated .50, .48, .52, and .49 with RWA scores.

INITIAL VALIDITY STUDIES

Does the DOG Scale measure what I mean by dogmatism? To test this, I slipped two measures of what seemed to me dogmatic behavior into the Secret Survey administered in January 1993.

Resistance to Changing Attitudes toward Homosexuals.   I had, in a recent lecture on prenatal development, explained to my classes the genetic and fetal androgenization theories of sexual orientation. I presented the evidence (Gorski et al., 1980; Dohler et al., 1984; Dodson, Shryne, and Gorksi, 1988; Allen and Gorski, 1992; Bailey and Pillard, 1991; Bailey, Pillard, and Agyei, 1993; Whitam, Diamond, and Martin, 1993; LeVay, 1991, 1993) connecting chromosome gender, gonadal gender, genital gender, and brain gender to genetic factors and the presence or absence of androgens during critical periods of embryonic development. I concluded that, according to the evidence, male homosexuality seemed at least partly determined by genetic and biochemical events in the womb over which the individual had no control. I further stated that for a male born with a brain "wired" to find other males sexually desirable, homosexuality would seem as automatic and "natural" as heterosexual attraction seemed for "straight" males. I said the explanation for lesbianism would probably turn out to be similar, but I knew of no human brain data on the topic yet.

My students had answered the Attitudes toward Homosexuals Scale (Exhibit 1.3) in September, as the first phase in this two-stage experiment. As they worked their way through the Secret Survey four months later—each in his or her chosen "safe place" for answering—they encountered the same twelve items again. I am sure many figured out I was looking to see if my recent lecture had had any effect on the class's attitude. I doubt any of them knew, however, that I was studying individual cases.

I had discretely encoded the Secret Surveys (see Chapter 2) with their fall survey numbers, and also whether the student had scored in the upper or lower quartile of the DOG Scale in October.[8] I also discretely indicated if the student had scored in the top quartile of the ATH Scale in September, expecting such a student to be the most challenged by the fetal androgenization findings.

Twenty-nine of these High ATH students also landed in the top quartile on the DOG Scale in October ("Dogmatic, Hostile toward Homosexuals"). Their initial ATH mean was 74.7 (scores can vary from 12 to 108, with 60 being neutral), and their mean after my fine lecture presenting the evidence for the fetal androgenization theory was 71.1, a nonsignificant drop of but 3.6 points.

Five other High ATH students had scored in the bottom quartile on the DOG Scale ("Nondogmatic, Hostile toward Homosexuals"—a small club). Their September mean ATH score had been 76.8, and on the Secret Survey their mean was 59.6, essentially neutral, a significant drop of 17.2 points.

So we have two groups, equally hostile toward homosexuals the previous fall. The members of the first scored high in dogmatism, and were unaffected by my lecture or any other "liberalizing" sources of information about homosexuals they might have encountered since September. But members of the second group scored low in dogmatism, and changed their attitudes when my lecture or other experiences during their first term at university came along.[9]

Experiments that ask students if the Experimenter has done an excellent job need to be held up to a light of Sirius brilliance and examined for social desirability effects. Maybe people sensitive to such pressures would know they should try to look flexible on the DOG Scale *and* tell the professor what a great job he had done. However, usually the High RWAs show more sensitivity to social desirability pressures, and they tended *not* to change in this experiment. Also, my students have been quite prepared to tell me to jump in the lake in the past on this issue, when answering in the superanonymous circumstances of the Secret Survey (*EOF,* pp. 226–228).

Now, I should acknowledge that what I am calling dogmatic attitudes toward homosexuals would be called "sensible resistance to malarkey" by others. Mysteriously, evidence that convinces me does not always convince others. And the shoe could easily be on the other foot. Some researchers believe that many psychological tests which I would pitch in the wastebasket have real value. To them, my resistance to the studies they find convincing must look like dogmatism. We lack consensus on many issues, do we not, and one person's "justified certainty" can easily look like dogged intransigence to another.

But I believe we eventually do figure out the truth, and our understanding of ourselves and our universe becomes more accurate every day. We can run experiments, and we *can* find out when we are wrong. People who believe homosexuals have chosen by free will to be sexually attracted to their own gender have, it seems to me, a lot of findings to explain away. If they cannot do so but still insist they are right, that smacks of dogmatism to me.

The "Ancient Scrolls" Experiment.   The study just described investigated the potential for change among people who thought homosexuals were disgusting, should be locked up, deserved to get AIDS, and so on. It amounted to a one-sided experiment in which only people who disliked homosexuals were put under the microscope; only High ATHs could look dogmatic. But in my second, 1993 Secret Survey experiment on the DOG Scale, I tested its ability to detect dogmatism among nonbelievers as well as believers in the divinity of Jesus.

I described my 1985 ancient scroll experiment in Chapter 6, where we found big differences in how much High and Low *RWAs* would change their beliefs if a major archaeological discovery disconfirmed their beliefs. In January 1993 I put the DOG Scale on the spot, when I placed either the Attis or Roman File proposition at the end of the Secret Survey.

Twenty-six of the students who got the "Attis: There Was No Jesus" version had scored in the top quartile on the DOG Scale and had answered a preliminary question about Jesus' divinity with either a $+3$ or a $+4$ ("Dogmatic Believers"). They indicated, after reading the ancient scrolls narrative, that a scientifically verified Attis discovery would lower their belief in Jesus 0.77 points on the -4 to $+4$ scale ($p > .10$). (Actually, only seven of the twenty-six changed; the rest stayed at $+4$.)

Seven other students who got the Attis version believed in Jesus' divinity just as strongly, but they had scored in the *bottom* quartile on the DOG scale ("Nondogmatic Believers"). Their scores dropped 2.71 points ($p < .05$), as six of the seven changed. So the DOG scores predicted fairly well who among the believers would prove relatively "unassailable" and who would change if facts strongly contradicted their beliefs.

Very few in the overall sample took extreme positions *against* Jesus' divinity (-4 or -3) before they got to the "Roman File: There Was a Jesus" narrative. Four such definite nonbelievers scored in the top quartile on the DOG scale ("Dogmatic Nonbelievers"), and they moved an average of 1.5 units toward greater belief in Jesus' divinity ($p > .20$). (Two of the four changed.) Six others were Nondogmatic Nonbelievers, and they moved 2.83 units toward greater belief ($p < .05$). (Five of the six shifted.) So the DOG Scale also did a fairly good job predicting who among the strong *non*believers would respond to evidence that went against their beliefs, and who would not.

To summarize this experiment, High DOG students on both sides of the issue typically said they would not be moved by strong evidence against their beliefs. Low DOG students on both sides usually said they *would*. The scale's predictions thus proved generally valid.[10]

THE FALL 1993 VALIDITY STUDIES

In September 1993 I administered a long booklet of materials to my students under the guise of the Psychometric Survey (*EOF*, p. 31). This booklet began with the RWA Scale, which was followed by the Religious Fundamentalism Scale described in Chapter 6. Next came a measure of *left*-wing authoritarianism, that I shall ask you to tuck away in the folds of your mind until Chapter 9. Then the students answered the DOG Scale. Three of my measures of authoritarian aggression followed (ATH, the Ethnocentrism Scale, and Posse-Radicals). Next appeared a new measure to be described below, which I call the Zealot Scale. Various demographic questions and the Religious Emphasis Scale finished the booklet.

Altogether 546 of the officially enrolled 600 students in my two sections answered this booklet. When the students had the unsurpassed thrill of taking their first hour exam in psychology a few weeks later, I invited these 546 to address envelopes home for a "parents' survey." Most (443) were happy to do so, and I ended up receiving completed booklets from at least one parent of 357 of them (340 mothers and 314 fathers). I shamelessly included nearly all the surveys given to the students, plus other things I was fiddling with, in the parents' long booklet, knowing from past and personal experience that moms and dads will do almost anything to help their gene carriers succeed at university.

The Zealot Scale.   In 1991 I began trying to measure how fired up people were about whatever they believed in most. How enthused were they about their beliefs, their causes? Were they consumed by them? Did they have a mission to make them dominant? Did disagreement anger them? Did they have the solution to all our problems? Did they proselytize? In short, were they zealots?

Exhibit 8.2   The Zealot Scale

Think of the *most important* "outlook" or way of understanding things you have in life. It may be a *religion*, a *philosophy*, a *social perspective*, a *scientific orientation*. What do you use, more than anything else, to make sense out of things, to understand "life"?

Then, when you have identified what your most basic outlook is, what your most basic way of understanding life is, please answer the questions below about it according to the following scale.

    0 = Not at all true of me

    1 = Slightly true of me

    2 = Mildly true of me

    3 = Moderately true of me

    4 = Decidedly true of me

    5 = Definitely true of me

    6 = Very definitely true of me

1. This outlook colors and shapes almost everything I experience in life. (3.04) [3.14]

2. I try to explain my outlook to others at every opportunity. (1.95) [1.50]

3. I am learning everything I can about this outlook. (2.85) [2.36]

4. I think every sensible person should agree with this outlook, once it has been explained. (1.50) [1.52]

5. I get excited just thinking about this outlook, and how right it is. (1.64) [1.56]

6. It is very important to me to support the leaders of this outlook. (1.97) [2.02]

7. Nothing else is as important in my life. (1.11) [1.23]

8. It angers me that certain people are trying to oppose this outlook. (1.44) [1.36]

9. No other outlook could be as true and valid. (1.17) [1.39]

10. It is my mission in life to see that this outlook becomes "No. 1" in our country. (0.88) [1.00]

11. This outlook is the solution to all of humanity's problems. (1.32) [1.60]

12. I am very committed to making this outlook the strongest influence in the world. (0.95) [1.10]

13. What is the nature of your most important outlook?

   0 = I don't have a basic, most important outlook. (102) [151]

   1 = A religious outlook. (77) [142]

   2 = A personal outlook all my own that I developed by myself. (215) [201]

   3 = A personal outlook that I developed with a few friends. (38) [38]

   4 = A *capitalist* social perspective; a capitalist theory of how society should operate. (16) [28]

   5 = A *socialist* social perspective; a socialist theory of how society should operate. (17) [27]

   6 = A scientific outlook. Science gives me my most basic understanding of things. (33) [30]

   7 = The feminist movement. (9) [0]

   8 = The environmental movement. (10) [12]

   9 = Some other "special cause" movement, such as "animal rights" or "right to die." (24) [21]

No response. (5) [4]

By the fall of 1993, I had a twelve-item scale assessing this zeal, Exhibit 8.2, which I included in the student and parent booklets just described. The thirteenth question asked the respondents to describe their particular outlook or cause. Notice the numerous possibilities. While being a zealot, like being dogmatic, originally had a religious connotation, I also wanted to find the zealots in the environmental movement, the feminist movement, science, capitalism or socialism, animal rights, whatever.

If you agree with me that zealots should, in general, be more dogmatic in their outlook than nonzealots, then the Zealot Scale can provide another validity test for the DOG Scale. A similar hypothesis that Religious Fundamentalists will also prove dogmatic was tested in this study.[11]

Results.   The psychometric properties of the RWA, Religious Fundamentalism, DOG, and Zealot Scales are given in Table 8.1. RWA and Fundamentalism banged out their usual reliability. You will note that both students and parents had low DOG scores overall, about 65 on a scale that could range from 20 to 180. Alpha for both was just under .90. Zealot means were also low, about 20 on a scale that could go from 0 to 72, with alphas just over .90. The means for the students and parents, respectively, are printed in Exhibit 8.2 after each item.

The four scales interlocked about as expected (Table 8.2). In particular, DOG scores correlated over .50 with RWA, nearly .60 with Fundamentalism, and about .45 with Zealot scores. So we have here a replication among parents of the previous student-based finding that right-wing authoritarians tend to be dogmatic. And in both samples, the DOG Scale predicted rather well who would hold fundamentalist religious views, and be zealots about *something.*[12]

Item Analyses.   To a certain extent none of this can surprise anyone, because the DOG Scale touches on some of the same sentiments covered by the Religious Fundamentalism and Zealot Scales. I mean, what is the difference between a DOG item that reads, "Anyone who is honestly and truly seeking the truth will end up believing what I believe," and a Fundamentalism item that says, "To lead the best, most meaningful life, one must belong to the one, true religion," and a Zealot item such as "No other outlook could be as true and valid"?

Table 8.1   Psychometric properties of tests used to assess DOG Scale validity

Scale	Sample	No. items	Scale mean	Scale variance	Mean Interitem	Alpha
RWA	Students	30	124.7	872	.20	.88
	Parents	30	146.1	1325	.23	.90
Religious	Students	20	69.6	827	.38	.93
Fundamentalism	Parents	20	80.0	1100	.40	.93
DOG	Students	20	60.2	400	.28	.88
	Parents	20	68.8	575	.30	.89
Zealot	Students	12	19.7	233	.50	.92
	Parents	12	19.7	222	.46	.91

Table 8.2   Intercorrelations among the tests used to assess DOG Scale validity

Scale	Sample	Religious Fundamentalism	DOG	Zealot
RWA	Students	.66	.52	.34
	Parents	.71	.53	.44
Religious Fundamentalism	Students		.57	.44
	Parents		.60	.55
DOG	Students			.43
	Parents			.52

However, these are the most direct "tautological" links I can find among the three measures. By and large, while they assess obviously related constructs, each scale goes off in its own direction, emphasizing different things. And *all* of the DOG items correlated significantly with Religious Fundamentalism and Zealot (and RWA) scores, in both samples.[13] So the DOG Scale connected solidly with the criterion measures of Religious Fundamentalism and Zealot scores because fundamentalists and zealots tended to be dogmatic in *all the ways* assessed by the DOG scale, not just the obvious content-sharing ways.[14]

A CLOSER LOOK AT PEOPLE WITH "CAUSES"

If you look at question 13 of Exhibit 8.2, you will find how often students (in parentheses) and parents (in brackets) said their "basic outlook" was religious, personal, and so on. Notice first that about 20% of each sample said they did *not* have a "basic, most important outlook." (I understand that better among the students than among the parents.) Second, you will see that the most common outlook was *personal,* developed by about 35% of the respondents by themselves, and by a few others with friends. Next came religion, more commonly important among parents than students. And after that it really falls off. If feminists and environmentalists were each their own species, needing others of their kind to reproduce, they would be endangered.

The only groups that produced much of a Zealot score were those who said their basic outlook was religious (means of 32.6 and 32.2 in the two samples), and the lonely nine student feminists (31.2).[15] You will apparently get mighty thin if you have to live off donations from zealous science enthusiasts (means about 19). Even people who have discovered their "own way" do not put on the dog about what they have figured out (means about 18).

As you would expect from Chapter 3, those who figured things out for themselves tended to be very *un*authoritarian. (Or to put it the other way,

High RWAs seldom said they had developed their own outlook.) "Own Out-looks" had the lowest mean RWA score among the students (115.7) except for those lonely feminists (108.0). "Own Outlooks" (141.6) proved less out-standing among the parents, but were only beaten to the bottom of the RWA ladder by the science enthusiasts (137.3) and the "socialists" (119.0).

By contrast, in both samples the religiously oriented scored highest not only on the Zealot Scale but also in authoritarianism (means of 152.7 and 168.2, respectively). As you would also surmise from Table 8.2, people who based their life outlook on religion also had the highest scores on the DOG Scale in both samples (means of 74.4 and 83.4).

Not many people in these samples said "capitalism" described their basic outlook in life, but they did catch your eye. They stood out among the students and parents on the high end of the RWA distribution (135.3 and 156.9, re-spectively), second only to the religious in both cases. The capitalist parents also scored highest *overall* on my three measures of authoritarian aggression: Ethnocentrism (first place), ATH (second place), and Posse-Radicals (second place). Among the students, the capitalists would have won the gold medal in all three tests if this had been the Authoritarian Hostility Olympics.[16]

You might accordingly infer that if capitalists looked really bad on these measures, socialists must have looked really good. This proved true among the parents, whose socialists scored lowest in RWA, fifth in DOG, fifth in Zealot, and lowest in Ethnocentrism, ATH, and Posse. But among the stu-dents, socialists ranked third in RWA, DOG, and Zealot scores, second in Ethnocentrism, fourth in ATH, and third in Posse-Radicals (*sic!*).

These findings naturally caught my eye, and I repeated the study in the fall of 1994. Capitalist parents ($N = 15$) and students ($N = 9$) again usually placed first or second on the RWA, DOG, Ethnocentrism, ATH, and Posse-Radicals Scales. The 24 parents who described their basic outlook in life as socialist tended to score quite low. Their worst showing was a fourth place in RWA. But unlike those in the 1993 study, the socialist students ($N = 15$) also scored *low* on the scales: fourth in RWA, fifth in DOG, ninth in Ethno-centrism, seventh in ATH, and sixth in Posse-Radicals.[17]

THE FALL 1994 PITTING EXPERIMENT

Being reasonably confident that the DOG Scale had some empirical validity, I pitted it against Rokeach's forty items in the fall of 1994 among 177 Mani-toba students. They answered a booklet that began with the RWA Scale, followed by the D and DOG Scales. The students then indicated the extent to which twenty questions about religion had occurred to them, and the extent to which they now had doubts about religion on each of the twenty grounds. Next they answered eight questions about how they had handled religious questions when they had arisen ("Read the Bible or other religious material?"

"Talk with people from other religions?"). They also said how likely they would be to change their present beliefs about religion (pro or con) if very strong evidence appeared indicating they were wrong, and the extent to which they felt they had found the truth about religion.

The original Dogmatism Scale had a mean interitem correlation of .09, which with its forty items produced an alpha of .79. The values for the twenty-item DOG scale were .29 and .89.

In terms of empirical validity, Rokeach's measure correlated .21 with the extent to which questions about religion had occurred to the student (which is in the wrong direction and statistically significant), .12 with present doubts (also in the wrong direction, but not significant), .14 with handling questions by going to "confirming" sources such as the Bible or parents, .03 with holding onto one's present beliefs in the face of major disconfirming evidence, and .03 with belief that one had captured the truth about religion.

The corresponding figures for the DOG Scale were −.20, −.33, .51, .33, and .43. All of these are in the expected direction, significant, and substantially larger than those obtained in this dogfight with the much longer D Scale. Moreover, the DOG Scale generally predicted these behaviors better than the RWA Scale did, though not by much. This surprised me, since one can find a fair amount of religious content on the latter, while the DOG Scale is content-neutral.

Dogmatism to this Point

Dogmatism has had a long and disappointing career in psychology. The most famous investigation of the subject, by Rokeach (1960), inspired a ton of studies during the 1960s and 1970s. But you would measure the current output in pounds and ounces. For all the studies run and papers published and grants obtained, I believe very little has been learned—though it has been dressed up at times to look like a million bucks. Rokeach's elaborate conceptualization failed to be represented on the Dogmatism Scale, which had almost minimal levels of internal consistency, and then shot itself in the foot (heart and head) by failing to control for yea-saying. Thus the primary measure had virtually no construct validity, and the die was cast.

I have offered here at least a simpler conceptualization of dogmatism as relatively unchangeable, unjustified certainty. The balanced DOG Scale that measures it has pleasing levels of internal consistency. It has shown some encouraging ability to predict dogmatic behavior among students in several contexts, and it correlates rather solidly in expected ways with such things as right-wing authoritarianism, religious fundamentalism, and being a zealot, among university students and their parents.

But while it appears to be a step in the right direction, the DOG Scale is just a pup, largely untried. I also suspect that the farther one gets from studying "the important things in life," the lower its empirical correlations will fall. I do not think it will have the predictive range or punch of the RWA Scale, because I do not sense dogmatism plays as important a role in human affairs as authoritarianism does. But if the world has been waiting for a good ten-cent cigar and a better approach to dogmatism, this may be one of them.

So where do we stand now in the quest for the "authoritarian on the left"? Following the trail of dogmatism has basically led us back to High RWAs. Maybe they are the only kind of authoritarians in the woods. But let us try the search again, following the procedures we used to discover the right-wing variety. Maybe we can find some *left-wing* authoritarians lurking in the shadows.

—9—
Left-Wing Authoritarianism

Let us go back forty-odd years, to the beginning of Chapter 8. *The Authoritarian Personality,* published a few years ago, has created quite a stir, providing a psychological explanation of the most terrible events of the era. The bad guys score high on this "fascism personality test." People who score low on it seemingly get the white hats. But then Shils (1954) points out that Communists would also score low, and they seem as "authoritarian" as fascists. Rokeach (1960) suggests dogmatism equals "general authoritarianism," and are not left-wingers dogmatic? So everyone goes looking for left-wing authoritarians. But nobody can find them, not with the D Scale anyway.[1] Is the "authoritarian on the left" like the Loch Ness Monster: an occasional shadow, but no monster?

The major paper on whether lots of authoritarians live on the left bank of the political spectrum was written by Stone (1980). He described Shils's criticisms and concentrated on the Dogmatism Scale. Reviewing the studies by Barker (1963), DiRenzo (1967), Hanson (1968), Knutson (1974), and Smithers and Lobley (1978), he found (as we did) no evidence that leftists were in general more dogmatic or general authoritarian than most people. Stone then asked: "Why has left-wing authoritarianism retained such a firm grip on the minds of social scientists? One answer is often heard from leftist activists themselves, who recall authoritarians they have known in their own circles. That such cases of left-authoritarianism do exist cannot be denied, but the idea that authoritarian personalities are equally drawn to communist and fascist movements now seems clearly false" (p. 12).

Two more recent lines of research on cognitive functioning bear on the issue. Tetlock (1983) found that a content analysis of the political statements of very conservative U.S. senators showed less cognitive complexity than those of their more moderate or very liberal colleagues. Interviewing British members of Parliament, he discovered that moderate socialists were less rigid than moderate conservatives (Tetlock, 1984). But farther out on the limbs, both extreme socialists and extreme conservatives showed less ability to differentiate and integrate aspects of complicated issues. Tetlock (1986) suggested persons who pursue two values (such as equality and freedom) have to think more complexly than those who pursue just one (equality for extreme leftists, freedom for extreme rightists).

Sidanius (1985) in turn has proposed that, besides (1) right-wing authoritarians, and (2) the possibility that one can find authoritarians on both extremes of the political spectrum, (3) persons on the far left and far right are often better informed, more motivated to change things, and more sophisticated in their analyses. In various studies, he and his colleagues have found evidence for 1 and 3, but not for 2.

Reviewing the literature on left-wing authoritarianism in 1993, Stone and Smith concluded that Roger Brown's (1965, p. 542) often-cited summation still stands: "It has not been demonstrated that fascists and communists resemble one another in authoritarianism or in any other dimension of ideology." I agree. But I also do not think we have gone searching with "the right stuff" yet, conceptually and instrument-ally. So I thought I would take a crack at it.

Defining Left-Wing Authoritarianism

Is the same personality structure visible on both ends of the political spectrum, singing quite different tunes naturally, but for basically the same underlying reason? Possibly. I have always qualified my studies of right-wing authoritarianism by saying what I just said: *right-wing*. That leaves a niche in my pantheon of beasties for a left-wing authoritarian, and even for a flightless, unwinged authoritarian critter somewhere in the middle.

Certainly I believe "authoritarians" have appeared on the left. I became convinced through experiences with Maoist students in the late 1960s, who resembled the people Stone (1980) mentioned. While small in number, they were quite militant and certainly had an authority whose teachings they pushed with the passion of the converted. They had "little red books" instead of brown shirts, but when they showed up at debates with baseball bats to intimidate speakers, and threatened to destroy the labs of professors whose research they did not like, I had trouble seeing much difference.

UNDERLYING CONFUSIONS

You may, however, in your fussy, nit-picking, dogmatic old way, be unwilling to agree that left-wing authoritarians exist because I say I ran into a few over twenty-five years ago. Can we therefore lay a conceptual foundation for a fresh expedition after the Loch Ness Monster of political psychology?

It would be nice, at the outset, to be able to define "left-wing" cogently. The phrase, like "liberal" and "conservative," is used by pamphleteers, pundits, politicians, and professors in many different contexts, with many different meanings. In North America, I think to be left-wing in economics means to prefer a centrally planned economy that emphasizes full employment. To be left-wing politically means to have Reagan and Bush's dreaded "L-word" stamped all over your political agenda, if not your forehead. In theology, left-wingers doubt God exists. In grocery stores, left-wing eaters head for the beans and sprouts. You may perceive left-wingers in education, theater, art, child rearing, newscasting, psychotherapy, and even hockey. What the world needs is a social psychological connotation for "left-wing." Here it comes.

A SOCIAL PSYCHOLOGICAL DEFINITION OF "LEFT-WING"

When I began talking about "right-wing" authoritarianism (*RWA*, p. 152), I was not using the phrase in an economic or political sense. Instead I was (brazenly) inventing a new sense, a social psychological sense that denotes submission to the perceived established authorities in one's life. In many instances the established authorities tend to be people who hold right-wing economic and political views—but not always. In Communist countries, the established authorities in society held a decidedly left-wing economic philosophy, but after so many years in power, the party leaders had become the Establishment. So I predicted persons who scored highly on the RWA Scale in the USSR would support the Communist leadership and oppose democratic reforms (*EOF*, p. 264), and by thunder they did.

Revolutions such as those in eastern Europe call off all bets for a while.[2] But the situation in stable countries seems more predictable. Psychological right-wingers (by definition) support the perceived established authorities in society, and psychological *left-wingers* (as I am using the term) oppose them.

I am not assuming anything about what the "opposers" stand for. Some may simply want society reformed so that disadvantaged groups can share more of the power. The African National Congress and civil rights groups in the United States come to mind. But others may want to seize all the power themselves, from either the far reaches of the political left (Communists) or the political right (Nazis, the Posse Comitatus, Lyndon LaRouche's National Caucus). Such extremist groups, while submissive to their own perceived "legitimate authorities," would be *psychological* left-wingers on a societal level during their opposition to the Establishment. But should their movement attain power in the flash of a revolution, their strong submission to the new societal authority would make them psychological right-wing authoritarians on that level, as they became in Germany and Russia.

I am proposing, in short, an underlying authoritarian personality that can be either psychologically left-wing or right-wing, depending on who holds power, and can be found at either extreme of the political spectrum.

A FORMAL DEFINITION OF LEFT-WING AUTHORITARIANISM

By "left-wing authoritarianism" I thus mean the covariation of three attitudinal clusters, which may be vaguely familiar:

1. Authoritarian submission—a high degree of submission to authorities who are dedicated to *overthrowing* the established authorities in one's society.

2. Authoritarian aggression—a general aggressiveness directed against the established authorities, or against persons who are perceived to support those authorities.

3. Conventionalism—a high degree of adherence to the norms of behavior perceived to be endorsed by the revolutionary authorities.

I mean by these terms the same things I meant when defining right-wing authoritarianism. We just have submission to very different, revolutionary authorities.[3] This conceptualization entails the same attitudes we have been dealing with all along when studying RWAs. Authoritarian submission, authoritarian aggression, and conventionalism make up generic authoritarianism, in a plain wrapper. When it is psychologically dedicated to serving the established authorities, it comprises our familiar right-wing authoritarianism. When it is dedicated to overthrowing those authorities, slap a left-wing authoritarianism (LWA) label on it.

But the underlying personality is authoritarian. It's "wingedness" depends upon which authorities you are talking about, and your perspective. So, to repeat a point from Chapter 1, American "militias" perceive the *proper* established authority to be their interpretation of the Constitution, God's will, and "American tradition." They reject the present federal government, which they think is undermining the original established authority. I would call them right-wing authoritarians because of their point of view; they think themselves, not revolutionaries, but restorers. Revolutionary Communists, on the other hand, perceived themselves as trying to overthrow the historical as well as contemporary "Establishment."

Not all psychological left-wingers (that is, people opposed to the established authorities) would be left-wing *authoritarians.* They may not be authoritarian at all, but may instead be highly independent individuals who want peaceful social reform. Color them "*un*authoritarians." Left-wing authoritarians are revolutionaries who (1) submit to movement leaders who must be obeyed, (2) have enemies who must be ruined, and (3) have rules and "party discipline" that must be followed. That is their social psychological orientation, whatever the ideology of the movement.

This conceptualization brings a great simplicity to our thinking. If the question is, what basic personality structure does an authoritarian on the political left share with an authoritarian on the political right?—the answer is (ta-dum!) being an authoritarian. Whatever their other differences, both submit to their authorities, aggress in their names, and adhere to their conventions.

The focus of the debate over the authoritarian on the left in democracies has been the Communist Party, ardent socialists, and transient groups such as the Weathermen. Although these groups represent only a tiny part of the "opposers" in North American society, I shall retain that focus in my investigations. I shall try to find, in the rest of this chapter, the authoritarian on the political left whom Shils talked about and Rokeach thought he would ensnare, but who has so far escaped scientific detection, much less capture.

Development of the LWA Scale

THE SEPTEMBER 1991 STUDY

I first tested items tapping my notion of left-wing authoritarianism in the fall of 1991, giving eight protrait and seven contrait items to 402 of my own students (Exhibit 9.1). Protrait items advocated submission to a revolutionary movement dedicated to overthrowing the Establishment, hostility toward those presently in power, and conformity to the rules of the revolutionary movement. Contrait items spoke out against these sentiments.

Exhibit 9.1   The Fifteen Items Used in the September 1991 LWA Study

1. When the time comes, we must stomp out the rich, powerful members of the Establishment who have exploited everyone else.

2. Our present society may have problems, but it would be a great mistake to think any revolutionary philosophy or radical leader has all the answers.*

3. Persons who belong to a group trying to overthrow the oppressive forces in society must conform strictly to the rules and norms of that group.

4. No political movement, even one dedicated to restoring social justice, has the right to tell its members how to act, dress, think, etc.*

5. Nothing is as low as the greedy bankers and industrialists who have lived off the hard work of others.

6. A revolutionary movement has the right to demand strict discipline among its members, who must follow the movement's rules in all aspects of their lives.

7. Most "revolutionary leaders" turn out to be dictators themselves, and should be treated with great suspicion.*

8. Society should be reformed *only* through *non*violent means.*

9. We should devotedly follow determined leaders who will fight the current social system.

10. When a reform movement begins dictating to its members whom they can associate with, where they have to shop, and what they can eat, it's time to leave it.*

11. Obedience and respect for a revolutionary leader is the most important thing the people can give the future.

12. The rich in our society create jobs, economic prosperity, and do much social good with their wealth.*

13. If certain people refuse to accept the historic restructuring of society that will come someday, they will have to be removed and silenced.

14. A social movement that aims to end injustice should have no rules for its members; it should instead encourage disagreement, individuality, and nonconformity among them.*

15. Our society cannot be truly, permanently changed unless people submit themselves to the revolutionary ideology that will overthrow the old order.

Note: Items are answered on a −4 to +4 basis.
* Item is worded in the contrait direction; the *left-wing* authoritarian response is to disagree.

To help the students understand that the "revolution" being mentioned would come from the economic or political "far left," I sprinkled about references to the "Establishment," to the "rich, powerful," "oppressive," "exploiting," "greedy bankers and industrialists who have lived off the hard work of others." I did not think any of my 1991 students would rise up, wave red flags, and rush out to build barricades. But I did expect enough variation in reactions to the items to indicate if I had touched on a system of ideas.

Responses to the fifteen items showed little *Les Miz* sentiment, averaging 4.02 on the 1–9 scale. But they also showed almost no internal consistency, their mean intercorrelation being only .07. The items I had tried did not uncover much of a "system of ideas."

THE OCTOBER 1991 STUDY

Uncontrollably gripped by a zeal to find the authoritarian on the left, I tried out twelve protrait and thirteen contrait items the following month, through a hired experimenter who tested 206 of the 402 students who had served in the first study. Most of the statements were reworked versions of those on my first try, usually stated in more extreme language.

Things went quite a bit better psychometrically (as they usually do when participants go over ground they have trod before). I combined the best intercorrelating six protrait and six contrait items as a mock LWA Scale. The mean interitem correlation equaled .24, producing an alpha of .79. The more strident tone of the protraits reduced the item means to 3.41 on the average.

Then I got quite a surprise. The correlation between RWA and LWA scores should, of course, be negative and big. One scale indicates willingness to bow down before the established authorities, the other a desire to kick them in the pants. But I found RWA scores correlated *plus* .18 (*p* < .05) with these students' mock LWA Scale scores?

In my Silas Marner way, I ran my fingers through the data, first examining the 49 students who formed the top quartile of the mock LWA Scale distribution ("High LWAs"). Who were these revolutionary firebrands who sat so dutifully before me in class, taking notes instead of knitting my name into the list of those to be deposed?

First of all, none of them scored highly on the mock scale in absolute terms. In fact, only 4 students (out of about 200, or 2%) even landed above the *neutral* point of 5.0. So the "greedy, bloodsucking exploiters of the masses" in my community can sleep soundly. There were no authoritarians on the left in this sample, no Loch Ness Monsters. But just as we use the Posse scores to indicate *potential* for right-wing pogroms, we can use LWA scores to look at those closest, under present circumstances, to endorsing left-wing authoritarian attitudes.

Second, when I looked at these 49 relatively high LWAs, I found 11 of them had also been High RWAs (where they really *were* high), but only 6 of them had been Low RWAs. These "High-Highs" killed any chance for a *big* negative correlation.

Then I looked at the 49 people who scored *low* (very low, in absolute terms) on the mock LWA Scale. I expected this group to be jam-packed with High RWAs, standing up for the Establishment. But I found nary a trace of them: only 6, who were outnumbered by 16 *LOW* RWAs. So these "Low-Lows" knocked the stuffing out of whatever chance remained that the correlation would even be negative. But do you see the implications? We have found something far more interesting than I at least ever anticipated.

THE FOUR COMBOS

The respectable interitem correlations show that sentiments of submission, aggression, and conventionalism *in a revolutionary context* do covary. But the logical expectation that Low RWAs would be High LWAs, and vice-versa, got clobbered by something *psycho*logical. What? We can tell by looking at the extremes of the RWA and LWA distributions—where the action is—and scrutinizing the four resulting combinations.

1. *Low RWAs, Low LWAs* (N = 16). Low RWAs tended to be Low LWAs, or Moderates, but *not* authoritarians on the left, not the despotic leftists Shils described. The "Low-Lows" were *un*authoritarian, period. They rejected submitting to the established authorities, and to revolutionary authorities as well. They rejected "stomping out the deviants" on the RWA Scale and "stomping out the Establishment" on the LWA Scale. They were against forcing conventions upon anyone, whether society's or those of a revolutionary movement. In short, with the integrity Low RWAs have often shown in other contexts, they rejected authoritarianism, however it was dressed and wherever it wanted to go. I would call them "Unauthoritarians."

2. *Low RWAs, High LWAs* (N = 6). A few Low RWAs scored *relatively* high on the LWA Scale. They come closest to fulfilling Shils's expectations, although none of them advocated overthrowing the Establishment. I would call them "Left-Wingers" (both in my social psychological and in the economic or political sense).

3. *High RWAs, Low LWAs* (N = 10). Some of the High RWAs (the "Highs" we have been talking about in all the previous chapters), scored low on the LWA Scale. They thus showed support for the established authorities on both tests, and I would call them "Right-Wingers" in my social psychological sense and in the usual economic or political sense.

4. *High RWAs, High LWAs* (N = 11). Some High RWAs scored *relatively* high on the LWA Scale. To be sure, their hearts and minds were captured more by the RWA Scale, where they punched up much higher numbers. But they seem to believe in submission, aggression, and conventionalism per se. So even though the LWA Scale talks about taking the Establishment out to the woodshed, the authoritarian sentiments in the items made it hard for these students to get a low score.

I would call these High-Highs "Wild-Card Authoritarians." I believe that in ordinary circumstances they would overwhelmingly support the established authorities, whom they prefer anyway and who, after all, have lots of power. But some High-Highs could see the established authorities as corrupt and evil, and join rebellious movements.

I think I can even tell you how to spot Wild-Card Authoritarians among the rest of the rebels. In this study, the High-Highs distinguished themselves, not only by upsetting my expectations, but also by their scoring high on two measures of (right-wing) authoritarian aggression that happened to be in the booklet. Seven of the 11 landed in the upper quartile on the Ethnocentrism distribution, and 9 of them were in the top quarter of the Attitudes toward Homosexual Scale. So they seem to be relatively hostile and prejudiced people.[4] Their hostility may lead them to join determined anti-Establishment groups.

To summarize, the Left-Wingers and Right-Wingers behaved as one would expect. But the RWA-LWA correlation came out positive because of the more numerous, and interesting, Unauthoritarians and Wild-Card Authoritarians.

THE NOVEMBER 1991 TO JANUARY 1993 STUDIES

I worked on the LWA Scale for another year, conducting six more studies, involving altogether 1,443 Manitoba students. (In other words, it took as many studies to develop this scale as it had to develop the RWA Scale, proving I had not learned a thing.) The mock scale assembled in October 1991 had benefited from those students' earlier experiences with my first batch of LWA statements. I would not see a mean interitem correlation of .24 again for some time.

Students would sometimes ask what was meant by the "Establishment," yet another indication I have inexplicably gotten old. So I added an introductory statement to keep the search focused in the direction Shils had indicated. This paragraph, and two unscored table-setters that lead off the LWA Scale, firmly equated the Establishment with the economic or political right-wing, and the revolutionary movement with the left-wing. I also used those winged phrases, and "socialist," and "conservative" to keep people who wanted a right-wing revolution from scoring highly on the LWA Scale. (These people interest and even terrify one, but we are searching here for Shils's monster.) I shall spare you the details of these six studies, except to say that the interesting results of the October 1991 experiment almost always reappeared. Mock LWA Scale scores stayed low. The four combos reappeared in similar proportions, with the Unauthoritarian Low-Lows and the Wild-Card High-Highs producing a *positive* if small correlation between RWA and LWA. The Wild Card Authoritarians always scored high on prejudice and other hostility scales.

THE FALL 1993 STUDENT-PARENT STUDIES

By the fall of 1993 I had a balanced twenty-item Left-Wing Authoritarianism Scale with good interitem correlations and an acceptable alpha (Exhibit 9.2). So I put it through its paces in the same big student and parent studies (described in the last chapter) I ran to test the DOG Scale.

Exhibit 9.2   The Left-Wing Authoritarianism Scale

In the items that follow, the "Establishment" refers to the people in our country who have traditionally had the most power, the greatest control over the economy: That is, the wealthiest people, the large corporations and banks who are often called the RIGHT-WING forces in Canada. Whereas a "revolutionary movement" denotes a LEFT-WING movement dedicated to overthrowing the Establishment, and taking away its power.

1. Communism has its flaws, but the basic idea of overthrowing the right-wing Establishment and giving its wealth to the poor is still a very good one.

2. Socialism will never work, so people should treat left-wing revolutionaries as the dangerous troublemakers they are.

3. People should do whatever a left-wing revolutionary movement against the Establishment decides.

4. The last thing our country needs is a revolutionary movement demanding total submission to its leaders, conformity among its members, and attacks upon the Establishment.*

5. The conservative, right-wing Establishment will never give up its power peacefully, so a revolutionary movement is justified in using violence to crush it.

6. There is a dangerous tendency for left-wing, anti-Establishment, revolutionary movements to demand too much conformity and blind obedience from their members.*

7. Anyone who truly wants to help our country should support left-wing revolutionary leaders stomp out the Establishment, and then devote themselves to the new way of life ahead.

8. Socialist revolutions require great leadership. When a strong, determined rebel leads the attack on the Establishment, that person deserves our complete faith and support.

9. When a leftist, anti-Establishment movement begins dictating to its members whom they can associate with, where they can shop, and what they can eat, it's time to leave it.*

10. The conservative Establishment has so much power, and is so unfair, we *have* to submit to the leaders and rules of a revolutionary movement in order to destroy them.

11. Our present society has its problems, but it would be a great mistake to think any leftist leader who wants to overthrow the Establishment has "the answers."*

12. The members of the Establishment deserve to be dealt with harshly, without mercy, when they are finally overthrown.

13. It would be a dreadful mistake for people in our country to unite behind leftist leaders, submit to their authority, and launch attacks upon the Establishment.*

14. Even a revolutionary left-wing movement dedicated to overthrowing the present, totally unjust right-wing system does NOT have the right to tell its members how to act, dress, think, etc.*

15. A leftist revolutionary movement is quite justified in attacking the Establishment, and in demanding obedience and conformity from its members.

16. It would be wrong to try to solve our problems by acts of violence against the conservative Establishment.*

17. We should devotedly follow determined leaders who will fight the Establishment.

18. If certain people refuse to accept the historic restructuring of society that will come when the Establishment is overthrown, they will have to be removed and smashed.

19. If people who want to overthrow the Establishment let revolutionary leaders become important authorities in their lives, they are just exchanging one set of masters for another.*

20. Even though the Establishment groups who control our country are quite repressive and unfair, society should *only* be reformed through NONviolent means.*

21. If the "Have-Nots" in our country are ever going to overthrow the "Haves," and give them the harsh treatment they fully deserve, the "Have-Nots" must follow the rules and leaders of the revolutionary movement.

22. One of the *worst* things people could do in Canada now would be to support the left-wing, revolutionary forces trying to overthrow the Establishment.*

Note: Only Items 3–22 are scored. Items are answered on a −4 to +4 basis.
* Item is worded in the contrait direction; the left-wing authoritarian response is to disagree.

These 546 students also showed no signs of revolutionary leftist tendencies. The item mean continued low (3.30), and only 12 students scored over 5.00 (× 20 = 100, the scale's neutral point). The *highest* score was 113. Their 642 responding parents were, as you would predict, even less likely to want to smash the Establishment to smithereens, with an item mean of 2.82. Only 20 scored over the neutral point, the highest being 117.[5] Thus we have nearly 1,200 people, and not a single high-scoring left-wing authoritarian in the bunch. We can again talk only about those closest to being such at thing, the upper quartile of the LWA distribution (who are none too close at that).

The mean intercorrelation of items 3–22 in Exhibit 9.2 equaled .22 among the students and .25 among the parents (a population in which I had not tried the LWA Scale before), producing alphas of .85 and .86. So even though the range of responses proved limited, the items covaried as hypothesized. The scale apparently measures sentiments of submission to revolutionary authority, aggression in its name, and conventionalism in following its norms.

RWA and LWA scores correlated .11 and .14 in the two samples, statistically significant (with the large N's), and quite the sort of thing I had gotten used to finding. Among the students, Low RWAs again tended to be Low LWAs (the Unauthoritarians), rather than High LWAs (the Left-Wingers), 41–22. High RWAs who were also Low LWAs (Right-Wingers) numbered 37; but more High RWAs (46) were also High LWAs (the Wild-Card Authoritarians).

The parents' data essentially replicated these results, with 56 Low-Lows, 26 Low-Highs, 35 High-Lows, and 45 High-Highs. Overall, we again have relatively large numbers of Unauthoritarians and Wild Cards, who make the RWA-LWA correlation positive. If, in the absence of any pinnable authoritarian on the left, you are willing to talk about who comes closest to being such a species, you can find some Low RWAs, the Left-Wingers, in the upper quadrant of the LWA distribution. But as always they were heavily outnumbered in that upper quadrant in both samples by High RWAs, the Wild-Card Authoritarians, 46–22 and 45–26.

A Closer Look at the Four Combos.   Table 9.1 presents the average scores that these four subgroups obtained on other instruments of interest in the booklets. Reading down, you can see that in both samples Low-Lows always had the lowest scores on the three authoritarian aggression measures and on the DOG Scale, whereas High-Highs usually had the highest scores. The dashed horizontal line that bisects each sample tells the story of statistical significance. Any two scale means on *opposite* sides of the line were significantly different; any two scale means on the *same* side of the line were not. (You may also notice that this horizontal line happens to separate the Low RWAs from the High RWAs.)

So Unauthoritarians showed almost no hostility nor dogmatism. Neither did Low-Highs (Left-Wingers). By contrast, High-Lows (Right-Wingers) always displayed significantly more hostility and dogmatism than these first two groups did, and so did the Wild Cards.

Interscale Correlations.   This knowledge of what was happening on the extremes of the distributions helps us interpret correctly the full-sample correlations between the LWA Scale and the other measures. Among the students, Left-Wing Authoritarianism correlated .14 with Ethnocentrism, .08 with Attitudes toward Homosexuals, .21 with Posse, and .21 with DOG. The same figures for the parents were .19, .11, .24, and .33. All but the .08 are statistically significant by a two-tailed test. But in each case the correlation was mainly due to the Wild-Card Authoritarians. As you can see from Table 9.1,

Table 9.1   Mean scores on various scales, by RWA and LWA position

			Students			
RWA	LWA	N	Ethno	ATH	Posse	DOG
Low	Low	41	58.0	27.3	12.4	45.1
Low	High	22	63.5	30.2	14.8	52.2
High	Low	37	79.6	63.8	27.0	77.5
High	High	46	89.6	61.5	28.8	76.8
			Parents			
RWA	LWA	N	Ethno	ATH	Posse	DOG
Low	Low	56	62.6	31.5	10.3	46.4
Low	High	26	65.2	35.1	12.5	64.7
High	Low	35	94.5	66.5	23.7	87.8
High	High	45	99.7	67.8	29.0	89.4

Note: Within each sample, any pair of scale scores on opposite sides of the dashed line were significantly different by a two-tailed test. Any pair of scale scores on the *same* side of the dashed line were *not* significantly different by a two-tailed test.

the outnumbered Left-Wingers (Low-Highs) among the High *LWAs* had rather low scores on these measures of aggression and dogmatism.[6]

THE NOVEMBER 1991 STUDY OF SASKATCHEWAN POLITICIANS

In November 1991, as part of the ongoing studies of right-wing authoritarianism among politicians that we shall cover in Chapter 11, I sent a one-sheet survey to the homes of the 66 New Democratic, 66 Liberal, and 66 Conservative candidates who had stood for election to the Saskatchewan legislature in October.[7] The survey began with the same 1982 RWA Scale used in previous studies of lawmakers. That was followed by an early rendition of the paragraph defining the Establishment, and six protrait and six contrait items that I was trying out then for the LWA Scale.

Saskatchewan provides a particularly good place to search for authoritarians on the left. The province gave birth to Canadian socialism during the 1930s, and eventually the New Democratic Party, which won this election in 1991. Furthermore, most of the NDP candidates were of my generation, which means they had been adolescents or young adults during the 1960s and 1970s when they could have been some of the left-wing radicals then about. Furthermore, by testing *candidates* rather than just those who were elected to office, I could collect opinions from NDPers who may have been too left-wing to get elected. In brief, if a "nest of pinko fellow-travelers" still existed in North America, this was one of the best places to look for it.

Twenty NDP, 33 Liberal, and 14 Conservative candidates sent back completed surveys. I shall save the RWA Scale results for Chapter 11, except to say that as always NDP politicians scored quite low, Liberals scored higher, and Conservatives scored highest of all. All differences were significant.

What happened with the LWA items?[8] Among the 67 candidates, they intercorrelated .19 on the average. But item means sank very low, averaging 2.30 on the 1–9 scale. The NDP mean was 2.57, that of the Liberals equaled 2.24, and the Tories came in at 2.07 ($F = 1.84$; $p < .17$). While the numbers proceed in the expected direction, their small and nonsignificant gaps underscore the fact that, as much as these parties split on other matters, none of them could be characterized as left-wing authoritarian.

How about the *individuals?* Well, one of the NDP candidates averaged 4.92 across the items, almost to the neutral point of 5.00. But *no* authoritarian on the left appeared. And one could find plenty of *right-wing* authoritarians, mainly among the Conservatives.

SO, CAN WE SAY THERE IS AN AUTHORITARIAN ON THE LEFT?

Is there an authoritarian on the left? No. Not if you are talking about Shils's left, not if you require scientific evidence. Lots of people have looked, in several different ways, in several different countries, for this creature of lore. But no one has found it yet.

In my own case, counting the item-development studies, I have now collected responses to left-wing authoritarian statements from 1,845 Manitoba students, 642 of their parents, and 67 politicians in Saskatchewan—over 2,500 persons. I have not yet found a single individual who even "slightly agreed" (+ 1, or 6.0) on average with the notion of an *authoritarian* left-wing movement.

Maybe that just shows the LWA Scale is no good. But it has a defendable internal consistency. It has at least face validity. While you may gag on some of its items because of their extreme language, many of the RWA Scale items also make me gag, and people agree with *them*. Besides, when I think back on some of the left-wing radicals I knew in days gone by, they talked that way. I just left out the "F-word" as the constant modifier of "Establishment."[9]

I think I have not found any authoritarians on the left because, *if* there ever were any, most of them have dried up and blown away and "nobody makes them any more." You don't have to be much of a weatherman to know which way the wind has been blowing for the past twenty-five years.

If you want Unauthoritarians on the political left, I have found plenty. If you want nonauthoritarians on the right, I have found some. If you want authoritarians on the right, I have found tons. But if you want a living, breathing, scientifically certifiable authoritarian on the left, I have not found a single one.

Well then, what about all those earlier "sightings," including Manitoba's militant Maoists? I suspect that the hostile, dogmatic, authoritarian people who sometimes appeared in such movements were usually Wild-Card Authoritarians, not Left-Wingers. I have no proof of this, since the instruments needed to find these "combos" did not exist at the time. But I offer Table 9.1 as evidence. Maybe the future will bless us (?) with a resurgence of radical left-wing movements in North America, so we can test this prediction. Or maybe the prediction can be tested right now elsewhere in the world. (But it would be important that such radicals answer as themselves, not as members of their movement.)

In closing this section, let me try to mine three nuggets of insight from the discovery of the Wild-Card Authoritarians. First, if we recall that Wild Cards almost always find the RWA Scale more to their liking than the LWA Scale, I think we can understand better the perplexing careers of Benito Mussolini, Lyndon LaRouche, and others who started out on the political left, but ended up way over on the political right. Some High RWAs can turn up in leftist movements. Second, you can see why left-wing organizations such as the Student Nonviolent Coordinating Committee and the Students for a Democratic Society eventually split into nonviolent and violent factions. The Left-Wingers and the Wild Cards could not work together forever. Third, these results may help explain why leftist revolutions so often become dictatorships if they succeed. Wild Cards tend to control things at the end of the war.

"Political Correctness" and Censorship

The issue of "political correctness," like that of affirmative action, has divided university campuses for several years now. A *Maclean's* magazine article in May 1991 put the matter this way:

Across Canada and the United States, many academics and people in other walks of life are finding themselves on the defensive for falling afoul of what some politicians and academics refer to as the "politically correct" posture on issues and ideas of the day. With temperatures rising, students, political activists and intellectuals are demanding, among other things, that seemingly disparaging references to color, sex or sexual preference be banned. As well, political correctness embraces a number of liberal causes—from feminism to homosexual and native rights.

This article gave three (Canadian university) examples of political correctness campaigns. The first campaign forced an anthropologist, Jeanne Cannizzo, to leave the University of Toronto following charges of racism. Professor Cannizzo had been curator of a museum exhibit depicting the treatment of Africans by white colonists. Although the exhibition was critical of white colonialism, some protestors said it humiliated blacks. After demonstrating outside the museum, they disrupted the professor's classes, hurling insults at her. Eventually, she took an extended medical leave of absence.

The second campaign involved the celebrated case of Philippe Rushton, a controversial psychology professor at the University of Western Ontario who suggested (among other things) that blacks do not have the intelligence of other races. Student protestors demanded he be fired.

The third, more general campaign featured feminist pressures to redress male dominance of the university curriculum and professorial ranks. Strong pressures were building to hire only female professors. Many students and professors were being intimidated into silence, the article said, for fear they would offend the reformers and be denounced as sexist.

Being myself strongly against political correctness (but not so strongly as to write a letter defending Professor Rushton, whose evidence I find most unconvincing) and being strongly in favor of affirmative action in hiring (but not so strongly as to resign to make way for a minority-group assistant professor), I wondered who these "political correctors" might be.[10]

In October 1991 I gave the same 206 students who served in the second LWA study the *Maclean's* magazine article, followed by six items that assessed their attitudes on the issues raised:

1. Should seemingly disparaging references to color, sex, or sexual preference such as the Cannizzo Exhibit, be banned at universities?

2. Should Philippe Rushton be kept on the faculty at the University of Western Ontario?*

3. Do you think the "politically correct" advocates want to intimidate potential opponents into silence by threatening to call them "bigots?"*

4. Should "jokes or unguarded statements about women, homosexuals, or members of racial minorities" be acceptable in university classrooms?*

5. Do you believe women should be given strong preference over men, provided they are minimally qualified, when universities are hiring new professors?

6. Would you like to see a "leftist" "political correctness" policy, such as that described in this article, established at the University of Manitoba?

It would probably surprise the editors of *Maclean's* that summed support for political correctness did *not* correlate with either mock LWA (.08) or RWA (.07) scores. Some students, to be sure, supported political correctness; however, they were not leftists as a rule but Wild-Card Authoritarians.

Exhibit 9.3   The Items Used to Measure Views on Censorship and Freedom of Speech

1. Persons with bad ideas about groups of people must be prevented from spreading them.

2. No one in a democracy has the right to silence a speaker because of his/her point of view.*

3. When you feel you have the right position on some issue, you should do whatever it takes to keep those with the wrong position from being heard.

4. Groups that won't let others speak freely are themselves a bigger threat to democracy than the speakers they oppose.*

5. Professors with wrong beliefs about certain groups should *not* be allowed to teach them.

6. Many ideas are so dangerous to our society, they should never be allowed to be taught or preached or published.

7. Our society should make sure all points of view on a controversial issue have a fair chance to be heard.*

8. Persons with certain points of view have no "right" to address the public.

9. Even if an idea seems wrong, it should have as much chance to influence others as an idea that seems right.*

10. Democracy cannot work if some people have the power to keep other people from expressing their opinions—however wicked or wrong.*

11. "Academic freedom" at universities does *not* mean a person with evil theories has a right to teach them to students.

12. Freedom of expression should *not* be denied, even if saying certain things might contribute to the oppression of others.*

Note: Items are answered on a −4 to +4 basis.
* Item is worded in the contrait direction; the "censorship" response is to disagree.

After the students had answered these six questions, they came upon a dozen items that dealt more generally with issues of censorship and freedom of speech (Exhibit 9.3). You can see that many of these statements spoke to the matters raised in the political-correctness article. The mean interitem correlation equaled .20, which with only a dozen items bore an alpha of .75. Scored in the direction of favoring censorship, these items basically drew low scores from the participants, with a mean of 46.9 on a scale that could vary from 12 to 108.

RWA scores correlated .24, and LWA scores .17, with favoring censorship ($p < .05$ in both cases). But before we conclude that this means both rightists and leftists oppose freedom of speech, we need to look at the scores of the four combos. Low-Lows (the 16 Unauthoritarians) averaged 41.9, Low-Highs (the 6 Left-Wingers) averaged 40.7, High-Lows (the 10 Right-Wingers) had a mean of 55.3, and that for the High-Highs (the 11 Wild Cards) was 52.0. This resembles the pattern seen in Table 9.1, and even with such tiny N's, the Low-Low mean was significantly less than that of the Right-Wingers and the Wild Cards. Again, leftists were not advocating political correctness or censorship. Again, even when the issues were raised in the context of leftist censoring, rightists wanted censorship more than anyone else.

I do not know if these results would apply to any debate on political correctness on your campus. After all, these data came from first-year students in the second month of their university experience, whereas the advocates for political correctness tend to be older undergraduates, graduate students, and faculty members. But the testable hypothesis looms that, when you find hostile and dogmatic "political correctors" at a university advocating censorship, you might be dealing not so much with leftists as with Wild-Card Authoritarians.

Results of the Expedition

We began at the same point we began Chapter 8: Is there an authoritarian on the "left" end of the political spectrum that counterbalances the one that clearly resides on the "right"? I agreed with Stone that it had not yet been demonstrated.

I then offered a new conceptualization of left-wing authoritarianism as submission, aggression, and conventionalism in a revolutionary cause. A scale with good internal consistency was eventually developed to measure this. It produced a very surprising positive correlation with right-wing authoritarianism that, when we took it apart, seemingly uncovered a little gold mine of insights. But although we looked in several populations, we never sighted an "authoritarian on the left." We *did* find some "Wild-Card Authoritarians" that may have led to rumors of the "monster" in the first place.

Then we considered evidence on political correctness and censorship. The data showed no connection between being a "leftist" and endorsing these stands.

Our discussion of censorship does not end with this chapter but instead propels us into the next. There we shall have to wrestle hard with the difficult issue of whether demonstrably false, wicked, and dangerous ideas should be allowed to circulate freely in a democracy. For turning to Chapter 10 will take us from the theoretical world of Shils's left to the terrifying world of *Schindler's List*.

—10—
The Effects of Hate Literature

On the evening of June 22, 1971, I was in a rather unusual place: the outer office of the National Socialist White People's Party (NSWPP) headquarters in Arlington, Virginia. The NSWPP was the American Nazi Party by another name, retitled by its founder George Lincoln Rockwell several months before he was assassinated by an ex-member in August 1967. This two-story office building on North Franklin Road had replaced the large rambling house in another part of Arlington that had been the center of American Nazism in Rockwell's day.

What was I doing here? I'll bet you can guess. I had written the NSWPP a month earlier, describing myself as a psychologist doing research on "political party affiliation and attitudes." I wanted to give out a survey to Nazis, and they had a corner on the market. I intended to be in the Washington, D.C., area in a few weeks and would pay four dollars per completed survey.

I did not expect the party leadership to jump at the chance to let me administer a psychological test to NSWPP members, and they did not even twitch. But when I got to Washington and phoned the headquarters, it was agreed I might come over that evening to talk with one of the party leaders.

The party occupied rooms on both floors of the building it shared (I recall) with an insurance agent and a dentist. (These tenants lived in apparent peace with their unusual neighbors, who often hung a large Nazi flag from the second floor.) The office on the ground floor was locked when I arrived, and I had to identify myself. I was admitted to a small anteroom containing a desk, a few chairs, and a rack of party literature. Large pictures of Adolf Hitler and Lincoln Rockwell hung on a wall. The receptionist was a young man wearing black trousers, a brown shirt, a swastika arm band, and a belt with a holstered .45 pistol.

While I was waiting for a party official to attend to me, I bought some of the literature. I began reading the party's paper, *White Power*. It carried some news about NSWPP activities, but it also presented stories from around the United States about Jews and blacks who had been convicted of various crimes. So and so had sold diseased meat; so and so had been convicted of distributing pornography; so and so had raped and murdered a white woman; so and so had sold drugs to elementary school children.

I had by 1971 received a Ph.D. and been teaching psychology for five years. I had always stressed critical thinking to my students. I knew a fair amount about how propagandists plied their trade, including the use of sensational stories, the ignoring of base rates, and out-and-out lying. But I was also the grown-up version of little Bobby Altemeyer, who had been taught (by lots of people) that the Jews had killed Jesus, and will always cheat you, and that "niggers" all carried razors and switchblades, and would "just as soon cut you up as look at you." As I sat there in the Nazi headquarters, I could feel my opinions of Jews and blacks slipping as I moved from one story to the next.[1]

Hitler's View Of Propaganda

If you have ever tried to read *Mein Kampf*, you know what Shirer (1960, p. 81) meant when he said it was the least-read best-seller in the Third Reich. But one particular section has been quoted often, in which Hitler explained his theory of propaganda: "The receptivity of the great masses is extremely limited, their intelligence is small, their forgetfulness enormous. Therefore all effective propaganda must be limited to a very few points and they should be used like slogans until the very last man in the audience is capable of understanding what is meant by this slogan" (p. 198).

This view, endorsed a thousand times since by Madison Avenue, made no distinction between the true and the false. Hitler had learned about propaganda firsthand during the war, from observing the effects of Allied leaflets on his comrades in the German trenches. He credited the British with inventing the Big Lie technique, as in their stories of atrocities supposedly committed by German soldiers. His solution was simply to tell bigger lies than anyone else, and tell them over and over and over.[2]

One particular lie, which Hitler fervently believed, said that Jews had ruined Germany and enslaved its people. Anti-Semitism became the central theme of Hitler's propaganda from the start. The Nazi Party newspaper, *Völkischer Beobachter,* carried a torrent of stories blaming the Jews for every imaginable problem in the Wiemar Republic, beginning with its formation. It was exceeded only by the extraordinarily vicious and vulgar weekly *Der Stürmer*, published by one of Hitler's closest henchmen, Julius Streicher. The stories in these publications were ludicrous. No sensible person, it seemed, would put any stock in them. But they kept appearing, issue after issue, and so did physical attacks on Jews. By 1933, the Nazis had been voted to power, and they used the resources of the state to implement the far wider policy of persecution and murder that eventually led to the Holocaust.

Freedom of Speech

The Nazis' attack upon Jews probably counts as the most destructive hate literature campaign of all time. If in retrospect you somehow had the power to stop it in 1930, to declare it verboten and make it disappear, would you have done so? Would you have denied Nazis freedom of speech when they used that freedom to create hatred against an identifiable minority?

What about today? Nazis still exist, and while they are selling the White Power brand of Aryan superiority, they still hate Jews and want others to hate Jews too. They are extremely active, through the mails, on the Internet, and on "early morning" radio. Should they have their chance to succeed?

In the United States, the Supreme Court has interpreted First Amendment rights "broadly" so that you can say almost anything. You do *not* have a right to stand up in a crowded theater and maliciously yell "Fire!" but you do seemingly have a right to stand up in that theater and yell "All Jews must die!" Because of this freedom, which can be interpreted as an overwhelming commitment to, and confidence in, democracy, the United States is the source of most of the neo-Nazi literature that gets smuggled into Germany these days (*Newsweek*, November 16, 1993), and into Canada too.

The Canadian Supreme Court has ruled that freedom of speech does *not* permit communications that promote hatred of identifiable groups. This ruling arose from a series of well-publicized trials of individuals who espouse Nazi beliefs and denied the Holocaust took place. These "communications" took the form of books and pamphlets in two cases, and lessons given by a high school teacher to his students in another.

As someone who most definitely would have outlawed the Nazi anti-Semitism campaign in Germany, given what happened afterward, but who feels (on most mornings) that people should be able to say whatever they want, when you do not know how things will turn out, I wondered about the Canadian Supreme Court decision. Were there any experimental data that "denial" propaganda actually affected people? Are not these ridiculous claims that the Holocaust never occurred dismissed out of hand by all but perhaps a tiny segment of the population? In what way did they constitute a "clear and present danger"? What was the evidence? I thought I might see.

The November 1992 Hate Literature Experiment

I opted to test the matter with an ordinary "pre-post-test" attitude change experiment in which two groups have their attitudes assessed, one receives some information, and then both have their attitudes assessed again. You have to avoid several traps in such a study. When the participants give their first opinions, they cannot have any idea that they will later serve in an experiment related to those answers. (If they do, that knowledge can affect what they put down.) Also, enough time has to pass before the second session so the subjects cannot remember exactly what they said the first time. Furthermore, since the issue involves prejudice, and the experiment obviously will track socially *un*-desirable change at the second session, people have to be anonymous, and know they are anonymous, on both occasions. Yet you have to be able somehow to match the first set of answers with the second. And you have to include a control group that receives no added information but still has a plausible reason for giving their opinions again.

The first session took place on October 5, 1992, when I administered a booklet of surveys to a large introductory psychology class under the secret-number conditions. The students signed nothing but instead put a number of their choosing at the top of the bubble sheet, supposedly so I could give them individual feedback later in the year. The second task in the eight-task booklet, right after the RWA Scale, asked for reactions to the statements shown in Exhibit 10.1. These measured how much the student believed the Holocaust had occurred. Some of the eight items dealt with general issues. Others were worded to catch any changes caused by specific points raised in the propaganda I intended to use later. Scores on the scale could go from 8 to 72, with 40 being the neutral point. A high score indicates belief that the Holocaust had happened.

Exhibit 10.1   The Eight Items Used to Assess Belief in the Holocaust

1. Six million Jews could not possibly have been killed by the Nazis during World War II; there were too many Jews alive *after* the war for that to be true.* (8.00)

2. The Nazis deliberately killed approximately six million Jews in an attempt to exterminate the Jewish population wherever they could. (7.98)

3. The films everyone has seen of the gas chambers and crematoria at Auschwitz leave no doubt that mass exterminations were carried out there during World War II. (7.98)[3]

4. Many impartial witnesses, including the Red Cross and United Nations officials, have testified there were *no* exterminations performed at Auschwitz.* (6.81)

5. The testimony of thousands of "Holocaust survivors" confirm that mass exterminations were carried out by the Nazis at extermination camps such as Auschwitz. (7.65)

6. There is an international Jewish conspiracy that uses fables about the "Holocaust" to help it dominate the world through control of banks, the news media, the movie industry, etc.* (7.04)

7. The stories about "exterminations" at Auschwitz are impossible, given the facts about the physical layout of the camp. Stories about "fires burning all night" and "foul smells" have quite ordinary explanations.* (7.44)

8. Jews are *not* trying to take over the world. That is simply a myth spread by bigots to make people fear and hate Jews. (7.70)

Note: Items are answered on a −4 to +4 basis.

* Item is worded in the contrait direction; the respondent has to *disagree* to indicate belief that the Holocaust occurred.

The 252 students' means are printed after each item in Exhibit 10.1. Adding them up, you can see that they average 60.6, about halfway between "moderately agree" and "strongly agree." The mean intercorrelation among the eight items equaled .41, producing an alpha of .84. Summed scores correlated significantly with RWA (− .21) and my Ethnocentrism measure (− .44).

Three weeks later I reappeared in this class with a list of the secret numbers the members had used. I invited the students to sign up for a second (undescribed) experiment, using just their secret numbers, to be run at either 3:30 or 4:30 P.M. on November 4.

Both of these sessions of the attitude-change experiment were held in a large classroom. A note on the board instructed participants to sit in alternate seats. At a signal from me, the students came to the front of the room to reclaim their bubble sheets, which were in numerical piles by secret numbers. Once the students had sat down again, I extracted a promise from them not to discuss the experiment "because other students will serve in it later." (I did this in all subsequent experiments as well.)[4] At the 3:30 session, attended by 74 students, I then distributed photocopies of excerpts from a pamphlet that denied the Holocaust had occurred. Reminding them that they were serving anonymously, I asked the students simply to read the article, and then respond on the bubble sheet to the statements that followed. (These were the same eight items given in Exhibit 10.1.) When the students turned in their materials, I gave them a feedback sheet extensively debunking the pamphlet.[5]

At the 4:30 session, attended by 14 students, the seating, anonymity, and distribution of the bubble sheets proceeded as above. However, instead of any "denial" material, I handed out copies of the booklet the students had completed in October. I explained the situation thus:

Today I am simply going to ask you to answer again some of the surveys you answered last time. That is because I am trying to determine the test-retest reliability of the questionnaires. All you have to do is answer according to how you feel today. Don't try to remember how you answered before. Don't try to *look* consistent. Just answer according to how you feel now.

   Let me remind you that you are answering anonymously. I never knew whose answers were whose the first time, and I never will know today.

The eight Holocaust items again made up the second task, after a batch of RWA Scale items. (However, to keep control subjects from being able to locate their first set of answers to the Holocaust items on the bubble sheet, I added a few statements to the RWA portion to throw the numbering off.)

THE DENIAL PAMPHLET

The Holocaust-denying material came from a pamphlet entitled *Auschwitz: A Personal Account by Thies Christophersen,* which someone had sent me. Christophersen was an SS officer stationed at Auschwitz during 1944, when a great number of the gassings took place. He was assigned to the Buna rubber project however, to supervise the cultivation of rubber plants by slave laborers. Although he was a minor cog in the operations at Auschwitz, I found a brief reference to him on page 418 of *Auschwitz Chronicle* (Czech, 1990). The female prisoners apparently nicknamed him "Locher" ("Puncher").

   Christophersen's pamphlet, first published in German in 1973, begins with his statement that he knows the atrocities said to have occurred at Auschwitz never happened. But he is fearful of telling the truth, because he could be prosecuted. Nevertheless, he will no longer keep silent.

   He starts with some vaguely referenced, uncheckable "population statistics" that "show" there were several million more Jews alive after World War II than there were before. Supposedly only 200,000 Jews died during World War II, "according to facts compiled by the UNO." And (rather inconsistently) "a book published in Brazil" stated that only 200,000 Jews died in the twelve years of Hitler's rule, from *all* causes. Several people are quoted as saying they saw no gas chambers while in concentration camps.

   Christophersen then begins his personal account. He talks about Germany's need for synthetic rubber. He had been wounded in the war and was sent to do a job in a rear area. He describes arriving at Auschwitz ("Auschwitz I," the original "show camp" constructed in 1940) and finding many of the camp's inmates walking around freely. The camp was guarded only at night, he says. He describes his supervisor and his roommate, fine fellows both. Some of his charges were Jehovah's Witnesses, and he let them practice their religion ("I had always been tolerant in matters of religion"). He describes the India rubber plant project. He relates that one of the staff agronomists found a former sweetheart among the prisoners. They were married and she was released. He mentions that "in Dresden more people died than had supposedly died in Auschwitz throughout all the years of the war."

Then Christophersen describes the daily routine at Auschwitz. The prisoners were awakened at 7:00 A.M. washed, showered, had breakfast and roll call, and then began work at 8:00 A.M. Lunch took place from 12:00 to 1:00, and the prisoners worked again until 5:00 P.M. Roll was called again at 7:00 P.M., and then the camp was put under guard. Mail was delivered daily. The prisoners routinely received packages from outside.

Christophersen tells of his wife's visit to Auschwitz in May 1944 for a second honeymoon, and how lovingly they were treated by the inmate assigned as his personal maid. His prisoners never went hungry, and any undernourished new arrivals were soon fattened up.

He describes a visit to Birkenau. He did not like this camp; it was crowded. But he points out that the British had done the same sort of thing during the Boer War. He needed some field workers, and female prisoners there were asked if they were interested. Many volunteered, and so the final 100 had to be selected. This was the "selection" at Birkenau that "was later completely misinterpreted." He never saw anything that indicated mass killings in gas chambers. The report that a smell of burning flesh hovered over the camp at times "was an infamous lie." There was a blacksmith nearby; the smell came from fitting shoes to horses. The fires that lit the skies at night came from a nearby mining camp.

Christophersen says he reported an SS guard for kicking a prisoner. His detachment of inmates from Birkenau "was a merry bunch," literally singing and dancing in the fields. There was a weekly movie. Church services were held. A theater group sprung up. Camp regulations became more generous all the time.

There were no secrets at Auschwitz. The Red Cross inspected the place and barely mentioned it in their report on German prisoner camps. Christophersen had extensive contact with the SS officers who ran other departments, and often heard them talk of their problems. But he never heard of anything offensive. Any medical experiments were humane and beneficial. "It is an absolute certainty that no people were shot at Auschwitz." But some of the prisoners spread a rumor one time that some hostages were to be shot. Christophersen expressed horror at the idea.

He concludes that it was impossible to kill as many people at Auschwitz as has been proposed. Why do the German people continue to believe that mass murders took place under the Nazi regime?

Christophersen's pamphlet features many photographs. He is shown leaning on a little horse-drawn buggy used by officers to move around the camp grounds. He and his wife are pictured strolling down a sidewalk. The two of them are seen enjoying dinner during the second honeymoon. Women inmates are shown working in the fields. A "visiting delegation" of about a dozen German soldiers smiles for the camera. A few overlapping pages of the Red Cross report, written in French, are displayed.[6]

Comment: This account of the Nazi death camp at Auschwitz differs so radically from any other of which I am aware, you would think it must have been on some other planet. Could Thies Christophersen really have had no idea what was happening around him? I think he *had* to know. For example, his residence and fields were in the village of Rajsko, just south of Auschwitz. He lived and worked right by the railroad tracks that brought trainload after trainload of prisoners into the camp, immensely more people than the facilities could hold. Did it never occur to him, "Where have all those prisoners gone?"

RESULTS

The mean pretest score for the control group was 63.3, and that on November 4 equaled 62.6, which obviously was *not* significantly different. We are talking about only 14 people here, but it does not appear that anything happened in the larger world during the intervening month that affected students' belief in the Holocaust.

The pretest mean among the other subjects was 60.4, which *dropped* to 52.3 after reading the Christophersen account ($p < .001$). To put this in perspective, if we consider the distance between the initial student mean of 60.4 and the neutral point of 40 to indicate how much the students positively believed the Holocaust occurred, Christophersen's pamphlet cut that nearly in half.

The effect was general, both in content and in who was duped. All of the items in Exhibit 10.1 showed a significant drop, except numbers 6 and 8 (which deal with the ancillary matter of the "international Jewish conspiracy"). Thus, most particularly, Christophersen's account not only affected beliefs on the specific points he raised (population figures, the source of the burning flesh smell, the Red Cross report), it also significantly lessened these students' general willingness to accept the testimony of Holocaust survivors, and it affected their belief that the Nazis had tried to destroy the Jewish people. This sad effect, which was accomplished in about fifteen minutes, affected Low RWAs just as much as Highs. The correlation between personal authoritarianism and being suckered by Christophersen's pamphlet was .12 (not significant).

DISCUSSION

First, I want to express my unease at the *pretest* means. The Holocaust has become one of the most heavily documented historical events of all time. It happened. No one can ever know the exact numbers of Jews who were murdered by the Nazis, but they *were* slaughtered on the most mind-numbing scale. It is no more a "matter of opinion" than belief that World War II occurred. There is no "other side" of the story worthy of consideration any more than there is "another side" to the story that manned lunar landings occurred.

But the first step in the denial campaign has been to make the Holocaust a matter of opinion, one with "two legitimate points of view." And it has been wildly successful. A widely reported poll (*Time,* January 3, 1994, pp. 9–11) found that one-third of the American people think it is "possible" the Holocaust never took place—compared with only 6% of the French and 16% of the British populations. Even more to the point of this experiment, 40% of American youth apparently do not even know what the Holocaust *was.*[7]

Second, I suspect Christophersen's pamphlet was so persuasive partly because of its simple, human tone. He was just a wounded soldier put in charge of a farm (he says, not revealing he was in the SS). He was so generous and fair, the inmates inevitably liked him. (Good Old "Puncher!") Could such a gentle, honorable man be part of anything horrible? Could a man who loved his wife so much lie now?

Certainly he could. But if you do not notice that the source of your information about the Holocaust is also the source of your information about the source of your information, you are ready to be "taken."

So was I, while reading the Nazi propaganda in the anteroom of the NSWPP headquarters. But that is the point. Critical thinking may be in desperately short supply. It is hard enough to find the truth in a fair fight. Most of us, especially scientists who assume everyone is dedicated to the truth, may be unprepared for the unfair fight when some people deliberately promote lies.[8]

So what? Well, would the Holocaust have occurred if the German people had seen through Hitler's Big Lie?

The January 1993 Experiment

As soon as I saw these results, I set out to repeat the experiment, administering the eight Holocaust items in a booklet given to another large section of introductory psychology on November 27, 1992. Some six weeks later, after the Christmas break, I reappeared in this class with the invitation to sign up for a second study via the secret numbers.

Two sessions were held on January 15, 1993. Sixty-three Controls served at 12:30 P.M., and then 38 experimental subjects appeared at 1:30 P.M. I had wondered if the students who received Christophersen's account in the first study had assumed I agreed with those ideas and if that assumption had contributed to the propaganda's effect. So I gave the following statement of neutrality to this batch of Experimentals.

Today I am simply going to hand out an article for you to read, and I'll ask you to answer some questions afterward. You should *not* assume, because I am giving you this article to read, that I agree with what it says. On the other hand, you should *not* assume that I *dis*agree with what it says either.

Let me remind you that you are answering anonymously. I never knew whose answers were whose the first time, and I never will know today.

The Controls got the test-retest instructions described earlier.

The control group's mean in November had been 59.3, while that in January was 59.5. Again, no sign appeared of change because of "external" events.

The experimental subjects started off with a somewhat low belief in the Holocaust, 55.4, which dropped to 48.2 after reading Christophersen's denial ($p < .001$). As a group, they now only "slightly agreed" that the Holocaust had occurred. Saying I did not necessarily endorse the article had no effect on *its* effect. All of the items showed a significant drop, except numbers 6 and 8. Again, Low RWAs were just as likely to be fooled by the propaganda as Highs ($r = .10$).

Replications On Other Campuses

Once I had replicated the finding, I asked Bruce Hunsberger at Wilfrid Laurier University and Bill Stone at the University of Maine to see what effect Christophersen's article had on their students. Hunsberger (personal communication, March 28, 1993) did a pre-post experiment over nearly a month, involving 48 introductory psychology students, and 19 upperclass students taking a psychology of religion course from him. All received the experimental treatment, with the "neutrality statement" given above.

These students too had a low initial level of belief in the Holocaust from the start, averaging 52.2. Christophersen's piece lowered that to 42.7 ($p < .001$). Significant changes occurred on all the items except numbers 6 and 8, and again no connection appeared between RWA scores and change.

Bill Stone (Stone and Yelland, 1994) ran a post-only experiment involving (1) a control group that read a four-page essay on a utopian community, (2) a denial group that read four pages taken from the Christophersen piece, and (3) a factual group given an account of Auschwitz taken from Rudolf Hoess's confession at Nuremberg (Hoess 1959). Subjects ($N = 131$) came from two sections of a social psychology course and worked through a booklet containing the RWA and other scales, one of the readings, and the eight-item Holocaust measure, while in class.

A significant main effect for the essays appeared ($F = 5.06$; $p < .01$). Those who had read the denial material believed less in the Holocaust afterward (the mean equaled 56.1) than those in the control (61.0) or factual (62.8) conditions. (The last two did not differ significantly.) While earlier studies showed a larger effect, these students read only a small part of Christophersen's pamphlet.

Stone found that High RWA students were significantly more likely to be persuaded by the denial than Lows ($F = 3.81$ for the interaction, $p < .05$).

The November 1993 Experiment

With these two cross-validations to comfort and frighten me, I set about exploring the nuances of the "denial effect" during the 1993–94 school year. My first experiment compared the effectiveness of the Christophersen piece with the confession of Rudolf Hoess. Hoess was the commandant of the Auschwitz complex until December 1943 (when he was promoted to supervise a *network* of camps). He had firsthand knowledge of the directive from above for the "final solution" and the way it was implemented at Auschwitz. After being found guilty of crimes against humanity at Nuremberg in 1946, he was turned over to Poland (in which Auschwitz is located), where he was tried again, found guilty, and hanged in 1947. During this period he wrote his autobiography, in which he confessed (with virtually no remorse) to his highly important role in the Holocaust.

I photocopied pages 206–218 of his autobiography, prefacing them with the title page of the book, and a note saying, "This article is taken from the autobiography of Rudolf Hoess, who was the Commandant of Auschwitz." Hoess begins these pages, an appendix to his autobiography, by describing the orders from Hitler through Heinrich Himmler in the summer of 1941 to eliminate the Jews, and the need to build a mass execution facility at Auschwitz. He details how Zyklon B was tested and chosen to kill the prisoners and describes the early days when relatively small numbers were gassed. He reveals that for a while the bodies were buried in mass graves, but toward the end of the summer of 1942 so many people were being killed in a day that the bodies were burned in huge piles in the open, "day and night, continuously." The bodies previously buried were also dug up and burned, on orders from Himmler, and the ashes distributed around the countryside and thrown in a river.

Hoess then relates how war industries were built at Auschwitz because of the availability of slave labor. The need for workers led to the "selection process" at the railroad siding, to separate those Jews who would be immediately gassed from those who would be worked until they succumbed to starvation or disease.

Hoess's biggest problem, he says, lay in the disposal of the dead bodies. Open air incineration spread the stench of burning flesh for miles and caused the whole neighborhood to talk about the burning of Jews. Moreover, the air defense services protested that the fires could be seen from great distances at night. Even after four new crematoria were built at Birkenau, the SS still had trouble disposing of all the murdered victims.

Food for the slave laborers was in such short supply at Auschwitz that even when Himmler ordered that some Jews be given extra food so they would last longer in the work projects, Hoess considered the order "sheer mockery." Unchecked disease began to kill large numbers of the workers too.

Hoess says he can only guess how many Jews died *at Auschwitz*. He "personally destroyed every bit of evidence which could be found in my office." Officers throughout the SS did the same thing, on orders, as the war came to a close. He remembered being told by Adolf Eichmann, and his deputies, that about two and one half million Jews had died at Auschwitz. It may have been less, however. The excerpted passage ended with Hoess's breakdown of how many Jews from different parts of Europe were killed in "the larger actions" at Auschwitz. That total comes to over a million.

These revelations involved about as much text as Christophersen's account of Auschwitz. They required fewer pages, however, because no photos accompanied them.

On November 17, 1993, students identifiable only by their secret numbers showed up for my third Holocaust-denial experiment. They had responded to the eight Holocaust items on September 29 as part of a booklet administered in their class. Those who made a 12:30 appointment ($N = 57$) received the Hoess confession just described. Those who showed up at 1:30 ($N = 52$) got the Christophersen denial. Those who appeared at 2:30 ($N = 49$) received both.

INSTRUCTIONS

I began with the usual pledge of secrecy and statement of neutrality in each condition. Then I added: "If you find some of the material too stressful to read, you should skip ahead a bit until you find you can continue. This may seem unnecessary to say, but I want you to know it is all right if you want to do so." I put this in because of the Hoess confession, a truly horrific account if you stop to think about what he describes so matter of factly. In the 2:30 session, I counterbalanced the order of presentation by giving everyone in alternate rows a booklet that started with Christophersen, and everyone in the intervening rows booklets that started with Hoess. You could easily tell from the front of the room which row was reading Hoess's account, for those students looked more intense, and sometimes showed expressions of pain. But I never saw anyone skip anything in Hoess's confession.[9]

RESULTS

The "September mean" score among the students who just got Hoess's confession was 59.8. After reading his confession, their scores remained virtually *un*changed, 60.4. By contrast, the students who read just Christophersen's account dropped from 56.9 to 48.9 ($p < .001$). And those who read both accounts *believed Christophersen;* their mean dropped from 58.0 to 50.7 ($p < .001$).

The Christophersen article thus proved as persuasive as before. In the 1:30 session, all the items showed significant changes except numbers 6 and 8. In the 2:30 session, item 5 also did not drop significantly. In both conditions employing Christophersen's denial, Low RWAs were as likely to be moved as Highs.

DISCUSSION

I cannot explain it. I do not know why students would take the word of a minor official who says nothing bad took place over that of a commander who confessed to operating a mass murder machine. If you were serving on a grand jury investigating a murder, which would you find more credible: the testimony of the driver of a get-away car who swears he saw nothing bad happen or the detailed confession of the person who says he pulled the trigger?

Could it be a "ceiling effect"? I doubt it. The subjects' pretest means left plenty of room to go up. Students are quite capable of answering a series of questionnaire items with +4s and −4s. Yet in the "Hoess only" condition, their opinions barely quivered; and in the "both" condition, Hoess's truthful narration could not even fight Christophersen's lies and distortions to a draw.

The January 6, 1994, Experiment

Maybe the Hoess confession would do better against a similarly "dry" account, one that denied the Holocaust had occurred, only without pictures. I had received another piece of revisionist material, a document entitled "Sixty-six Questions and Answers on the Holocaust" published by the major source of denial material, the Institute for Historical Review, located in Costa Mesa, California. The document documents nothing, demonstrates nothing, proves nothing. But it amounts to a *lot* of nothing, taking up both sides of a legal-sized sheet of paper. It operates mainly on the level of bald (and largely false) assertion. Take questions 1 and 2, for example:

1. What proof exists that the Nazis practiced genocide or deliberately killed six million Jews? [Answer:] None. The only evidence is the testimony of individual "survivors." This testimony is contradictory, and few "survivors" claim to have actually witnessed any gassing. There is no hard evidence whatsoever: no mounds of ashes, no crematoria capable of doing the job, no piles of clothes, no human soap, no lamp shades made of human skin, no records, no credible demographic statistics.

2. What evidence exists that six million Jews were not killed by the Nazis? [Answer:] Extensive evidence, including that of a forensic, demographic, analytical and comparative nature, exists demonstrating the *impossibility* of such a figure, an exaggeration of, perhaps, 1000%.

"Sixty-six Questions" only partly overlaps the material Christophersen brought up. It concentrates much more on the difficulty in gassing and burning so many people. (In one subterfuge it demonstrates that six million Jews could not have been killed *at Auschwitz*.) But the Red Cross report is mentioned ("rumors of gas chambers could not be confirmed").[10] And it is claimed that after the war "it was American, British, French and Soviet policy to torture German prisoners in order to exact confessions." In Hoess's case, he was supposedly "tortured by Jewish interrogators in British uniform, as one of them has subsequently admitted."

The document specifically states that the Holocaust story, while false, is used by Jews and the state of Israel to further their ends—which Christophersen never said explicitly. But it does not cover the "foul smells" issue brought up in item 7 of Exhibit 10.1.

PROCEDURE

On November 25, 1993, I administered a booklet of surveys to another large section of introductory psychology under the secret-number conditions. The eight-item Holocaust Scale used in the previous studies was included. Students recruited from this class then served in a two-condition experiment on January 6, 1994. The same set of instructions used in the November 1993 study was employed again. At 1:00 P.M. 51 persons received both "Sixty-six Questions" and the Hoess confession in counterbalanced order. Then they answered the Holocaust Scale again. At 2:30 P.M., 39 other students responded to the scale after receiving just the "Sixty-six Questions."[11]

RESULTS

The "Sixty-six Questions" (2:30 session) moved the students' mean from 59.4 to 55.3 ($p < .05$). When pitted against the Hoess confession, the propaganda dropped scores even more, from 60.9 to 54.1 ($p < .001$). In the former case, only items 1, 2, and 3 from Exhibit 10.1 showed a significant drop. In the latter case, in which students received both pieces, all of the items showed a significant drop, except number 8. In both conditions, Low RWAs were as affected by the propaganda as Highs.

DISCUSSION

Overall, "Sixty-six Questions and Answers on the Holocaust" appears a little less convincing than Christophersen's "personal account." It lacks the "homey touch" and the nice photos. But this is like saying a heart attack is not as bad as a malignant tumor. Both pieces of denial propaganda proved much more convincing than the confession of the man who supervised an enormous amount of the killing. His admissions were simply ignored.

In retrospect, I think the Hoess confession misfired because it is so gruesome. Students may have avoided thinking about it for that reason, and so remained unmoved. Strong fear-arousing communications can do this (Insko, 1967). If so, it provides a final ironic injustice to the victims of the Holocaust. They, along with many other Nazi prisoners, were brutalized and murdered by the powerful forces in German society. These Nazis, because they were powerful and still influential, often escaped from Europe afterward, sometimes with the active help of Allied governments. Even those captured, tried, and convicted usually had their sentences commuted for reasons of political expediency as the Cold War developed. And now, people may not want to know the truth about the Holocaust precisely because it was so horrible.

But why should people be influenced by the "Sixty-six Questions"? It boils down to crass assertions. Suppose I were to assert no atomic bombs were dropped on Japan. It's all a lie, I could insist, with fake photos, false records, contradictory evidence from "survivors," and affidavits obtained by torture. Hiroshima and Nagasaki, I could say in all perfect insincerity, were destroyed by intense conventional bombing. The fraud was originally perpetrated by the United States to intimidate the Soviet Union, to keep it from overrunning western Europe in 1945. Actually, America had no atomic bombs until 1946 I assert. Now the Japanese use the fake atomic bombings to make Americans feel guilty and generous toward Japan.

If I make up sixty-six questions and answers about the Manhattan Project and the Enola Gay and how quickly radiation kills a person, asserting the atomic bombing never happened, will that cause university students today to believe less strongly in a thoroughly established, undeniable major historical fact? Maybe it would.

Overall it seems, from these six Holocaust-denial studies, that people are spring-loaded to move in just one direction on the Holocaust. And the direction truly alarms me.[12]

Hate Literature against Homosexuals

During the summer of 1993 I received another pamphlet through the mail, with the pithy title "Intolerance of, Discrimination against, and the Death Penalty for Homosexuals Is Prescribed in the Bible." It was sent me by its author, Pastor Peter J. Peters of Fort Collins, Colorado, perhaps in the hopeless hope I would change my beliefs and be saved. This polemic begins with various biblical tracts, one of which does indeed prescribe the death penalty for homosexuals.[13]

The pamphlet goes on to make three main points. (1) Law by its very nature is intolerant and discriminatory. The police, for example, will not tolerate your driving over the speed limit and will discriminate against you for speeding by giving you a ticket. (2) The Bible must be obeyed in America according to Public Law 97-280. (Peters reproduces this "law," which is clearly labeled as merely a Congressional resolution designating 1983 as the "Year of the Bible.") (3) Homosexuals are trying to kill heterosexuals, so heterosexuals have to kill homosexuals.

The pamphlet abounds in biblical quotations supplementing Pastor Peters's analogies and arguments. He also attacks "luke-warm hypocrites like those so-called Christians in the Churches" who have not heeded the pastor's call for a bloodbath. He says Jesus will spit them out of his mouth (Revelations 3:15–16).

The January 1994 Study

I decided to see if something as ridiculous as this pamphlet would affect university students' opinions about homosexuals. So on November 10 and 15, 1993, I administered a booklet in two other sections of introductory psychology that contained eight items that would later prove relevant to Pastor Peters's appeal. (An asterisk indicates, as usual, a contrait item where the nonhostile, supportive-of-homosexuals response was to disagree.)

1. Laws should be passed protecting homosexuals from discrimination and intolerance.

2. Homosexuals are an abomination in the sight of God.*

3. It is unChristian to hate homosexuals.

4. Discrimination and intolerance are a way of life, and there is nothing wrong with them per se.*

5. The *true* Christian believes homosexuals should have NO "rights" in our society.*

6. If there is a Heaven, homosexuals have as good a chance of getting there as anyone else.

7. Homosexuals are NOT plotting to kill whoever opposes them.

8. Homosexuals should be put to death.*

The 269 students from the two classes, who answered their booklets in the secret-number situation, showed *mild* support of homosexuals, averaging

54.8 on a scale that could go from 8 to 72, with 40 being neutral. On the average, the eight items intercorrelated .32, giving an alpha of .79. RWA scores correlated .52 with degree of hostility shown toward homosexuals.

I recruited members of these classes for a three-condition experiment as soon as they returned from their Christmas break. At 10:30 A.M. on January 7, 1994, 46 students served in a control condition. However, they did not receive the "test-retest reliability" cover story. Instead, after they had picked up their bubble sheets, sat back down, and committed themselves to secrecy, I handed out a booklet that began with the statements listed above. I simply asked them to respond to those items and not turn the page until I gave them the signal. When I could see all had finished, I asked them to read the (Peters) article that followed. Then they responded to the eight items again.

The 47 students who attended a session at 12:30 P.M. got the experimental procedure used in the last two Holocaust-denial studies, including the statement of neutrality.

The 38 students at a session at 11:30 A.M. also got the usual experimental treatment, except that I told them: "I want to say that I personally do NOT agree AT ALL with the contents of this article. I think it is COMPLETELY wrong. But other people would disagree with me, and agree with the article."

RESULTS

The control group's average score over the eight intervening weeks went from 54.0 to 56.3 (at the very beginning of the session), a nonsignificant rise. The 12:30 P.M. students who read Pastor Peters's arguments after my neutrality statement had their scores *drop* significantly, from 55.9 to 49.2 ($p < .01$). The 11:30 A.M. students who read the article after I had denounced it were less affected by it, but their mean still *fell* from 54.0 to 50.0 ($p < .05$).[14]

In the neutral situation, items 1, 2, 4, and 7 in the list above all fell significantly, and RWA scores correlated significantly (.31) with the change produced by Pastor Peters—perhaps because of all the biblical quotes. In the denounced-by-Experimenter condition, items 4, 5, and 7 rose significantly, and there was no connection between personal authoritarianism and change ($-.06$)—perhaps because the Experimenter's denunciation offset the biblical references.

DISCUSSION

I think we can lay to rest the suspicion that the students did not really change their attitudes in all these studies, but merely pretended to, to please the Experimenter. For subjects here were still affected by an article that the Experimenter condemned—not as much as when the Experimenter insisted he be considered neutral, of course, but almost as much.

This result disturbs me, because Peters's arguments, like those of the Holocaust deniers, overwhelm me with their flimsiness and stupidity. They are Hitler's Big Lie. Yet after reading them, these university students became less in favor of legislation protecting homosexuals from discrimination, became more convinced homosexuals are an abomination in the sight of God, believed more strongly that there was nothing wrong with discrimination and intolerance, and believed more strongly that homosexuals are plotting to kill their opponents.

We cannot be proud of these effects as educators. Our students do not appear to examine critically what they read; they just chugalug it down. Furthermore, the fact that Pastor Peters moved them even when his arguments were denounced by the Experimenter suggests one cannot present such material to uncritical thinkers, simply denounce it, and think it will do no harm.

Effects of an Anti-Feminist Article

The autumn of 1994, with its bounty of new students, presented opportunities for more experiments on hate literature. Professor Karen Grant of our Sociology Department had called my attention to a Canadian magazine article entitled "Fembo in Academe" (*Western Report,* January 7, 1991). This piece presented (in my opinion) an unfair picture of Women's Studies programs. By citing misleading statistics, using unrepresentative quotes, and concentrating on the most radical writers in the field, the article created the impression that Women's Studies departments are dominated by lesbian, man-hating, family-destroying "separatists" who care little about truth or academic standards and everything about "the Cause."

I would not argue that this article constitutes "hate literature" the way the Christophersen, "Sixty-six Questions" and Peters pieces do. But it comes close. Like more flagrant attacks, it presented its targets as immoral, single-minded deviants who are growing ever more powerful and out to get us. It was not Rush Limbaugh, but it was the step right before him. I thought that someone who was influenced by the article would likely become more prejudiced against feminists in general.

Following my usual procedure, I administered the following eight items in a secret-number booklet answered by 394 students in October 1994. (As usual, an asterisk indicates a contrait item.)

1. Most feminists want to destroy the family.*

2. Hiring more women than men as professors in the future will *not* hurt academic standards at this university.

3. Most female professors who teach in Women's Studies programs are lesbians.*

4. Women's Studies is as much an academic discipline as any other program at this university. It is a scholarly field that is taught, not an ideology that is preached.

5. The chief purpose of Women's Studies courses is to promote hatred against men and to instill contempt for non-feminist women.*

6. Radical feminist views should be offered in courses at this university. If they are wrong, they will be exposed by other scholars, as always, in the usual way.

7. There is nothing wrong with giving women extra scholarships or research grants to encourage them to enter programs that men traditionally dominate.

8. Most feminist professors are not really interested in scholarship or normal academic standards. All they really care about is "the Cause."*

Scores could again vary from 8 to 72, with a high score representing *support* of Women's Studies and 40 being neutral. The students' mean was 51.3. With an average interitem correlation of .28, alpha equaled .76. As you would predict, High RWAs tended to score low in support for feminists ($r = -.33$); the correlation with gender was even greater (.47), with women scoring higher than men.

Six weeks later I recruited 160 students from these classes, who signed up by their secret numbers, for an experiment being run at 11:30, 12:30, and 1:30 on November 16. Participants in the first two sessions ($N = 117$) simply answered a booklet of surveys for me under the usual (control) "test-retest reliability" instructions. This booklet ended with the eight "Fembo" items. The 43 students who attended at 1:30, however, got the Fembo article with the statement of Experimenter neutrality and answered the same eight items afterward.

The control students had had a mean of 51.2 in October, and they posted a very similar 50.9 in November. Thus attitudes on the issues do not appear to have changed for extraneous reasons over the interval.

Those in the third session had a slightly higher October score of 53.8 ($p > .20$), which dropped nearly 10 points to 43.9 following the Fembo article. Significant losses occurred on the first five items and the last. By a bit of sampling misfortune, only 8 men served in the experimental condition. They dropped 10.4 points overall, from 45.8 to 35.4. But the 35 females in this condition were affected nearly as much ($55.6 - 45.9 = 9.7$). Overall, Low RWAs were as likely to be affected by the attack as Highs ($r = -.12$; not significant).

To summarize, after a month at university the students expressed moderate support of feminism, female professors, and Women's Studies programs. Six weeks later, a short magazine article effectively wiped out that support. While that may bring joy to the editors of the magazine, it troubles me no end. As proved true for Jews and for homosexuals, feminists appear quite vulnerable to those who would promote hostility against them.

The Effects of *Schindler's List* upon Holocaust Denial

Shortly after my last experiment using Holocaust-denial material, the Academy Award–winning movie *Schindler's List* opened in Winnipeg. This film presents in a most gripping, harrowing way the cruelty and savagery of the Holocaust. It was well attended in my city, as elsewhere, and became available on video cassette the following autumn.

I wondered whether the movie would help protect university students against Holocaust-denial material, and so I administered my usual eight items to 415 introductory psychology students under secret-number circumstances in early October 1994. The mean score was 60.6, the same value I had found in my first hate literature study two years earlier. (I was surprised, expecting the movie to have increased belief that the Holocaust had occurred.)

On November 17, 46 of these students serving as a control group reanswered these items at the end of a "test-retest reliability" booklet. *Their* October mean of 60.4 had shifted just a touch to 60.0 over the six weeks. So again we have a stable attitude, unaffected by events over the pre-post test interval.

The next day 85 (non-Jewish) students on whom I had October scores were given the Christophersen piece with the neutrality statement. They then reanswered the eight items and also told me whether they had seen *Schindler's List,* before or since the October survey. I also asked them to identify what Oskar Schindler had manufactured at his first factory, to verify they had indeed seen the movie. Thirty-four of the students said they had seen the movie before October, 3 had seen it since, and 48 said they had not seen it at all. All but one of the viewers knew that Schindler had manufactured cooking pots.

The 33 persons whom I was reasonably sure had seen the movie before October had shown significantly higher belief in the Holocaust in the pretest (mean = 64.8) than the 48 who had not (57.2) ($p < .01$). The nonviewers were affected, as usual, by Christophersen's fairy tale about Auschwitz, dropping nearly 7 points to 50.4. But so were the 33 persons *who had seen the movie,* who went from 64.8 to 57.9. Both drops were statistically significant beyond the .01 level.

We cannot say that *Schindler's List* had any effect on belief in the Holocaust. The students who chose to see the movie may have known about the Nazis' systematic annihilation of the Jews before they went; those who did not know, and did not want to know, may have generally avoided the film. What we can say, unfortunately, is that the non-Jewish students who saw the movie were not protected against later Holocaust denial. They fell for Christophersen just like everyone else. I was quite disappointed.

Are the Effects of Hate Literature Short-Lived?

Do the disturbing effects we have uncovered last, or do they evaporate with the next thought? We do not know. I *suspect* they are strongest when gauged immediately after students have read an inciting piece, but before they have had a chance to reflect upon it, or just plain forget it, or hear counterarguments. But I also suspect the effect seldom disappears entirely. People may not reflect further, and even if they forget the particular "facts" raised in the hate literature, they may still carry around the conclusion in their heads. We should also recall the several experiments which showed that students, when presented with hate literature and the truth, overwhelmingly believed the hate literature.[15]

So while I would like to think that hate literature has no lasting effect, I could simply be sticking my head in the sand. After all, something *has* had a significant long-term effect on many Americans' belief in the Holocaust. And people who come into contact with anti-Semitic, homosexual-hating, feminist-despising groups will be given one piece of hate literature after another. There are many, many books and pamphlets that tell the same lies so consistently, it could seem to many "there must be some truth to this."

What Should We Do?

It appears that many kinds of hate literature "work" on university students. Can we wonder, then, why it attracts disgruntled, undereducated, disaffected young people to violent "skinhead" organizations? Can we wonder how it might convince people who join "militias" that they are victims of a gigantic Jewish, black, Communist conspiracy to take away their guns and enslave them?

Considering the historic evidence that hate literature can turn a nation against a vulnerable minority, where does freedom of speech end? Is it an absolute right more important than any other? Do not people have a right to be protected against false and vicious attacks that, if believed, could lead to their destruction? The Canadian Supreme Court ruling appeals to me a lot more after doing these experiments than it did before. Should the Institute for

Historical Review be allowed to publish things like its "Sixty-six Questions"? Should the "Personal Account by Thies Christophersen" and "The Bible Says Homosexuals Should Be Killed" be allowed to circulate?

I used to say "Yes" *automatically,* because I do not think you can have a "truth police" in a democracy, and because I believed that a completely free and open marketplace of ideas provided the best antidote to the poison of hate literature. One *can* easily expose the distortions, frauds, and subterfuges of the hatemongers. Let them have their say; then others can show how distorted and unconvincing their "evidence" is. But what happens if the people in the marketplace cannot tell truth from falsity? What happens if they do not care, like Pastor Niemoeller in Hitler's Germany, so long as *their* group is not being persecuted.

I *still* feel freedom of speech should extend to hate literature; but like my affected subjects, I am now closer to $+1$ than to $+3$. I also know that the hate spreaders count on people like me to defend this right, which they do not believe in at all; that they despise us for our "weakness" in doing so, that civil rights advocates would be among the first they would eliminate if they came to power, and that they would never give anyone any freedoms at all, but only their place in the execution line, if they had their murderous way.

Short of bringing "mind pornographers" into court, several things must obviously be done. We cannot let the lies go unchallenged but must instead continually expose their falseness.[16] We also have to do a much, much better job teaching people how to think critically. If the students we have taught fall for absurd arguments, ridiculous reasoning and ersatz evidence—including even the Low RWAs—then we should have to give back part of our salaries. For we have failed worse than they. I think we have to make strenuous, positive efforts to tell the truth. If we do not, we leave the field to those who would destroy all we have struggled to accomplish, while they tell the Big Lie that they are trying to protect democracy.

Summing Up a Lot of Bad News

We have covered nine attitude-change experiments on the effects of hate literature upon university students. The studies showed such propaganda "worked." It made people believe *less* that the Holocaust occurred, it made them less accepting of and more hostile toward homosexuals, and it effectively wiped out support for feminist professors. I would have bet that Low RWAs would prove more resistant to hate literature than others, and I would almost always have been wrong.

Several lines of evidence indicate the changes genuinely occurred and were not caused by "demand characteristics" or other experimental artifacts. We do not know that the shifts would have lasted over time, had not the participants been immediately debriefed. But the possibility exists. Moreover, three of the studies found that students were *not* influenced by truthful accounts of the Holocaust, but instead believed denials that it had even occurred. That is, when they were given credible truth and a preposterous lie, they believed the lie. The superficiality and absurdity of the propaganda used illustrate that Big Lies still work, and raise large questions about our critical thinking abilities. I do not advocate reducing freedom of speech to control hate literature; I hope I have more confidence in democracy than that. But we do need to counteract it vigorously.[17]

My mother warned me, as a young man, never to bring up three topics in casual conversation: religion, sex, and politics. She said people quickly become very emotional if you do. Well, play the processional theme from "Pictures at An Exhibition," for we are moving on to the last of the dangerous subjects. Fools rush in.

—11—
The Authoritarianism of Legislators in North America

What for you was the most amazing thing that happened on this planet as the twentieth century drew to a close?

For me, it was the overthrow of all those Communist regimes in eastern Europe. I can still see, in my mind's eye, the enormous crowds filling the central squares of Prague, Budapest, Sofia, Bucharest, and Leipzig, demanding that the Communist Party relinquish power. Television cameras could hardly show us the hundreds of thousands of people in those vast seas.

As a psychologist, I was particularly amazed because behavioral scientists have always thought that societies have overwhelming power to shape the beliefs and attitudes of their members. Yet these regimes, which had exercised crushing monolithic control over what a whole generation learned in school, read in the papers, saw in the cinema, and so on, had failed completely. They were solidly detested by the vast majority of the citizens they had tried to shape, who now filled the central squares with one message: "*No more. Out!*"

In democracies, we put our rulers out the same way we put them in, not by filling central squares but by filling voting booths. We make changes quite often. None of the prominent presidents and prime ministers who were in power at the end of the 1980s were still around by the middle of the 1990s. In North America, we turned out parties as well as leaders in the autumns of 1992, 1993, and 1994. The people have "clout," and the politicians know it.

How do we choose? Do politicians stand for anything, besides their own election to power? Do the political parties stand for anything, except the same? Is it all, as extremists have claimed, one gang of crooks who have worked out a deal whereby we get to choose between one half of the gang or the other? Who are these people who want to impress us, curry our favor, and garner our vote, so they can govern us?

We can hardly know, once we get past the municipal level where we might know a candidate personally. Instead, we usually meet politicians on their terms, through their staged events, their carefully crafted commercials, and their appearances on interview programs. Our image of them is manufactured to specifications. They try to be many things to different people. Handlers and public relations experts put "spin" on the positions and "spin" on the candidates, but the electorate gets spun around the most in the end.

Discovering the Person behind the Politician's Mask

How *do* you find out what politicians are "really like"? They excel, after all, in impression management, and part of their craft involves disguising what they actually think and feel. If you interview them, I think you can count on getting whatever public image they want to project. You can do content analyses of their speeches, as Tetlock (1983, 1984) did of U.S. senators and British members of Parliament (MPs). But those too are public presentations, carefully "packaged." (Tetlock's analysis convinces one because the politicians could not have known, as they were making their speeches, that some day the *complexity* of their thinking would be inferred from their words.) Every now and then someone thoughtfully tape records himself, "warts and all," and we get to listen in later. You can wait until officeholders die, and then dig at their diaries and papers. Canadians discovered that one of their longest serving prime ministers, William Lyon Mackenzie King, had stalked Ottawa's streets at night looking for prostitutes and gotten advice on the affairs of state from his (dead) mother through a bird. (And Americans think they have loopy leaders!)

Another approach, seldom tried because it seems fruitless, simply asks politicians to take psychological tests. Only a foolish office-seeker would agree to do so, right? But suppose the politician was guaranteed anonymity, and suppose the test involved not ink blots or questions about childhood but social attitudes? Might such responses produce insight into what politicians are really like, what they personally believe in, what they truly stand for?

Let me tell you why I raise the possibility. You see, I have this test, the RWA Scale, whose purpose people can almost never divine, which also posts some pretty good numbers when it comes to validity. It correlates with various liberal versus conservative outlooks, so it seems germane to politics. How would professional politicians answer it?

Just to recollect your recollection from Chapter 1, I sent the RWA Scale to four Canadian provincial and four American state legislatures during the years 1983–1985.[1] Thirty-four percent of the Canadians and 24% of the American lawmakers returned completed questionnaires to me. Almost everywhere, the consistency of their answers produced astounding alphas of .94 or higher. Legislators responded to the scale almost as if they were reciting a catechism. In Canada, the test separated the lawmakers into their political parties almost as cleanly as a role-call vote. New Democrats scored very low, Conservatives scored high, and the middling Liberals plopped in the middle. The point-biserial NDP versus Conservative correlations averaged a wee .87. The American data found Democrats much less authoritarian than Republicans in California, but proved inconclusive elsewhere.

Subsequent Canadian Studies

I have sent the RWA Scale to three more groups of Canadian politicians in the past few years: to the Saskatchewan candidates (described in Chapter 9), in November 1991, to the Alberta Legislative Assembly in January 1994, and to most of the members of (the federal) Parliament from the western provinces (Manitoba, Saskatchewan, Alberta, and British Columbia), also in January 1994.

SASKATCHEWAN CANDIDATES FOR THE LEGISLATIVE ASSEMBLY

This marked the only time I sought RWA scores from all the people who ran for office, as opposed to just those who won. I wrote the Saskatchewan candidates at their home addresses, asking them to complete an opinion survey for my research on social attitudes. The letter arrived a few weeks *after* the election, when the recipients would know their answers could not affect the electoral outcome this side of the Twilight Zone.[2]

Twenty of the 66 NDP candidates, 33 of the Liberals, and 14 of the Progressive Conservatives kindly responded to this request. The NDP scores ranged much more widely than they had in previous studies, from 73 to 190. Their mean equaled 119.0. The Liberals ranged even more, from 49 to 225, with a mean of 146.7.[3] The Tory scores went from 105 to 223, averaging 182.7. The overall F equaled 12.8 ($p < .001$); all parties differed significantly from one another. Cranking out the RWA point-biserial correlation between being an NDP versus being a Conservative candidate produced a .70.

As in previous studies, the RWA Scale was answered with strong internal consistency by these politicians. The mean interitem correlations averaged .34, producing an alpha coefficient of .94.

The candidates indicated whether they had won or not, in an election that saw the NDP take 55 seats, the Liberals 1, and the Conservatives 10. The only elected Tory I heard from had an RWA score virtually identical to the mean of the other 13 (defeated) Conservative respondents. I did not hear from the 1 Liberal victor. The mean of the 13 NDP respondents who were elected to the legislative assembly (115.8) did not differ significantly from that of the 7 NDP participants who were defeated. Overall, it appears that the *elected* candidates represented their party's field of standard-bearers when it comes to authoritarianism.

These results basically replicated those obtained earlier in the three-party legislatures in Ontario and New Brunswick, and extended the base of generalization from elected officials to *candidates* for election. In most places the NDP candidates were apt to be unauthoritarian, the Tories tended to be highly authoritarian, and the Liberals, as always, left their footprints all over the RWA Scale's range.

THE 1994 ALBERTA LEGISLATIVE ASSEMBLY STUDY

Early in 1994 I sent a fifty-item survey to the newly elected 83 members of the Alberta Legislative Assembly. The Conservatives' 51 seats controlled the legislature, with the Liberals' 32 members providing the opposition.

The survey consisted of two table-setters and the RWA Scale, plus the ten Economic Philosophy items shown in Exhibit 11.1,[4] plus eight of the items Pratto (personal communication, January 10, 1993) had included in an early report of the effort to develop a Social Dominance Orientation Scale: "Some groups of people are simply inferior to other groups." "Group equality should be our ideal." "If certain groups stayed in their place, we would have fewer problems." "We should strive to make incomes as equal as possible." "It's probably a good thing that certain groups are at the top and other groups are at the bottom." "All groups should be given an equal chance in life." "We would have fewer problems if we treated people more equally." "Sometimes other groups should be kept in their place."[5]

Exhibit 11.1   The Ten Economic Philosophy Items Sent to Alberta Legislators

33. The biggest problem we have in Canada is that, even though the federal government takes most of our money, it still can't balance its budget.

34. The Canadian economy will perform best if the *government* basically decides what should be made, and how much things will cost.*

35. Whatever is good for business is good for Canada.

36. The more government gets involved in the economy, the more red tape, waste, and inefficiency will drag us down.

37. The wealth of Canada should be spread out much more evenly; right now, too much is owned by too few.*

38. The *less* government interferes with business and tries to regulate it, the better.

39. The government should increase the federal deficit to create jobs, rather than waiting for business and industry to create them.*

40. There should be *higher* taxes on corporate earnings in Canada than there are now.*

41. If you let capitalism and the "free market" run unchecked and unregulated, the country will be controlled by the greediest and most dishonest people among us.*

42. People in Canada who earn lots of money should have their taxes *lowered*, so they can still have a reason to keep on striving.

Note: Items are answered on a − 4 to + 4 basis.

* Item is worded in the contrait direction; the economically conservative response is to disagree.

Results. I received completed surveys from 9 (28%) of the Liberal lawmakers, and 8 (16%) of the Conservatives. The Liberal scores on the RWA Scale ranged from 73 to 154, and averaged 117.7. The Tories went from 125 to 203, with a significantly higher mean of 170.9. The point-biserial correlation between party affiliation and authoritarianism was .69. The mean interitem correlation on the RWA Scale equaled .35, producing an alpha of .94.

Conservative lawmakers scored higher on all the statements on the Economic Philosophy Scale, with significant differences appearing—despite the tiny samples—on items 35, 37, 38, and 41. Having a right-wing economic philosophy correlated .69 with party affiliation and .43 with RWA scores. The ten statements intercorrelated .21 on the average, producing an alpha of .72.

The Tory respondents also scored higher on all but the first of the Social Dominance items used, and significantly so on half of the statements. They believed *less* than Liberals did that "Group equality should be our ideal," and that "We would have fewer problems if we treated people more equally." Instead they believed *more* that "If certain groups stayed in their place, we would have fewer problems," and "Sometimes other groups should be kept in their place."

The Social Dominance Orientation items intercorrelated .32 on the average, producing an alpha of .80. Their summed scores correlated .74 with RWA scores, .47 with party affiliation, and .32 with having a conservative economic philosophy. The Conservative mean was 35.0, when scores could range from 8 to 72, with 40 being neutral.

Discussion. As far as economic philosophy goes, I doubt it would have surprised many people in Alberta in 1994 that members of their Tory government were against increasing deficits to create jobs. I suspect they also could have readily guessed that Conservative lawmakers tended to believe,

"Whatever is good for business is good for Canada," and tended to endorse capitalism and the free market. They might not even have been surprised to learn that Tory lawmakers were against distributing the wealth of Canada more equally. (Only two of the Conservatives thought that "right now, too much is owned by too few.")

But I think Albertans might have been disturbed to learn that members of their government were less in favor of *equality among people* than were members of the opposition. After all, equality is one of the principal values of democracy. Furthermore, the Tory respondents did not see inequality as the source of problems to the same extent that the Liberals did. Instead, they believed that problems were more often caused because "certain groups" did not stay "in their place" *and* that these groups "should be kept in their place." In short, the Conservative respondents believed significantly more, not in equality, but in social dominance. These attitudes smack of right-wing authoritarianism, and indeed the Conservatives scored much higher on the RWA Scale than the Liberals did. But this amounts to very old news by now.

I find the Liberal mean of 117.7 more interesting, since it lands appreciably lower than Liberal means obtained elsewhere (136.5 in Ontario, 170.5 in New Brunswick, 146.7 in Saskatchewan). I infer that Alberta politics are polarized, just as they were in Manitoba and British Columbia when I did my earlier studies, with no body in the political center to hear the shells passing overhead. But in Alberta the Liberal Party, not the NDP, has become the viable alternative to the right-wing party. So it attracts, and even occasionally elects, Low RWA candidates to the legislature.

THE ISSUE OF SAMPLE SELF-SELECTION

Since I am now lobbing interpretations of whole provincial political systems on the basis of seventeen questionnaires, maybe we should wrestle here with the issue of subject self-selection in all these politician studies.

I do not believe, for a second, that the people who responded to my request perfectly represented their caucuses. Perhaps the better educated, or more altruistic, or less wary, or less busy legislators tended to invest the fifteen minutes it took to answer my survey. Maybe the respondents enjoyed stating their opinions more, or maybe (like me) they could not stand to be doing nothing, so they just ground away at all the stuff piled up on their desk, even a survey from a distant academic. Perhaps all of these factors operated, here and there.

I do not see, however, how any of these could have artificially produced the result that keeps turning up in study after study. If there really is *no difference* in the overall authoritarianism of the people you find in the different caucus rooms in legislatures, then how come we keep getting the same split? Why do basically just the Lows in one of the rooms answer, while basically just the Highs in the other respond? Got any ideas, short of vast conspiratorial theories to deceive nosy scientists?

To summarize then, I do not believe that the RWA Scale means I have gotten from (roughly) a quarter of the caucus memberships would equal the means I would have gotten if everyone had responded. I *suspect* that High RWA Canadian legislators are less likely to answer surveys from psychologists than Lows are, other things being equal. Thus the mean in each party would probably go up if I had been blessed with a 100% response rate. But I do not think the *differences* between the parties would change much. If they did, the differences could well *increase,* not disappear (*EOF,* pp. 249–251).

THE JANUARY 1994 WESTERN MEMBER OF PARLIAMENT STUDY

The October 1993 federal election in Canada saw a dramatic reversal in fortunes for the ruling Conservative Party, as its holdings in the House of Commons shrank a tad from 153 to 2. It lost its Quebec seats to a new separatist party, the Bloc Quebecois, it lost its seats in the Maritimes and Ontario to the Liberals, and it lost most of its western seats to another new entry, the right-wing Reform Party. The NDP also suffered dramatic setbacks, as the country headed in many directions, but mainly away from the Tories and toward the "center."

Only the four western provinces of Canada showed much diversity in the candidates elected to the House of Commons. All the others voted overwhelmingly Liberal or Bloc Quebecois. But the 85 seats from Manitoba to British Columbia were held by 51 Reform Party victors, 27 Liberals, and 7 NDPers.

At the beginning of 1994 I asked these members of Parliament—except 6 from the Winnipeg area (all Liberals) who might have been familiar with my family name—to fill out a fifty-item survey. This time the questionnaire ended with twelve Ethnocentrism items (Exhibit 11.2) and the first six Social Dominance items mentioned above.

Exhibit 11.2   The Ethnocentrism Items Used in the Member of Parliament Study

33. Foreign religions like Hinduism, Judaism, and Islam are not as close to God's truth as Christianity, nor do they produce as much good behavior in the world. (.52)

34. There is nothing wrong with intermarriage among the races.* (.42)

35. Canadians are NOT any better than most of the other people in the world.* (.25)

36. Certain races of people clearly do not have the natural intelligence and "get up and go" of the white race. (.27)

37. The Pakistanis and East Indians who have recently come to Canada have mainly brought disease, ignorance, and crime with them. (.10)

38. It's good to live in a country where there are so many minority groups present, such as blacks, Asians, and Latin Americans.* (.32)

39. Every person we let into Canada from overseas means either another Canadian won't be able to find a job, or another foreigner will go on welfare here. (.32)

40. Jews can be trusted as much as everyone else.* (.20)

41. Black people are NOT, by their nature, more violent than white people.* (.26)

42. It is a waste of time to train certain races for good jobs; they simply don't have the drive and determination it takes to learn a complicated skill. (.25)

43. As a group, aboriginals (Indians) are lazy, promiscuous, and irresponsible. (.26)

44. The Vietnamese and other Asians who have recently moved to Canada have proven themselves to be industrious citizens, and many more should be invited in.* (.39)

Note: Items were answered on a −4 to +4 basis. Numbers in parentheses indicate the item's correlation with party (NDP versus Reform) affiliation.

* Item is worded in the contrait direction; the ethnocentric response is to disagree.

RWA Scale. I heard from 2 NDPers (29%), 5 Liberals (24%) and 10 Reformers (20%). The 2 NDP members both scored very low on the RWA Scale, 71 and 77, for a mean of 74. The Liberal results ranged from 57 to 188, averaging 121.6. The Reform MPs had RWA scores from 114 to 241, with a mean of 172.3. Even with the minuscule samples, all three groups were significantly different from one another. The point biserial, NDP versus Reform, correlation with authoritarianism equaled .77.

The mean interitem correlation among the RWA Scale items for these 17 national legislators was .49, producing an alpha of .96.

Ethnocentrism. The Reform MPs scored highest on nearly all of the prejudice items, producing a range on the summed scores from 17 to 50. The Reform mean equaled 31.3. The Liberals' scores went from 12 to 38, with a mean of 23.4. The 2 NDP respondents had scores of 14 and 17, for an average of 15.5. The NDP mean was significantly lower than the Reformers', giving a point-biserial correlation of .53. Over all 17 responding MPs, the sum of these twelve Ethnocentrism items correlated .62 with RWA scores.

Responses to the dozen Ethnocentrism items intercorrelated .37 on the average, for an alpha = .85.

Social Dominance.   The six Social Dominance items also differentiated the three parties, with the Reform Party members almost always showing the least commitment to equality. The largest difference appeared on "We should strive to make incomes as equal as possible," which 8 out of 10 Reformers disagreed with, Liberals split upon, and both NDP members strongly agreed with.

The mean intercorrelation among these six items equaled .24, which with but six items produces an alpha of only .62. The Reformers ranged from 6 to 30 and had a mean of 17.9. The Liberals went from 12 to 20, and their mean of 15.2 was not significantly lower than the Reformers'. The NDPers scored 6 and 8, with a mean of 7.0, significantly lower than the Reform average. The correlation for all 17 MPs between Social Dominance and RWA was only .24; that with the sum of the Ethnocentrism items was .45. The Reform versus NDP r equaled .50.

Discussion.   The setting and the cast may have changed, but the play unfolded as always before. On the *national* level, the left-wing, center, and right-wing parties scored miles apart on the RWA Scale. The Conservatives were gone, but (in western Canada at least) the Reform Party had taken their place, supplying authoritarian lawmakers to those ridings that wanted them. The Reform legislators also proved relatively ethnocentric and less egalitarian in their thinking.

I hasten to emphasize the word "relatively" in that last sentence. You could not fairly characterize the 10 Reform respondents as "prejudiced" or "non-egalitarians," based on their answers to my survey. None of the members scored over the neutral point on the Ethnocentrism and Social Dominance sums.

Still, I think the answers speak to the differing inclinations and priorities of these caucuses. The Ethnocentrism scores particularly bear examination, because the Reform Party has often been accused of advocating racist immigration and domestic policies. It had to remove local leaders for making statements that smacked of bigotry, and it was not long before one of its newly elected MPs compared the largely poverty-stricken reserves upon which many aboriginal people live with "South Sea island paradises." Reform Party candidates, as the least tolerant and least egalitarian candidates seeking election, may have been the party of choice for bigots. (See also note 15 to Chapter 1.)

We can test this possibility by examining the political party preferences of the 654 parents who filled out a booklet of surveys for me in October 1993, just before the election on October 25. In response to my standard question about party preference, 177 said they were Liberals, 119 said they were Conservatives, 63 said they supported the Reform Party, and 49 said they preferred the NDP. (The rest were Independents and Undecideds.)

These parents also filled out my twenty-item Ethnocentrism Scale. The Reform Party supporters had the highest mean of all, 101.0. The Progressive Conservatives came in at 83.1. Then came the Liberal boosters with 78.5, and the New Democrats with 76.8. The overall one-way F equaled 5.27 ($p < .001$). The Reform mean was significantly higher than all of the others. So the Reform party appears to have been the choice of the most prejudiced people.[6]

Reform Party supporters also had the highest RWA scores (mean = 163.5), DOG scores (77.9), (hostile) Attitudes toward Homosexuals scores (62.6), Posse-Radical scores (23.8), and Zealot scores (24.2) in the sample. The large percentage of "High-High, Wild-Card Authoritarians" among the Reform enthusiasts also gave them the second-highest LWA Scale scores in the sample.[7]

SUMMARY OF STUDIES OF CANADIAN LEGISLATORS

Figure 11.1 shows the RWA Scale means of the left-wing and right-wing parties represented in my seven studies of Canadian lawmakers. It seems clear that in the multiparty *Canadian* system, the politicians in these "winged" parties differ greatly in the personality variable of authoritarianism. When you are talking about left-wing politicians in Canada, you are almost always talking about Low RWAs, probably with all that implies given what we have seen in the past chapters. When you are talking about right-wing politicians in Canada, you are almost always talking about High RWAs, and probably all *that* implies.

These differences are as clear, consistent, powerful, and compelling as any others you can find in the behavioral sciences. The RWA Scale, with its mean alpha of .94 in these studies, taps a powerful ideological dimension operating in the minds of Canadian lawmakers. And this dimension strongly differentiates the political parties. The mean left-right party-RWA correlation equaled .82, a connection so close to perfect it likely exceeds any other difference you could find between these parties.

Subsequent American Studies

Very well. What about the "Yanks"?

I never expected to find as big a difference between Democratic and Republican lawmakers as I had between New Democrats and Conservatives in Canada (*EOF*, pp. 253–258). The principals in a two-party system necessarily involve coalitions of many diverse groups. Both try to capture the political center. I also anticipated much greater regional disparity than I had found

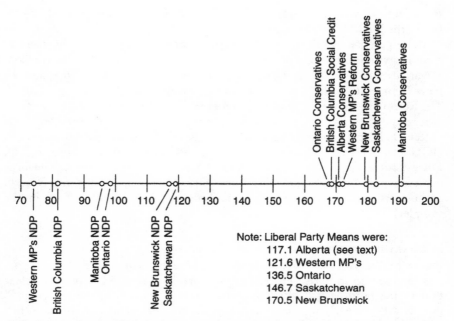

Figure 11.1   Mean RWA Scale scores of Canadian legislators in left-wing and right-wing parties

from sea to shining sea in Canada. But I did expect an RWA *r* of (say) .30 between Democrats and Republicans.

Since my first inconclusive surveys, I have conducted eight new studies of American state legislators, involving altogether forty state lawmaking bodies. If you are an American who lives in any state other than Alaska, Arkansas, Delaware, Hawaii, Idaho, Montana, Rhode Island, or West Virginia, plus California and Mississippi (which I surveyed earlier), I recently studied the authoritarianism of the people who write the laws in your state. What do you think I found?

THE APRIL 1990 RWA AND ECONOMIC PHILOSOPHY STUDY

In my first study, I sent the RWA Scale and my ten Economic Philosophy items to the members of the Arizona, Colorado, Illinois, Michigan, New York, and Virginia Houses of Representatives and to the Michigan Senate.[8] I received answers from 84 (24%) of the 348 Democrats contacted and 69 (24%) of the 287 Republicans. The state-by-state breakdown is given in Table 11.1.

Table 11.1 Results of the April 1990 state legislator RWA and Economic Philosophy study

State	Party	No. of replies	Response rate (%)	RWA Scale				Economic Philosophy Scale			
				Range	Mean	Interitem corr.	Corr. with party	Range	Mean	Interitem corr.	Corr. with RWA
Arizona	Dem.	6/26	23	52–217	153.2	.50	.37	33–61	55.0	.33	.72
	Rep.	11/34	32	137–221	190.4			53–80	69.8		
Colorado	Dem.	15/26	58	71–180	118.2	.39	.68	22–60	44.0	.33	.45
	Rep.	9/39	23	116–250	175.7			45–82	67.1		
Illinois	Dem.	12/66	18	95–211	145.9	.39	.36	27–58	46.0	.47	.36
	Rep.	12/51	24	128–231	174.8			49–82	66.0		
Michigan (House)	Dem.	11/61	18	78–194	122.3	.37	.58	29–63	45.2	.41	.67
	Rep.	10/49	20	100–208	168.3			45–88	67.1		
Michigan (Senate)	Dem.	8/18	44	49–163	102.6	.54	.74	32–59	41.2	.44	.62
	Rep.	5/20	25	157–243	184.6			73–84	76.8		
New York	Dem.	15/92	16	73–186	129.9	.36	.57	27–61	45.1	.26	.69
	Rep.	9/56	16	100–231	180.8			62–71	66.9		
Virginia	Dem.	17/59	29	92–198	144.9	.36	.56	40–75	53.5	.25	.73
	Rep.	13/38	34	121–257	185.8			58–81	69.5		
All	Dem.	84/348	24	49–217	131.2	.41	.57	22–75	47.1	.35	.62
	Rep.	69/287	24	100–257	180.0			45–88	68.5		

RWA Scale. The RWA Scale had a mean interitem correlation of .41, yielding an alpha of .95. As anticipated, the distribution of scores among Democrats and Republicans overlapped considerably in each state—much more than the NDP and Conservatives had in Canada. You can also see that scores varied quite a bit from one state to the next. But in each chamber Republicans scored higher, significantly so in all cases except Arizona. The overall Democratic mean was 131.2, compared with the Republican average of 180.0—quite a sizable gap. The point-biserial correlation equaled .57, much larger than I had expected.[9] Republicans scored significantly higher than Democrats on all 30 of the RWA Scale items.

Economic Philosophy. The Economic Philosophy items had a lower level of interitem correlation (.35; alpha = .85). But their sum distinguished Democrats from Republicans even better than the RWA Scale did, its point-biserial correlation with party being .75. Republicans scored significantly higher on all ten of the items, with large differences occurring on numbers 35, 36, 37, 39, 40, and 41 in Exhibit 11.1. The Republicans especially wanted support for business and capitalism, with a minimum of government involvement in the economy. They did not want corporate taxes increased, and they were against the redistribution of income in the United States. Only 10 (14%) of the GOP legislators thought that "right now, too much is owned by too few." Instead, most of the 69 Republicans either *strongly* disagreed with that item (17), or *very strongly* disagreed (22).[10] Having a conservative economic philosophy correlated .62 with RWA scores.

Discussion. Five things should be noted from this study. First, the question about whether Republican legislators are more authoritarian than Democrats seems to have been decisively answered.

Second, these data reinforce the conclusion from the 1986 study that the RWA Scale measures a powerful ideological dimension among American lawmakers. We can see this directly by comparing the two measures used in this study. The Economic Philosophy Scale, with its ten items, has only 45 interitem correlations, all basically dealing with one thing: the operation of the American economy. The mean interitem correlation on this short, focused test equaled a very respectable .35. But the mean intercorrelation on the much larger (435 intercorrelations!), much wider-ranging, rambling-to-the-point-of-being-indecipherable RWA Scale proved even higher: .41.

The strength of these interconnections amazes me all the more because I know economic ideologies have been formalized, become known as "schools," been taught in universities, and been presented and debated in many public forums. I believe politicians have been exposed to at least some of this discussion and have often adopted an "economic philosophy." But I doubt that anyone ever taught them a *system* of responses to the many issues raised by the RWA Scale. And yet, those answers are *better* interconnected, more systematic than the economic ones. If you believe these politicians have economic ideologies, they have an even stronger one regarding authoritarian submission, authoritarian aggression, and conventionalism.

Third, although economic philosophy was not as well organized in the answers of these lawmakers as their authoritarian "catechism" was, it *did* distinguish the parties better. So while Republicans differed considerably from Democrats in RWA scores, they differed even more in Economic Philosophy.

Fourth, if you look at Table 11.1, you will notice that the better the response rate from a chamber, the larger the party correlations with RWA and Economic Philosophy scores. The respective rank order correlations equaled .43 and .84.

We generally assume that the better the return rate, the truer the picture we see. So it would appear that the correlations would have been *higher,* not lower, if we had heard from everyone. You will find the same trend in nearly all of the subsequent studies, meaning self-selection bias has probably attenuated the true difference between Democrats and Republicans. The real gaps are even bigger.

Finally, I feel I should comment on the number of *extraordinarily high* RWA scores uncovered in this study. Except for one Reform Party member who soared into the "Hitler range" on the test with a 241, the highest score in any of my Canadian politician samples was a 225. Normally, the *most* authoritarian Canadian legislator came in at about 215. But you can see in Table 11.1 that this was topped in almost all of the assemblies in this study. Three state lawmakers scored *over* 240, including one (to me, almost unbelievable) legislator who racked up a 257—the highest score I can recall seeing in tens of thousands of participants.[11]

THE JUNE 1990 RWA AND MIRROR-IMAGE STUDY

Let's clean up some unfinished business. Remember back in Chapter 5, when I presented the results of the Moscow State (USSR) and Harvard-Potsdam-Tulane studies of mirror-images of American and Soviet behavior? I also presented the mirror-image scores of a Group X, who showed a pronounced nationalism compared with the student samples. I promised I would unmask them later. Behold, they are state legislators who answered a survey I sent out in June 1990.

This survey, sent to the Florida, Iowa, Oregon, Texas, and Wisconsin lower chambers, contained the RWA Scale and the two versions of the mirror-image task. Some of the legislators received form A, which began, "The Soviet Union has the right to intervene militarily when one of its neighbors shows signs of becoming allied with the United States." Others got form B, which began,

"The United States has the right to intervene militarily when one of its neighbors shows signs of becoming allied with the Soviet Union."

I received replies from 120 lawmakers, 71 (23%) of the 311 Democrats solicited and 49 (23%) of the 215 Republicans.

RWA Scale.   RWA scores had a mean interitem correlation of .41 and an alpha of .95. Republicans again scored higher than the Democrats in each assembly, significantly so at all sites except Texas (see Table 11.2). The overall Democratic mean equaled 126.8, the Republicans', 177.6. Party affiliation correlated .63 with authoritarianism. This correlation was again much larger than I had expected to find in the two-party, regionally complicated American system.

You will note that all of the assemblies except Wisconsin had at least one "Very High RWA" (with a score over 200) among their respondents. A Texas Democrat even tied the Virginia Republican from the last study with a chilling 257.

Mirror Images.   Sixty-one of the lawmakers answered form A of the mirror-image survey and 59, form B. The means of these responses are given in Table 5.1 under Group X. You can see that the legislators collectively exhibited significant double standards and judgments favoring the United States on ten of the twelve issues raised. So while it was wrong for either side to invade a neighbor to control its international alliances, it was "wronger" for the Russians to do so than for the Americans. The United States wanted world peace appreciably more than the Soviet Union did. Its foreign aid was more altruistic. While neither country was thought likely to launch a sneak attack with intercontinental ballistic missiles, the Russians were still more likely to do this than the Americans. And so on.[12]

These elected officials accordingly had the highest net nationalistic image score of any of the five samples. Table 11.2 shows that, in each legislature, high RWAs tended to see the world in black-and-white terms, with the overall correlation being .66—much stronger than the connections of .38 to .47 found among the university students. Republicans consistently had bigger double standards and nationalistic image scores than Democrats (.49).

Discussion.   While these results reinforce our earlier discoveries about High RWAs' ethnocentrism and compartmentalized thinking, I must say I was still surprised. I thought a lot of the Cold War rhetoric I heard over the years was just "for domestic consumption." I believed that politicians, even on the state level, knew the many ways the public's perception of "the enemy" can be manipulated in a democracy. I expected them to have a more detached private view of U.S.-USSR actions. But to the contrary, they personally be-

Table 11.2 Results of the June 1990 RWA and mirror-image study

State	Party	No. of replies	Response rate (%)	Range	RWA Scale Scale mean	RWA Scale Interitem corr.	RWA Scale Corr. with party	RWA Scale Corr. with "image"*
Florida	Dem.	12/72	17	67–207	135.7	.39	.48	.50
	Rep.	6/48	12	124–225	182.7			
Iowa	Dem.	18/61	30	75–189	119.2	.43	.77	.71
	Rep.	12/39	31	136–229	188.8			
Oregon	Dem.	5/32	16	70–151	99.0	.56	.65	.74
	Rep.	5/25	20	101–237	170.6			
Texas	Dem.	21/90	23	85–257	155.8	.34	.29	.56
	Rep.	11/60	18	132–227	180.5			
Wisconsin	Dem.	15/56	27	50–170	97.7	.40	.79	.73
	Rep.	15/43	35	112–191	166.8			
All	Dem.	71/311	23	50–257	126.8	.41	.63	.66
	Rep.	49/215	23	101–237	177.6			

* An "image" score was calculated for each respondent by comparing his or her attitudes toward the United States with those expressed toward the USSR. A positive score means the person was more favorable toward the United States (which everyone was). The positive RWA Scale correlations in this column, in turn, mean authoritarians had a bigger gap, a larger nationalistic orientation, in their images than nonauthoritarians did.

lieved "the official account" more than the university students did. (Whether they believed it more than other groups of Americans is admittedly another matter.)

Another thing surprised me. Item 30 on the survey these legislators answered reads, "The biggest threat to our freedom comes from the Communists and their kind, who are out to destroy religion, ridicule patriotism, corrupt the youth, and in general undermine our whole way of life." This McCarthyist perception of a powerful subversive Communist movement in America was soundly rejected by most of the lawmakers serving in this 1990 study. But 36 of them (30%) still agreed with this cancerous self-doubt in the American psyche. They tended to be High RWAs (.61) and Republicans (.45). The phrase "Communists *and their kind*" may have opened the door to non-McCarthyist fears. But I was still taken aback. The item was far too dated to be used in ordinary samples by 1990.

THE FEBRUARY 1991 RWA AND ETHNOCENTRISM STUDY

Toward the beginning of 1991, when state legislatures would usually have started the year's session, I undertook two new investigations of lawmakers' attitudes. In the first, I sent the RWA Scale and twelve Ethnocentrism items to the Houses of Representatives in Kansas, Kentucky, Minnesota, South Carolina, Vermont, and Washington. The Ethnocentrism items were identical to those I later used in the western Canadian member of Parliament study (Exhibit 11.2), except I substituted "Americans" for "Canadians" (and made similar changes throughout), and item 43 was worded "Most Hispanics and Mexican-Americans are lazy and irresponsible."

RWA Scale. I received completed surveys from 107 (25%) of the 424 Democrats, 96 (32%) of the 299 Republicans, and both members of the Progressive Coalition Party in the Vermont House. Overall, these 205 state lawmakers answered the RWA Scale with even greater internal consistency than their predecessors, belting out a mean interitem correlation of .45 and an alpha of .96.

Republicans scored significantly higher than Democrats in each of the bodies tested, with overall means of 181.0 versus 136.7. The state-by-state breakdowns are given in Table 11.3, which also shows that the electorate in most of these states chose at least one Extraordinarily High RWA to write their laws. A Vermont Democrat raised the all-time record to 258. (On the bright side, someone in the same caucus produced a 35!) The correlations between party affiliation and authoritarianism across the states averaged .53.[13]

Ethnocentrism. Responses to the twelve Ethnocentrism items intercorrelated .40 on the average, producing an alpha of .88. Scores ranged from the minimum possible (12) to 83.

Table 11.3 Results of the February 1991 RWA and Ethnocentrism study

State	Party	No. of replies	Response rate (%)	RWA Scale				Ethnocentrism items			
				Range	Mean	Interitem corr.	Corr. with party	Range	Mean	Interitem corr.	Corr. with RWA
Kansas	Dem.	16/63	25	75–192	123.1	.48	.64	12–61	28.9	.33	.71
	Rep.	7/62	11	100–239	188.4			25–61	41.7		
Kentucky	Dem.	15/68	22	96–250	170.7	.42	.42	16–81	40.2	.44	.72
	Rep.	8/32	25	156–255	208.6			42–78	56.5		
Minnesota	Dem.	25/81	31	59–216	128.6	.45	.52	12–60	27.8	.29	.58
	Rep.	21/53	40	97–236	175.2			12–53	33.4		
S. Carolina	Dem.	21/78	27	102–222	171.5	.20	.33	15–70	38.8	.34	.81
	Rep.	14/42	33	148–247	193.0			23–83	51.0		
Vermont	Dem.	17/73	23	35–258	114.0	.49	.64	12–55	24.6	.45	.72
	Rep.	30/73	41	106–249	177.7			14–67	40.1		
Washington	Dem.	13/61	21	59–215	103.8	.49	.59	12–42	20.4	.42	.67
	Rep.	16/37	43	100–245	167.2			14–64	32.8		
All	Dem.	107/424	25	35–258	136.7	.45	.53	12–81	30.5	.40	.71
	Rep.	96/299	32	97–255	181.0			12–83	40.3		

Republicans proved more ethnocentric than Democrats in all the legislatures, significantly so in all but Minnesota, and significantly so on all twelve of the items except number 44. The largest differences between Republicans and Democrats appeared on item 36 (certain races not as good as the white race), item 33 (Christianity the best religion), item 37 (Pakistanis and East Indians bring disease, ignorance, and crime), and item 42 (waste of time training certain races for good jobs). Overall, Democrats averaged 30.5, while Republicans had a mean of 40.3. Ethnocentrism correlated .38 with party affiliation, on the average, and an eye-popping .71 with RWA.

Discussion. You have probably already noticed that these American legislators proved appreciably more ethnocentric than the Canadian members of Parliament discussed a few pages back. There, the highest mean was the Reform Party's 31.3, barely different from the Democrats' 30.5. It may be invalid to compare *national* lawmakers with *state* legislators. Still, a lot (43) of the elected American officials scored higher than the 50 posted by the most ethnocentric Canadian lawmaker.

Much more impressive, however, stands the .71 correlation between right-wing authoritarianism and ethnocentrism among these lawmakers. It rates as the highest such relationship yet discovered, the previous record being a .69 found with an anti-black survey administered to white South Africans (Duckitt, 1992). It is so large, it even supports the original Berkeley group's premise that prefascist personalities and ethnocentrism compose two sides of the same coin.

I hasten to add the usual caution about the low level of the Ethnocentrism scores. Ninety percent of these American lawmakers ended up on the "unprejudiced" side of the neutral point. But I also hasten to add again that the data speak to the probable priorities of these decision makers. In a world of limited resources, how likely are High RWA legislators to vote funds for programs that will mainly benefit minorities, when the dollars could be spent instead to benefit the "get up and go" white race? How likely have they been in the past?

THE FEBRUARY 1991 RWA AND ABORTION STAND STUDY
In my second 1991 American legislator study, I sent surveys to the lower houses in Connecticut, New Jersey, North Carolina, Ohio, Oklahoma, and Wyoming, and to the Wyoming Senate. This time the RWA Scale was followed by a reminder of anonymity and three questions:

Now I want to ask your opinion on what is probably the most contentious issue facing society today: abortion. As always, the answers you give will be *completely anonymous.*

1. What is your personal opinion on the abortion issue, and *why* do you think this is right?

2. What would be the provisions of the *ideal* abortion bill, in your opinion?

3. To what extent is the abortion controversy a moral, legal, religious, or personal (or other) issue, or some combination of these?

These questions were developed with Bruce Hunsberger, who agreed (with another researcher, who shall go nameless because he later finked out) to score the legislators' answers for "cognitive complexity."

Things went smoothly at all sites, save the caucus room of the Wyoming Senate Democrats. Seven of the ten members sent me a letter saying my survey was so crummy and stupid, "it is difficult to believe this constitutes serious research."[14]

RWA Scale. Altogether I received 169 answers from the 644 legislators contacted, 88 (23%) of the 375 Democrats and 81 (30%) of the 269 Republicans. Table 11.4 presents the usual state-by-state breakdown. The crummy and stupid RWA Scale had a mean interitem correlation of .43 and an alpha of .96. Republicans again walloped the Democrats, 175.7 to 138.8, when it came to being "prefascists," significantly so in all states except Oklahoma. The RWA-party correlations averaged .43. A Republican representative from Wyoming can claim the distinction of producing the highest RWA score I have ever seen: 259.

Abortion Stands. All but 18 of the respondents described their stands on abortion (but I could not figure out what 6 of them meant). *No* correlation appeared between authoritarianism and cognitive complexity. Some High RWAs had very simple stands ("Abortion is wrong because the Bible does not allow it"). But so did some Lows ("I feel a woman should have the right to choose").

A strong connection did appear, however, between authoritarianism and *which side* the lawmakers took in the debate. Forty-seven of the 145 participants with interpretable stands said they would sharply cut back on the number of abortions being performed under *Roe v. Wade*—most frequently limiting abortion to cases involving rape, incest, or serious threat to the mother's physical health. They averaged 200.7 on the RWA Scale, a very high group mean. The other 98 legislators said they would stay with *Roe* ($N = 43$), or lessen its restrictions further ($N = 12$), or have no legal restraints and no law on abortion at all ($N = 43$). The mean RWA scores in these groups came in at 131.5, 144.3, and 133.4, respectively. None of these differs significantly from another, but all differ significantly from those who would cut back from *Roe*.

Table 11.4 Results of the February 1991 RWA and abortion-stand study

State	Party	No. of replies	Response rate (%)	RWA Scale Range	RWA Scale Mean	Interitem corr.	Corr. with party	Abortion Stand* ≤ Roe	Abortion Stand* > Roe	Abortion Stand* NR	Corr. with RWA
Connecticut	Dem.	23/89	26	56–211	123.8	.36	.31	19	2	2	.46
	Rep.	16/62	26	74–210	148.5			13	2	1	
New Jersey	Dem.	7/43	16	77–228	138.3	.46	.54	7	0	0	.31
	Rep.	4/36	11	148–212	190.8			3	1	0	
N. Carolina	Dem.	11/81	14	85–223	163.8	.32	.41	8	1	2	.67
	Rep.	14/39	36	117–241	198.4			3	7	4	
Ohio	Dem.	16/61	26	37–201	134.0	.50	.52	9	5	2	.69
	Rep.	8/38	21	115–231	189.9			3	4	1	
Oklahoma	Dem.	19/69	28	59–228	163.6	.43	.21	9	4	6	.65
	Rep.	8/32	25	141–229	185.8			1	6	1	
Wyoming (House)	Dem.	11/22	50	72–201	111.5	.45	.55	8	1	2	.73
	Rep.	20/42	48	103–259	168.4			11	9	0	
Wyoming (Senate)	Dem.	1/10	10	117	—	.38	—	0	0	1	.57
	Rep.	11/20	55	107–237	176.8			4	5	2	
All	Dem.	88/375	23	37–228	138.8	.43	.43	60	13	15	.60
	Rep.	81/269	30	74–259	175.7			38	34	9	

*The heading "≤ Row" indicates legislators who favored the *Roe v. Wade* ruling or would place fewer restrictions on abortion. The heading "> Roe" indicates lawmakers who would place tighter restrictions on abortion than those allowed in the *Roe* ruling. "NR" indicates legislators who did not answer the question.

Lumping these last three groups together enables one to compare the 47 lawmakers who wanted to make abortions much harder to obtain with the 98 who would make them as available as they are under *Roe* or more so. The point-biserial correlation with RWA scores equaled a very sizable .60 across the states. The state-by-state results are presented in Table 11.4.[15]

Discussion.   One lawmaker wrote, in his response to my question, "[Abortion is] overrated in its importance compared to other legislative issues. I've been a legislator 14 years, cast over 5,000 votes, only one of which dealt with it." Yet many others spoke of the personal and political anguish they had experienced on this matter: "It is a no-win, deep-seated issue that makes enemies of friends." Opinions were generally polarized. Feelings ran very high on both sides. Conflict was inevitable.

I found the strong connection with RWA scores instructive. Virtually all of the very right-wing authoritarian legislators wanted to restrict abortions greatly. (You do not get a *group mean* of 200 with a lot of moderates in your ranks; the "moderate" RWAs were almost always against them.)[16] Thirteen said abortion should be legal only to save the mother's life, and 7 others said abortion should never be permitted.

The 47 legislators who wanted to place much greater restrictions on abortion sent a shiver down my spine. They scored significantly higher than their legislative colleagues on *every* statement on the RWA Scale. As you would probably predict, the biggest differences occurred on items with religious tones or overtones. But the "restricters" also firmly believed that children should learn "obedience and respect for authority" above all else, that we should use more physical punishment on "troublemakers," that we should enforce laws "without mercy," "crack down harder on deviant groups," and "stomp out the rot." Incongruously (unless you have read Chapters 4 and 5), they also did *not* believe in treating dissenters with an open mind.

If a group can be characterized as right-wing authoritarian, and well down the road to fascism, it would seem to be these pro-life advocates with their sky-high RWA scores. They believe in far more, far more extremely, than just protecting the unborn. They *are* marching to the beat of a "different drum," but I do not think it is God's.

THE MARCH 1991 RWA AND HODGE-PODGE STUDY

In March 1991, as winter in Winnipeg turned into late winter, I sent off two more surveys to state lawmakers. The first, dispatched to both houses of the legislatures located in Atlanta, Indianapolis, Boston, and Santa Fe, dealt with a hodge-podge of issues. Items 33 and 34 on the questionnaire read: "Wife abuse is one of the most serious problems in our country today" and "Our country needs much stricter gun-control laws." Then I asked a question about capital punishment: "Which crimes (if any) should be punished by *execution* in your opinion? That is, for which crimes would you make capital punishment available to a judge/jury at sentencing?" Finally, I asked the lawmakers to give me their responses to Rokeach's (1973) value-ranking task. Specifically:

> Below are listed a number of *goals* or *values* that a person might have in life, both for oneself and for others. Please look over the list. Which one of these is *most important to you?* Please write a "1" down beside your most important goal/value. Which one of the remainder is the next most important? Write a "2" beside it, please. And so on. Rank the remainder from "3" to "9."

_____ A Sense of Accomplishment

_____ A World at Peace

_____ Equality

_____ Family Security

_____ A Comfortable Life

_____ Freedom

_____ Mature Love

_____ Happiness

_____ National Security

RWA Scale.   I heard from 116 (23%) of the 486 Democrats and 65 (31%) of the 208 Republicans. As for the RWA Scale, if you are sick to death of hearing the same old results in study after study, cheer up. This time the test fell short. The interitem correlations averaged only .35, causing alpha to plummet to .94. More noteworthy, while Republicans scored higher than Democrats in all of the eight chambers surveyed, the difference attained significance only in the Indiana Senate. The final score was much closer than usual, 174.2 versus 158.6, and the RWA-party correlations averaged a mere .25. (See Table 11.5).

Wife Abuse.   Legislators agreed that wife abuse was one of the most serious problems. Lows RWAs thought it was a little more serious than Highs did (r −.19), as did Democrats compared with Republicans (−.18).

Gun Control.   Much sharper disagreement appeared over stiffer gun control laws. In general, Lows favored them and Highs were opposed (r = −.49). Democrats wanted tougher gun-control laws than Republicans did (−.47).

Table 11.5   Results of the March 1991 hodge-podge study

State	Party	No. of replies	Response rate (%)	RWA Scale Range	RWA Scale Mean	Interitem corr.	Corr. with party
Georgia (House)	Dem.	30/144	21	68–246	171.1	.32	.03
	Rep.	12/34	35	120–214	174.0		
Georgia (Senate)	Dem.	12/45	27	151–232	185.6	.17	.26
	Rep.	5/11	45	187–233	201.2		
Indiana (House)	Dem.	10/52	19	113–252	178.6	.39	.10
	Rep.	15/48	31	104–257	187.2		
Indiana (Senate)	Dem.	6/24	25	95–178	131.2	.19	.58
	Rep.	4/26	15	150–177	163.2		
Mass. (House)	Dem.	23/122	19	56–230	138.8	.35	.19
	Rep.	4/36	11	119–232	162.0		
Mass. (Senate)	Dem.	6/24	25	70–217	128.7	.35	.38
	Rep.	8/16	50	128–185	160.2		
New Mexico (House)	Dem.	18/49	37	61–221	159.2	.37	.10
	Rep.	9/21	43	142–223	168.2		
New Mexico (Senate)	Dem.	11/26	42	54–224	149.0	.33	.21
	Rep.	8/16	50	133–205	165.8		
All	Dem.	116/486	24	54–252	158.6	.35	.25
	Rep.	65/208	31	104–257	174.2		

Capital Punishment.   I simply counted the number of crimes each legis-lator listed. Some (31) said, unambiguously, "none." The others answered with varying detail, which compromised my tallying. Someone who said sim-ply "Murder" got a score of 1. But someone who said, "First-degree murder, second-degree murder, manslaughter" got a score of 3. Maybe the first person meant all three as well. But even with this "noise" in the measurements, RWA scores correlated .47 with the extent to which a legislator wanted to give judges and juries the option of execution. Republicans favored capital pun-ishment more than Democrats (.21).

Values.   Rokeach designed the value-ranking procedure to measure the relative standing of Equality and Freedom, arguably the two most basic values of democracy. He discovered that people generally ranked Freedom higher, and that prejudiced persons ranked it much higher than Equality.

Everyone—Low, Moderate, and High RWAs—tended to rank Freedom first. But rather shockingly in a study of state lawmakers, Equality was ranked sixth *overall,* behind Freedom, Family Security, Happiness, a World at Peace, and a Sense of Accomplishment. Low RWA legislators ranked Equality *third,* while Highs ranked it *seventh.* The correlation between RWA scores and the ranking of Equality (if you will tolerate such a statistic) equaled − .38.

Lows and Highs differed most on Equality. But Highs also put Family Security, National Security, and a Comfortable Life significantly higher than Lows did.

Discussion.   Were you surprised that High RWA lawmakers downplayed wife abuse a bit and seldom saw a need for stiffer gun control legislation in the United States? Or that they favored the use of capital punishment more? Neither was I.

We might have been surprised that Equality had such a low priority among authoritarians—lower than almost everything else on the list—had we not already seen the data on the Economic Philosophy Scale. Authoritarian legislators, who help write the tax laws for their states, did *not* feel in that earlier study that there was anything wrong with the huge *in*equality in the distribution of wealth in America.

The large gap in Highs' rankings of Freedom and Equality would have led Rokeach to predict that High RWA legislators would tend to be more prejudiced than Lows. And he would have been right, as we saw in the study of RWA and ethnocentrism. Highs' greater valuing of family security and national security also fits in with the evidence that authoritarians are more fearful than most people. So, for that matter, does the desire for guns.

As for equality and freedom, I think it takes a special kind of mind to disconnect the two. If you are seriously "less equal" than others (like most of the animals in *Animal Farm*), you do not have the freedoms the "more equal" people have. Hence both values, freedom *and equality,* were forcefully asserted in the Declaration of Independence. But we know Highs have that "special kind of mind" which can, and does, disconnect all kinds of things that are closely connected.[17]

THE MARCH 1991 RWA FREEDOM AND EQUALITY LAWS STUDY

I study authoritarianism partly because it has turned out to be a crackerjack mystery, with many inner puzzles. I want to see how it comes out in the end, and I am pleased that the various pieces are fitting together now. So I am hooked on the scientific quest. But mainly I have spent over twenty-five years trying to understand what Nevitt Sanford and his associates first uncovered because, like them, I suspect "It *can* happen here." I perceive a potential for the acceptance of totalitarian rule in our countries, a bedrock authoritarianism that never goes away. High RWAs usually think they are the biggest patriots of all, but it turns out they care little for democracy. They need only to have their ranks swelled during a crisis to sweep our form of government away, I fear.

Please understand. I do not think we presently teeter on the brink. Our Constitutions and our institutions present formidable obstacles to any Hitler. But if we ever suffer the hammer blows that have pulverized other nations, people could turn to a dictator who promised glory, prosperity, and law and order.

When it comes to legislators, democracy can most obviously be destroyed through laws that undermine equality and freedom. Equality already sits all but forgotten on the back burner among authoritarians. What about freedom?

I doubt many American lawmakers would vote for an amendment to repeal freedom of speech outright. Even High RWAs believe in it, certainly for themselves. But I suspect authoritarian legislators would often support bills that whittled away our freedom of speech, when they did not like the speech. They would do the same for freedom of the press. And even though the First Amendment prohibits the establishment of a state religion, we have reason to suspect right-wing authoritarians would vote for a law to have *their* religion taught in public schools.

I tested this perception that High RWA legislators would tend to favor certain laws that restricted freedom, and *also* tend to oppose bills that promoted equality, through a survey sent to members of the Alabama, Maine, Missouri, Pennsylvania, and Utah Houses of Representatives, and the Missouri Senate, in March 1991. After they had answered the RWA Scale, the lawmakers were asked to indicate on a -4 to $+4$ basis if they would like to pass certain laws, even though some of them might violate the Bill of Rights.

The U.S. Supreme Court sometimes rules a state law unconstitutional. But state lawmakers still have things they would *like* to do. So, *regardless of what the Court might someday say*, how *in general* would you react to the following proposed laws?

_____ A bill giving police much wider, much less restrictive wiretap, search-and-seizure, and interrogation rules. (.56)

_____ A law requiring "affirmative action" in state hiring that would give priority to qualified minorities (i.e., they would get more than their per capita "share" until they caught up). (.51)

_____ A bill outlawing the Communist Party and other radical political organizations. (.58)

_____ A law requiring Christian religious instruction in public schools. (.50)

_____ A law extending "equal rights" legislation to homosexuals by prohibiting discrimination in housing and employment on the basis of sexual orientation. (.68)

_____ A law that would prohibit television broadcasts (such as CNN's from Baghdad) from a foreign country when the United States is at war with that country. (.49)

_____ A law raising the income tax *rate* for the rich, and lowering it for the poor. (.40)

_____ A law restricting anti-war protests to certain sizes, times, and places—generally away from public view—while American troops are fighting overseas. (.63)

_____ If the Equal Rights Amendment ("ERA") were still up for ratification, would you vote for it? (.60)[18]

Five of these proposed laws would *reduce freedoms* that the American people presently enjoy, mainly under the First Amendment. The other four would *increase the chances for equality* and help level the playing field.

RWA Scale.   Sorry, we are back to the same old story. The mean interitem correlation on the RWA Scale among the 113 Democrats and 84 Republicans equaled .43. Alpha therefore climbed back up to .96. Republicans continued their uninterrupted "winning streak" of outpointing Democrats in authoritarianism, with an overall difference of 179.2 to 134.3 ($r = .41$). But the differences in Alabama and the Missouri Senate were not statistically significant (see Table 11.6). A Pennsylvania Republican tied the Wyoming Republican from the February 1991 study for the highest score ever, 259. (Is there someone somewhere, the Babe Ruth of fascists, who can hit 260?)

The Proposed Laws Affecting Freedom and Equality.   Most of the respondents indicated they would *not* support the laws reducing freedoms that Americans presently enjoy. The mean responses ranged from 2.74 (outlawing Communists and other radicals) to 3.80 (giving police much wider powers). But in every case, High RWAs favored these laws more than anyone else. The correlations are printed after each item above, and ranged from .49 to .63. And *most* Highs would have voted both to give police much greater powers and keep anti-war protests small and away from view during wartime.[19]

Opinions on the bills to increase equality proved much more divided, with means landing from 4.28 (for affirmative action in state hiring) to 5.51 (for changing the tax rate). Again, RWA scores predicted all these stands, the correlations ranging from .40 to .68. As we would expect from all that has

Table 11.6 Results of the March 1991 freedom and equality laws study

State	Party	No. of replies	Response rate (%)	RWA Scale				Proposed freedom/equality laws*			
				Range	Mean	Interitem corr.	Corr. with party	Range	Mean	Interitem corr.	Corr. with RWA
Alabama	Dem.	9/82	11	112–241	170.9	.30	.26	9–68	34.8	.38	.83
	Rep.	6/23	26	143–211	191.0			43–67	50.7		
Maine	Dem.	36/96	38	52–239	111.2	.45	.47	9–60	23.0	.36	.86
	Rep.	18/53	34	96–249	163.2			20–63	42.2		
Missouri (House)	Dem.	33/97	34	62–243	142.9	.34	.38	10–69	30.9	.36	.79
	Rep.	20/65	31	68–232	176.1			23–76	48.0		
Missouri (Senate)	Dem.	6/23	26	105–174	141.8	.31	.47	17–34	25.3	.27	.60
	Rep.	5/11	45	117–230	174.0			37–53	45.2		
Penn.	Dem.	22/107	21	47–219	133.3	.54	.51	11–52	25.9	.45	.89
	Rep.	19/96	20	102–259	187.5			32–74	50.5		
Utah	Dem.	7/31	23	125–185	161.6	.28	.37	25–42	32.3	.13	.62
	Rep.	16/44	36	113–230	190.0			23–59	46.2		
All	Dem.	113/436	26	47–243	134.3	.43	.41	9–69	27.5	.36	.84
	Rep.	84/292	29	68–259	179.2			20–76	47.0		

*Responses to nine proposed laws that would either take away freedoms or increase equality. A high score means the lawmaker would reduce freedom and hinder equality. Summed scores could vary from 9 to 81, with 45 being neutral.

286 The Authoritarian Specter

come before, most High RWA legislators were firmly opposed to laws that would make America a land of more equal opportunity.

We can combine these nine answers to produce an index of how much each lawmaker *would undermine freedom and equality,* if he or she could vote on such acts. Rather amazingly, considering the wide range of topics involved, responses to these proposals intercorrelated .36 on the average—when scored as being *in favor* of restricting freedom and *against* increasing equality. Thus we have an ad hoc, balanced "Legislative Undermining of Democracy Scale" with an alpha of .84.

So who "Just says, 'No' " to freedom and equality? The right-wing authoritarians do. The correlation across all 197 legislators was a very powerful .84. The Democrat versus Republican correlation equaled .66.

Discussion. These results overwhelm me, given that they came from *lawmakers.* I would bet that right-wing authoritarians fly the biggest flags in town on July 4, but as we have seen over and over again, that does not mean a thing. High RWA legislators have greatly compartmentalized their love of America from what America set out to be. Besides caring little about the undeniable inequality of opportunity in their society, they actually have little commitment to freedom—at least *other people's* freedom. Many would outlaw political groups *they* consider "radical." Many High lawmakers would prohibit the press from reporting a war from the "other side." Many would require, not just prayer, but Christian religious instruction in public schools. Most of them would subvert protestors' constitutional right to reach the public. Though they might insist it is not so, Highs would give police much greater power to spy on and seize Americans as they wished.

It was precisely because of the danger such lawmakers would pose to democracy that the Bill of Rights was added to the U.S. Constitution in 1791, two hundred years before this study was done. While they would undoubtedly deny it to others, and perhaps to themselves, many of the right-wing authoritarian politicians who today claim the American government has taken away people's rights would destroy those rights if they had the chance. They care not a farthing about equality, and stand ready to undermine our hard-won freedoms. Without losing a world war, or enduring economic catastrophe, or suffering crippling internal strife, these High RWAs have forsaken democracy.

THE JANUARY 1993 RWA AND LWA STUDY

At the beginning of the 1993 legislative sessions, I sent a forty-four-item survey to the Maryland House, the Nebraska Unicameral, and both chambers of the North Dakota legislature. After the usual table-setters and RWA Scale items, the survey ended with the explanatory paragraph that precedes the

LWA Scale, and items 3, 16, 15, 9, 6, 12, 17, 14, 5, 11, 7, and 19 from Exhibit 9.2.

RWA Scale. I received completed surveys from 43 (22%) of the 196 Democrats contacted and 42 (30%) of the 140 Republicans. RWA Scale items intercorrelated .37 for an alpha of .95. Table 11.7 shows Republicans always scored significantly higher than Democrats, with the final totals being 177.1 and 137.1. The RWA-party point-biserial correlations averaged .45.

LWA Items. The twelve LWA Scale items intercorrelated .25 overall, giving their sum an alpha of .77. As usual, scores were low; only one legislator had a leg up on the neutral point of 60. Democrats scored higher overall, 27.1 versus 24.7 (2.26 versus 2.06 on a per item basis). But this was not statistically significant. As usual, RWA and LWA scores correlated very little, only this time negatively so (−.17) and nonsignificantly.

Discussion. The LWA results largely replicate our earlier findings, including those obtained with a somewhat different set of items in November 1991 among Saskatchewan electoral candidates. Whereas one can find plenty of High RWAs in state legislatures, almost no one scores on the "authoritarian" side of the neutral point on LWA Scale items.

Switching to relative differences then, Democrats in this study scored a little higher on the LWA Scale than Republicans, just as New Democrats opened up a small gap on Conservatives in Saskatchewan. But in neither case was the difference significant. So we can find no evidence for the alleged authoritarian on the left in American legislatures either.

THE JANUARY 1993 RWA AND DOG STUDY

Hang on! You have reached the last study in this book, involving the lower chambers of the Louisiana, Nevada, New Hampshire, South Dakota, and Tennessee legislatures, and the Tennessee Senate.[20] This time, the survey ended with fourteen DOG statements: items 1, 5, 7, 8, 20, 18, 6, 3, 4, 14, 13, and 11 from Exhibit 8.1, plus the contrait "I would change my beliefs about important things in life if certain discoveries occurred, and certain facts were established," and the protrait "It is dangerous to be 'open-minded' about the really central issues in life."

RWA Scale. Answers came in from 59 (23%) of the 257 Democrats contacted and 64 (35%) of the 185 Republicans. The RWA Scale faltered again, with a mean interitem correlation of .32 and an alpha of .93. More remarkably, Louisiana became the only state in which Republicans scored *lower* (though nonsignificantly so) than Democrats, 171.3 versus 189.1 (see Table

Table 11.7 Results of the January 1993 RWA and LWA study

State	Party	No. of replies	Response rate (%)	RWA Scale				Left-wing author. items			
				Range	Mean	Interitem corr.	Corr. with party	Range	Mean	Interitem corr.	Corr. with RWA
Maryland	Dem.	20/116	17	73–201	137.6	.35	.39	12–61	24.1	.25	.01
	Rep.	8/25	32	138–208	174.5			12–38	23.6		
Nebraska	Dem.	5/22	23	80–216	146.4	.44	.40	31–44	36.0	.24	−.42
	Rep.	5/26	19	155–214	182.6			12–27	20.2		
N. Dakota (House)	Dem.	11/33	33	59–217	130.9	.42	.52	13–55	29.3	.22	−.41
	Rep.	22/65	34	120–246	177.4			12–40	25.7		
N. Dakota (Senate)	Dem.	7/25	28	88–194	138.9	.25	.47	15–57	29.7	.43	.06
	Rep.	7/24	29	136–205	175.0			25–27	26.0		
All	Dem.	43/196	22	59–217	137.1	.37	.45	12–61	27.1	.25	−.17
	Rep.	42/140	30	120–246	177.1			12–40	24.7		

11.8).[21] This reversal of form shrunk the overall Republican "superiority" to 179.3 versus 156.8. The RWA-party correlations averaged .34, also pulled down by the Louisiana data.

DOG Items. The DOG items intercorrelated .27 overall, producing an alpha of .83. As was true of Manitoba students and parents, sums proved rather low, with only 9 lawmakers clearing the neutral point of 70. Still, GOP lawmakers rang up higher totals in every legislature, significantly so overall ($r = .30$). The RWA-DOG correlation equaled .50.

Discussion. It makes sense to me that lawmakers would be nondogmatic. The legislative process requires endless compromise, and if you do not compromise you might have to shape up or ship out. The *relatively* dogmatic lawmakers tended to be High RWAs and Republicans. If you take dogmatism to be Rokeach's "general authoritarianism," we again find no evidence for the authoritarian on the left. As we saw in Chapter 8, dogmatism is largely a right-wing mind-lock.

Critique and Conclusions

CHALLENGING THE DATA

We set out to discover what American lawmakers are truly like, what they really believe in. What some of them are truly like proved to be truly disturbing. We had better take one last look before proceeding. Was our methodology sound? Is the test we used valid in this group? Did the legislators answer it truthfully? Were the samples representative?

As for methodology, all the politicians in these eight studies answered the same (1982) version of the RWA Scale, for the same researcher, for the same reason, in exactly the same format, with exactly the same instructions. Only the year of testing (1990, 1991, or 1993) and how much postage it took to get the answers back to Canada, systematically varied.

As for validity, the RWA Scale's *construct* validity in this population has broken all records for the test. The mean interitem correlation across all respondents averaged .41—higher even than that among the Canadian legislators—producing a Cronbach alpha of over .95. That means the signal-to-noise ratio in these data exceeds 19:1, giving the phrase "less than .05" a new meaning. You will have trouble finding many psychological test administrations that produced such loud, clear, and clean data with the primary measure.

As for *empirical* validity, we have witnessed a stream of powerful RWA Scale relationships with right-wing economic outlook (.62), nationalism (.66), ethnocentrism (.71), abortion (.60), and sabotage of equality and freedom (.84). The RWA Scale also predicted other important attitudes, such as those

Table 11.8 Results of the January 1993 RWA and Dogmatism study

State	Party	No. of replies	Response rate (%)	RWA Scale				Dogmatism Items			
				Range	Mean	Interitem corr.	Corr. with party	Range	Mean	Interitem corr.	Corr. with RWA
Louisiana	Dem.	15/83	18	149–227	189.1	.15	–.31	28–84	52.6	.26	–.09
	Rep.	6/16	38	133–206	171.3			47–71	54.5		
Nevada	Dem.	15/29	52	68–198	128.5	.37	.52	14–65	41.8	.23	.62
	Rep.	6/13	46	159–245	177.3			43–55	48.0		
New Hampshire	Dem.	11/35	31	75–223	135.4	.35	.34	17–66	36.9	.27	.62
	Rep.	22/65	34	67–232	169.3			23–80	49.8		
S. Dakota	Dem.	5/29	17	95–192	156.0	.24	.38	31–52	39.4	.25	.52
	Rep.	20/41	49	136–241	185.6			21–72	46.4		
Tennessee (House)	Dem.	7/63	11	149–215	182.9	.22	.49	23–68	47.4	.44	.59
	Rep.	4/36	11	180–231	207.0			42–88	66.2		
Tennessee (Senate)	Dem.	6/18	33	127–189	155.8	.23	.50	17–57	41.0	.25	.49
	Rep.	6/14	43	155–248	186.3			39–66	51.0		
All	Dem.	59/257	23	68–227	156.8	.32	.34	14–84	44.0	.27	.50
	Rep.	64/185	35	67–248	179.3			21–88	50.2		

on gun control ($-.49$) and capital punishment ($.47$). In almost every case, the test predicted outlooks *better* in this population than it has in any other.

As to whether the politicians answered truthfully, we have to realize, first, that except in a few cases when respondents signed their names to the surveys, we do not know for certain that *any* lawmaker wrote down the responses. Assuming the answers came from their own hands, and not an aide's, did the legislators reveal their true attitudes to us? We cannot say, of course. We can only observe that they knew they were anonymous, that their answers would not affect anything, that very few people can detect what the wide-ranging, balanced RWA Scale measures, that the politicians were not asked about their party affiliation until the very end, and that they were asked to participate only if they freely chose to do so.

Well then, how representative are these samples of the population of legislators writing laws in American state capitols? As I said when discussing the Canadian data, a lot of self-selection biases probably twisted and turned here. But this can be said of almost every poll result you will ever see. The question is, what effect did these biases have on the results?

I have indicated my *suspicion* that Low RWAs were more likely to turn up in my mailbox than Highs, and several features of the data (for instance, the abortion stands) support this hunch. We also know that usually, the greater the response rate from a chamber, the greater the gap between Democrats and Republicans. The correlation between response rate and the size of this gap averaged .69. So it seems probable that (1) High RWAs responded less than others did, and (2) if I had heard from all, the parties would have separated *more* than they did, not less.[22]

If you believe the politicians filled out the scales themselves—and not one piece of evidence indicates otherwise—then we apparently have trustworthy data from a valid measure of authoritarianism on 1,233 of the most powerful people in the United States—people who decide state criminal codes, taxation policies, human rights laws, educational funding, gun control, abortion bills, capital punishment, industry regulations, inner city programs, and a great deal more. What did we find?[23]

DEMOCRATS VERSUS REPUBLICANS

I did not expect to find nearly as strong a difference in RWA scores between the two mainstream American parties as appeared between the NDP and Conservative parties in the more strung out Canadian system. Altogether, the eight studies just described collected RWA scores from 682 Democrats and 549 Republicans (and two Vermont Progressive Coalition members). Figure 11.2 shows the party scores by state, plus those from my first, 1986 study.

This picture says at least a thousand words to me, but I shall be pithy and make just five observations. First, notice that we are employing a different

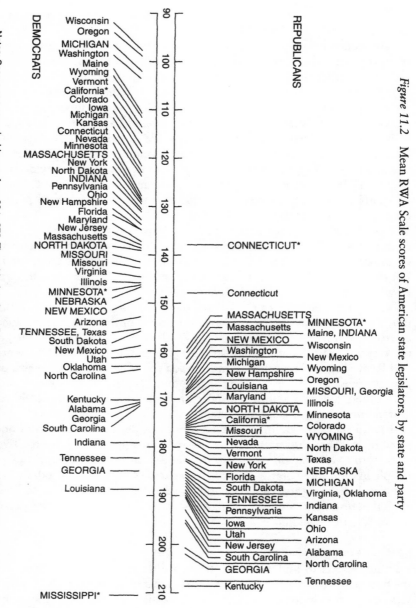

Figure 11.2   Mean RWA Scale scores of American state legislators, by state and party

Notes: Scores can conceivably vary from 30 to 270. The midpoint of possible scores is 150. Sample includes 549 Republican legislators and 682 Democrats. Scores from upper chambers are presented in larger print: e.g. CONNECTICUT vs. Connecticut.
* indicates results from the initial, 1986 study. No Connecticut Democratic senator, and only one Mississippi Republican answered.
Only one Wyoming Democratic senator answered in a 1991 study, and hence no score is listed.

DEMOCRATS

90
Wisconsin
Oregon
MICHIGAN
Washington
Maine
100
Wyoming
Vermont
California*
Colorado
110
Iowa
Michigan
Kansas
Connecticut
Nevada
Minnesota
120
MASSACHUSETTS
New York
North Dakota
INDIANA
Pennsylvania
Ohio
130
New Hampshire
Florida
Maryland
New Jersey
Massachusetts
NORTH DAKOTA
140
MISSOURI
Missouri
Virginia
Illinois
MINNESOTA*
150
NEBRASKA
NEW MEXICO
Arizona
TENNESSEE, Texas
South Dakota
160
New Mexico
Utah
Oklahoma
North Carolina
170
Kentucky
Alabama
Georgia
South Carolina
Indiana
180
Tennessee
GEORGIA
Louisiana
190
200
210
MISSISSIPPI*

REPUBLICANS

CONNECTICUT*

Connecticut

MASSACHUSETTS
Massachusetts   MINNESOTA*
NEW MEXICO   Maine, INDIANA
Washington   Wisconsin
Michigan   New Mexico
New Hampshire   Wyoming
Louisiana   Oregon
Maryland   MISSOURI, Georgia
NORTH DAKOTA   Illinois
California*   Minnesota
Missouri   Colorado
Nevada   WYOMING
Vermont   North Dakota
New York   Texas
Florida   NEBRASKA
South Dakota   MICHIGAN
TENNESSEE   Virginia, Oklahoma
Pennsylvania   Indiana
Iowa   Kansas
Utah   Ohio
New Jersey   Arizona
South Carolina   Alabama
GEORGIA   North Carolina
Kentucky   Tennessee

part of the RWA Scale continuum than we needed in Figure 11.1 for the Canadian data. It starts and ends about 20 points higher, because we found no extremely low averages in the United States, but there were some notably high ones, just as some extraordinarily high individuals turned up.

Second, GOP caucuses proved substantially more authoritarian than Democratic ones. The mean score of the responding Republicans was 178.2, while that of the Democrats was nearly *forty* points lower (140.3). Republicans scored higher on *all* the RWA Scale items; they registered much stronger belief in authoritarian submission and authoritarian aggression, as well as conventionalism. The average of the correlations between party affiliation and authoritarianism across the forty-nine chambers was .44—about half the .82 found between New Democrats and Conservatives in Canada, but still rather higher than I expected it to be.

Third, you can see that the Republican means bunch together. Almost all of them fell in the 160–200 range. By contrast, the Democrats splattered all over the place. They had the lowest score, and the highest one too. Most of them landed *below* 150, the midpoint on the RWA Scale. But some of the Democratic caucuses put up big numbers, as scary as the higher GOP scores.

This pattern of tight and scattered scores basically parallels the Canadian results, where the means of the conservative parties also clustered together, in the same neighborhood where the Republicans live. But both the NDP and the Liberals showed more diversity. You could say, then, that the Democratic Party in the United States attracts the same kind of politicians who join the NDP and Liberals in Canada. But it also contains a lot of High RWAs. Have you noticed that the Democrats show as much "caucus discipline" in Congress as do the members of an average psychology department?

Fourth, you can see a pretty clear pattern of regional differences in Figure 11.2. Northern states tend to score lower than southern states, and have bigger differences between Democrats and Republicans. I was surprised that the parties did not flip-flop in the South. I expected southern Democratic lawmakers (as the long-ruling party) to prove *more* authoritarian, and upstarts to join the Republicans. But we saw that flip-flop only in Louisiana. There *were* lots of High RWA Democrats in the South, but the Low RWA legislators south of the Mason-Dixon Line were almost always Democrats too. Outside Connecticut, Low RWAs seeking political careers either do not often join the Republican Party or do not advance in it unless they change their beliefs.

Fifth, draw a vertical line at the 150 mark. Look who is at the left of this line, and look who is at the right. Would you say that, in general, the political forces that have been trying to promote equality and freedom in America during your lifetime lay to the left of that line, and to the right lay the political forces that have been resisting it? If so, can you see who outnumbers whom? (Draw the same line in Figure 11.1, sketching in the means for the Liberals.

What do you notice? The corresponding difference between the social programs of the two countries may be just a coincidence. Then again, it may not.)

HOUSES OF REPRESENTATIVES VERSUS SENATES

These studies enable us to compare the authoritarianism in *both* chambers of
nine state legislatures (Georgia, Indiana, Massachusetts, Michigan, Missouri,
New Mexico, North Dakota, Tennessee, and Wyoming). Let us ask, what
kind of representative is likely to move up to the Senate? Are Low RWAs
more likely to advance, or Highs? Maybe it makes a difference which party
they are in.

The House Democrats averaged 153.3 on the RWA Scale, and the Senate
Democrats came in significantly *lower*, at 141.7. The House Republicans averaged 176.5, and so nearly did the Senate Republicans (176.3). Taking into
account the differences in the parties to start with, I would say being a High
RWA usually hurts your chances of advancement in the Democratic Party but
does *not* hurt you if you are a Republican.

Projecting these data onto the national scene, I would expect national Democratic leaders to be, usually, pretty Low RWAs—lower than their state-level
associates. And I would expect leaders of the national Republican Party to
be, usually, as High as the nest of Republican scores in Figure 11.2. (It would
also seem that no matter which *party* controls Congress, High RWAs will be
in the majority.)

These projections may be quite wrong. But if you look at the Canadian
results in Figure 11.1 again, where we *do* have data from national lawmakers,
you will see that is precisely what appears when you compare provincial and
federal legislators in the New Democratic and Liberal versus conservative
parties.

DO OTHER FINDINGS ABOUT HIGH RWAS NECESSARILY APPLY TO
AUTHORITARIAN LEGISLATORS?

When you look back at the earlier chapters in this book, and see all the
disturbing things that have been associated with High RWAs, it cannot bring
joy to the hearts of Republicans (and some Democrats too) that their politicians scored so high on this measure of prefascist personality. But it does not
necessarily follow that research findings about authoritarians in general will
apply to particular groups. Any particular group can have some feature in its
background, or ideological outlook, that cancels a general attribute of High
RWAs. We have no scientific evidence that authoritarian lawmakers are self-
righteous, show double standards in criminal sentencing situations, use lots
of electric shock in bogus learning experiments, are likely to join "posses,"
have trouble making correct inferences from evidence, are more likely to make
the fundamental attribution error when they like the message, are blowhards

when it comes to self-understanding, tend to be religious fundamentalists, and so on.

To be sure, High legislators have confirmed every finding thrown their way, usually more strongly than anyone ever did before. But I doubt that *all* the other findings about High RWAs would apply to authoritarian *lawmakers*. These people are just too sophisticated, I would bet, to think that society is about to be destroyed, or that punishment will solve all our social problems, or that you can trust a politician who says what you want to hear.

DO RWA SCORES NECESSARILY PREDICT HOW LEGISLATORS WILL VOTE?

Heck no. For starters, attitudes only sometimes predict behavior, as most social psychology textbooks quickly point out. In the case of politicians and their votes as legislators, the connection positively trembles. Caucus discipline, trade-offs, pressure from colleagues and special interest groups, signals of what the "folks back home" think can all produce votes "out of character"— or at least an absence when a vote is taken.

But it still seems naive to believe that the personalities of lawmakers have no influence on their decisions. We all have our values, our priorities, our attitudes, which can shape what is decided in caucus and in those fabled smoke-filled rooms out of public view. If RWA Scale scores have no connection to the stands people and parties take on the issues, then you should have been very surprised by the relationships that turned up regarding abortion, gun control, taxation policies, calls to restrict anti-war protests, and so on. Well, how surprised *were* you?

THE MATTER OF EQUALITY

In both the Canadian and the American studies, High RWA lawmakers *admitted* they opposed greater equality in society. Does *that* not surprise you? Conservatives will usually say they oppose increased taxes on the wealthy, and on corporations, because such taxes would hurt the economy. They may believe this. And it may be true, for all I know—although the "trickle down" theory was given its chance during the 1980s, and things bubbled upward instead. But Highs' answers to the Economic Philosophy Scale, their low ranking of Equality in the hodge-podge study, and their responses to the "equality" proposals in the freedom and equality study, all show that whatever else they may say, these authoritarian legislators want the rich to stay rich, and the rest can divvy up the trickles.

THE LIBERAL-CONSERVATIVE DIMENSION

Although the terms "liberal" and "conservative" carry enough common meaning that people can generally communicate with them, they also bring along enough confusion to make their use problematic, especially to a scientist. I submit that when journalists, educators, and politicians themselves talk about liberals and conservatives on the issues of our day, they are usually talking about the dimension measured by the RWA Scale. In fact, that scale probably provides our best current measure of the very real, very important liberal-conservative dimension, conceptually, psychometrically, and empirically: *Conceptually,* because we do have a fairly detailed definition of right-wing authoritarianism, which we do not have for liberalism and conservatism. *Psychometrically,* because we have a measure of right-wing authoritarianism that has shown good internal consistency in every North American sample tested thus far (and in samples from other countries as well), which again we do not have for any measure of "L-Word" and "C-Word." And *empirically,* because the measurements produced by the RWA Scale correlate well, especially among politicians, with a wide range of attitudes, behaviors, and affiliations that people commonly identify as liberal and conservative, which we do not have . . .

For me, the most amazing feature of the studies of North American lawmakers was the high interitem correlation of the RWA Scale. This occurred partly, I think, because legislators read and answer things quite carefully. But that in itself will not produce record-breaking internal consistency. (Their answers to the social dominance, left-wing authoritarianism, and dogmatism items did not hang together amazingly well, compared with other samples.) Instead, we saw that lawmakers' responses to the RWA Scale were *more* tightly organized than those to the much more focused Economic Philosophy Scale. As I said earlier, I think the RWA Scale items interconnect so strongly because we are dealing with an important ideological dimension that guides lawmakers.

Thus when I hear Rush Limbaugh, Jesse Helms, or Pat Buchanan say that the liberals favor guaranteeing equal rights for homosexuals, I say to myself, "Actually, *Low RWAs* do, and it connects to much else in their thinking." And when I hear Gary Trudeau, Edward Kennedy, and Barbara Jordan say that the conservatives oppose abortion and favor the death penalty, I say to myself, "Actually, if you understand that it's *High RWAs* who do these things, you'll realize why and a lot, lot more." When people are "conservatives"— politically, religiously, economically—the odds are pretty good that they are High RWAs. That is not an opinion, but a scientifically established fact.

You can see the connections among many things, you can perceive how many events tie together, you can grasp that much of your newspaper reports different versions of the same underlying story, if you understand the role that right-wing authoritarianism plays in our world.

AN ITEM ANALYSIS FOR THE ROAD

Whenever I give a talk on authoritarianism, I include examples of items from the RWA Scale so the group can get a feel for how I measure the construct. I always cite, as an example of a statement mainly tapping authoritarian aggression, the following item from the 1982 version of the test: "Once our government leaders and the authorities condemn the dangerous elements in our society, it will be the duty of every patriotic citizen to help stomp out the rot that is poisoning our country from within." The audience usually laughs out loud at this statement, which I have nicknamed the "Holocaust Premise" item because it could have come from some Nazi "cheerbook." It seems to be such a preposterous, "extreme" sentiment. People, even students, have interrupted my presentation to challenge me, saying, "Surely nobody agrees with that" and "Only an out-and-out Nazi thinks that way."

Here is how the 1,233 American lawmakers responded to this item. Sixty-six percent of them disagreed, most of them "very strongly" or "strongly." Eight percent either said they were neutral or did not answer it. And the other 26% said they *agreed* with it. David Duke is not a one-in-a-million speck on the American political scene, as we saw from the steady froth of Very High and Extraordinarily High RWA lawmakers in the studies of forty state legislatures.

Remember when I said earlier that I study authoritarianism mainly because I sense a bedrock of right-wing authoritarianism that never goes away and that needs only to be supplemented during a crisis to wipe out hundreds of years of democratic government? Well, behold this test drilling that shows how far down, and how thick, and where the bedrock lies.

On my optimistic days, I say, "There is nothing to worry about. A solid majority of these American legislators rejected the premise underlying the Holocaust." But on my pessimistic days, I realize, "The *lawmakers* who want the public to help stomp out whomever they consider to be 'the rot' already stand half-way to being the majority."

A CRISIS THAT HAPPENED, AND ANOTHER THAT MIGHT

In October 1970, a terrorist group in Quebec kidnapped two prominent officials. When ten days of intense police activity failed to locate the kidnappers, the (Liberal) federal government invoked the War Measures Act. This act, similar to laws many democracies have on the books for use in the gravest national emergencies, suspended many of the civil liberties of Canadian citizens. It could be promulgated in peacetime, however, only in the case of an "apprehended insurrection." The government insisted an insurrection was imminent in Quebec.

Some 87% of the people of Canada, including me, believed the government and supported the loss of our rights, since that was the only way (we were told) to save the nation. It turned out later, however, that *no* danger of an insurrection had existed, and the government had knowingly, massively misrepresented the situation. But *we* believed the government's deceit, and thus had risked the loss of our democracy (*RWA*, pp. 3–4). We had our "Reichstag

Fire Test," and we failed it. Fortunately for us, the prime minister was not intent on establishing a dictatorship (though he may have been mightily interested in having his party win the upcoming provincial election in Quebec).[24]

In closing, let me tell you a story you have probably *not* heard of a similar crisis in the United States that did not occur, but still might. On July 5, 1987, the *Miami Herald* reported that Oliver North had drawn up a top-secret plan for the National Security Council calling for the "suspension" of the United States Constitution under certain conditions. The "conditions" involved such things as a *nuclear* holocaust, but North also included "national opposition to a U.S. military invasion abroad" as ground for casting aside Congress, the Supreme Court, the Bill of Rights, whatever. (If you have not heard of this plan, it is probably because, curiously, very few newspapers or news broadcasts ever reported the story. Representative Jack Brooks tried to have the matter placed on the agenda of the Iran-Contra hearings, but he was overruled—not because the report was untrue, but because the issue was so highly classified; see the *New York Times,* July 14, 1987, p. A11.)

I myself am not privy to whether the National Security Council ever adopted this plan to overthrow the Constitution of the United States—which all American military officers take an apparently compartmentalizable oath to defend. I do not know whether, if the Executive Branch did once approve this plan, it still holds it at the ready. But the revelation shows that extreme rightwing authoritarianism has, at times in the past, been alive and well in the highest reaches of democratic government, from which it could have sent us to the lowest depths.

Conclusion:
A Few Last Words on the Subject

A year has passed since I began writing this book. Some of the twenty stories from the Introduction that were in the news in the fall of 1993 have disappeared. The Pentagon's policy on gays and lesbians has not led to the ruin of the armed forces. And atrocities in Brazil have not drawn much ink lately. Instead, we are hearing of atrocities committed in Argentina during the "dirty war."

Other stories limped off the pages. The "Democrat-controlled" Congress never passed a health bill in 1993–1994. The Chinese government slapped its dissenters back into jail as soon as it lost its Olympic bid, and the Clinton administration decided to disconnect human rights concerns from its trade negotiations with China. (No other country, including Canada, was pushing the issue when discussing trade with Beijing.)

Other stories happily took a turn for the better. A significant peace accord was reached by a new Israeli government and the PLO. (Whereupon Jewish and Muslim fundamentalists, who want to keep on fighting, did their best to wreck the chances for peace, mostly by killing unarmed civilians.) Free elections were held in South Africa, and Nelson Mandela's Freedom Party swept to power. The IRA announced a cease-fire, which "hard-liners" resisted. Also, I consider it a plus that Oliver North did not get elected to the Senate.

But I still see right-wing authoritarians at work in every paper, every day. The Bosnian Serbs are still pursuing their "final solution." Another doctor was killed outside an abortion clinic in Florida. Vladimir Zhirinovsky brought a little comic relief to the world scene by announcing he would help reverse Russia's declining birth rate by fathering children all over the country. (But the Parliament his party controlled granted full pardons to all the conspirators who had been convicted of trying violently to overthrow the new democracy. And people hurt by the economic reforms have begun to support a rejuvenated Communist Party.) Senator Jesse Helms told the president of the United States that if he dared visit any military bases in North Carolina, he had better bring bodyguards. And Rwandans on all sides learned, as the German people did in 1945, the horrific price that ultimately must be paid *by everyone* when the right-wing authoritarians within a population gain absolute control.

The Outcomes of the Studies

THE HIGHS

At the beginning of this book I observed that we often swap a lot of stereotypes when discussing liberals and conservatives. I promised to let the scientific method do the talking, and I hope you agree that the evidence presented in this book cannot be dismissed as "just opinions." Exhibit 12.1 lists fifty noteworthy results of the experiments I conducted, all based on completely objective scoring, not "dream interpretations." The studies turned out the way they did because that is apparently the way things are. Furthermore, in nearly all these cases the RWA relationships proved quite substantial, sometimes ranking among the strongest findings we have ever uncovered in the behavioral sciences. Moreover, RWA Scale findings have a very good record of replication by other researchers, just as some of my findings are replications of others' discoveries.

This summary does not paint a pretty picture of right-wing authoritarians, and it only gets worse when you add in findings by other researchers, such as High men's greater tendency to assault women sexually (Walker, Rowe, and Quinsey, 1993). It may seem one-sided to someone who has not worked through the evidence. But after all, we are talking about people who have Nazi-like inclinations.

As you consider Highs' demonstrated inclinations and orientations, recall my statement at the beginning of this book that, their denial notwithstanding, many conservatives differ from the Oklahoma City bombers more in degree than in kind. Here is the evidence.[1]

Exhibit 12.1   Summary of Scientific Research Findings regarding High RWAs.

Compared with others, right-wing authoritarians are significantly more likely to:

Score on the "Hitler" end of the RWA Scale.

Accept unfair and illegal abuses of power by government authorities.

Trust leaders (such as Richard Nixon) who are untrustworthy.

Weaken constitutional guarantees of liberty, such as the Bill of Rights.

Punish severely "common" criminals in a role-playing situation.

Admit they get personal pleasure from punishing such people.

But go easy on authorities who commit crimes and people who attack minorities.

Not hold responsible the authority who caused the attacks in the "Milgram experiment."

Attack "learners" in an "electric shock" experiment.

Be prejudiced against many racial, ethnic, nationalistic, and linguistic minorities.

Be hostile toward homosexuals.

Support "gay-bashing."

Volunteer to help the government persecute almost anyone.

Be mean-spirited toward those who have made mistakes and suffered.

Insist on traditional sex roles.

Be hostile toward feminists.

Conform to opinions of others, and be more likely to "yea-say."

Be fearful of a dangerous world.

Be highly self-righteous.

Strongly believe in group cohesiveness and "loyalty."

Make many incorrect inferences from evidence.

Hold contradictory ideas leading them to "speak out of both sides of their mouths."

Uncritically accept that many problems are "our most serious problem."

Uncritically accept insufficient evidence that supports their beliefs.

Uncritically trust people who tell them what they want to hear.

Use many double standards in their thinking and judgments.

Be hypocrites.

Help cause and inflame intergroup conflict.

Be bullies when they have power over others.

Seek dominance over others by being competitive and destructive in situations requiring cooperation.

Believe they have no personal failings.

Avoid learning about their personal failings.

Use religion to erase guilt over their acts and to maintain their self-righteousness.

Be "fundamentalists" and the most prejudiced members of whatever religion they belong to.

Be dogmatic.

Be zealots.

Be less educated.

Sometimes join left-wing movements, where their hostility distinguishes them.

But much more typically endorse right-wing political parties.

Be Conservative/Reform Party (Canada) or Republican Party (United States) lawmakers, who (1) have a conservative economic philosophy; (2) believe in social dominance; (3) are ethnocentric; (4) are highly nationalistic; (5) oppose abortion; (6) support capital punishment; (7) oppose gun-control legislation; (8) say they value freedom but actually want to undermine the Bill of Rights; (9) do not value equality very highly and oppose measures to increase it; (10) are not likely to rise in the Democratic Party, but do so among Republicans.

THE LOWS

If Low RWAs had as little integrity as Highs have, if they were as fearful and self-righteous, if they were as hostile and destructive, if they were as unfair, if they were as defensive and as blind to themselves, if they were as prejudiced, and so on, then the experiments would have turned out differently. Lows had as good a chance of acting these ways as Highs did. But the Lows did not.

Instead, they tended to object strongly to any abuse of power, no matter who was in control and who the victim was. You would wait quite a while for a posse of Lows to help run down some "varmints." They tended to be moderate and evenhanded in their punishment of criminals, responding more to the crime, not to who the criminal was. Their thinking was much less compartmentalized, much more consistent. They were more likely to make correct inferences from facts. They were more willing to admit things about themselves they did not like. When given bad news about their personalities, they faced the news squarely. They were much more open-minded, much less dogmatic than Highs, and more independent, more peaceful and peace-seeking, and much less biased. The dogmatism and hostility one sometimes finds in leftist groups does not seem likely to have sprung from Low RWAs, but instead probably comes from the Wild-Card Authoritarians we discovered.[2]

CHALLENGING THE RESULTS

If you think I got these results only because I "set up" the Highs by my choice of issues, and manipulations, I think you are wrong. I tried to give both Lows and Highs equal opportunities to show their good and bad sides. Sometimes Lows behaved badly too, as in their double standard regarding Quebec separation and their greater shift toward intolerance following the 1995 Quebec referendum. They also were just as likely as Highs to cheat on their lovers, and equally susceptible to Holocaust-denial material. Twice they acted *worse* than Highs; see the University of Pittsburgh experiments described in note 13 to Chapter 1. But the point is, Lows *could* have looked bad many other times as well in my studies; but they did not. Never? Hardly ever.

Let me repeat one more time: if the difference between ordinary High RWAs and neo-Nazis is a matter of degree, so also is the difference between Lows and Highs. I would not be surprised if some day researchers find worse things about Lows than we presently know. But considering the overall evidence, I would much rather be a Low RWA than a High.

If you nonetheless think my research has been very unfair to Highs, that they have talents and strengths that I have ignored, then take heart from the fact that all of these findings are based on experiments. That means researchers around the world can design their own studies and determine how limited my findings are. And this will happen in due course, automatically, if these results peak anyone's curiosity. Science is basically a cooperative human adventure, with massive long-run controls for the truth.

Similarly, where my *interpretations* are wrong, we can go beyond arguing—which gains us little because anyone can "talk the talk"—and demonstrate my errors. If, for example, the liberal—conservative dimension in politics is *not* basically synonymous with the Low RWA–High RWA scale, if the political dimension can be better conceptualized in some other way, then that can be proven scientifically. It will take a well-defined alternate conceptualization, and a sound way of measuring it, and then experiments that demonstrate its superiority. But it can be done, and we shall advance when it happens. We know much more on this subject than we knew when we thought we knew a lot. And we shall learn more. There is room for optimism.

Controlling Authoritarianism within Our Societies

My students sometimes challenge my optimism, demanding, "What good does it do to understand bad things if you cannot change them?" I respond, as many have before: "When you understand, you know better how to produce change." That said, I still have to work some to compose a Top Ten list of recommendations for protecting society against right-wing authoritarianism.

1. We are helped, both ethically and practically, by the fact that right-wing authoritarians themselves typically do not want to be so authoritarian. When High RWAs learn they are Highs, about 80% of them are surprised and upset, and they say that they want to change (*EOF*, pp. 312–317). Mind you, they

do not aspire to be Lows; rather, they want to be "average"—which is predictable, but still a big step forward.

We cannot give the RWA Scale to everybody, however, much less tell them their scores. And we know that Highs will usually think these findings apply to someone else, not them. But studies have led to some practical suggestions (*EOF,* chapter 8).

2. Anti-discrimination laws can be quite beneficial. Ordinary authoritarians appear more likely to obey laws they dislike than others are. (It comes from being an authoritarian.) Such laws, *when enforced,* not only protect the vulnerable minorities, but also bring Highs into more contact, as equals, with the people they would otherwise avoid. Recall that Highs who got to know a homosexual usually lost some of their prejudice.

3. Brother Bernard, my favorite teacher in high school, would not like what I am going to say next, but secular education also helps High RWAs move in wider circles of acquaintances. Highs drop significantly in authoritarianism during public university education mostly, I think, because of the exposure to more diverse people and opinions. Parents should have the right to send their children to private schools. But doing so probably costs all of us in subtle ways.

4. News media that value freedom of the press might resist the temptation to overplay the crime and violence stories. Hyping a "dangerous world" increases right-wing authoritarianism in the population, which could lead to authoritarian leaders. What do dictators seize first after a coup?

5. Similarly, churches that value freedom of religion could do much to *discourage* ethnocentrism, authoritarianism, and self-righteousness, and produce a wonderful *negative* relationship between religiousness and prejudice. (I know many try, and they are often dealing with "hard, hard hearts.")

6. Reformers who value the right to protest should proceed nonviolently, for many reasons. Violent demonstrations appear to drive the population toward right-wing authoritarianism. Reformers should watch out for the "wild cards" in their ranks, who are most likely to become violent.

7. Groups in conflict with other groups should note the mirror-image studies. The people shouting in the front ranks on the other side are apt to be like the people screaming in the front ranks on your side: right-wing authoritarians. Lows and Moderates in both camps have to see past them and their hatred, and reach over them to one another, to reduce the conflict.

8. We have to speak out against the hatemongers in our society by independently presenting the truth and exposing their lies. Hate campaigners would use freedom of speech to take it away from us. We have to use it to keep it.

9. It is not my place to tell anyone how to vote. But it seems very unwise to elect High RWAs, from any party, to govern a democracy.

10. Finally, I think we should learn a humbling lesson from the experiments on Holocaust denial. Everyone—Lows, Moderates, and Highs—could have done better, just as I could have in the anteroom of the National Socialist White People's Party headquarters. If you know who "Pogo" was, you know who the real enemy is.

Ordinary People

Sometimes, when I tell people that I study authoritarian personalities, they say things like, "Oh, you mean neo-Nazis and the Klan." When these people are psychologists at conventions or the president of my university, I say "Right," because I know they will probably instantly forget whatever I reply. But I am more forthcoming with others.

Most people seem surprised when I say, "No, I study normal folks, not Nazis." Few people, unless they are familiar with the history of fascism, understand that people as ordinary as you and I, and our friends and neighbors, might bring down democracy if the going got tough enough. But *we* are the people who, driven by fear and cuddling in our self-righteousness, could create the wave that would lift the monsters among us to power. And once the monsters acquire the powers of the state, their evil explodes.

Can one credibly talk about fascism in the North American context as we approach the year 2000? Is it even remotely possible that the horrors of Nazi Germany could someday occur in Canada or the United States? When I talk about prefascist personalities, do I seriously propose that many North Americans could act like Hitler, Himmler, Hoess, and so on?

I have little doubt that most of the "230s," "240s," and "250s" could. But, although the Nazis did monstrous things, it is a mistake to think that only ardent fascists and psychopathic killers became Nazis. Adolf Eichmann struck some as a bland person, not particularly anti-Semitic, who basically wanted to advance his career and so worked hard to impress his superiors. His evil was "banal" (Arendt, 1977). I can also imagine that many of those who made the arrests and transported the victims to the death camps would have been described as "good, decent people" by their families and neighbors. So would many of those who ran the slave labor camps in which hundreds of thousands of prisoners perished and maybe even the SS soldiers who massacred whole villages. You can be an ordinary Joe, or Lieutenant Calley, and still do terrible things. One of the first things Americans learned about the militias, in an Associated Press story dated April 27, 1995, was that they were "ordinary people who feel pushed."

If you think our countries could never elect an Adolf Hitler to power, note that David Duke would have become the governor of Louisiana if it had just been up to the white voters in the state. Many people vote for extraordinarily High RWA candidates today. Many more would want one during a crisis. About a quarter of American state legislators are already poised to "stomp out the rot." And if you think a North American dictator could not find the people he needed to kill Jews, or professors, or Communists, or trade union leaders, or defiant clergy, or religious minorities, or the mentally "unsuitable," or whomever he wanted to eliminate, then you might recall what Milgram found.

I am now writing the last page in my last book about authoritarianism. So for the last time, I do *not* think a fascist dictatorship lies just over our horizon. But I do not think we are well protected against one. And I think our recent history shows the threat is growing.

Fascism has proven as vile and persistent in this century as prejudice, which has shown it can be quietly passed from generation to generation even when the state vigorously discourages it. And unlike Communism, fascism cannot be expected to fail because it makes some fatally wrong assumptions about human nature. Instead, democracy seems to be fighting the current here: by depending on tolerance, when fear and dislike come so easily; by asking for generosity of spirit, when selfishness is so natural; by championing equality, when hierarchy seems so inevitable.

We cannot secure the blessings of liberty to ourselves, and our posterity, if we sit with our oars out of the water. If we drift mindlessly, circumstances can sweep us to disaster. Our societies presently produce millions of highly authoritarian personalities as a matter of course, enough to stage the Nuremberg Rallies over and over and over again. Turning a blind eye to this could someday point guns at all our heads, and the fingers on the triggers will belong to right-wing authoritarians. We ignore this at our peril.

Notes • References • Index

Notes

1. Previous Research on Right-Wing Authoritarianism

1. It gives some psychologists pause that I have defined a *personality* variable in terms of *attitudes*. By "personality" I mean an individual's unique and enduring behavior patterns. By "attitude" I mean a characteristic evaluative orientation toward some stimulus. Attitudes are thus an example of unique and enduring behavior patterns, i.e., an aspect of personality.

   Defining right-wing authoritarianism as a set of attitudes means that it should be measured with an attitude scale. This brings an immediate advantage, since personality tests traditionally are phrased in the first person (e.g., "I have strange thoughts while in the bathtub"), and attitude surveys usually are not ("Bathtubs should keep to 'their place' in a house"). Thus, a personality test involving attitudes can easily be passed off as an opinion survey.

2. Most of these elaborations were originally given in my first book, *Right-Wing Authoritarianism*, pp. 147–155, which should be consulted for a fuller account. I could find no reason to change anything by the time I wrote my second book (*Enemies of Freedom*). (We'll discuss dogmatism in chapter 8.)

3. Mixon (1971) and Greenwood (1983) would not agree with me about the Teachers' perceptions. They would say instead that Milgram's subjects were willing to hurt the Learner but did not believe they were permanently harming him. Orne and Holland (1968) in turn hold that Milgram's subjects saw through the deception and knew the Learner was not really being shocked. See Blass (1992a), pp. 304–308). Blass (1991), arguing against the "situationalist view," observes that Milgram's experiments did not always produce noticeably different levels of obedience in very different situations.

4. Both leaders and followers can be "authoritarian." Hitler, for example, believed his authority to do what he wanted superseded all human rights, laws, treaties, etc. He was an authoritarian leader. Millions of Germans in turn gladly accepted his authority over the state and everything in it. They were authoritarian follow-

ers, exhibiting authoritarian submission. Psychologists have mainly tried to understand the authoritarianism of the *followers*. In this sense, our focus has been upon the multitudes at the Nuremberg rallies, not the figure on the podium. Why? For one thing, potential followers vastly outnumber would-be dictators, and so permit powerful statistical analyses and defendable generalizations. But also, without supporters, demagogues are just comical eccentrics on soapboxes, as Hitler himself was before World War I (Payne, 1973, pp. 86–87). We shall probably always have potential dictators in our midst. They pose no great threat to an established democracy until multitudes lift them aloft.

5. Do you notice how seldom authoritarians aggress against others in a fair fight? The victim is usually already under control, as in a prison, or else caught unawares, outnumbered, or overwhelmingly outweaponed. Women, children, and others unable to defend themselves are typical targets. Attacks occur at night by hooded men, or when the victim has been isolated or when his or her back is turned. Undoubtedly authoritarians fear retaliation and legal punishment. But doesn't their behavior suggest an enjoyment of power per se? *Something* else is at work here, for authoritarian aggression is done in the name of some higher authority. This authority gives the attack legitimacy in the minds of the aggressors, and they will often say they are proud of what they did. Yet what they did was almost always extraordinarily cowardly.

6. These samples were recruited as part of a series of "pitting experiments" designed to test the new RWA Scale's validity against that of its famous forerunner, the California Fascism Scale (Adorno et al., 1950), mentioned earlier in conjunction with Milgram's experiments. Also included were Rokeach's (1960) Dogmatism Scale, Wilson's (1973) Conservatism Scale, Lee and Warr's (1969) "Balanced F Scale," and Kohn's (1972) Authoritarianism-Rebellion Scale. (The RWA Scale proved to be rather better than the others: *RWA*, chapter 4.)

7. The people who so kindly helped me were my friends David Hanson at SUNY-Potsdam, Roger Brown and Gregg Solomon at Harvard, Irene Frieze and Richard Moreland at the University of Pittsburgh, and Richard Rozelle and Steven Cardozo at the University of Houston. Dan Perlman and Jim Barton at the University of British Columbia, Edgar O'Neal and Paul Frankel at Tulane University, and Doris Becker at San Francisco State University also helped me collect data which I shall describe later. But the samples were too small (i.e., less than 100) to yield a trustworthy estimate of alpha, as was another Manitoba nonstudent sample (Wylie and Forest, 1992).

8. I shall call all of the various RWA Scales used since 1981 "the RWA Scale." The first version had twenty-four items and was published in 1981, along with a succeeding thirty-item version, in *RWA*. Many of the studies in this review used one or the other of these versions. Most of those that did not instead used the 1982 version of the test given in *EOF* or the slightly different 1986 version given in that same book. While these tests (and the revisions that followed) vary some, they still share many items and intercorrelate highly, as shall be demonstrated in the next chapter.

The summary presented in Table 1.1 includes all the studies I know of—including unpublished ones that have come my way down the electronic superhighway—that gathered RWA scores from at least 100 subjects. I have excluded from this table, and the subsequent review on empirical validity, any study that used a "condensed version" of the RWA Scale, no matter what its sample size. I understand well that in some circumstances, time and space considerations force researchers to choose between full versions of a few scales and short versions of many. My preference is for the former, in the hope of being more certain about a few things rather than less certain about many. I want to encourage researchers to use the entire RWA Scale, so even though I shall thereby pass up some delicious findings, it is expedient for me to ignore studies that only used bits and pieces of the test. I can be a person of strong principle, when it is expedient.

I shall not say much about *mean* RWA scores here. The topic is complicated by whether the scale employed was twenty-four or thirty items long, which items were used, and whether a 3-, 5-, 6-, 7-, or 9-point response scale was used. But I must observe that the Soviet/Russian data obtained in the late 1980s indicate that the Russian people were then quite *un*authoritarian. Compensating for the factors just described, the mean of the Moscow and Estonian samples tested by McFarland and his colleagues (1990) was about 120, on a scale from 30 to 270. Brief, Comrey, and Collins (1994) found a mean of 131 among 440 St. Petersburg police officers, soldiers, and government trainees. Manitoba parents in turn averaged about 175 on that (1986) version of the test, and Manitoba students averaged about 150. McFarland's 463 Kentucky adults also averaged about 175.

9. People sometimes ask me, "What score makes one a High RWA?" That is like asking, "What height makes one tall?" The answer is different when assembling a submarine crew and a basketball team. But some people are definitely tall no matter what the context, and the same applies to authoritarianism. In the case of the RWA Scale, my answer depends on which version of the test is involved and which response scale is used—as noted above. I think scores in the 180s on the RWA Scale given in *EOF* are "high" in absolute terms. When they approach 200, I start to shudder.

10. A Gallup poll taken in the last days of Nixon's presidency found that 24% of the American people still approved of the way he was doing his job. Nixon knew these people, who-would-believe-him-no-matter-what, were "out there" and would support him to the end. The Watergate tape of April 25, 1973, contains the following exchange with his chief of staff, H. R. Haldemann, over his deteriorating position in the polls: "I think there's still a hell of a lot of people out there . . . [who] want to believe. That's the point isn't it?" Haldemann replied, "Why sure. Want to and do" (*New York Times,* November 22, 1974, p. 20). Many people count on this gullibility of High RWAs for their incomes, social standing, and election to public office, as we shall see in Chapter 4.

11. Two other studies, not as concerned with democracy-threatening submission, have also shown RWA Scale connections to authoritarian submission. A "Kohlberg-type" survey in 1973 among Manitoba students found High RWAs were much more inclined to use relatively primitive thinking ("The law is the law and meant to be obeyed") and punishment-oriented thinking as their basis for moral

reasoning (*RWA*, pp. 192–196). Second, a famous astronomer wrote me in 1989, wondering if there were RWA connections with more "animalistic" signs of submission, such as bowing to a superior. I developed a scale of drawn stick-figures showing increasing angles of inclination, and asked 178 Manitoba students to mark the deepest bow they would presently show to their father, the president of a company where they worked, an important religious leader, etc. The answers did not reveal a whole lot of throwing oneself flat on the floor at the feet of a superior. But RWA scores did correlate significantly with degree of bowing in all eight cases presented, ranging from .21 to .46. The correlation with the "sum of bows" equaled .43.

12. Educational attainment averaged 13.0 years among the respondents, virtually the same as that obtained with parents of university students. However, education correlated − .46 with RWA in this sample, a much larger figure than the − .20 to − .30 usually found among parents. This result reveals a larger self-selection bias for education than occurs in my parent studies. The strong correlation with education means some RWA Scale findings may really be due to low education, not authoritarianism per se. There is a statistical way, called a "partial correlation," to set aside the effects of education and then see how well authoritarianism correlates with things by itself. Partialling out the effects of education in this study reduces the correlation between RWA scores and sentences from .52 to .43. Similar drops would occur in most of the other RWA relationships we shall encounter from Wylie's study.

13. This finding, obtained both times in two studies using Manitoba students, was *not* replicated in the 1990 sample of University of Pittsburgh students (nearly all of whom were women). In fact, the *Low* RWAs showed a significant double standard in that study, punishing the anti-gay leader more than the pro-gay one. This same sample also showed another Low RWA double standard. They believed the testimony of a liberal U.S. senator implicated in the Charles Keating Savings and Loan scandal more than that of a conservative U.S. senator, when the facts were identical in each case. These are the only instances in which I have found Low RWAs showing a significant double standard, relative to Highs.

14. I had run three earlier versions of this experiment in 1971–72, using both student and nonstudent subjects, as I was developing the RWA Scale. A significant RWA—Shock correlation appeared in each of these studies. At the *end* of each session in these four studies, the Experimenter (played by a mild-mannered male graduate student) instructed the Teacher to deliver a shock to the learner from a separate device labeled "Danger: Very Severe Shock." Between 86% and 91% of the subjects complied, usually in a matter of three or four seconds. The major hesitations (not counting the few people who refused to obey) occurred because the Teachers were afraid *they* would receive the shock if they touched the button. Once they were shown the device was safe, they pushed it (*RWA*, pp. 273–274). (Nothing happened. The Experimenter then "discovered" a high-voltage connection had "come loose.")

I did not try to run a laboratory aggression study again until 1983. In the meanwhile, I discovered in 1981 that 48% of a sample of introductory psychology students at my university said they knew about Milgram's experiment by the time they matriculated. So in 1983 I attempted to disguise the experiment as a game of Battleship in which subjects could give blasts of noise to (supposed) opponents to confuse them. But nearly half the students wrote on a post-experimental questionnaire that the real purpose of the study was to see how aggressive they would be. (See *EOF*, pp. 131–132, n. 3.) In the fall of 1994 I asked 191 introductory students if they knew of Milgram's experiment. This time 31% said they had heard of it. So the experiment might be losing some of its fame.

15. Please note the wording: "Compared with others [Highs] dislike almost every group that is different." Scores on my Ethnocentrism Scale (which can vary from 20 to 180) tend to average between 70 and 75 among Manitoba students and about 10–15 points higher among their parents. Most High RWA students, and about half of the High RWA parents, thus score *below* the neutral point of 100 on the scale.

When I call High RWAs "equal-opportunity *bigots*," I am assuming that social desirability affects the answers people give to an obvious prejudice scale. That is, people probably pull their punches so as not to look as prejudiced as they might actually be. I am also assuming that Lows and Highs tend to pull their punches equally. I have often found, however, that High RWAs give significantly more prejudiced answers when answering anonymously than when they know they can be identified (just as exit polls of elections involving a black and a white candidate sometimes find more people saying they voted for the minority candidate than actually did). I have never found Low RWAs to score significantly lower in prejudice when answering anonymously, compared to when they are identifiable. High RWAs may thus be cloaking their ethnocentrism *more* than most. More of them would probably land above the neutral point if they answered more truthfully.

16. The disconfirmation may *partly* be due to the use of AZT treatments as an index of hostility toward homosexuals. Not everyone who contracts AIDS is a homosexual, and even homophobes may feel some sympathy for homosexuals who are HIV-positive. I tested this interpretation in the fall of 1994, when I asked 191 University of Manitoba students to recommend cuts to provincial programs supporting businesses, people on welfare, the disabled, homosexuals, and private schools. (I stole this procedure, without permission, from the fertile minds of Geoffrey Haddock and Mark Zanna.) For half the students the homosexual program was described as: "Gay-Lesbian Political Support. This program supports homosexual organizations, helping them pursue complaints to the Human Rights Commission, seek equal rights, etc." On average, students recommended a 4.93% cut in the budget for this program (the deepest cut of the five possibilities), and RWA scores correlated .43 with wielding the ax here. The other half of the sample was asked about an AZT program: "AZT Subsidies. This program provides AZT, an expensive drug that prolongs the lives of homosexuals and others who have AIDS, but does not cure them." Students whacked at this budget significantly less (3.16%, in third place), and the correlation with RWA was only .26 (not significantly different with these sample sizes, but in line with the expectation).

17. I have found a noticeable drop in ATH Scale scores among Manitoba introductory psychology students lately. The mean of the scale shown in Exhibit 1.3 among 105 students in the fall of 1990 was 52.1. It was 50.0 among 559 students the following autumn. In the fall of 1992, it had dropped to 46.2 for 413 students. By the next autumn it had plummeted to 41.8 among 803 students—firmly on the "acceptance" side of the neutral point (60) on a scale whose scores can range from 12 to 108. The September 1994 mean equaled 41.5 among 456 students.

    I attribute this drop to many factors, such as a more sympathetic treatment of homosexuals in the media and more openness among homosexuals. (In Winnipeg, one of the best known city counsellors is openly gay, and he won his seat by an enormous majority in the last election.) To test the coming-out effect, I ran an experiment in 1985 with my own introductory students, in which I (falsely) told half of them I was gay and asked for their anonymous evaluations of me *and* homosexuals. Compared with those from the other half of my students, who got no such information, my personal ratings dropped some but ratings of homosexuals in general rose (*EOF*, pp. 226–230). (The *New York Times* picked up this study but did not include the incidental fact that I was lying when I told my students I was gay. This gave my father-in-law quite a jolt at breakfast one morning.)

    Beyond these effects, however, the scientific evidence indicating that sexual orientation might be determined before one is born (e.g., LeVay, 1993) has likely affected the attitudes of heterosexuals. In the fall of 1989 I briefly described the "fetal androgenization" theory (Brown, 1986, pp. 358–362) in a booklet administered to 372 Manitoba students. Then I asked them to indicate on a 0–4 scale "how blame-worthy, how morally at fault would a person be for being a homosexual" if this theory proved true? The mean was 0.43, with 74% of the sample saying "0." As you would expect, however, some Highs *still* thought homosexuals would be morally at fault: $r = .31$.

18. Some of these data on male sexual aggression were collected for Kathryn Ryan of Lycoming College.

19. I do not mean to criticize my good friends Tim Fullerton and Bruce Hunsberger. I helped compose the Christian Orthodoxy Scale and probably put in all the sexist language.

20. I found it interesting that almost none of the reviews of *Enemies of Freedom* mentioned the extensive connections between authoritarianism and religiousness presented in the book. Maybe the reviewers thought, "Everybody knows that already." (You can hardly miss the connection between religious fundamentalism and militant right-wing movements in the United States.) Or maybe they felt this would be a "sensitive subject" and thus best passed over.

    It certainly *is* sensitive, for some people. No matter how often you remind readers that findings are generalizations with exceptions, and that you are *not* saying, "All religious people are fascists" (e.g., *EOF*, pp. 201, 217), some people will still accuse you of overgeneralizing and "smearing" religion. (Sometimes they tell me I shall go to hell for this. Or at least they hope I shall.)

    If you think this reaction occurs only among nonscientists, I fear you are mistaken. An editor of *The International Journal for the Psychology of Religion* solicited a paper on authoritarianism and religion from Bruce Hunsberger and me. I agreed, with the understanding that my phraseology would be tolerated and editing would be limited to correcting my more outrageous grammatical violations and spelling mistakes. We submitted a paper reporting five studies on authoritarianism, religious fundamentalism, and prejudice. The editor then had our paper critiqued, and the assessor complained we had overgeneralized our findings (which proved rather unfavorable to religion). In fact, we had gone out of our way to point out the limitations of our data, in one paragraph qualifying our findings three times. But you can never qualify unflattering findings about religion enough for some. Religion is a *very* sensitive topic. You can offend more people in ten minutes by presenting "negative" findings about religion, than you can by parading Bill the Cat around the New York City Cat Show all day, and then giving him first prize. Oh well, just another episode in the "raw and violent world of international archeology" (Circus, 1970).

21. Vladimir Ageyev presented these results at a meeting of the International Society of Political Psychology in Helsinki, in July 1991. He then returned to Moscow, and shortly thereafter hard-liners in the Communist Party staged their attempted coup against Mikhail Gorbachev and his democratic reforms. While I was out playing golf, Vladimir and his wife were in the crowd that faced down the tanks in front of Moscow's White House for three tense days and nights. For some of us, the study of authoritarianism is far more than an "academic" exercise.

22. I had done a similar role-playing experiment in early 1974, asking students at the University of Western Ontario to answer the RWA Scale as they thought the Canadian prime minister, Pierre Trudeau, or the American president, Richard Nixon, or Adolf Hitler would have responded (*RWA*, p. 210). "Hitler's" score was near the top of the possible range, about a 230 or 240 in terms of a thirty-item test answered on a -4 to $+4$ basis. "Trudeau" ended up surprisingly close to the students' own mean, toward the center of the possible range. "Nixon" placed in between, but closer to "Hitler" than to "Trudeau."

23. If this literature review seemed long and tedious, it could have been much worse. For a test published fifteen years ago, the RWA Scale has a relatively small literature, which has undoubtedly been to its advantage. Nearly all of the people who have used the measure thus far have been, first and foremost, interested in studying authoritarianism, and they have proceeded with some background knowledge and skill.

Doesn't everyone? Well, when a scale gets "hot" in the journals, I perceive some people latch onto it just to get publications. They may not have much background in the area, nor have thought much about their studies, nor even know what they are doing. (I have seen RWA Scale papers in which the authors did not realize you have to reverse the scoring key for the contrait items.) It is so *easy* to do studies in which you just copy down a scale and give it out with some other scales. Roger Brown (1965) called this response to a new test the "hula hoop effect."

I suspect Ph.D. dissertations also contribute a lot of error variance to a scale's literature. The researcher tends to be inexperienced, and the studies often get rushed in at the end of the term. Moreover, dissertations are shaped by faculty committees, and each member basically gets to put in whatever he or she wants ("Why don't you just put in the _____ Scale to see what happens?") James Rest (1979, p. xix), talking about the huge demand for his Defining Issues Test, spoke wonderfully of the letters he receives that go something like this: "Dear Sir: My dissertation committee says I have to include a measure of moral development in my study. I tried to use Kohlberg's test, but since I'm not that interested in moral judgment, I'd like to use yours, which I heard is quick and easy. Please send me a copy of the test right away because I'm supposed to collect data next week." So the RWA Scale has not become "popular." Papers using the California F Scale still appear more often in the journals (which I do not mind at all, if you follow my drift).

24. As was true with the review of the RWA Scale's internal consistency, I have excluded from this presentation any study that used a condensed version of the test. Actually, almost all such studies produced confirmatory results. However, such confirmatory results are one of the reasons I am wary of studies that use only part of a test. You can, if you choose the items carefully, get an appreciably stronger relationship between a miniversion of a scale and some target variable of interest than you could with the scale as a whole. It will then appear to the uncritical reviewer that the construct validity of the test *as a whole* has been splendidly verified. (This is an old trick, but it apparently still works.) Another potential "sleight of hand" maneuver involves using just the items with the best intercorrelations on the test. This also ignores the probability that those items no longer faithfully represent the construct for which the test was conceived and named.

Scales sometimes go through a life cycle in which they are presented, generate excitement, then prove disappointing, and are reborn in some picked-over form. But they are not reconceptualized, or even renamed, and people seldom appear to look at the "surviving items" to see what they are measuring, compared with the items that went onto the bone pile. (You cannot get around this need to reconceptualize with another old trick, showing a high correlation between the shortened version and the original; they share many items.) *Too often, construct validity takes a back seat to "p < .05." We should be trying to* explain *things, not just find statistically significant relationships.* If a measure has weak, seriously compromised construct validity, you are essentially wasting your time from a scientific point of view when you use it.

However, with the exception of the "Condensed Cream of RWA" studies, I have included every investigation I know of that reported tests of the RWA Scale's ability to predict what seemed to me authoritarian submissive, authoritarian aggressive, or conventional behaviors. I have not, by a long shot, reported *all* of the results from all of these studies, which are sometimes quite numerous. But I have left out no study or finding because I thought it disconfirmed the validity of the test. If you know of such, please tell me.

25. Lewis Goldberg (whose name appears in the Acknowledgments) has had considerable sport with the statistical "expertise" I displayed while making this analysis in *Enemies of Freedom.* You see, I simultaneously partialled out the mutual cor-

relations that RWA and (say) Attitudes toward Homosexuals had with my measures of fear and self-righteousness. Then I compared the *square* of the remaining correlation with the *square* of the original RWA-ATH correlation, and (usually) found there was little left to "account for." I had never seen this procedure done before, but it seemed legitimate to me, since I had learned in statistics class that the square of a Pearson product-moment r is a proper measure of the size of an effect. (I admit that I spent a lot of time in statistics classes thinking about women. But this was also in the text.)

Goldberg holds that plain old r better interprets the "variation accounted for" than r-squared. John Loehlin wrote in agreement that r, not r-squared, is the proportion of variance that two variables share, despite what we were all taught in statistics. So if two variables correlate .50, they share half of their variance, not a quarter. If you are trying to *predict* the variance of one variable from another, then that is r-squared. If you are trying to *explain* variance shared (which I certainly was in my analysis of authoritarian aggression), then that is r. I have since learned from Ozer (1985) that this point was made earlier by Jensen (1980). The upshot is that my partialling out the "explanatory variables" of fear and self-righteousness did not explain *most* of the RWA-aggression variance, as I claimed—just a lot of it. So I have made a less striking imitation of a puffer fish in this book and given a more subdued statement of the finding.

26. An ironic twist to the fame of "Adorno et al."—one of the most frequent citations in the 1950s and 1960s—was that Theodore Adorno was the least involved member of the Berkeley research team. As Brewster Smith (1988) observed, Adorno only joined the project late in the proceedings, at the insistence of the funders. He was not even at Berkeley, traveling from Los Angeles on weekends to meet with the other researchers. The founder and center of the Berkeley team was Nevitt Sanford, who graciously proposed alphabetical listing of the authors to resolve conflict within the team over second and third authorships. Where's the irony? Adorno's original name was Wiesengrund-Adorno, until he shortened it in 1943 (Stone, Lederer, and Christie, 1993, p. 13).

27. Two elements of the Berkeley model that researchers often cite these days are Intolerance of Ambiguity and Rigidity. However, while both were "observed" in the pivotal Berkeley study of ethnocentric people (i.e., the study thoroughly criticized by Hyman and Sheatsley, 1954), neither one is an element or cluster in the definition of the authoritarian personality that underlay the F Scale.

28. If you want a highly critical review of my research program, you should read Ray's review of *Enemies of Freedom* in *Canadian Psychologist* (see Ray 1990). You might also consider my response, which follows his piece in the same journal.

29. The RWA Scale *correlates* with many things, but that does not mean the other things are what the RWA Scale "really measures," nor that they are *integral* to the construct. From the start, for example, ethnocentrism connected to RWA scores but never strongly enough that I could reconceptualize the construct as the covariance of *four* attitude clusters (*RWA*, chapter 3). Similarly, I have experimented with, and discarded, over two hundred items as candidates for the test since 1973. They almost always correlated significantly and "well" (in the .30s)

with the rest of the scale. But statements have to interlock with the others much more than that to earn a spot. (Corrected item-whole correlations on the RWA Scale now average about .50.)

2. Studying Authoritarianism

1. Perhaps I should explain a little about the thinking behind psychological testing, for readers who have not taken a thrilling course on the subject. The first item on the 1996 RWA Scale (number 5 in Exhibit 1.1) states, "Our country desperately needs a mighty leader who will do what has to be done to destroy the radical new ways and sinfulness that are ruining us." What I *want* from reactions to this statement is an indication of the extent to which a respondent believes in authoritarian submission ("Our country desperately needs a mighty leader"), believes in authoritarian aggression ("who will do what has to be done to destroy"), and believes in conventionalism ("the radical new ways and sinfulness that are ruining us"). I may *get* what I want from some subjects. But I am also likely to get a whole lot else, for the following ten reasons.

Right off the bat, we have to realize that words inevitably mean different things, evoke different meanings, to different people. One person might give a +3 to item 5, and be thinking of a "mighty leader" like Hitler. Another might give the same response but be thinking of Mahatma Gandhi. As far as that item goes, both respondents would look equally authoritarian. "No. 5 is alive!"—with potential ambiguity. So are all the other items.

The same person could easily give a somewhat different answer tomorrow. Anger over being deprived of a seat on the bus that morning, or a space in the parking lot, may trigger more agreement with "do whatever has to be done to destroy" on one day than on another.

Some people tend to be "yea-sayers" and will agree with lots of statements they have not thought about or understood. Their +3 does not necessarily mean they are ripe for Nazi recruiters. They may just have learned to act agreeably when unsure of themselves. (There are also rarer "nattering nabobs of negativism," naysayers, who disagree with almost every thing you say to them.) (Know any?)

Some people will try to guess what the researcher thinks is right. This too can lead to yea-saying, as subjects tend to think the experimenter is voicing his or her own opinions on a survey.

Some people will purposely put down the opposite of what they feel. This is called the "Screw You Effect." In a variation, motivationally challenged and time-pressed subjects may just slop down answers at random.

Two persons may have the same real opinion, when all is said and done, but have different response styles. If one of them is less educated, for example, he or she will tend to be more emphatic (+4 rather than +2.) Conversely, some respondents seldom take extreme positions but instead hover carefully around the neutral point.

People will often give "socially desirable" and "guarded" answers, especially if they fear their answers could cost them something. This is often called "impression management" when consciously done, "self-deception" if unconscious.

People will sometimes answer as members of a group rather than as individuals. If you know you are in a study because you are a Muslim, you might well give the answers you think Muslims *should* give. But if you know you are in a study because you are a lawyer . . .

Some respondents give the exact opposite of their true opinions about an issue because they miss a key word such as "no" or "not" in a statement. (This is why negatives are sometimes repeated in important communications: e.g., "You may not, repeat, NOT, stay out until 2:00 A.M. tonight!")

People sometimes mistakenly blacken a different bubble than they intended, often on the opposite end of the scale (e.g., a -4 instead of a $+4$), just as people sometimes hit the wrong key when tyqing.

You can see that many things can affect the bubbles people blacken on a personality test, besides the trait you are trying to measure. Most of these things produce error, "noise," in the measurements. The more ambiguous the items, the more sensitive they are to swings of mood; the more yea-saying influences the test score, the more people wish they were doing something else, and so on, the more wretched and useless the scores obtained.

I have gotten over 50,000 people to answer the RWA Scale for me over the years. If p is the percentage of them who positively *wanted* to do so, to the point of giving it their full attention and devotion, then probably $p < .001$. Given that, how wretched and useless are RWA scores? They are good only in comparison with various other tests. But a certain amount of effort has gone into reducing the RWA Scale's vulnerability to measurement error. The twenty-year item-testing program has produced relatively unambiguous statements. (Would someone who started off item 5 thinking about Gandhi continue to do so when the statement went on to mention *destroying* "radical new ways and sinfulness?") And while any one item can be misconstrued, or interpreted "peculiarly," it takes an awful lot of systematic misconstruing to get a high score.

As for mood susceptibility, the test-retest reliability of the RWA Scale is about .95 over one week, .85 over twenty-eight weeks, and .75 over four years (*EOF*, pp. 29, 94). The scale is balanced with equal numbers of protrait and contrait items, so yea-saying will tend to cancel itself out, as will naysaying. Whatever the inducement, I still try to get people to *choose* consciously to serve in my experiments, which cuts down on the "Screw You Effect." And so on. Nevertheless, scores on the RWA Scale are hardly error-free.

2. The improvement would be: [the square root of (the new alpha divided by the old alpha)] minus one. So if alpha goes from .88 to .90—which incidentally takes a lot more work than getting an alpha from .78 to .80—the improvement in empirical validity would be about 1%. Which I tried not, repeat, not to think about while busting a gut to get the RWA Scale's alpha from .88 to .90.
3. The 1993 version of the test correlated .86 with the 1973 version and .92 with the 1986 model. The last two correlated .90. Don't be impressed—these scales share many items.
4. I am *not* saying you need only evidence of internal consistency to establish a scale's construct validity. It also has to predict relevant behavior, as we saw in Chapter

1. The empirical findings give you terrific feedback about whether you are measuring what you set out to measure. I *am* saying that if a scale intended to measure a psychological construct or variable has very little internal consistency, you will have a devil of a time correctly interpreting whatever you find with it. There are many reasons why test X *can* correlate with variable Y, when test X goes all over the place.

Cronbach 1970 (p. 142) put it this way, when describing construct validity. "[Some] items would probably correlate with criteria . . . and would probably be judged to have 'content validity' . . . but the test cannot be interpreted as a measure of a coherent psychological quality . . . The interpretation of a test is built up very gradually, and probably is never complete. As knowledge develops, we arrive at a more complete listing of the influences that affect the test score . . . Whereas predictive validity is examined in a single experiment, construct validity is established through a long-continued interplay between observation, reasoning and imagination."

5. In case you do not know, an eigenvalue is the value of an eigen. "Oh." Okay, it is a way of telling how powerful a factor is, how much variance it can account for. But we have to rotate the factors before we can get (we hope) psychologically meaningful factors to care about.

Uh, "rotate"? Yes, there *are* some esoteric concepts involved here. And while others who know a lot more about factor analysis than I do will disagree, my experience has been that you can get markedly different results depending on how you extract the factors, how you decide what number of factors to retain, how you rotate the factors, and (especially) how you interpret what you have left when you are done. (Beware of tables in journal articles that tell you how much an item loaded on only one factor, rather than on all of the factors.)

6. People sometimes ask me why factor analyses of the RWA Scale should not produce three highly correlated factors: one for authoritarian submission, one for authoritarian aggression, and one for conventionalism. The answer is that the three components are thoroughly intertwined among the items on the test. All of the items tap at least two, and some (such as number 5) tap all three. It would therefore be nigh impossible to find, say, an authoritarian submission factor in such a tangle. (But the "tangle" is consistent with the definition of right-wing authoritarianism as the *covariation* of the three.)

7. By my experience, you cannot perform a common factor analysis in SPSSx, its assurance notwithstanding, if you call for a principal factor ("PAF") extraction in FACTOR. The program still puts 1.0s in the diagonal of the correlation matrix before extracting factors. Supplying the squared multiple correlations yourself through a DIAGONAL statement will not change things. You will still get a principal-components analysis at the beginning, and a lot of factors that probably mean little or nothing.

8. An interesting difference of opinion developed in the factor analysis literature over whether principal components and common factor analyses will give you substantially different results. Velicer (1977; Velicer, Peacock, and Jackson, 1982; Fava and Velicer, 1992) has argued through both empirical data and Monte Carlo

simulations that it really makes no difference. Comrey (1978; Lee and Comrey, 1979) has illustrated instead that principal-components analysis, *the way it is usually done* (following the "Kaiser rule" of retaining all factors with eigenvalues greater than 1.0), retains too many factors, elevates the factor loadings on major variables, and gives rotated solutions that are easily misinterpreted.

My experience would support Comrey. I performed a principal components analysis on the 1993 RWA Scale data obtained from the 762 students mentioned at the beginning of the chapter. SPSSx cranked out six components with eigenvalues greater than 1.0. The first two proved substantial (eigens of 7.55 and 3.00, respectively), while the rest were more piddling (1.48 to 1.05). Some researchers, using various subjective rules, would lop off the last four components, giving the same result as a common factor analysis. But as Goldberg and Digman (1994) illustrate, you can get almost anything you want with such subjective rules. Fortunately, more objective criteria are now emerging.

I gather it is widely agreed today that automatically retaining all the components with eigenvalues over 1.0 will "overextract" a matrix (Velicer and Jackson, 1990; Goldberg and Digman, 1994). You will ordinarily get a "component" for every three or four items on a scale, regardless of the actual number of components underlying the data. Yet, almost every factor analysis of the RWA Scale I have seen performed by someone else used a principal-components extraction and followed the Kaiser rule (even though a principal-components analysis was the wrong way to test hypotheses about the factor structure of the scale to start with).

9. My feedback sessions, held in regular classes at the end of the school year, begin with the explanation that I have been doing research on "my topic" for many years. Thousands of people, I continue, have been told afterward what I was studying. But they promised me they would not tell anyone. "And because they kept their word, you very likely did not know what I was investigating when you filled out my surveys. That means that your data 'count.' I can trust the results. So not only did you get credit, but our science, our knowledge advanced because of you. It is important that this tradition continue. So is there anyone here who cannot promise me, [pause] they won't reveal to anyone what I am about to reveal?" (There never has been a public decliner.)

10. I used to give respondents a fifth possibility: "None of the above. This survey is a mixture of statements about many unrelated things." But this always got the fewest votes; subjects believed I was investigating *something*. So I dropped this option.

11. Surprisingly, knowledge of the RWA Scale's purpose may not lower respondents' scores much. In January 1987, I had 97 students read a draft of the first chapter of *Enemies of Freedom*. This short chapter gives the definition of RWA, and reviews the findings linking high RWA scores to acceptance of government injustices, punitiveness, prejudice, "Hitler's score," and other things. Then the students anonymously answered the 1986 RWA Scale. Their mean score was 137.4, only about 10 points lower than the usual value at that point in the academic year.

12. I have also tracked the mean interitem correlation among the Continuing Twelve over the years (*RWA*, pp. 247–248; *EOF*, pp. 26–29). For about ten years it

dropped like a stone, which might have been caused by diminished reading skills or by items losing their social relevance and psychometric cohesion. Then it climbed back up to about .17 (nowhere near the 1973 value of .25, but higher than the bottoming out value of .13 in 1984). It has stayed around .17 since, which you will recall was also the mean interitem correlation of the *whole* 1973 test in 1993. As our students' reading skills have not noticeably increased since the mid-1980s, these results appear to favor the "psychometric cohesion" explanation.

The "ungluing" and "gluing" thus involved can be illustrated by the fall and rise of one of the Continuing Twelve items, which states, "A 'woman's place' should be wherever she wants to be. The days when women are submissive to their husbands and social conventions belong strictly in the past." This item lost much of its connections with the rest of the test for a while, because almost everyone strongly agreed with it. So I dropped it from the scale (*EOF*, pp. 26–28). But lately, enough disagreement has emerged—an exception to the general trend that students of the nineties are somewhat less authoritarian—that the item has recaptured a place on the RWA Scale.

13. I shall continue my practice of not automatically giving standard deviations after each mean. No one has ever written me to ask for one. I am also not going to report routinely "*t*'s," "*z*'s," and "*d.f.*'s" in this book. (I shall, however, give you the important information: estimates of effect sizes and *p*.) If you want some particular "*s.d.*," "*t*," or "*z*" value, write me.

Incidentally, since most of the hypotheses I test in my research are based on lots of previous findings and fairly obvious theoretical expectations, most of my tests of significance are one-tailed. (I will use two-tailed tests when this is not the case, however, as in Chapter 9 when I go off into the wild blue yonder.) In the vast majority of cases, the findings would be significant by a two-tailed test anyway, as you can see for yourself from the correlation coefficients and sample sizes.

14. I do *not* give students veridical personal feedback, despite this statement at the beginning of some of my surveys. I do, however, explain when I give feedback to these classes why I lied to them, and why it would be wrong and potentially harmful to give them their RWA scores, and other results.

15. To illustrate, the Secret Survey I administered in January 1994 began with a question about gender and then asked whether the person was a virgin. If not, it went on, how many times had the person had intercourse, and with how many different partners? At what age did intercourse begin? Had the person ever "cheated" on a lover, and how often? About how many times per month did the person masturbate? Changing topics, I asked if the subject had doubts about the existence of God. If so, when did these doubts begin? Next came one of two versions of a hypothetical tale of "ancient scrolls" (to be discussed in Chapters 6 and 8). Finally, the person was asked to describe the time in life when he or she had been most afraid (or most angry), and to rate the strength of that emotion then. All this material was asked on (two sides of) an 8½-by-14-inch sheet and answered on a bubble form.

16. Some years, when I want to determine correlations between the students' and parents' attitudes, I discretely code the students' survey numbers onto the answer sheets sent home. But I then destroy the master list, and the parents *do* answer anonymously.

17. Two self-selection biases tend to cancel each other out during this process (*EOF*, p. 21). First, Low RWA students—who are more likely to be estranged from their parents, or at least "fiercely independent" after the tuition has been paid—are usually a little less likely to address envelopes home. But, second, the parents of High RWA students are usually a little less likely to complete the surveys, perhaps because of lower formal education.

18. For example, the October 1993 parent survey began with forty-four RWA Scale items, followed by twenty items measuring religious fundamentalism, twenty-four left-wing authoritarianism items, and a like number of statements assessing dogmatism. The parents were then asked to respond to the twelve Attitudes toward Homosexuals statements and to my twenty-item Ethnocentrism Scale. Four statements about the Holocaust followed, as well as a thirteen-item "Zealots Scale" and an eight-item "Posse-Radicals" survey. Then the parents were asked to decide how different they were from the friend who was least like them. Whereupon I asked six questions about media preferences. Finally, they got to the demographic section and the end. This survey took ten sides of 8½-by-11-inch paper to reproduce. It must have taken one to two hours to complete. And yet the parents were extremely cooperative. What was the biggest data loss? Twelve of the 654 respondents did not answer the left-wing authoritarianism items.

19. One would expect social desirability to be correlated with RWA scores, insofar as one of the defining elements of right-wing authoritarianism is conventionalism. You can raise RWA scores by telling subjects to make socially desirable images. In a 1974 experiment (*RWA*, pp. 243–244), students asked to "fake good"—to make as socially acceptable a picture of themselves as possible—produced significantly higher scores on the RWA Scale than did students answering normally. Others asked to "fake bad" produced significantly lower totals. But these extreme instructions raised or lowered scores only about 10%, the same effect obtained by telling students about right-wing authoritarianism before they answer the test. These instructions probably had little effect because people tend to believe their opinions *are* the right ones.

20. The Berkeley researchers themselves tried to develop contrait items but found it too difficult. Test makers will probably agree it is easier to write protrait than contrait items. Usually you have a better idea of what you are trying to measure than its opposite quality. This leads to contraits that are simply negations of protrait sentiments (i.e., items that use "no," "not," and "never," which tend to have low reliabilities because subjects often fly right over the all-important negative). In addition, constructs sometimes have several conceivable "opposites." What is the conceptual opposite of right-wing authoritarianism? Left-wing authoritarianism? Democracy? Anarchy? In a way, each is.

21. Why was it so bollixed up? Well, how could you tell who was "authoritarian" when the only measure of the trait then was the F Scale? What was wrong with

it? Among other things, it might be seriously contaminated by yea-saying. But maybe that is part of being authoritarian. Let's get some authoritarians and see. How can we identify them? (We are back where we started.) This dog-chases-tail muddle was straightened out when the adequately balanced F Scale made it clear the original *was* affected by response sets. That research led to a new conceptualization and measure of right-wing authoritarianism. Studies with that scale, as we are about to see, established that authoritarians *are* somewhat more likely to yea-say on tests than others are. It only took twenty-five years to straighten out the vicious circle.

22. About 1% of the parents and others who can candidly tell me what they think of my "survey of public opinion" (the RWA Scale) tell me that it really stinks. They write such things as "This is an outrageous statement" and "What a loaded question!" on the booklet. Sometimes these people cannot even finish the scale, they are so outraged at the extremity of the wording. The scientific value of the study seems nonexistent, they say. Some of these respondents appear to think the items represent *my* beliefs, and since they are often extreme, I must be an extremist. Still others seem to see the survey as a trap; I am trying to trick them into saying something terrible. So when they come to statements with which they strongly disagree, they throw a rod rather than simply saying " – 4."

In December 1995 I asked 168 parents who had just answered the RWA Scale to say, on a 0–6 basis, "how ambiguous" and "how biased, one-sided" the items had been. The respective means of 2.58 and 3.01 did not set off alarms in my mind. As I suspected, Lows and Highs proved equally likely to find fault with the test.

23. Only part of my nonsense is as sensible as I am trying to make it look. For the truth is, after having spent a summer designing the next batch of studies, typing up the surveys, running them off, compiling the booklets, and so on, I am just too curious to hold back testing until November. I can barely keep from handing out booklets in the Student Union during Freshman Orientation Week! I *do*, however, purposely handicap the RWA Scale to be relatively certain that when I tell other scientists I have discovered something, I really have. In other words, I make the RWA Scale swim with lead weights attached when I throw it into my subject pool. But the person I am most trying to protect from "gossamer findings," and years of fruitless research, is myself.

Unfortunately, I have a good example of a very frustrating "Type II" (believing a falsehood) error in my files that was supposed to become a chapter in this book. In 1989–90 I attempted to reduce High RWAs' prejudice against aboriginal peoples through Rokeach's (1973) "value-confrontation" technique. It was an elaborate, three-stage experiment done over a ten-month period ending in an expensive mail survey after the school year had ended. But at its conclusion I had $p < .05$ evidence that High RWAs who had experienced a value confrontation were amazingly willing to set aside some of the university's scholarship funds just for aboriginal students (compared with equivalent Highs who had not gone through the manipulation). A follow-up phone survey six months later, on the issue of aboriginal "self-rule" in Canada, indicated (again, $p < .05$) that the value-confrontation manipulation had had a long-lasting, general, wonderful effect.

My first reaction to any discovery, especially a surprising, or dramatic one, is to keep quiet and repeat the study—which I did over 1990–91. Again, the manipulation appeared to work on the Experimentals. But the control group of High RWAs, who had received no value confrontation, also liked the idea of exclusively aboriginal scholarships. Believing this was probably an anomaly, I presented the results of the two experiments at the Ontario Symposium on Prejudice in June 1991, though I was appropriately cautious in my conclusions (Zanna and Olson, 1994, pp. 131–148). However my third study, run in 1991–92, could produce only $p < .15$ evidence for the value-manipulation effect. And a fourth experiment conducted in 1992–93 found the value confrontation had virtually no effect on Highs; in fact, the Control Highs were almost significantly more willing to set up the aboriginal scholarships than the Experimental Highs were. Put all four studies together, with all the work and money involved (*my* money!), and you get nothing.

We have to remember that every now and then when p is $< .05$, nothing is actually there. But if a "gossamer finding" materializes the *first* time you study something, it may take you years to discover you are chasing "the stuff that dreams are made of."

3. The Personal Origins of Right-Wing Authoritarianism

1. Falconer (1989, pp. 173–176) outlines the assumptions underlying this formula and explains why actual human heritability is likely to be *lower* than the estimate it gives.
2. I never again found that the Group Cohesiveness Scale correlated better with the Ethnocentrism Scale than the RWA Scale did (although Pratto et al.'s [1994] Social Dominance Scale certainly did). This could have been due to my revisions, of course. But in a follow-up January 1992 study, the twenty-two *original* Group Cohesiveness items correlated .34 with Ethnocentrism, compared with the RWA Scale's .41 with Ethnocentrism.
3. Whenever I ask people through the mail to complete a survey for me, I try to have the survey fit on just one piece of paper. I think that increases the response rate. The page usually is a legal-size sheet, and the back side often has more jammed onto it than the front. The instructions and the RWA Scale take up about 75% of the total space, leaving only a little room for anything else.
4. The 1976 study was mainly devoted to developing new items for the RWA Scale. It involved 548 students then, whose scores on the Continuing Twelve are given in Figure 2.1. The 138 alumni to whom I mailed surveys in 1994 constituted about half of those from 1976 for whom the university had (supposedly) current addresses. I am saving the other half for another study in about 2001, when the children of these alumni should be young adolescents. I would like to thank L. Rankin, executive director of the University of Manitoba Alumni Association, and his supervisor of records, M. Nayar, for their invaluable assistance in conducting this study.
5. On balance, the alumni indicated they had become slightly more religious over the years in both beliefs (mean = 3.18) and practice (3.17), on a 1–5 scale where

3.0 indicates no change. There was a small but significant tendency for those who became more religious to show *less* of a drop in their levels of authoritarianism (r's of $-.19$ and $-.25$, respectively).

6. I always wonder how consistent the archival evidence is. For example, Sales (1973) argued that an increase in the number of astrology books and magazine stories showed people became more superstitious during the 1930s. I am ready to believe this; we probably turn to superstition, and Busby Berkeley type escapism, when things seem beyond our control. But did the number of ghost stories also increase? Were there more articles about dowsers, fortune tellers, vampires, numerology, and "lucky signs"? I also am bothered that researchers can find archival evidence for things that are probably not there. The Berkeley theory (the one from the university, not Busby) *did* state that superstition was an integral part of the authoritarian personality. But the "superstition" items on the F Scale (which included an item specifically about astrology) never correlated highly with the core of the test. I know of no literature demonstrating that people scoring high on the *F Scale* were highly superstitious—unless you want categorically to equate being religious with being superstitious (which I would not). Certain famous right-wing individuals may believe in astrology, but you can "prove" anything with individual cases. We shall see in the next chapter that High RWA students are *not* particularly likely to believe in astrology, perhaps because it is often condemned by religions.

7. Unfortunately I can report a real-world replication of this role-played finding. Canada is presently going through a crisis over Quebec separation, and in the fall of 1995 the separatist government in Quebec held a referendum seeking a mandate to take the province out of confederation. Many thought the future of the country was at stake, and the referendum failed to pass by the slimmest of margins. I had developed a balanced Attitudes toward Quebec Scale some time back. It basically measures hostility towards Francophone Quebecois, with an alpha of .90 (see Chapter 5). In the routine of things, I had collected responses to fourteen items from this scale from 468 Manitoba parents in the autumn of 1994. I got 373 other Manitoba parents to answer it a few weeks after the 1995 referendum. Overall, hostility had gone up significantly if not greatly, from 76.6 to 79.2. Who had changed?—not the High RWAs, whose means equaled 84.4 and 84.0 in the two samples. The increase had come from the Lows, whose mean jumped from 63.9 in 1994 to 69.4 after the referendum ($p < .05$). They were still less hostile than the Highs were; but they had become more like the Highs.

4. The Cognitive Behavior of Authoritarians

1. In September 1995 I gave my introductory psychology students two optional extra credit assignments: to critique the account of Noah and the flood in the Bible, and to criticize Darwin's theory of evolution. Contrary to my expectation, Highs proved as willing as Lows to find fault with the story of Noah (and the theory of evolution, too, of course). Moreover, they made as many valid criticisms of the biblical account as Lows did—at least in my judgment. These results indicate that authoritarians *can* criticize their religious beliefs, if motivated. But the data from

the "Sufficient Evidence" studies show they usually do not. (Highs' criticisms of evolution were less impressive. They apparently have often been told that Darwin claimed we descended from chimpanzees or monkeys, and asked, "so where is the Missing Link?")

2. The two positions do not *logically* exclude each other. You could try to stop producing criminals while cracking down on the ones you already have. But with limited resources, the two approaches compete for scarce dollars, and people tend to emphasize one over the other.

3. Thanks to the pioneering research of Tajfel and his associates (1978; Tajfel et al., 1971; Tajfel and Turner, 1979), we know that collections of people rather automatically divide the world into in-groups and out-groups. Called the Minimal Group Effect, this tendency has been widely observed in natural groups and even in artificial groups whose members know they have been composed on a purely random basis (Billig and Tajfel, 1973).

   If the Minimal Group Effect is the mainspring of ethnocentrism, this spring should be wound a little tighter in right-wing authoritarians than in others. In September 1990, I asked the students who had just answered an abstract reasoning test to predict which of my two sections of introductory psychology would score higher. In both classes, most students (sensibly) checked the alternative "There will be no difference between the two sections." The students who *did* think a difference would appear almost always said their class would prove smarter. High RWAs were twice as likely (30 out of 113) to show this net in-group preference as were Lows (15 out of 114) ($p < .02$).

   I repeated this experiment the following fall, when my two classes had answered the inferences test used by Wegmann (1992). This time Highs proved three times as likely to show the Minimal Group Effect (31 of 93 versus 10 of 91; $p < .01$). However, when I tried "which class has better looking students" and "which class is more moral" on other occasions, I found *non*significant High RWA leanings toward the Minimal Group Effect. So I do not know yet why the relationship sometimes appears and sometimes does not.

5. Inconsistency and Blindness in the Authoritarian Mind

1. I have also tried three times to find a double standard about affirmative-action programs and not yet gotten a consistent result. Overall, both High and Low RWA university students strongly favor "hiring the best person" and have little sympathy for affirmative-action hiring.

2. I am *not* saying the Soviet Union represented the "good guys" in the Cold War and the United States, the "bad guys." I am *not* saying the United States acted as badly, overall, as the Soviet Union did. I am *not* saying one can never decide, objectively, that one side proved more noble, or reprehensible, than the other. Events have revealed clearly how much the peoples in Communist countries ultimately supported their old dictatorial governments. But I would say that both governments lied, to the world and to their own peoples. Both governments made disarmament proposals for public-relations reasons on the world stage, that they knew the other side would never accept. Both governments gave foreign aid, not

for humanitarian reasons, but to advance their own interests. Both invaded other nations to control their international allegiance. Both became active in the internal affairs of other countries, trying to influence elections and supporting uprisings. And so on.

3. In *Enemies of Freedom* (pp. 196–197) I mentioned in a note an unpublished experiment Professor Gerry Sande and I had conducted on intergroup conflict. We discretely created All-Low, and All-High RWA teams of male students to serve in an "international simulation" involving NATO and Warsaw Pact teams. The two teams, placed in adjacent rooms, thought they were playing each other, and each team thought it was NATO. In reality, each team was independently playing against the Experimenter, who made the moves for the Warsaw Pact. The simulation began with some ambiguous military moves by the "Warsaw Pact." The NATO team could make peaceful overtures, do nothing in response, or make threatening military and/or nonmilitary moves of various magnitudes. The "Warsaw Pact" responded with a "see you and raise you just as much" strategy. If a team of students responded to the ambiguous initial moves with 25 points of "threat points," the "Warsaw Pact" retaliated with 50 threat points, and it was NATO's turn again. So teams reaped what they sowed, and some sowed the whirlwind.

In our first run of this experiment, in November 1987, the five Low RWA teams made a total of 14 threat points, on the average, over the course of an hour. Basically, they responded calmly to the ambiguous initial moves of the Warsaw Pact, and things stayed calm. The five High RWA teams, by contrast, tended to "act tough" in response to the ambiguous moves, which produced even larger countermoves by the Warsaw Pact. So they escalated further. By the end of the game, they had averaged a total of 141.7 threat points—ten times as many as the Lows ($p < .05$). Most of the High teams had created an "international crisis" by threatening themselves in the mirror.

We then tried to lower High RWAs' aggressiveness by giving them a "perfect Star Wars" defense against nuclear attack that the Warsaw Pact did not have. It took several runs (and years) to find a way to explain this defense to students, so they could see the implication: the NATO team had nothing to fear. For purposes of comparison, we also developed a condition in which the *Warsaw Pact* had the perfect nuclear defense, and NATO had everything to fear. Continuing with this unpublished series of experiments, in the fall of 1989 we ran six groups of Lows and six groups of Highs through each of these two conditions. (That is, we ran twelve sessions, with a Low and a High team in each one, supposedly playing each other.) Again, all teams thought they were NATO, and the Experimenters played the Warsaw Pact according to the same "see you and raise as much" rule used before. The simulation began with the same ambiguous moves.

When Low RWA teams thought they were unbeatable, they averaged a total of only 2.5 threat points. But when High RWA teams thought they were unbeatable, they showed two different patterns. Three of the six teams became *nonbel*ligerent. Their totals were 5, 15, and 25 threat points. But the other three High RWA teams who knew they were unbeatable acted aggressively; their totals were

100, 335, and 375 threat points. Overall the Highs ended up with virtually the same mean as in the first experiment: 142.5—over fifty times that of the Lows!

I expected High RWA teams with a foolproof defense to become less belligerent, because their fear should have evaporated. And it apparently did, sometimes. But I did not anticipate that some of the High teams, once they felt perfectly safe, would become perfect bullies. One of their members explained it this way afterward: "We wanted them to realize we could wipe them out at any time." A member of another very threatening High team put it more graphically: "We had all the power, and we wanted them to kiss our asses." So why do some Highs act as aggressively as they do? Among many reasons, High RWAs may fear others would treat *them* the way they would treat others unfortunate enough to be under their power. In their "Ungolden Rule," they don't want others to do unto them what they would do unto others, if they could.

The data in the "Warsaw Pact with Star Wars" condition also surprised me. Some *Low* RWA teams became very threatening—which is fairly idiotic when you know you can be crushed. Overall these Low teams averaged 112.5 threat points. High RWA teams were even bigger idiots, averaging 211, their highest score of all. Can you guess why teams with everything to lose became threatening from the start? Their most common explanation afterward was that they wanted the Warsaw Pact team to realize they would not be intimidated. (They did not realize that a stronger opponent with benign intentions would thereby be driven to defend against *them*.)

4. One of these facilitators got his corn pone in the Altemeyer household, along with many tellings of Dr. Seuss's "The Lorax." This family connection enabled me to rent the Global Change Game at a bargain rate.

5. I recruited the Low and High RWA teams from five large introductory psychology classes, whose members had answered a batch of surveys for me a few weeks earlier under the secret-number condition. Sign-up booklets for a three-hour experiment in which "players would be assigned at random to different regions of the earth and challenged to solve the problems of the future" were circulated in these classes. However, a student could participate only if his or her secret number was listed on the front of the booklet. The secret numbers had supposedly been drawn at random, with separate drawings for the game on two consecutive nights. Students signed up by putting down their secret number, sex, and faculty, which were checked to make sure no "uninviteds" got in. (None did.)

6. I asked the Lows, who of course were not debriefed about why they had been recruited for the experiment, not to discuss the Global Change Game with anyone they might know who was going to participate the following evening.

7. For *my* money, the most interesting person on Low RWA night was the Pacific Rim Elite, who showed leadership in developing global cooperation. The most interesting player on the second night was the Middle East Elite. I would bet that if the random assignment had put him in a superpower, rather than in the Middle East, he would have controlled the whole world by the end of the game. He seemed to know just what "buttons" to push on the other Highs. (By the end of the game, though, the other Elites seemed to be "on to" him, and his impoverished region

felt betrayed—but submissive.) The warlike CIS was also interesting. By the luck of the draw, it consisted of four males and one female. The men were all in favor of waging war, and completely ignored the woman. She sat apart the whole night, literally exiled in Siberia.

8. Namely, *Hamlet,* act 1, scene 3, line 78. Polonius is speaking.

9. These students had scored low on the RWA Scale the previous September. On another point, sample sizes will bounce around in follow-up studies such as these, depending on who came to class the day the experiment was run.

10. Do these experiments demonstrate that right-wing authoritarians are "anti-intraceptive," as the Berkeley researchers proposed? That is, are they opposed to the subjective and tender-minded, and against concern with what people think and feel? They are only if you look at just half the data. Highs were quite interested in learning about the self-esteem measure when they thought they had scored high on it, and they usually wanted to be told if they were *un*prejudiced.

6. Authoritarianism and Religion

1. Would non-Christian Low RWAs similarly "run away" from an archaeological discovery that strongly supported the *existence* of a divine Jesus of Nazareth? In October 1986 I asked 430 students to react to both the hypothetical Attis discovery and another hypothetical unearthing: the Roman "file" on Jesus (*EOF,* pp. 235–237). I said these scrolls contained the reports of spies who verified the miracles. Most important, the file supported completely the account of the Resurrection given in the New Testament. As before, most strongly believing Christian Highs (54%) said the discovery of the Attis legend would have no effect whatsoever on their beliefs. What about the strongly *dis*believing Lows? First of all, they are rare; only 21 of 107 Lows strongly doubted Jesus' divinity. Of these 21, only 7 (33%) said they would be *un*affected by the discovery of the Roman file ($p < .001$). Thus Low nonbelievers proved significantly *more* likely to be influenced by scientific evidence contradicting their beliefs than High believers were. Most of these disbelieving Lows said they would have to change, whereas most of the believing Highs said they would not change at all.

2. It is no accident, accordingly, that many violent white-supremacist groups in the United States tend to consider themselves the "true Christians." From the burning crosses of the Ku Klux Klan to the Church of Jesus Christ Christian (Aryan Nations), extremists present themselves as the true disciples of someone who preached against prejudice and advocated loving thy neighbor. The most prominent white-supremacist groups in South Africa portrayed themselves similarly.

3. I realize that the classification problems go back to the original studies. Some authors would call weekly attendance "moderate," and others "high." The reviewer is stuck with their published categories. But the problem still remains. Another thing bothers me about these ranges: they are highly unequal. Usually when you break up a continuum of responses into a few categories, you follow meaningful breaks in the criterion or else try to get the sample evenly distributed in the categories. Here the breaks for attendance were: Lows 0–3 times per year; Moderates 3–52 times; and Highs 52–365 times. Were these ranges picked to

spread out the sample evenly? In my studies, a majority of affiliates would be Moderates, depending on where the "weeklies" were placed. If weekly attenders are Moderates, there would be very few Highs.

4. Even the linear relationship has its problems in these twelve studies, only six of which showed more active church members to be significantly less prejudiced than less active church members.

5. The initial work was done by a Harvard student, W. Cody Wilson (1960), who composed a fifteen-item Extrinsic Religious Values Scale with Allport's help and gave it out to various groups during the late 1950s. Curiously, Allport and Ross (1967) criticized this instrument for being unidirectionally worded, but judging from Wilson's examples, it was not.

Feagin (1964) took up the challenge next, administering twelve Extrinsic and nine Intrinsic items that Allport's seminar had "revised" to members of five churches in the spring of 1963. Feagin (p. 3) says Allport's concept of the intrinsically oriented person (at that point) was someone who was "truly devout," who "lives for his religion; his creed is a part of the pattern of his personality. He will have a tendency to be more mystical and devout."

Allport and Ross (1967) used the same scale Feagin used, except they dropped one Extrinsic statement. So the Intrinsic Scale was based on Allport's *earlier* conceptualization, not the rather different one he presented in Allport 1966, in which he never once used the word "devout" (much less "mystical") to describe the intrinsic orientation.

Allport's conceptualization of "intrinsic" roamed even farther than this. Hunt and King (1971) cited eleven different ways he distinguished the intrinsic orientation from the extrinsic. This strikes me as singularly unusual, for Allport was justly known for the care he took in defining concepts such as "personality" and "prejudice."

6. Allport and Ross (1967, p. 435) probably thought that having about half the items in their scale worded in the intrinsic direction, and the rest worded in the extrinsic direction, would control for yea-saying. But that assumes and requires that intrinsic and extrinsic be on opposite ends of one dimension, and Feagin (1964) had already shown that the two scales seemingly measured two *different* dimensions. The result was a unidirectionally worded Intrinsic Scale, subject to response sets. And ditto, for the Extrinsic Scale.

7. In the interest of clarity, I am overriding the self-reversing scoring key Allport and Ross used. They scored the Extrinsic items such that "Definite Agreement" was a "5." They scored the Intrinsic items such that "Definite *Disagreement*" was a "5." Therefore, they were expecting a high *positive* correlation between the two scales, and obtained only a + .21. But their scoring confuses people who expect the scales to be negatively correlated. So I have flip-flopped the flip-flop.

8. I am sure some researchers will protest this seemingly flippant disregard of a literature. I would simply say that literatures enormously bigger than that of the Intrinsic and Extrinsic Orientation Scales (e.g., the Fascism Scale's, the Dogmatism Scale's) have in the long run amounted to surprisingly little (Altemeyer, 1981, chap. 1; see also Chapter 8 in this book). So the size of a literature proves nothing

about its ultimate worth. To demonstrate that these orientation scales have notable value, someone must show that they measure the construct for which they were named and for which measurement is claimed; show that the scores obtained with the scales are not seriously contaminated by response sets; and show that the studies using these scales, when you look at all of them, speak with essentially one voice. I think the literature on the Intrinsic and Extrinsic Scales fails all these tests of construct validity.

9. Allport may have assumed that people for whom Christianity is very important would "get" this intrinsic message. But it ain't necessarily so. For one thing, some people, who go to a lot of sporting events, believe the intrinsic message in the New Testament is John 3:16. You also hear about being "born again" now and then. One group of American white supremacists, featured in the Canadian documentary film "Blood in the Face," think the most significant passage in the Bible is Genesis 9, where God makes a covenant with Noah and his sons, giving them dominion over the earth. In particular, they cite Genesis 9:5, "And surely your blood of your lives will I require." This neo-Nazi group interprets this brief passage to mean God gave the earth only to white folks. "How do they figure that?" you may well ask. Well, they believe only white people can blush, showing their blood.

10. Allport (1966, p. 455) also expected "fundamentalists" would prove more prejudiced. He thought they were a version of his extrinsic orientation. "While most extrinsics are casual and peripheral churchgoers, a few are ideological extremists. With equal fervor they embrace some political nostrum along with the tenets of some religious (usually fundamentalist) sect. In such cases religious extremism is found to be ancillary to a prejudiced philosophy of life. I am thinking here of the right-wing groups whose ardent desire is to escape from the complexities of modern life."

11. The Fundamentalism-Ethnocentrism correlation has been tested in six subsequent Manitoba studies and always proved statistically significant. The mean of the correlations equals .28.

12. Our study was strongly criticized by Gorsuch (1993). Our reply immediately follows his observations.

13. I have left out half of the discoveries reported in Altemeyer and Hunsberger 1992. We made a determined effort to increase the size of Batson's Quest Scale and balance it against response sets, eventually producing eight protrait and eight contrait items that had a mean interitem correlation of .31 and an alpha of .88. Both Professor Batson and Professor S. McFarland have said they think our "new, improved" Quest Scale has too much "fundamentalism" in it, despite the fact that all but two of these sixteen items correlated better with the sum of the other fifteen Quest statements than they did with the Religious Fundamentalism Scale. (This was all done before Batson's twelve-item, partially balanced revision of the Quest Scale appeared in the fall of 1991.) In case you care, our "Fundy-tainted Quest Scale" correlated $-.67$ with RWA, $-.79$ with Religious Fundamentalism, $-.26$ with Ethnocentrism, $-.39$ with ATH, $-.34$ with Posse, and $-.27$ with Trials. It makes sense to me that Fundamentalism and Quest would correlate very highly

and negatively. One is saying, "I already know the religious meaning of life," and the other is saying, "I am searching for some religious answers." But we have no wish to corrupt someone else's scale (we have our own to corrupt), and so have not proceeded with the matter. Hence I have not discussed our Quest findings here.

14. I am always honored to do research with Professor Hunsberger, a winner of the William James Prize for research in the psychology of religion awarded by the American Psychological Association. He fully qualifies as a coauthor of this chapter. (He is not interested in publication credits, however, and has graciously let me become the target of the fundamentalists' reaction to our findings.)

7. Sex and the Single Authoritarian

1. By way of comparison Michael et al.'s (1994) justly lauded, *much* more representative sample of 3,432 American English-speaking adults comprised 79% of the 4,369 they set out to study. (However, they gathered the data in face-to-face interviews, which one suspects produces less truthful answering than anonymous secret surveys.)

2. The sample sizes bounce around a little in these analyses. The data shown in Figure 7.1 excluded married students and those who would be virgins except for having been raped. This analysis of willingness for first intercourse includes those. So, for example, the female *non*virgin sample totals 149, not just the 135 used for the 1987 computation for Figure 7.1. Similar (small) shifts of denominators will occur in other calculations. In addition, students who answered one question occasionally did not answer another.

3. Let me hasten to add that this does not mean the guys in my class had copulated 30 times on the average, and the women 50 times. We are excluding the virgins. If you include them, then the median number of acts of intercourse for all the males in the sample equaled 2, and for all the females, 1—quite a different picture from 30 and 50.

4. Since the women are having intercourse with men, where are these men? One explanation would be that a few guys are having a tremendous amount of sex. But that is not so. Instead, the partners are not in this sample. They are probably older than my female students and not likely to be taking introductory psychology.

5. Every now and then, someone answers with "Oh, just one person at a time."

6. The January 1996 data were gathered too late to be included in the figures for this book. Here are the results if you want to sketch them in. Figure 7.1: 35% of the females were virgins, and 37% of the males. Figure 7.2: 43% of High RWA females were virgins, and 51% of the High RWA males. Figure 7.3: 28% of the Low females and 22% of the Low males were virgins. Figure 7.4: 75 times for the females, and 45 times for the males (same as 1995). Both male and female nonvirgins had 2.0 partners (median). Apart from the figures, the age of first intercourse rose for the first time in years, to 15.9 and 16.5 years, for the women and men, respectively. Are young people becoming more hesitant about sex?

7. The numbers who mentioned these dislikes can be misleading. For example, the fact that only 8 women complained about anal intercourse does not mean everyone else had no problem with it. We do not know how many women had undergone the experience.

8. I am sure these women would welcome a world in which women could be as forthright about their sexual desires as men are permitted to be. But that is not our world, yet. Remember Martina Navratilova's comment that society would label her a "slut" if she had had as many sexual partners as people found "understandable" and even magnificent in Magic Johnson's case.

9. All of my sex surveys have involved introductory psychology students. I wondered how their situation might change over time, so in February 1996 I sent another secret survey and a self-addressed stamped envelope to 471 of my students from 1993–94—all for whom the university had a mailing address.

I do not know how many of my former students I reached, but by March 21 I had received 216 replies. This sample included a greater percentage of females than the larger study had two years earlier, 65% instead of 58%. But otherwise it seemed representative. For example, 31% of the women and 36% of the men said they had been virgins at the time of the first study, almost exactly the percentages obtained in January 1994 (see Figure 7.1). A solid majority of the 216 respondents (76%) said they were presently full-time university students. Another 12% attended school part-time, 1% had graduated; 12% were taking a breather from higher education.

The first thing I wondered was, how many of the 216 respondents who said they had been virgins in January 1994 ($N = 68$) were virgins now? The answer, which surprised me, was 45, or 66%. I asked the 23 students who had ceased to be virgins why it had happened. More than anything else (13 out of 23, 10 of them women), they said they had met "the right person" and fallen in love. (This fits with the January 1996 secret survey, which found that the biggest reason for virginity was that the student had not yet found the right person and fallen seriously in love.) Of the 23 former virgins, most (15) had only had sex with one person.

Most of the 45 *continuing* virgins fell into two camps. Some ($N = 17$) said they were still looking for the right person. Nearly all of these had engaged in oral-genital sex as a substitute for intercourse. But a determined group of 19 virgins had shunned intercourse for religious reasons. While some of them said they had engaged in oral-genital sex (up to a hundred times), by and large they had only "held hands," "kissed," or petted. One of them had not even held hands or danced with anyone; she wrote, "I give 'virgin' a whole new meaning."

As mentioned above, the men were more likely to be virgins than the women two years earlier. But now 21% of the males were virgins, and 22% of the females. But the fellows were still far behind in number of acts of intercourse; their median equaled 95, while that for the sexually active women was 170. (The figures two years earlier had been 45 and 95, respectively; so over the two intervening years the men had averaged about 50 more acts of intercourse, and the women 75. The latter were probably still more likely to be involved in long-term relationships, where most intercourse occurs.)

I found it interesting that the median number of sexual partners for the non-virgins remained low, at 3.0. The median in 1994 had been 1.7. So these respondents had hardly been engaging in a lot of casual sex while at university.

I also asked how many times, if ever, the respondent had cheated on a lover. In 1994, 29% of the women said they had done so at least once. By 1996 the figure had climbed to 35%. Among the men, the 33% of two years ago had increased to 41%. For both genders, the vast majority of "cheaters" had done so once or twice.

I again inquired if they had ever tried to make someone have sexual contact with them by threatening or using physical force. Everyone said "never."

I asked what impact the feedback lecture about the secret survey had had upon their attitudes or behavior. Most said "none," beyond being surprised at various results. The most common answer came from the virgins, who said they had been relieved to learn they were not the only ones left. Only one person said the lecture had changed his behavior: "It forced me to realize a distinctive cheating pattern . . . Since then I have not cheated and have discovered that sexual intercourse should not be taken lightly."

This last comment was echoed over a hundred times when I asked my former students what advice they would give my present ones about sex. The overwhelming answer was, "Use protection." (I passed the message along as "advice you might be giving someone in two years if the same sort of things happen to you that happened to your predecessors.")

8. Dogmatism

1. On February 27, 1985, Rokeach wrote me to ask if I had developed a balanced version of the Dogmatism Scale. I had not. No one to my knowledge ever has, perhaps because Rokeach (1967) himself discouraged it. Haiman (1964) wrote five contrait versions of D Scale items for a balanced thirty-item test to measure open-mindedness. And Druckman (1967) developed a balanced forty-eight-item "Dogmatism Scale," but only sixteen of the statements came from Rokeach's test. Predictably, it had a very low split-half reliability.
2. Or else, respondents *dis*agreed with both the original and its reversal. By and large, people disagree with most of the F and D Scale sentiments.
3. The usual alibi at this point, when you have a mess of barely intercorrelating items in your "scale," is to say that the thing you are trying to measure is "multifaceted." Thus the test inventor attributes his poor results to Mother Nature, rather than to his own theory or ability. But be assured, Mother Nature has the last say in the matter.
4. The only reason the Dogmatism Scale achieves reliabilities around .80, even with response sets producing some artificial internal consistency, is because it has so many items. You can produce "acceptable reliability" among a set of barely connecting statements that measure gobs of different things if you simply assemble enough of them. Wilson and Patterson (1968) had fifty "catchphrases" in their Conservatism Scale (*RWA*, pp. 91–104).

5. Are warning bells going off inside your head over this maneuver? Such overlapping ranges and cross-categorizations can easily create anomalies. Some "leftists" in (say) the dogmatic camp could easily have had more conservative PEC scores than some "moderates" in the nondogmatic camp. Many subjects might have been called one thing when, if they had been "dogmatic" rather than "nondogmatic," they would have been called something else. I interpret the "semi-interquartile range" Barker specified to be the half of the distribution between the first and fourth quartiles (i.e., the same range I usually call "Moderates"). If instead he meant the 25% of the distribution centered on the mean (the fourth and fifth "octupiles," if you please), the problem would occur less frequently but still remain.

6. DiRenzo used a brief version of the Dogmatism Scale prepared by Schulze (1962) at Michigan State University, who acknowledged the help he received from Rokeach. For reasons that elude me, Schulze performed a Guttman scalogram analysis of the forty D Scale items, and predictably had trouble coming up with a subset that met Guttman's .90 target Coefficient of Reproducibility. The ten items he selected had a coefficient of only .83, which raised questions about unidimensionality. But Schulze noted such questions existed about the forty item scale anyway, so his was not any worse ("equally bad is good").

The ten-item version correlated only .76 and .73 in two samples with the forty-item version (which had the same ten items in it, providing a perfect match with one quarter of the criterion). Such a low overall figure strongly implies that the ten items chosen did not adequately represent whatever the forty items measure. Indeed, the correlation of the Chosen Ten with the Rejected Thirty was given for the second sample and equaled only .46, a terribly low figure. Brevity represented this miniscale's only virtue, then. If you are going to *not* measure what you set out to measure, you might as well do it quickly.

7. Smithers and Lobley's (1978) study comes closest of these to supporting Rokeach's central premise of a curvilinear relationship between left-right social attitudes and D Scale scores. The subjects were 539 Bradford University (England) students. But, as Stone (1980) pointed out, no test of the significance of the curvilinear relationship was presented.

Smithers and Lobley *did* used the entire forty-item version of the Dogmatism Scale that Rokeach developed. That has become increasingly unusual. Many other researchers have instead used Troldahl and Powell's (1965) twenty-item abridgment, which has muddied the muddy waters even more. Troldahl and Powell based their choice of items upon field studies each had done using the original forty items. Troldahl had read the statements to 227 "Boston suburbanites who subscribed to a county agricultural newspaper," while Powell had let 84 Lansing, Michigan, residents answer the D Scale in the usual "self-administered" way. They each calculated the item-whole correlations for each statement, and ranked the items according to how well each correlated with the sum of all forty.

Then they tried ten-item, fifteen-item, and twenty-item versions, seeing how well each correlated with the forty-item scores. Inevitably, the twenty-item version did best, since besides being longer, it had twenty perfect correlations with the criterion. The authors did not present the correlation between the twenty items they chose and the twenty items they dropped. But we would expect it to be good, as the "twenty-forty" correlation came in at about .95.

I spoke in Chapter 1 about the dangers of using this technique to shorten scales. In this case, the whole schmear of forty items has almost no underlying meaning, judging by their intercorrelations, so a twenty-item measure of this set, like the ten-item "quickie" Schulze (1962) developed, has little to lose. The items Troldahl and Powell selected *could* simply be those most susceptible to response sets.

Finally, shortening a scale on the basis of two studies (a doctoral dissertation and a master's thesis) involving altogether 311 persons seems rather preliminary to me. Would the same items be discarded in studies involving other, larger samples? The inherent instability of such choices is driven home by a comparison with Schulze's ten items (chosen on the basis of two studies involving altogether 272 university students). You would expect the ten items Schulze picked to make the Top Twenty on Troldahl and Powell's list, would you not, if the procedure were valid? But only five of them did, exactly chance on a twenty item version of a forty-item scale.

Noting this, and attributing it to the difference in populations sampled, Troldahl and Powell (p. 214) said, "These findings illustrate the need for a different abbreviated scale in field studies than in the classroom." *Their* quickie was for field studies of the general population, not for the usual student study. Do you think many dogmatism researchers paid any attention to that stated limitation, which was even included in the title of Troldahl and Powell's article, once the twenty-item version was published? Or do you suspect that once a scale is *published*, its appearance in print becomes a kind of universal license to go hunting with it, no matter what the article says?

8. I then destroyed the attendance sheets linking the students' names with their responses. As they told me all about their sex lives, guilty deeds, and other things on the Secret Survey, they were totally anonymous.

9. These results were replicated in my January 1995 Secret Survey experiment.

10. I did not particularly trust these results, especially those based upon the small N's, so I repeated the experiment in January 1994. I again ended up with twenty-six Dogmatic Believers who happened to get the Attis proposition. They shifted 0.85 units ($p > .10$). (Only six of the twenty-six moved; the others did not budge a bit.) But eleven Nondogmatic Believers shifted an average of 2.36 units ($p < .05$). (Seven of them shifted.)

Among the scarce "firmly *non*believing," there were only three High DOG Nonbelievers who had to deal with the implications of a Roman File. They moved an average of 3.33 units (thanks to two of them), which was not significant with such a sliver of an N. Five other Nonbelievers who got the Roman File version were Low DOGs. They shifted 3.60 units ($p < .05$), with four of the five moving. The difference between these two small groups appears to me largely fortuitous.

At this point, it seems that in general firm *Non*believers are willing to change more than firm Believers (who are much more numerous). The DOG scale predicts this willingness within each group but seems to do a better job among the Believers. High DOG Believers in Jesus' divinity appear quite resistant to change.

11. The Zealot Scale, like my other 0–6 measures such as the Religious Emphasis Scale, does not control for response sets. So the interitem correlations and alphas on these scales are doubtless inflated, perhaps considerably. And their correlations with other unbalanced measures will also be pumped up. But their correlations with balanced measures such as the RWA, Religious Fundamentalism, and DOG Scales would be *lessened*, not increased.

12. In case you care, here are the *student-parent* correlations for the various measures common to the two booklets; RWA, .38 (already reported in Chapter 3); Religious Fundamentalism, .61; Dogmatism, .29; Zealot, .23; ATH, .36; Ethnocentrism, .31; Posse, .16.

13. In fact, with three exceptions all of the items on all four of these scales correlated significantly with the summed scores of the other three scales, in both samples. That's a 489 out of 492, or .994, batting average. You can look at any item on any of those scales, and almost always correctly infer that people who answered it in a certain way also tended to be more authoritarian, fundamentalist, dogmatic, or zealous. You might make the same kind of inferences when interpreting other instruments' relationships with things, but it will often be wrong even with very large samples (*RWA*, pp. 205–208). Relatively unidimensional scales bring you this kind of consistent performance and ease of interpretation on a silver platter.

14. DOG scores also correlated significantly with the three measures of authoritarian aggression in the booklets: Ethnocentrism (about .25), ATH (about .40), and Posse (about .30). But as was true with the links between Religious Fundamentalism and aggression that we saw in the last chapter, these relationships disappear when you partial out the mutual connections with right-wing authoritarianism.

15. The one-way ANOVA of Zealot scores by the ten categories given in question 13 produced $p < .001$ for both students and parents. The same was true for "Nature" breakdowns of RWA, DOG, and Fundamentalism scores, and indeed for nearly all of the variables measured in the booklets.

16. Some people might even call this "dog-eat-dog" capitalism. But not I.

17. In a fall 1995 survey of 501 parents, 26 self-declared capitalists scored moderate on the RWA Scale, but again proved more ethnocentric than any other group. They also scored highest on Pratto et al.'s (1994) Social Dominance Scale. In contrast, the 18 self-described socialists scored lowest on all three measures.

9. Left-Wing Authoritarianism

1. Eysenck (1954) had proposed that Communists and fascists are both "tough-minded." While the premise certainly appeals, Christie and Rokeach pointed out many disturbing, unbelievable flaws in Eysenck's evidence (*RWA*, pp. 80–91).

2. By definition, revolutions change the system. Who constitutes the "established authorities" then, that High RWAs will support in their hearts? I think it depends largely on who they were taught were the legitimate authorities when they were growing up (though this is not necessarily chiseled in stone forever). Thus I suspect many Russians who grew up honoring the czar did not accept their new Communist masters, even after the civil war and foreign interventions ended. Rather amazingly, they apparently transmitted their devotion to the czar to some of their

descendants, for a small czarist party exists in Russia today, over seventy-five years after Nicholas II was murdered.

But most present-day Russians were taught that the Communist Party was the legitimate authority in their country. While many became disenchanted with the Communist regime and cheered its demise, other Russians have come to long for the return of the Politburo. We have the spectacle of Communists and czarists, one of whose founders deposed and murdered the leader of the other, allied now in opposition to democracy in Russia today—along with the nationalists, fascists, and anti-Semites. What do you suppose all these groups have in common?

3. If it seems strange that authoritarians could hold such varying *beliefs,* recall that even among the right-wing authoritarians we have considered so far, strong differences can appear. How much do you think fundamentalist Christians agree with fundamentalist Jews or fundamentalist Muslims? Remember the front ranks on both sides of the Cold War were filled with High RWAs. One High RWA group can thus attack another High RWA group, and indeed much of the trouble caused by the FBI's Hostage Rescue force at Ruby Ridge, Idaho, and Waco, Texas, can be seen in this light.

4. I immediately wondered how much of the "bad rep" I had been handing out to High RWAs was really just due to the Wild-Card, High-High authoritarians, who could also be called "High *LWAs.*" But there were still lots of prejudiced and hostile High RWAs who were *not* also High LWAs. Setting aside the High-Highs, RWA scores correlated .46 with Ethnocentrism and .54 with ATH scores in the rest of the sample.

5. Among the students, the scale mean equaled 65.9, with a variance of 298. Among the parents, the scale mean was 56.5, and the variance 439.

6. The booklets contained other scales besides these. In case you care, LWA correlated for students and parents, respectively, .16 and .22 with Religious Fundamentalism, and .11 and .17 with Zealot Scale scores, it correlated −.17 with education among the parents. All of these are attributable to the High-Highs. Also, LWA correlated nonsignificantly with gender (−.04 and .04).

7. The accompanying letter soliciting their cooperation made it clear that the former candidates would be answering anonymously. They were approached *not* as members of their party but simply as people who had sought office. The *last* item on the survey asked for party affiliation.

8. Please note I am not calling these a "scale," and I did not use them as an "abbreviated version of the LWA Scale." There was no LWA Scale in November 1991. These were just items I was testing at the time, most of which (with modification) made it to the final version of the test.

9. You could easily write less extreme LWA items. That would raise the item means, and you might eventually get some people to score high on the measure in absolute terms. But if you had to drop the submission, aggression, and conventionalism content to pull this off, you would not be measuring authoritarianism (by my definition at least). Nor would you if the internal consistency dropped appreciably as the items became mellower. You can quickly come up with items on which left-wingers will score highly. But you cannot demonstrate there is an *authoritarian* on the left with statements such as "The rich should share their wealth more."

10. I have a white son in graduate school who could become a professor and would probably make a good one. But he knows he has much less of a chance of becoming one than others do because of his gender and Caucasoid genes. The woman (let's say) who gets the job he might have gotten in a blind competition did not cheat him out of his chance. I did. For generations, white guys such as I have had it easy, competing only with one another, consciously and unconsciously keeping the cream of the professional jobs within "our club." We have undeniably prospered, because we benefited from the unfairness of the world. I think we have no right to start crying out now about "reverse discrimination" and how "two wrongs don't make a right." Where were we when it was just "one wrong," for generation after generation? So if anybody "owes" my son, because his future will be less fair than it should be, it is not the long disadvantaged groups who are finally getting a little of what *they* are owed. It is I.

10. The Effects of Hate Literature

1. We shall leave the story at this point, but in case you care, the party leaders decided to let me give out my surveys, which I did to twenty-four members following an interesting demonstration on the Fourth of July across from the White House. I also administered a second questionnaire to forty-four Nazis on September 5, following another demonstration. At the time I was thrilled by the data. But over the years I have seen their virtual uselessness since the participants, sitting in their Stormtrooper uniforms in front of the party headquarters, filling out a psychological survey only because they had practically been ordered to do so by the party leaders, were hardly answering as individuals.

   I did, however, obtain some demographic information from the Stormtroopers at each testing that may be of interest. In the first study, the respondents ranged in age from 17 to 38, with a mean age of 24.6 years. Eleven had blue-collar jobs (e.g., truck driver, machinist, roofer). Four were white-collar workers (two school teachers, a computer programmer, an office manager). Three were college students, one was a farmer, and one was unemployed. So basically these Stormtroopers were young, blue-collar workers, and males, although most had wives or girlfriends with them in support.

   The larger, September 1971 sample (which included thirty-four persons who had not answered the July survey, most of them from out of town) varied more. Ages ranged from 17 to 52, with a mean of 26.1 years. Blue-collar workers still outnumbered white-collar ones, but only by sixteen to twelve. Twelve of the Stormtroopers were still students, seven in high school. The mean level of formal education was 13.0 years, with a range from 6 to 18. Most of those who had attempted university had failed to complete their studies, however. Only four of the forty-three Nazis who answered this question had college degrees.

2. Paul F. Boller, Jr., and John George (1989) have compiled a delightful book of fake quotes, misquotes, and misleading attributions that they entitled *They Never Said It*. As one reads through the scores of things that people *never* said, so far as anyone can tell, but that other people say they *did*, one finds that the misquoters tend to be political extremists with an ax to grind—which does not exactly bowl

you over, right? It also becomes obvious as you read the book that the political right has done a lot more "inventive quoting" than the political left has. From Jimmy Swaggert's claim that Charles Darwin renounced the theory of evolution on his deathbed, to several dozen things Joseph McCarthy, the John Birch Society, and others put into the mouth of Lenin, to attacks on everything from trade agreements to deficit spending, the far right has shown much less respect for the truth, and a much greater tendency to accept quotes from other people in their "tight circles," without checking on the accuracy of the information. For example, one enterprising author, Eustace Mullins, Jr., who once wrote a piece entitled "Adolf Hitler: An Appreciation," also invented a book entitled *A Racial Program for the Twentieth Century,* which he attributed to a nonexistent "leading British Communist," Israel Cohen. The book revealed a nonexistent Zionist plot to destroy the United States through racial unrest. During debate on a civil rights bill in June 1957, Mississippi Congressman Thomas G. Abernathy quoted it into the *Congressional Record.* "The phoney quote continued to circulate among bigots in the 1980s" (Boller and George, 1989, pp. 15–16).

Professors Boller and George note this right-wing gift for distortion in their preface (p. x): "For some reason, American reactionaries have gone in more for quote-making than American radicals. This is possibly because the former feel more of a need for authoritative quotes than the latter. Radicals have plenty of quotations from Karl Marx, anyway, and probably see no need to add to the Marxist treasure-house. Extreme rightists in America have a real problem, in any case; they would like to cite the Founding Fathers, but rarely find what they want in Franklin, Washington and Jefferson. Hence the quote-faking."

Just the kind of analysis you'd expect from a couple of young whippersnapper Ivy League profs, huh? But Paul Boller is Professor of History Emeritus at Texas Christian University in Fort Worth, and John George is Professor of Political Science and Sociology at Central State University in Edmond, Oklahoma.

3. Item 3 was badly worded. The films most people have been shown of Nazi concentration camps were taken in western Europe by American and British armies. In particular, the shots most of us have seen of shower rooms and skeletons in ovens were made at Dachau. While many horrendous things happened there, it was not a site of mass gassings, which mainly took place at Birkenau, near Auschwitz, often called "Auschwitz II." I know of no motion picture films of the actual mass gassings that took place at Birkenau or of the burning of the bodies. The physical evidence of the mass execution facilities was largely destroyed toward the end of the war. One of the four crematoria at Birkenau was destroyed during a prisoner revolt on October 7, 1944, and two others were damaged. Their remains, the one still undamaged, and the gas chambers themselves were blown up by the Nazis on January 26, 1945, as they abandoned the area to the Russian Army advancing from the east. (Important blueprints for the gas chambers and crematoria, captured by the Russians in 1945, have recently become public, and were presented in a Public Broadcasting System *NOVA* program aired on February 7, 1995.)

When I realized my mistake in item 3, I reworded it to read, "The films everyone has seen of the concentration camps and piles of dead bodies leave no doubt that mass executions of Jews were carried out by the Nazis during World War II." As you would probably expect, this made no difference in the results of subsequent studies.

I regret my reference to the "gas chamber films from Auschwitz," and not only because it was erroneous. Any such mistake is seized upon by Holocaust deniers to "show" that the Holocaust never occurred. Everything you say has to be exactly right, and nothing they say has to be true, the way the Holocaust deniers play.

4. Two things probably contributed to the integrity of the manipulations across conditions in these experiments, besides extracting this promise not to discuss it. First, the study normally took about twenty minutes; the last subject had usually left the room within half an hour. That meant there were no students standing around in the hall, waiting for the next session to begin, when "experienced" participants were leaving. Second, many students may have been too embarrassed to bring up the subject with others, once they had read the debriefing.

5. In this and all subsequent experiments, I visited the classes involved at the end of the school year to give the results of the Holocaust-denial experiment. I used this opportunity to discredit again the revisionist material used.

6. In this, my first experiment, I left out a few pages from Christophersen's account that dealt mainly with the synthetic rubber project. One of the subjects, noticing that pages were missing (they contained the photograph of several overlapping pages of the Red Cross report), accused me of "suppressing the information in the pamphlet" that would prove Christophersen correct. It was vital, he told me, "to present the whole story." Thereafter I used Christophersen's entire twenty-four-page account in my experiments.

7. Lest we just single out American youth, in the fall of 1995 I asked 184 Manitoba introductory psychology students to say (on a -4 to $+4$ basis, converted to the usual 1–9 format) how false or true various statements were. The mean of answers to "The United States dropped atom bombs on Japan at the end of World War II" was 7.49. This happened about eight weeks after numerous television programs aired marking the fiftieth anniversary of the bombing of Hiroshima and Nagasaki. The figure of 7.49 matches students' belief in the Holocaust, and was mainly due to students who said they did not know, one way or the other. Also, in the fall of 1993, 654 parents of my introductory psychology students responded to items 1, 5, 6, and 8 of Exhibit 10.1. Their scores, which averaged 30.1 (or an item mean of 7.52), were *not* that much higher than those usually obtained from students. Presumably, British and French parents would know better.

8. I was surprised that the Low RWA students did not prove more resistant to Christophersen's influence. But they were not *that* much better than the Highs at critical reasoning in the experiments described in Chapter 4. The correlations were often in the .20s, which is about what has turned up overall in my hate literature experiments.

9. A small percentage of the students taking introductory psychology at my university are Jewish, and they could sign up for the experiment as easily as anyone else. (I could identify them by the answers they had given on the bubble sheets to my

demographic questions about their home and present religions.) No Jewish students signed up for my first two experiments. One or two did for the subsequent Holocaust-denial experiments, but I dropped their responses from the others in the analyses to be reported because I wanted to study the effect of revisionist propaganda on non-Jews.

10. I have found two reports of Red Cross visits to Auschwitz. Yahil (1980, pp. 450–451) says that in February 1944 the head of the German Red Cross was taken to a special "family camp." These families were displayed in good circumstances, with the children even receiving schooling. After the visit, the families were murdered. Mirchuk (1976, pp. 125–126), who was a Ukrainian political prisoner at the original Auschwitz "labor camp," tells of how one day in September 1944 his block was evacuated, cleaned, equipped with beds, and turned over to new Jewish prisoners who were given good clothing and fed large amounts of good food. The next day an inspector from the International Red Cross was given a tour of this facility. All the other prisoners were taken from the camp for that day. The next day everything returned to its normally brutal state. The International Red Cross inspector did not visit Birkenau, three kilometers away, with its vast facilities for death and destruction.

11. To be precise, the students got only sixty-four of the questions and answers. The photocopy of the original sheet sent to me did not catch the bottom two questions on the front side. I later sent away for an original sheet of my own and discovered the missing questions covered how many Jews were in areas that came to be controlled by the Germans before the war and how such a mass program (of extermination) could have been kept secret from Jews who were scheduled for extermination. I do not think their omission makes much difference in the document's effect. If you would insist upon using all sixty-six questions, you would have a problem. There apparently is no definitive version of these questions and answers. The set I received from the Institute for Historical Review differed in numerous ways from the set I was originally sent. For example, the answer to question 1 now excludes the passage "no piles of clothes." ("Oh, there are still piles of clothes? Well, never mind. We'll just drop that one.") Want to bet that the "Institute" says the current version is a revision of an earlier one?

12. The only group to whom I have ever described this finding is the "Saturday Night Discussion Group" in Winnipeg, a lively gathering of Jewish women and men my age (and even older) who invited me to speak on the psychology of fascism in early 1993. Like many Jews of this generation, some of the people in the room had lost loved ones in the Holocaust, and several had been in concentration camps during the war. I told them of my first two experiments. They argued with me, and with each other, about what the data meant. But they were quite concerned.

When we had finished tearing my experiments apart, I asked them what I should do with the results. I pointed out that these findings will encourage the very people who want to kill them, their children, and their grandchildren. I revealed that, so far as I knew, no one had ever done scientific experiments on the effects of the denial literature, and perhaps no one else ever would. So what should I do? Should I ever publish these results? It would probably increase the circulation of hate literature directed against Jews in North America, with obviously dangerous possibilities. I asked them for guidance.

No one said to suppress the evidence. Some said, do more studies before you conclude anything. But the basic consensus was, "If it is true, it should not be denied or hidden," which I found very courageous. (In the end I decided *not* to publish my findings, for the reasons described above, plus the fact that I had not found a way to counteract hate literature. When I sent off the manuscript for this book to prospective publishers in March of 1995, it did not have this chapter in it. Then the Oklahoma City bombing occurred, and we found out a lot more about the "militias," the distortions being drummed out on the Internet, "hate radio," and so on. It seemed obvious that denial literature was spreading rapidly anyway and probably having a terrible effect on certain people. That led me to include this chapter, so as to document the power of these lies.)

13. The passage can be found in Leviticus 20:13. Numbers 15:32–36 in turn prescribes the death penalty for picking up sticks on the Sabbath.

14. The control group's mean fell from 56.3 at the beginning of the session to 48.1 after they had read Peters' article ($p < .01$). These students would have most definitely known they were in a pre-test, post-test attitude change experiment, and they might have assumed I agreed with Pastor Peters, since I gave them the article. Their change (-8.2) was the largest observed, but it was not much greater than the -6.8 produced in the neutral Experimenter condition. Like the rise produced even when I condemned the article ($+4.0$), it indicates that the major factor influencing attitude change was not a desire to please the Experimenter, but the article itself.

15. We could test the issue by giving hate literature to students and not testing their beliefs until, say, a month later. But that would mean spreading the lies and letting them go unchallenged for a long time.

16. But I would not debate them in a forum that gave them an audience they did not already have.

17. In November 1995 I ran another three-condition experiment on Holocaust denial. Having a student confederate "spontaneously" speak out against the Christophersen piece while others read it had, at best, a small effect on the propaganda's impact. The mean still dropped from 64.1 to 59.0 ($p < .01$). Extracts from an Auschwitz survivor's horrific account of her experiences (Perl, 1948), which was suggested, assembled, and supplemented with photographs by an undergraduate honors student, Kevin Del Ben, did not raise belief in the Holocaust significantly. The mean went from 61.4 to 63.3 ($p > .15$). But this article, when paired with the Christophersen denial, prevented the latter's usual persuasive effect. The mean only went from 57.9 to 57.0 ($p > .30$). As usual, the two articles were counterbalanced for order of presentation, and a significant primacy effect appeared. Students were influenced more by whichever article came first.

11. The Authoritarianism of Legislators in North America

1. See *EOF*, p. 356, for the soliciting letter sent to the lawmakers. I used the 1982 version of the RWA Scale shown on pages 22–23 of *Enemies of Freedom* in all

of my studies of politicians, including those being reported now for the first time. But I always added a clarifying paragraph to the standard instructions printed at the beginning of the survey and two table-setting items at the very beginning of the questionnaire.

The clarifying paragraph read, "Finally, it is always difficult to communicate complex ideas in a sentence or two. It is understood that a person's answers to these statements can vary quite a bit, depending on how terms are defined. But previous research indicates there is a common understanding as to what these statements are referring to, or getting at. If you find yourself saying, What does he mean by _____? the answer is likely 'What do you think most people mean by it?' "

The two "lead off" items, designed to get a strong positive and a strong negative reaction, respectively, were: (1) The number of nuclear weapons in the world should be reduced. (Thus the statement does not get into more involved issues such as how the number should be reduced, unilateral disarmament, etc. It simply says, do you think the number of nuclear weapons in the world should be reduced?) and (2) The use of illegal drugs in Canada (the United States) is *not* a serious problem today.

The politicians always answered anonymously. I did, however, ask them (at the bottom of the "flip side" of the survey, as the last thing on the questionnaire) which caucus they belonged to. When it became clear in my first studies that all respondents were willing to answer this item, I discretely coded the surveys so I could make sure the answers were reliable, not somebody's idea of a good joke on the researcher. Over 99% of the answers I have received since have corresponded to the precoded designation. That is, the lawmakers told the truth about their party affiliation.

2. I was amused to have two of my solicitations returned by the postal service because the (defeated) candidates had already moved and left no forwarding address. It restored in my mind the original meaning of the contemporary expression "Get out of town!"

3. In my Manitoba parent studies, the top eighth of the distribution usually scored 200 or higher on the 1982 version of the RWA Scale used in these legislator studies. If the top *quartile* of the distribution comprises the "High" RWAs, I call scores over 200 "Very High." You can see that some of the candidates were Very High RWAs.

4. Preliminary studies among Canadian and American introductory psychology students had led to these ten items. Progress was slow because such students have almost no discernable economic philosophy.

Additional item development, aided by a discussion with my friend Professor Larry Morse of North Carolina A & T University, has led to a better scale. A December 1995 booklet answered by 168 parents produced a balanced sixteen-item Economic Philosophy Scale with a mean interitem correlation of .24 and an alpha of .84. Scoring "conservative" on this scale correlated .42 with the RWA Scale and .44 with the Ethnocentrism Scale. I was prepared to blame economists for the lack of economic philosophy in my earlier subjects, but it appears the philosophy is there to a reasonable degree. Nevertheless, let's blame the economists anyway—and the lawyers.

5. Since I object to other people using parts of the RWA Scale in their research, I should explain that the Social Dominance Orientation Scale was under development at this time. In fact, as I noted in Chapter 1, the version I had received consisted of ten (American) nationalism items and eighteen others concerned with equality among different groups of people. The nationalism items have since been dropped (Pratto et al., 1994), and the published version of the scale consists of eight protrait and eight contrait items concerned with equality.

6. If you believe that political parties know which issues draw which supporters, then you might conclude that the Reform Party knows it has cornered the "bigot vote." But that card must be played with finesse. I did a series of experiments in 1983–84 on the factors that would affect High RWAs' liking for a new political figure on the scene. In one of the experiments, the newcomer was overtly racist, saying things like "Perhaps the biggest mistake those muddle-headed liberals in Ottawa have made is to allow all the coloured people into the country . . . And the Jews, with all their dirty money and secret control of things, are not going to be too welcome either. I guess we're stuck with our native Indians, but if they want to drink themselves to death, I won't stop them" (EOF, p. 322). This depiction turned *off* High RWA students (as well as Lows, of course). Bigotry sells much better if one can find *other* grounds, socially defensible ones such as "state's rights" or "immigration needs" that will achieve discriminatory ends. As we have seen, most highly prejudiced people do not think they are highly prejudiced. Covert racism works much better with them than overt racism.

7. These placements reappeared in two subsequent Manitoba parent studies. In the fall of 1994, 35 Reform Party supporters in a sample of 468 scored highest in RWA, Ethnocentrism, (hostile) Attitudes toward Homosexuals and (hostile) Attitudes toward Quebec. The following autumn 40 parents who preferred the Reform Party (out of 501 respondents) again scored highest in RWA and Ethnocentrism. The ATH and Attitudes toward Quebec Scales were not included in this booklet. Instead the parents were asked to answer Pratto et al.'s (1994) full Social Dominance Scale, Spence and Helmreich's (1978) sex-role survey, and a set of items measuring concern for the environment. Reform Party supporters scored highest in Social Dominance, believed strongest in traditional sex roles, and had the least concern for the environment.

8. I also sent surveys to the Tennessee House, but they got trapped in the bureaucracy. (I had made the mistake of sending them to the Speaker's Office, rather than to the Office of the Clerk.)

   You will see that I mainly sampled the "lower houses" of these state legislatures in these eight studies. I reasoned representatives, more numerous to start with, would also be more likely to fill out my surveys than senators.

9. When calculating the overall correlation between party *affiliation* and some other variable, I took the average of the state-by-state results rather than just cranking the value out for all the legislators involved. This method kept states with large assemblies from having an undue influence on the final figure in these sensitive

comparisons. (You also have to convert correlation coefficients to numbers on an equal interval scale—called a "z-transformation," to get the true average. Just averaging the coefficients will usually give too low a figure.)

10. How much of the wealth in the United States do you think is owned by the wealthiest 20% of its households? According to an analysis of Federal Reserve figures presented in a *New York Times* Service article written by Keith Bradsher that appeared in the *Toronto Globe and Mail* on April 17, 1995, it controls over 80% of the country's wealth. That means the other 80% of the country owns less than 20% of its wealth. Comparisons with other nations show the United States is the *least* egalitarian of industrialized countries. And that situation is just fine, in the view of High RWA lawmakers.

11. I was not entirely unprepared for this result from the American study. One of the Mississippi senators who responded in my 1986 study pulled down a 245. And a Minnesota senator came in at 248. Both lawmakers, incidentally, were Democrats.

12. I am *not* saying the Soviets were the good guys in the Cold War, and the Americans the bad guys. See note 2 to Chapter 5.

13. The two Vermont Progressive Coalition lawmakers averaged a very low 60.5 on the RWA Scale and an equally low 19.0 when the Ethnocentrism items were summed.

14. I wrote each of the seven signatories and tried to explain how they could give qualified answers with the nine-point response scale. But I was unconvincing. I had, however, heard from one member of their caucus, before the "Cheyenne Seven" got organized. This person turned in a low 117 on the RWA Scale.

15. You can see that, if the 169 respondents were their own state legislature, a bill to place greater restrictions on abortion would never pass. And yet many states have recently passed such laws. This reinforces my suspicion that I tended to hear from Low and Moderate RWA legislators, while Highs tended to decline participation. The implications for how many Very High RWA lawmakers, how many prejudiced lawmakers, and so on one can find writing legislation in state capitols is obvious, and yet *more* disturbing.

16. Recall from Chapter 1 that Moghaddam and Vuksanovic (1990) administered the RWA Scale to 74 pro-life activists in Montreal and found a *mean* of 220! I cannot recall any higher group score.

17. It can be objected that no one intended, or promised, *complete* equality in democracy. I agree. But no one intended, or promised, complete freedom either. I am not advocating dividing a country's wealth by the number of citizens, and giving all their share at the post office. Nor do I think freedom of speech should have no bounds, or freedom of the press, or the right to bear arms. But we have done a much better job establishing civil *freedoms* in Canada and the United States than we have at establishing *equal opportunity*. It is not a "level playing field." Lots of people are born in deep holes and have little chance at "the pursuit of happiness." And lately, some of the few ladders that enabled people to escape those holes have been pulled up.

Some people appear to forget completely that democracy means more than just freedom. During the 1968 presidential campaign, Ball-Rokeach, Rokeach, and Grube (1984) report, campaign workers for Hubert Humphrey, Eugene McCarthy, Richard Nixon, Ronald Reagan, Nelson Rockefeller, and George Wallace were asked to rank eighteen values, including Equality and Freedom. Overall, the workers in most camps ranked Freedom very high, and Equality somewhat lower. But the gaps varied considerably from camp to camp. The Reagan workers put Equality seventeenth, and the Wallace workers did them one better, and put it dead last. The same study also cited an analysis by the syndicated columnist David Broder of President Reagan's speeches. Noting that "words are important symbols, and for 200 years the words 'freedom' and 'equality' have defined the twin guideposts of American democracy," Broder observed that Reagan had used forms of "freedom" or "liberty" forty-four times in his speeches, and "equality" or "equal rights" just twice.

18. I also had a tenth proposed law, one "which imposes *very* stiff fines upon companies that seriously pollute the environment." I was testing my perception that High RWA legislators do not take environmental issues as seriously as Low RWA lawmakers do. Most respondents said they definitely would impose such fines (the mean equaled 7.63). But Highs ($r = .30$) and Republicans (.37) were less enthusiastic than Lows and Democrats.

19. If you exclude the Utah representatives, who for an understandable reason most strongly opposed a law requiring Christian instruction in public schools, then most of the High RWA lawmakers were also in favor of *that* law too—which also clearly violates the Bill of Rights. Seen from this perspective, the legislators' data replicated the student-based studies (Chapter 5), which showed the double standard High RWAs have over religious instruction in public schools. High students supported such laws when they were in the majority but opposed them when in the minority. Here, most High lawmakers outside Utah wanted America's majority religion, Christianity, taught in public schools. But Utah Highs did not think it was proper.

20. The New Hampshire House of Representatives consists of about 400 elected members. At the time I did this study, 100 of them listed their party affiliation as (just) Democrats, and 190 others were (just) Republicans. But others were both. And others were still more complicated. I sent surveys to the first 35 "just Democrats" and 65 "just Republicans" on the alphabetical list supplied by the Clerk's Office.

21. Is it a coincidence that the Louisiana Republican Party came under strong pressure from the national party to "moderate itself" after America's most famous one-time Nazi, David Duke, won the GOP gubernatorial nomination and very nearly the governorship itself?

22. Since Republicans were more likely to respond than Democrats (return rates of 29% and 24%, respectively, over all eight studies), the simplest explanation that fits all the facts would be that Republican Very Highs were particularly unlikely to respond, compared with Democratic Very Highs. It could also be that some of the difference in Republican versus Democrat response rate arose because most of the state houses I sampled were controlled by the Democrats, who may consequently have been busier.

23. I have already told the legislatures what I found. I sent individual sheets to all the lawmakers contacted, which explained the purpose and outcome of the particular study I asked them to serve in, and which outlined the results of the other studies (done to date). Stapled to this sheet was a copy of an article I had written on right-wing authoritarianism (Altemeyer, 1990). I also sent, to the majority and minority leaders of most of the chambers involved, a thirty-one-page, single-spaced summary of the studies, asking them to make it available to any member of their caucus who was interested.

     Was I besieged by angry (or happy) lawmakers? Altogether, I believe I have heard from six, most of them Republicans who did not believe what I had found or who wanted to point out that gun-control laws could also be unconstitutional, etc. The vast, overwhelming response to these results has been a gigantic *yawn*. ("You know psychologists. They're like psychiatrists. Or sociologists. Or economists. It's all opinion.")

24. In 1977 I asked a sample of Canadian soldiers who had just finished their basic training what they would do if the prime minister suspended the civil liberties of Canadians and declared Parliament closed, when "there are no laws giving the prime minister such powers." Seventy-six percent said that they would obey orders to take up positions on Parliament Hill to keep the House of Commons from meeting. Ninety-two percent said they would arrest a member of the House of Commons who tried to enter the Parliament buildings. Sixty-three percent said they would, if ordered, shoot at demonstrators who gathered to protest the destruction of democracy (*RWA*, pp. 274–275).

Conclusion

1. Ordinary High RWAs, one predicts, will find this preposterous and cite the surface differences that conceal the underlying similarities. But High RWAs, we have seen, have less insight into themselves than most people do. They would probably find just as preposterous the statement that they were psychological twins of the Communists in the Soviet Union.

2. Some people have asked me whether High RWAs might not make better "managers" than Lows do. The issue can be tested. I would bet it will depend a lot on the situation (e.g., running a platoon versus running a social service agency). But the times we have given Highs a chance to "run things" (the NATO–Warsaw Pact simulations, the Global Change Game), they performed just dreadfully when left to themselves. *If* it turns out that Highs are generally better at "making the trains run on time," we still have to worry about what they might load onto the trains.

References

Adorno, T. W., E. Frenkel-Brunswik, D. J. Levinson, and R. N. Sanford. 1950. *The Authoritarian Personality*. New York: Harper and Row.

Allen, L. S., and R. A. Gorski. 1992. "Sexual Orientation and the Size of the Anterior Commissure in the Human Brain." *Proceedings of the National Academy of Sciences of the U.S.A.*, 89, 7199–7202.

Alliger, G. M., and K. J. Williams. 1992. "Relating the Internal Consistency of Scales to Rater Response Tendencies." *Educational and Psychological Measurement, 52*, 337–343.

Allport, G. W. 1966. "The Religious Context of Prejudice." *Journal for the Scientific Study of Religion, 5*, 447–457.

Allport, G. W., and J. M. Ross. 1967. "Personal Religious Orientations and Prejudice." *Journal of Personality and Social Psychology, 5*, 432–443.

Allport, G. W., P. E. Vernon, and G. Lindzey. 1960. *Manual for the Study of Values*, 3d ed. Boston: Houghton Mifflin.

Altemeyer, B. 1981. *Right-Wing Authoritarianism*. Winnipeg: University of Manitoba Press.

———. 1988. *Enemies of Freedom: Understanding Right-Wing Authoritarianism*. San Franscisco: Jossey-Bass.

———. 1990. "The Authoritarian Personality." *Harvard Mental Health Letter*, 7 (September).

Altemeyer, B., and B. Hunsberger. 1992. "Authoritarianism, Religious Fundamentalism, Quest, and Prejudice." *International Journal for the Psychology of Religion*, 2, 113–133.

Altemeyer, B., and A. Kamenshikov. 1991. "Impressions of American and Soviet Behaviour: RWA Images in a Mirror." *South African Journal of Psychology, 21*, 255–260.

Arendt, H. 1977. *Eichmann in Jerusalem: A Report on the Banality of Evil*, rev. ed. New York: Penguin Books.

Bailey, J. M., and R. C. Pillard. 1991. "A Genetic Study of Male Sexual Orientation." *Archives of General Psychiatry,* 48, 1089–1096.

Bailey, J. M., R. C., Pillard, and Y. Agyei. 1993. "A Genetic Study of Female Sexual Orientation." *Archives of General Psychiatry,* 50, 217–223.

Bailes, D. W., and I. B. Guller. 1970. "Dogmatism and Attitudes towards the Vietnam War." *Sociometry,* 33, 140–146.

Baker-Brown, G., E. J. Ballard, S. Bluck, B. DeVries, P. Suedfeld, and P. Tetlock. 1992. "Scoring Manual for Integrative and Conceptual Complexity." In J. Atkinson, D. McClelland, and J. Veroff, eds., *Handbook of Thematic Analysis,* pp. 401–418. New York: Springer-Verlag.

Ball-Rokeach, S. J., M. Rokeach, and J. W. Grube. 1984. "The Great American Values Test." *Psychology Today,* 18 (November), 34–41.

Bandura, A. 1973. *Aggression: A Social Learning Analysis.* Englewood Cliffs, N.J.: Prentice-Hall.

———. 1977. *Social Learning Theory.* Englewood Cliffs, N.J.: Prentice-Hall.

Barker, E. N. 1963. "Authoritarianism of the Political Right, Center, and Left." *Journal of Social Issues,* 19, 63–74.

Barry, D. 1990. *Dave Barry Turns Forty.* New York: Ballantine.

Batson, C. D. 1976. "Religion as Prosocial: Agent or Double Agent?" *Journal for the Scientific Study of Religion,* 15, 29–45.

Batson, C. D., C. H. Flink, P. A. Schoenrade, J. Fultz, and V. Pych. 1986. "Religious Orientation and Overt versus Covert Racial Prejudice." *Journal of Personality and Social Psychology,* 50, 175–181.

Batson, C. D., S. J. Naifeh, and S. Pate. 1978. "Social Desirability, Religious Orientation, and Racial Prejudice." *Journal for the Scientific Study of Religion,* 17, 31–41.

Batson, C. D., and C. T. Burris. 1994. "Personal Religion: Depressant or Stimulant of Prejudice and Discrimination?" In M. P. Zanna and J. M. Olson, eds., *The Psychology of Prejudice: The Ontario Symposium,* vol. 7, 131–148. Hillside, N.J.: Lawrence Erlbaum.

Batson, C. D., and P. A. Schoenrade. 1991. "Measuring Religion as Quest: Reliability Concerns." *Journal for the Scientific Study of Religion,* 30, 430–447.

Batson, C. D., P. A. Schoenrade, and W. L. Ventis. 1993. *Religion and the Individual: A Social-Psychological Perspective,* 2d ed. New York: Oxford University Press.

Batson, C. D., and W. L. Ventis. 1982. *The Religious Experience: A Social Psychological Perspective.* New York: Oxford University Press.

Billig, M., and H. Tajfel. 1973. "Social Categorization and Similarity in Intergroup Behavior." *European Journal of Social Psychology,* 3, 27–52.

Billings, S. W., S. J. Guastello, and M. L. Rieke. 1993. "A Comparative Assessment of the Construct Validity of Three Authoritarianism Measures." *Journal of Research in Personality,* 27, 328–348.

Blass, T. 1991. "Understanding Behavior in the Milgram Obedience Experiment: The Role of Personality, Situation, and Their Interaction." *Journal of Personality and Social Psychology,* 60, 398–413.

———. 1992a. "The Social Psychology of Stanley Milgram." In M. P. Zanna, ed., *Advances in Experimental Social Psychology,* vol. 25, 227–329. San Diego, Calif.: Academic Press.

————. 1992b. "Right-Wing Authoritarianism and Role as Predictors of Attributions about Obedience to Authority." Paper presented at the annual meeting of the Eastern Psychological Association, Boston.

Boller, P. F., and J. George. 1989. *They Never Said It.* New York: Oxford University Press.

Bouchard, T. J., Jr., and M. McGue. 1981. "Familial Studies of Intelligence: A Review." *Science,* 212, 1055–1059.

Bouchard, T. J., Jr., D. T. Lykken, M. McGue, N. L. Segal, and A. Tellegen. 1990. "Sources of Human Psychological Differences: The Minnesota Study of Twins Reared Apart." *Science,* 250, 223–228.

Brief, D. E., A L. Comrey, and B. E. Collins. 1994. "The Comrey Personality Scales in Russia: A Study of Concurrent, Predictive, and External Validity." *Personality and Individual Differences,* 16, 113–122.

Bronfenbrenner, U. 1961. "The Mirror Image in Soviet-American Relations: A Social Psychologist's Report." *Journal of Social Issues,* 17, 45–56.

Brown, R. W. 1953. "A Determinant of the Relationship between Rigidity and Authoritarianism." *Journal of Abnormal and Social Psychology,* 48, 469–476.

————. 1965. *Social Psychology.* New York: Free Press.

————. 1986. *Social Psychology: The Second Edition.* New York: Free Press.

Burt, M. R. 1980. "Cultural Myths and Supports for Rape." *Journal of Personality and Social Psychology,* 38, 217–230.

Byrne, D. G., M. I. Reinhart, and P. C. L. Heaven. 1989. "Type A Behaviour and the Authoritarian Personality." *British Journal of Medical Psychology,* 62, 163–172.

Campbell, D. T., C. R. Siegman, and M. B. Rees. 1967. "Direction-of-Wording Effects in the Relationships between Scales." *Psychological Bulletin,* 68, 293–303.

Cattell, R. B., H. W. Eber, and M. M. Tatsuoka. 1970. *Handbook for the Sixteen Personality Factor Questionnaire.* Champaign, Ill.: Institute for Personality and Ability Testing.

Check, J. V. P., N. M. Malamuth, B. Elias, and S. A. Barton. 1985. "On Hostile Ground." *Psychology Today,* April, 56–58, 60–61.

Circus, M. P. F. 1970. "Archeology Today." *Series 2, Show 8,* 6th minute.

Colby, B. N., S. I. Mishra, R. Newcomb, and J. Ashurst. 1987. "Adaptive Potential, Coherence Scope, and Authoritarianism." Unpublished manuscript, University of California at Irvine.

Colby, B. N., L. C. Milanesi, T. Cesario, S. I. Mishra, N. D. Vaziri, and S. Yousefi. 1992. "On the Possible Consequences of Altruistic Social Support and Authoritarianism for Health and Immunological Functioning among Older Japanese-American and Anglo-American Women." Unpublished manuscript, University of California at Irvine.

Comrey, A. L. 1973. *A First Course in Factor Analysis.* New York: Academic Press.

————. 1978. "Common Methodological Problems in Factor Analytic Studies." *Journal of Consulting and Clinical Psychology,* 46, 648–659.

Cronbach, L. J. 1942. "Studies of Acquiescence as a Factor in the True-False Test." *Journal of Educational Psychology,* 33, 401–415.

————. 1946. "Response Sets and Test Validity." *Educational and Psychological Measurement,* 6, 475–494.

————. 1970. *Essentials of Psychological Testing,* 3d ed. New York: Harper and Row.

Crowne, D. P., and D. Marlowe. 1964. *The Approval Motive.* New York: Wiley.

Czech, D. 1990. *Auschwitz Chronicle, 1939–1945.* New York: H. Holt.

D'Andrade, R., and J. Dart. 1990. "The Interpretation of *r* versus *r*², or, Why Percent of Variance Accounted for Is a Poor Measure of Size of Effect." *Journal of Quantitative Anthropology,* 2, 47–59.

Darley, J. M., and C. D. Batson. 1973. "From Jerusalem to Jericho: A Study of Situational and Dispositional Variables in Helping Behavior." *Journal of Personality and Social Psychology,* 27, 100–108.

Delgato, J. M. R. 1963a. "Effect of Brain Stimulation on Task-Free Situations." *EEG Clinical Neurophysiology,* supplement 24, 260–280.

———. 1963b. "Cerebral Heterostimulation in a Monkey Colony." *Science,* 141, 161–163.

———. 1964. "Free Behavior and Brain Stimulation." In C. C. Pfeiffer and J. R. Smythies, eds., *International Review of Neurobiology,* pp. 349–449. New York: Academic Press.

———. 1965. "Pharmacology of Spontaneous and Conditioned Behavior in the Monkey." In *Proceedings of the Second International Pharmacology Congress,* vol. 1, 133–156. Oxford: Pergamon Press.

DiRenzo, G. J. 1967. "Professional Politicians and Personality Structures." *American Journal of Sociology,* 73, 217–225.

———. 1968. "Dogmatism and Presidential Preferences in the 1964 Elections." *Psychological Reports,* 22, 1197–1202.

———. 1971. "Dogmatism and Presidential Preferences: A 1968 Replication." *Psychological Reports,* 29, 109–110.

———. 1986. "Presidential Preferences and Dogmatism: A Progress Report on Longitudinal Analysis." *Psychological Reports,* 59, 1320.

Dixon, W. J., ed. 1990. *BMDP Statistical Software Manual.* Berkeley: University of California Press.

Dodson, R. E., J. E. Shryne, and R. A. Gorski. 1988. "Hormonal Modification of the Number of Total and Late-Arising Neurons in the Central Part of the Medial Preoptic Nucleus of the Rat." *Journal of Comparative Neurology,* 275, 623–629.

Dohler, K.-D., A. Coquelin, F. Davis, M. Hines, J. E. Shryne, and R. A. Gorski. 1984. "Pre- and Postnatal Influence of Testosterone Propionate and Diethylstil-Bestrol on Differentiation of the Sexually Dimorphic Nucleus of the Preoptic Area in Male and Female Rats." *Brain Research,* 302, 291–295.

Doty, R. M., and R. J. Larsen. 1993. "Authoritarianism and Emotional Reactivity: A Psychophysiological Study." Paper presented at the annual meeting of the International Society of Political Psychology, Boston, July.

Doty, R. M., B. E. Peterson, and D. G. Winter. 1991. "Threat and Authoritarianism in the United States, 1978–1987." *Journal of Personality and Social Psychology,* 61, 629–640.

Druckman, D. 1967. "Dogmatism, Prenegotiation Experience, and Simulated Group Representation as Determinants of Dyadic Behavior in a Bargaining Situation." *Journal of Personality and Social Psychology,* 6, 279–290.

Duckitt, J. 1989. "Authoritarianism and Group Identification: A New View of an Old Construct." *Political Psychology,* 10, 63–84.

———. 1992. *The Social Psychology of Prejudice.* New York: Praeger.

Dunlap, R. E., and K. D. van Liere. 1978. "The New Environmental Paradigm: A Reexamination." *Journal of Environmental Education*, 9, 10–19.

Edwards, A. L. 1957. *The Social Desirability Variable in Personality Assessment and Research.* New York: Dryden.

———. 1990. "Construct Validity and Social Desirability." *American Psychologist*, 45, 287–289.

Edwards, D., and P. Leger. 1993. "Psychometric Properties of the Right-Wing Authoritarianism Scale in Black and White South African Students." Paper submitted to the *International Journal of Psychology.*

Eigenberger, M. 1994. "Physique, Temperament and Beliefs: A Philosophical and Empirical Exploration of W. H. Sheldon's Constitutional Psychology." Master's thesis, University of Wyoming, Laramie.

Elms, A. C., and S. Milgram. 1966. "Personality Characteristics Associated with Obedience and Defiance toward Authoritative Command." *Journal of Experimental Research in Personality*, 1, 282–289.

Eysenck, H. J. 1954. *The Psychology of Politics.* London: Routledge and Keagan Paul.

Falconer, D. S. 1960. *Introduction to Quantitative Genetics.* Glascow: Robert MacLehose.

———. 1989. *Introduction to Quantitative Genetics,* 3d ed. Essex, Eng.: Longman Scientific and Technical Publishers.

Fava, J. L., and W. F. Velicer. 1992. "An Empirical Comparison of Factor, Image, Component, and Scale Scores." *Multivariate Behavioral Research*, 27, 301–322.

Feagin, J. R. 1964. "Prejudice and Religious Types: A Focused Study of Southern Fundamentalists." *Journal for the Scientific Study of Religion*, 4, 3–13.

Feather, N. T. 1993. "Authoritarianism and Attitudes toward High Achievers." *Journal of Personality and Social Psychology*, 65, 152–164.

Fenigstein, A., M. F. Scheier, and A. H. Buss. 1975. "Public and Private Self-Consciousness: Assessment and Theory." *Journal of Consulting and Clinical Psychology*, 43, 522–527.

Fowler, J. W. 1981. *Stages of Faith.* San Francisco: Harper and Row.

Fruchter, B. 1954. *Introduction to Factor Analysis.* New York: Van Nostrand.

Fullerton, J. T., and B. E. Hunsberger. 1982. "A Unidimensional Measure of Christian Orthodoxy." *Journal for the Scientific Study of Religion*, 21, 317–326.

Garzon, J. S. A. 1992. "Creencias Sociales Contemporaneas, Autoritarismo y Humanismo." *Psicologia Politica*, 5, 27–52.

Goldberg, L. R., and J. M. Digman. 1994. "Revealing Structure in the Data: Principles of Exploratory Factor Analysis." In S. Strack and M. Lorr, eds., *Differentiating Normal and Abnormal Personality.* New York: Springer-Verlag.

Goldberg, L. R., and T. K. Rosolack. 1991. "Comparing the Big Five Factor Structure with Its Competitors: I. Eysenck's P-E-N Model." Address to the Conference on the Development of the Structure of Temperament and Personality from Infancy to Adulthood, Netherlands Institute for Advanced Study, Wassenaar.

Gorski, R. A., R. E. Harlan, C. D. Jacobson, J. E. Shryne, and A. M. Southam. 1980. "Evidence for a Morphological Sex Difference within the Medial Preoptic Area of the Rat Brain." *Journal of Comparative Neurology*, 193, 529–539.

Gorsuch, R. L. 1993. "Religion and Prejudice: Lessons Not Learned from the Past." *International Journal for the Psychology of Religion*, 3, 29–31.

Gorsuch, R., and D. Aleshire. 1974. "Christian Faith and Ethnic Prejudice: A Review and Interpretation of Research." *Journal for the Scientific Study of Religion*, 13, 281–307.

Granberg, D., and G. Corrigan. 1972. "Authoritarianism, Dogmatism, and Orientation toward the Vietnam War." *Sociometry*, 35, 468–476.

Greenwood, J. D. 1983. "Role-Playing as an Experimental Strategy in Social Psychology." *European Journal of Social Psychology*, 13, 235–254.

Griffin, G. A., R. L. Gorsuch, and A. Davis. 1987. "A Cross-Sectional Investigation of Religious Orientation, Social Norms, and Prejudice." *Journal for the Scientific Study of Religion*, 26, 358–365.

Haiman, F. S. 1964. "A Revised Scale for the Measurement of Open-Mindedness." *Speech Monographs*, 31, 97–102.

Hanson, D. 1968. "Dogmatism and Authoritarianism." *Journal of Social Psychology*, 76, 89–95.

———. 1974. *Dogmatism and Authoritarianism: A Bibliography of Doctoral Dissertations*. Washington, D.C.: American Psychological Association.

Harman, H. H. 1967. *Modern Factor Analysis*, 2d ed. Chicago: University of Chicago Press.

Heaven, P. C. L. 1984. "Predicting Authoritarian Behaviour: Analysis of Three Measures." *Personality and Individual Differences*, 5, 251–253.

Hilgard, E. R. 1973. "A Neodissociation Interpretation of Pain Reduction in Hypnosis." *Psychological Review*, 80, 396–411.

———. 1977. *Divided Consciousness: Multiple Controls in Human Thought and Action*. New York: Wiley.

Hite, S. 1989. *Women and Love*. New York: St. Martin.

Hitler, A. 1943. *Mein Kampf*. Boston: Houghton Mifflin.

Hoess, R. 1959. *The Autobiography of Rudolf Hoess*. London: Weidenfeld.

Hogan, R., and R. A. Nicholson. 1988. "The Meaning of Personality Test Scores." *American Psychologist*, 43, 621–626.

Hoge, D. R., and J. W. Carroll. 1973. "Religiosity and Prejudice in Northern and Southern Churches." *Journal for the Scientific Study of Religion*, 12, 181–197.

Holms, V. L. 1989. "Career Commitment, Family Commitment, and Family/Career Conflict among Young Adults." Ph.d. diss., University of Manitoba, Winnipeg.

Hopf, C. 1993. "Authoritarians and Their Families: Qualitative Studies on the Origins of Authoritarian Dispositions." In W. F. Stone, G. Lederer, and R. Christie, eds., *Strength and Weakness: The Authoritarian Personality Today*. New York: Springer-Verlag.

Horgan, J. 1993. "Eugenics Revisited." *Scientific American*, June, 122–128, 130–131.

Hunsberger, B. 1996. "Religious Fundamentalism, Right-Wing Authoritarianism, and Hostility toward Homosexuals in Non-Christian Groups." *International Journal for the Psychology of Religion*, 6, 39–49.

Hunsberger, B., M. Pratt, and S. M. Pancer. 1994. "Religious Fundamentalism and Integrative Complexity of Thought: A Relationship for Existential Content Only?" *Journal for the Scientific Study of Religion*, 33, 335–346.

Hunt, R. A., and M. King. 1971. "The Intrinsic-Extrinsic Concept: A Review and Evaluation." *Journal for the Scientific Study of Religion*, 10, 339–356.

Hyman, H. H., and P. B. Sheatsley. 1954. "The Authoritarian Personality: A Methodological Critique." In R. Christie and M. Jahoda, eds., *Studies in the Scope and Method of "The Authoritarian Personality."* Glencoe, Ill.: Free Press.

Ilfeld, F. 1976. "Further Validation of a Psychiatric Symptom Index in a Normal Population." *Psychological Reports*, 39, 1215–1228.

Insko, C. A. 1967. *Theories of Attitude Change.* New York: Appleton-Century-Crofts.

Jensen, A. R. 1980. *Bias in Mental Testing.* New York: Free Press.

Jones, E.E., and V. A. Harris. 1967. "The Attribution of Attitudes." *Journal of Experimental Social Psychology*, 3, 1–24.

Kalin, R., and P. J. Tilby. 1978. "Development and Validation of a Sex-Role Ideology Scale." *Psychological Reports*, 42, 731–738.

Karabenick, S. A., and R. W. Wilson. 1969. "Dogmatism among War Hawks and Peace Doves." *Psychological Reports*, 25, 419–422.

Kerlinger, F., and M. Rokeach. 1966. "The Factorial Nature of the F and D Scales." *Journal of Personality and Social Psychology*, 4, 391–399.

Kirkpatrick, L. A., and R. W. Hood. 1990. "Intrinsic-Extrinsic Religious Orientation: The Boon or Bane of Contemporary Psychology of Religion?" *Journal for the Scientific Study of Religion*, 29, 442–462.

Knutson, J. N. 1974. "Psychological Variables in Political Recruitment." Unpublished paper, Wright Institute, University of California, Berkeley.

Kohn, P. M. 1972. "The Authoritarianism-Rebellion Scale: A Balanced F Scale with Left-Wing Reversals." *Sociometry*, 35, 176–189.

Koss, M. P., and T. E. Dinero. 1987. "Predictors of Sexual Aggression among a National Sample of Male College Students." In R. A. Prentky and V. L. Quinsey, eds., *Human Sexual Aggression: Current Perspectives*, pp. 113–147. New York: New York Academy of the Sciences.

Krosnick, J. A. 1991. "Response Strategies for Coping with the Cognitive Demands of Attitude Measures in Surveys." *Applied Cognitive Psychology*, 5 (May–June special issue), 213–236.

Leak, G. K., and B. A. Randall. 1995. "Clarification of the Link between Right-Wing Authoritarianism and Religiousness: The Role of Religious Maturity." *Journal for the Scientific Study of Religion*, 34, 245–252.

Lederer, G. 1993. "Authoritarianism in German Adolescents: Trends and Cross-Cultural Comparisons." In W. F. Stone, G. Lederer, and R. Christie, eds., *Strength and Weakness: The Authoritarian Personality Today.* New York: Springer-Verlag.

Lee, H. B., and A. L. Comrey. 1979. "Distortions in a Commonly Used Factor Analytic Procedure." *Multivariate Behavioral Research*, 14, 301–321.

Lee, R. E., and P. B. Warr. 1969. "The Development and Standardization of a Balanced F Scale." *Journal of General Psychology*, 81, 109–129.

LeVay, S. 1991. "A Difference in Hypothalamic Structure between Heterosexual and Homosexual Men." *Science*, 253, 1034–1037.

———. 1993. *The Sexual Brain*, Cambridge, Mass.: MIT Press.

Likert, R. 1932. "A Technique for the Measurement of Attitudes." *Archives of Psychology*, no. 140.

Lorge, I. 1937. "Gen-Like: Halo or Reality?" *Psychological Bulletin,* 34, 545–546.

Lykken, D. T., T. J. Bouchard, Jr., M. McGue, and A. Tellegen. 1990. "The Minnesota Twin Registry: Some Initial Findings." *Acta Geneticae Medicae et Gemmellologiae,* 39, 35–70.

Malamuth, N. 1981. "Rape Proclivity among Males." *Journal of Social Issues,* 37, 138–157.

McCarthy, J., and R. C. Johnson. 1962. "Interpretation of the 'City Hall Riots' as a Function of General Dogmatism." *Psychological Reports,* 11, 243–245.

McFarland, S. 1989a. "The Current Status of Authoritarianism in Kentucky." Unpublished paper, University of Western Kentucky, Bowling Green.

——. 1989b. "Religious Orientations and the Targets of Discrimination." *Journal for the Scientific Study of Religion,* 28, 324–336.

——. 1990. "Religiously Oriented Prejudice in Communism and Christianity: The Role of Quest." Paper presented at the annual convention of the Southeastern Psychological Association, Atlanta.

McFarland, S., V. Ageyev, and M. Abalakina. 1990. "The Authoritarian Personality in Russia and North America." Symposium held at the annual meeting of the International Society of Political Psychology. Washington, D.C., July.

McFarland, S., V. Ageyev, and M. Abalakina-Paap. 1992. "Authoritarianism in the Former Soviet Union." *Journal of Personality and Social Psychology,* 63, 1004–1010.

McFarland, S., V. Ageyev, and N. Djintcharadze. 1995. "Russian Authoritarianism Two Years after Communism." *Personality and Social Psychology Bulletin,* 22, 210–217.

McFarland, S., V. Ageyev, M. Abalakina-Paap, and N. Djintcharadze. 1993. "Why Are Russians Less Authoritarian Than Americans?" Paper presented at the annual meeting of the International Society of Political Psychology, Boston.

Meloen, J. D. 1993. "The F Scale as a Predictor of Fascism: An Overview of Forty Years of Authoritarianism Research." In W. F. Stone, G. Lederer, and R. Christie, eds., *Strength and Weakness: The Authoritarian Personality Today.* New York: Springer-Verlag.

Michael, R. T., J. H. Gagnon, E. O. Laumann, and G. Kolata. 1994. *Sex in America.* Boston: Little, Brown.

Milgram, S. 1965. *Obedience* (film). New York: New York University Film Library.

——. 1974. *Obedience to Authority.* New York: Harper and Row.

Mirchuk, P. 1976. *In the German Mills of Death.* New York: Vantage Press.

Mischel, W. 1968. *Personality and Assessment.* New York: Wiley.

Mixon, D. 1971. "Further Conditions of Obedience and Disobedience to Authority." Ph.d. diss., University of Nevada, Reno. (University Microfilms no. 72-6477.)

Moghaddam, F. M., and V. Vuksanovic. 1990. "Attitudes and Behavior toward Human Rights across Different Contexts: The Role of Right-Wing Authoritarianism, Political Ideology, and Religiosity." *International Journal of Psychology,* 25, 455–474.

Mosher, D. L. 1988. "Aggressive Sexual Behavior Inventory and Revised Guilt Inventory." In C. M. Davis, W. L. Varber, and S. L. Davis, eds., *Sexuality Related Measures: A Compendium.* Lake Mills, Iowa: Graphic.

Myers, D. G. 1992. *Psychology,* 3d ed. New York: Worth Publishers.
————. 1993. *Social Psychology,* 4th ed. New York: McGraw-Hill.
Newcomb, T. M. 1961. *The Acquaintance Process.* New York: Holt, Rinehart, and Winston.
Nie, N. H., D. H. Bent, and C. H. Hull. 1970. *SPSS: A Statistical Package for the Social Sciences.* New York: McGraw-Hill.
Orne, M. T., and C. H. Holland. 1968. "On the Ecological Validity of Laboratory Deceptions." *International Journal of Psychiatry,* 6, 282–293.
Oskamp, S. 1965. "Attitudes toward U.S., and Russian Actions—a Double Standard." *Psychological Reports,* 16, 43–46.
Ozer, D. J. 1985. "Correlation and the Coefficient of Determination." *Psychological Bulletin,* 97, 307–315.
Payne, R. 1973. *The Life and Death of Adolf Hitler.* New York: Praeger.
Perl, G. 1948. *I Was a Doctor in Auschwitz.* New York: International Univerities Press.
Perrott, S. B. 1991. "Social Identity Patterns in the Police: Attitudinal and Performance Implications." Ph.d. diss., McGill University, Montreal.
Peters, L. 1990. "Faith, Doubt, and Authority: The Religious Nature of Quest, and the Relationship of Intrinsic and Quest Religiosity with Right-Wing Authoritarianism." Unpublished manuscript, University of Waterloo, Ontario.
Peterson, B. E., R. M. Doty, and D. G. Winter. 1993. "Authoritarianism and Attitudes toward Contemporary Social Issues." *Personality and Social Psychology Bulletin,* 19, 174–184.
Piaget, J. 1965. *The Moral Judgment of the Child.* New York: Free Press.
Plant, W. T. 1960. "Rokeach's Dogmatism Scale as a Measure of General Authoritarianism." *Psychological Reports,* 6, 164.
Ponton, M. O., and R. L. Gorsuch. 1988. "Prejudice and Religion Revisited: A Cross-Cultural Investigation with a Venezuelan Sample." *Journal for the Scientific Study of Religion,* 27, 260–271.
Pratto, F., J. Sidanius, L. M. Stallworth, and B. F. Malle. 1994. "Social Dominance Orientation: A Personality Variable Predicting Social and Political Attitudes." *Journal of Personality and Social Psychology,* 67, 741–763.
Ray, J. J. 1985. "Defective Validity in the Altemeyer Authoritarianism Scale." *Journal of Social Psychology,* 125, 271–272.
————. 1990. "Comment on 'Right-Wing Authoritarianism.'" *Canadian Psychologist,* 31, 392–393.
Rest, J. W. 1979. *Development in Judging Moral Issues.* Minneapolis: University of Minnesota Press.
Rokeach, M. 1960. *The Open and Closed Mind.* New York: Basic Books.
————. 1967. "Authoritarianism Scale and Response Bias: Comment on Peabody's Paper." *Psychological Bulletin,* 67, 349–355.
———— 1973. *The Nature of Human Values.* New York: Free Press.
Rorer, L. G. 1965. "The Great Response Style Myth." *Psychological Bulletin,* 63, 129–156.
Rosenberg, M. 1965. *Society and the Adolescent Self-Image.* Princeton, N.J.: Princeton University Press.

Rosenblum, A. L. 1958. "Ethnic Prejudice as Related to Social Class and Religiosity." *Sociology and Social Research,* 43, 272–275.

Ross, L. 1977. "The Intuitive Psychologist and His Shortcomings: Distortions in the Attribution Process." In L. Berkowitz, ed., *Advances in Experimental Social Psychology,* vol. 10, pp. 173–220. New York: Academic Press.

Rubinstein, G. 1996. "Two Peoples in One Land: A Validation Study of Altemeyer's Right-Wing Authoritarianism Scale in the Palestinian and Jewish Societies in Israel." *Journal of Cross-Cultural Psychology,* 27, 216–230.

Russell, D., L. A. Peplau, and C. E. Cutrona. 1980. "The Revised UCLA Loneliness Scale: Concurrent and Discriminant Validity Evidence." *Journal of Personality and Social Psychology,* 39, 472–480.

Sales, S. M. 1972. "Economic Threat as a Determinant of Conversion Rates in Authoritarian and Nonauthoritarian Churches." *Journal of Personality and Social Psychology,* 23, 420–428.

———. 1973. "Threat as a Factor in Authoritarianism: An Analysis of Archival Data." *Journal of Personality and Social Psychology,* 28, 44–57.

Schultz, P. W., and W. F. Stone. 1994. "Authoritarianism and Attitudes toward the Environment." *Environment and Behavior,* 26, 25–37.

Schulze, R. H. K. 1962. "A Shortened Version of the Rokeach Dogmatism Scale." *Journal of Psychological Studies,* 13, 93–97.

Schwendiman, G., K. S. Larsen, and S. C. Cope. 1970. "Authoritarian Traits as Predictors of Candidate Preference in 1968 United States Presidential Election." *Psychological Reports,* 27, 629–630.

Shakespeare, W. 1604. *The Tragicall Historie of Hamlet, Prince of Denmark* (second quarto). In *The Yale Shakespeare.* New Haven, CT: Yale University Press.

Shelley, M. 1818. *Frankenstein, or, The Modern Prometheus.*

Sherif, M., O. J. Harvey, B. J. White, W. E. Hood, and C. W. Sherif. 1961. *Intergroup Conflict and Cooperation: The Robber's Cave Experiment.* Norman: University of Oklahoma Book Exchange.

Shils, E. A. 1954. "Authoritarianism: Right and Left." in R. Christie and M. Jahoda, eds., *Studies in the Scope and Method of "The Authoritarian Personality."* Glencoe, Ill.: Free Press.

Shirer, W. L. 1960. *The Rise and Fall of the Third Reich.* New York: Simon and Schuster.

Sidanius, J. 1985. "Cognitive Functioning and Sociopolitical Ideology Revisited." *Political Psychology,* 6, 637–661.

Skitka, L. J., and P. E. Tetlock. 1993. "Providing Public Assistance: Cognitive and Motivational Processes Underlying Liberal and Conservative Policy Preferences." *Journal of Personality and Social Psychology,* 65, 1205–1223.

Smith, M. B. 1965. "An analysis of Two Measures of 'Authoritarianism' among Peace Corps Teachers." *Journal of Personality,* 33, 513–535.

———. 1988. Foreword to B. Altemeyer, *Enemies of Freedom: Understanding Right-Wing Authoritarianism,* pp. xi–xvi. San Francisco: Jossey-Bass.

Smithers, A. G., and D. M. Lobley. 1978. "The Relationship between Dogmatism and Radicalism/Conservatism." In H. J. Eysenck and G. D. Wilson, eds., *The Psychological Basis of Ideology.* Baltimore, Md.: University Park Press.

Snook, S. C., and R. L. Gorsuch. 1985. "Religion and Racial Prejudice in South Africa." Paper presented at the annual convention of the American Psychological Association, Los Angeles.

Snyder, M., and S. Gangestad. 1986. "On the Nature of Self-Monitoring: Matters of Assessment, Matters of Validity." *Journal of Personality and Social Psychology*, 51, 125–139.

Spence, J. T., and R. L. Helmreich. 1978. *Masculinity and Femininity: Their Psychological Dimensions, Correlates, and Antecedents*. Austin: University of Texas Press.

Spilka, B., R. W. Hood, and R. L. Gorsuch. 1985. *The Psychology of Religion: An Empirical Approach*. Englewood Cliffs, N.J.: Prentice-Hall.

Stern, G. G., M. I. Stein, and B. S. Bloom. 1956. *Methods in Personality Assessment*. Glencoe, Ill.: Free Press.

Stone, W. F. 1980. "The Myth of Left-Wing Authoritarianism." *Political Psychology*, 2, 3–19.

Stone, W. F., and P. E. Schaffner. 1988. *The Psychology of Politics*, 2d ed. New York: Springer-Verlag.

Stone, W. F., and W. P. Schultz. 1992. "Authoritarianism and Rigidity." Unpublished paper, University of Maine, Orono.

Stone, W. F., and L. D. Smith. 1993. "Authoritarianism: Left and Right." In W. F. Stone, G. Lederer, and R. Christie, eds., *Strength and Weakness: The Authoritarian Personality Today*. New York: Springer-Verlag.

Stone, W. F., and L. Yelland. 1994. "Belief in the Holocaust: Effects of Personality and Propaganda." Paper presented at the annual meeting of the Eastern Psychological Association, Providence, R.I.

Stone, W. F., G. Lederer, and R. Christie, eds. 1993. *Strength and Weakness: The Authoritarian Personality Today*. New York: Springer-Verlag.

Tajfel, H., ed. 1978. *Differentiation between Social Groups*. New York: Academic Press.

Tajfel, H., and J. C. Turner. 1979. "An Integrative Theory of Social Conflict." In W. Austin and S. Worchel, eds., *The Social Psychology of Intergroup Relations*. Monterey, Calif.: Brooks/Cole.

Tajfel, H., M. G. Billig, R. P. Bundy, and C. Flament. 1971. "Social Categorization and Intergroup Behavior." *European Journal of Social Psychology*, 1, 149–178.

Tarr, H., and M. Lorr. 1991. "A Comparison of Right-Wing Authoritarianism, Conformity, and Conservatism." *Personality and Individual Differences*, 12, 307–311.

Taylor, D. A., and I. Altman. 1966. "Intimacy-Scaled Stimuli for Use in Research on Interpersonal Exchange." San Diego Naval Medical Research Institute.

Tellegen, A., D. T. Lykken, T. J. Bouchard, Jr., K. J. Wilcox, N. L. Segal, and S. Rich. 1988. "Personality Similarity in Twins Reared Apart and Together." *Journal of Personality and Social Psychology*, 54, 1031–1039.

Tetlock, P. E. 1983. "Cognitive Style and Political Ideology." *Journal of Personality and Social Psychology*, 45, 118–126.

———. 1984. "Cognitive Style and Political Belief Systems in the British House of Commons." *Journal of Personality and Social Psychology*, 46, 365–375.

————. 1986. "A Value Pluralism Model of Ideological Reasoning." *Journal of Personality and Social Psychology,* 50, 819–827.

Thompson, R. C., and J. B. Michel. 1972. "Measuring Authoritarianism: A Comparison of the F and D Scales." *Journal of Personality,* 40, 180–190.

Tomkins, S. S. 1965. "Affect and the Psychology of Knowledge." In S. S. Tomkins and C. E. Izard, eds., *Affect, Cognition and Personality.* New York: Springer-Verlag.

Tourangeau, R., and K. A. Rasinski. 1988. "Cognitive Processes Underlying Context Effects in Attitude Measurement." *Psychological Bulletin,* 103, 299–314.

Trappnel, P. 1992. "Vocational Interests and the Facet Structure of Factor V." Paper presented at the symposium "Intelligence and Openness in the 'Big Five' Personality Structure," annual convention of the American Psychological Association, Washington, D.C., August.

Troldahl, V., and F. A. Powell. 1965. "A Short-Form Dogmatism Scale for Use in Field Studies." *Social Forces,* 44, 211–215.

Twain, M. "Corn-Pone Opinions." In *The Family Mark Twain.* New York: Harper, n.d. (Originally published 1900.)

Vacchiano, R. B., P. S. Strauss, and L. Hochman. 1969. "The Open and Closed Mind: A Review of Dogmatism." *Psychological Bulletin,* 71, 261–273.

Velicer, W. F. 1977. "An Empirical Comparison of the Similarity of Principal Component, Image, and Factor Patterns." *Multivariate Behavioral Research,* 12, 3–22.

Velicer, W. F., and D. N. Jackson. 1990. "Component Analysis versus Common Factor Analysis: Some Issues in Selecting an Appropriate Procedure." *Multivariate Behavioral Research,* 25, 1–28.

Velicer, W. F., A. C. Peacock, and D. N. Jackson. 1982. "A Comparison of Component and Factor Patterns: A Monte Carlo Approach." *Multivariate Behavioral Research,* 17, 371–388.

Walker, W. D., and V. L. Quinsey. 1991. "Authoritarianism, Attitudes toward Women, and Sexual Aggression." Unpublished manuscript, Queens University, Kingston, Ontario.

Walker, W. D., R. C. Rowe, and V. L. Quinsey. 1993. "Authoritarianism and Sexual Aggression." *Journal of Personality and Social Psychology,* 65, 1036–1045.

Waller, N. G., B. A. Kojetin, T. J. Bouchard, Jr., D. T. Lykken, and A. Tellegen. 1990. "Genetic and Environmental Influences on Religious Interests, Attitudes, and Values: A Study of Twins Reared Apart and Together." *Psychological Science,* 1, 1–5.

Walsh, J. A. 1990. "Comment on Social Desirability." *American Psychologist,* 45, 289–290.

Watson, G., and E. M. Glasser. 1980. *Critical Thinking Appraisal Manual.* New York: Psychological Corporation.

Wegmann, M. F. 1992. "Information Processing Deficits of the Authoritarian Mind." Ph.d. diss., Fielding Institute, Santa Barbara, Calif.

Whitan, F. L., M. Diamond, and J. Martin. 1993. "Homosexual Orientation in Twins: A Report on Sixty-one Pairs and Three Triplet Sets." *Archives of Sexual Behavior,* 22, 216–230.

Wiggins, J. S. 1966. "Substantive Dimensions of Self-Report in the MMPI Item Pool." *Psychological Monographs,* 80, no. 630.

Wilson, G. D., ed. 1973. *The Psychology of Conservatism.* New York: Academic Press.

Wilson, G. D., and J. R. Patterson. 1968. "A New Measure of Conservatism." *British Journal of Social and Clinical Psychology,* 7, 264–269.

Wilson, W. C. 1960. "Extrinsic Religious Values and Prejudice." *Journal of Abnormal and Social Psychology,* 60, 286–288.

Wylie, L., and J. Forest. 1992. "Religious Fundamentalism, Right-Wing Authoritarianism, and Prejudice." *Psychological Reports,* 71, 1291–1298.

Yahil, L. 1980. *The Holocaust.* New York: Oxford University Press.

Zanna, M. P., and J. M. Olson. 1994. *The Psychology of Prejudice.* The Ontario Symposium, vol. 7. Hillsdale, N.J.: Lawrence Erlbaum Associates.

Zwillenberg, D. F. 1983. "Predicting Biases in the Punishment of Criminals as a Function of Authoritarianism: The Effects of Severity of the Crime, Degree of Mitigating Circumstances, and Status of the Offender." Ph.d. diss., Columbia University, New York. (University Microfilms no. 8311876.)

Index

Harvard University Press is a member of Green Press Initiative
(greenpressinitiative.org), a nonprofit organization working to
help publishers and printers increase their use of recycled paper
and decrease their use of fiber derived from endangered forests.
This book was printed on 100% recycled paper containing
50% post-consumer waste and processed chlorine free.

CPSIA information can be obtained
at www.ICGtesting.com
Printed in the USA
JSHW030843211222
34210JS00011B/36

9 780674 053052